THE WILEY BICENTENNIAL—KNOWLEDGE FOR GENERATIONS

*E*ach generation has its unique needs and aspirations. When Charles Wiley first opened his small printing shop in lower Manhattan in 1807, it was a generation of boundless potential searching for an identity. And we were there, helping to define a new American literary tradition. Over half a century later, in the midst of the Second Industrial Revolution, it was a generation focused on building the future. Once again, we were there, supplying the critical scientific, technical, and engineering knowledge that helped frame the world. Throughout the 20th Century, and into the new millennium, nations began to reach out beyond their own borders and a new international community was born. Wiley was there, expanding its operations around the world to enable a global exchange of ideas, opinions, and know-how.

For 200 years, Wiley has been an integral part of each generation's journey, enabling the flow of information and understanding necessary to meet their needs and fulfill their aspirations. Today, bold new technologies are changing the way we live and learn. Wiley will be there, providing you the must-have knowledge you need to imagine new worlds, new possibilities, and new opportunities.

Generations come and go, but you can always count on Wiley to provide you the knowledge you need, when and where you need it!

WILLIAM J. PESCE
PRESIDENT AND CHIEF EXECUTIVE OFFICER

PETER BOOTH WILEY
CHAIRMAN OF THE BOARD

Project Management

Stanley Portny

Certified Project Management Professional (PMP)

Samuel J. Mantel, Jr.

University of Cincinnati

Jack R. Meredith

Wake Forest University

Scott M. Shafer

Wake Forest University

Margaret M. Sutton

with Brian Kramer

BICENTENNIAL

1807

WILEY

2007

BICENTENNIAL

Credits

Publisher
Anne Smith

Project Editor
Beth Tripmacher

Marketing Manager
Jennifer Slomack

Senior Editorial Assistant
Tiara Kelly

Production Manager
Kelly Tavares

Project Manager
Shana Meyer

Production Assistant
Courtney Leshko

Creative Director
Harry Nolan

Cover Designer
Hope Miller

Cover Photo
Jon Feingersh/Blend/Getty Images

Wiley 200th Anniversary Logo designed by: Richard J. Pacifico

ISBN-13 978-0-470-11124-6

Printed in the United States of America

10 9 8 7 6 5

PREFACE

College classrooms bring together learners from many backgrounds with a variety of aspirations. Although the students are in the same course, they are not necessarily on the same path. This diversity, coupled with the reality that these learners often have jobs, families, and other commitments, requires a flexibility that our nation's higher education system is addressing. Distance learning, shorter course terms, chunked curriculum, new disciplines, evening courses, and certification programs are some of the approaches that colleges employ to reach as many students as possible and help them clarify and achieve their goals.

Wiley Pathways books, a new line of texts from John Wiley & Sons, Inc., are designed to help you address this diversity and the need for flexibility. These books focus on the fundamentals, identify core competencies and skills, and promote independent learning. The focus on the fundamentals helps students grasp the subject, bringing them all to the same basic understanding. These books use clear, everyday language, presented in an uncluttered format, making the content more accessible and the reading experience more pleasurable. The core competencies and practical skills focus help students succeed in the classroom and beyond, whether in another course or in a professional setting. A variety of built-in learning resources promote independent learning and help instructors and students gauge students' understanding of the content. These resources enable students to think critically about their new knowledge, and apply their skills in any situation.

Our goal with *Wiley Pathways* books—with its brief, inviting format, clear language, and core competencies and skills focus—is to celebrate the many students in your courses, respect their needs, and help you guide them on their way.

Wiley Pathways Pedagogy

To meet the needs of working college students, all *Wiley Pathways* texts explicitly use an outcomes and assessment-based pedagogy for the books: students will review what they have learned, acquire new information and skills, and apply their new knowledge and skills to real-life situations. Based on the recently updated categories of Bloom's Taxonomy of Learning, *Wiley Pathways Project Management* presents key topics in project management (the content) in easy-to-follow chapters. The text then prompts analysis, synthesis, and evaluation with a variety of learning aids and assessment tools. Students move efficiently from reviewing what they have learned, to acquiring new information and skills, to applying their new knowledge and skills to real-life scenarios.

With *Wiley Pathways*, students not only achieve academic mastery of project management *topics,* but they master real-world *skills* related to that content. The books help students become independent learners, giving them a distinct advantage in the field, whether they are starting out or seek to advance in their careers.

Organization, Depth and Breadth of the Text

▲ **Modular format.** Research on college students shows that they access information from textbooks in a non-linear way. Instructors also often wish to reorder textbook content to suit the needs of a particular class. Therefore, although *Wiley Pathways Project Management* proceeds logically from the basics to increasingly more challenging material, chapters are further organized into sections that are self-contained for maximum teaching and learning flexibility.

▲ **Numeric system of headings.** *Wiley Pathways Project Management* uses a numeric system for headings (for example, 2.3.4 identifies the fourth sub-section of section 3 of chapter 2). With this system, students and teachers can quickly and easily pinpoint topics in the table of contents and the text, keeping class time and study sessions focused.

▲ **Core content.** Topics in the text are organized into fourteen chapters.

PART I: Defining Your Project

Chapter 1, Defining Project Management Today, introduces the basics of projects and project management skills. The chapter examines what constitutes a successful project and compares project management with general management. An introduction to various roles within projects and common types of projects provides an overview of work within project-based organizations.

Chapter 2, Identifying Project Needs and Solutions, explains how any project can be defined in terms of its needs, strategies, objectives, boundaries, and unknowns. The Statement of Work is a frequently used tool for establishing and focusing new projects. The chapter also highlights the pros and cons of managing projects utilizing project-management software.

Chapter 3, Organizing Projects, discusses how projects can fit into various types of companies, including traditional companies which are often organized centrally or functionally. Because projects are even more common in companies with matrix and mixed organizations, the chapter discusses the challenges of managing multiple deadlines, resources, and expectations within these often demanding environments.

Part II: Project Planning and Control

Chapter 4, Planning Projects, anchors the process of project management around the concept of the project life cycle. From the conceive phase through the close phase, projects require specific actions from a variety of participants. A Work Breakdown Structure and Linear Responsibility Chart are tools to identify and describe the responsibilities and deadlines for every person and group associated with a project. Project managers have a variety of ways to create, develop, and display Work Breakdown Structures and Linear Responsibility Charts, and this chapter highlights some of the most popular and useful formats. The chapter concludes by offering advice for working with multi-disciplinary teams and avoiding project plan failure.

Chapter 5, Budgeting Projects, introduces readers to various techniques and rationales for estimating how much projects will cost, including top-down and bottom-up budgeting. Methods of improving the accuracy of estimates and responses to budget uncertainty are covered in the chapter as well.

Chapter 6, Establishing Project Schedules, focuses on the technical methods and graphical representations of project tasks and timelines. The processes of planning, sketching, and refining network diagrams is covered in detail with detailed examples to make this important but often theoretical topic more understandable and relevant. Ways to more accurately estimate activity durations and identifying time constraints are discussed, as our formats for display schedules.

Chapter 7, Estimating and Allocating Resources, discusses methods for effectively estimating and assigning resources—including human resources, materials, and equipment—to projects. The chapter explores ways to optimize resources through the process of resource loading and leveling. The challenges of allocating scarce resources and juggling limited resources among multiple projects are also examined.

Part III: People: The Key To Project Success

Chapter 8, Being an Effective Project Manager, provides a wealth of real-world strategies that readers need to succeed and excel as project managers. This chapter covers the essential criteria for selecting a project manager, as well as ways to get an off-track plan back on-track. The daily challenges of leadership, team member accountability, delegation, and micromanagement are defined and strategic responses are explored in detail.

Chapter 9, Involving the Right People in Projects, explores the various people that constitute a project's audience. Drivers, supporters, and observers for a project exist at various levels within and outside of an organization, and project managers can identify these groups with audience lists and other communication tools.

Chapter 10, Managing Project Teams, focuses on the most prevalent organizational structure within companies today—the project team. By accurately defining team members' responsibilities and roles, a project manager can increase the likelihood of project success. New project teams require special consideration and planning on the part of the project management, while motivating team members is an important challenge throughout the life of projects.

PART IV: Steering the Ship

Chapter 11, Tracking Progress and Maintaining Control, is devoted to the project manager's ongoing duties of planning, monitoring, and controlling various aspects of projects, particularly budgets and schedules. Data is an essential tool for monitoring and control, and this chapter covers ways to accurately collect, analyze, report, and share data to continually improve projects. An explanation of Earned Value Analysis shows how to easily assess whether projects are on-schedule and on-budget. The process of establishing monitoring/control systems and minimizing scope creep are discussed as well.

Chapter 12, Communicating and Documenting Project Progress, covers the various forms that communication can take within organizations and project teams. The chapter focuses on two critical types of communications—reports and meetings. Strategies for drafting effective meetings are complemented by advice on how to hold empowering, useful meetings throughout a project's life cycle.

Chapter 13, Managing Risk, confronts the uncertainty that resides within all projects and examines techniques for identifying, assessing, and analyzing risks. Project managers can deal effectively with risk, plan ahead, and respond to negative events through the creation and implementation of a comprehensive risk-management plan.

Chapter 14, Evaluating and Ending Projects, explains the necessary tasks that occur for projects near completion. Project managers are frequently responsible for evaluating the highs and lows of projects and producing reports to help future projects run more smoothly. The project audit, a more formal evaluation by a third party, is also discussed and compared to project evaluations. Finally, the chapter outlines ways to terminate projects in a positive manner.

Pre-reading Learning Aids

Each chapter of *Wiley Pathways Project Management* features the following learning and study aids to activate students' prior knowledge of the topics and orient them to the material.

▲ **Pre-test.** This pre-reading assessment tool in multiple-choice format not only introduces chapter material, but it also helps students anticipate the chapter's learning outcomes. By focusing students' attention on what they do not know, the self-test provides students with a benchmark against which they can measure their own progress. The pre-test is available online at www.wiley.com/college/portny.

▲ **What You'll Learn in this Chapter.** This bulleted list focuses on *subject matter* that will be taught. It tells students what they will be learning in this chapter and why it is significant for their careers. It will also help students understand why the chapter is important and how it relates to other chapters in the text.

▲ **After Studying this Chapter, You'll Be Able To.** This list emphasizes *capabilities and skills* students will learn as a result of reading the chapter. It focuses on *execution* of subject matter that show the relationship between what students will learn in the chapter and how the information learned will be applied in an on-the-job situation.

Within-text Learning Aids

The following learning aids are designed to encourage analysis and synthesis of the material, support the learning process, and ensure success during the evaluation phase:

▲ **Introduction.** This section orients the student by introducing the chapter and explaining its practical value and relevance to the book as a whole. Short summaries of chapter sections preview the topics to follow.

▲ **"For Example" Boxes.** Found within each chapter, these boxes tie section content to real-world examples, scenarios, and applications.

▲ **Figures and tables.** Line art and photos have been carefully chosen to be truly instructional rather than filler. Tables distill and present information in a way that is easy to identify, access, and understand, enhancing the focus of the text on essential ideas.

▲ **Self-Check.** Related to the "What You'll Learn" bullets and found at the end of each section, this battery of short answer questions emphasizes student understanding of concepts and mastery of section content. Though the questions may either be discussed in class or studied by students outside of class, students should not go on before they can answer all questions correctly.

▲ **Key Terms and Glossary.** To help students develop a professional vocabulary, key terms are bolded in the introduction, summary, and when they first appear in the chapter. A complete list of key terms with brief definitions appears at the end of each chapter and again in a glossary at the end of the book. Knowledge of key terms is assessed by all assessment tools (see below).

▲ **Summary.** Each chapter concludes with a summary paragraph that reviews the major concepts in the chapter and links back to the "What You'll Learn" list.

Evaluation and Assessment Tools

Each *Wiley Pathways* text consists of a variety of within-chapter and end-of-chapter assessment tools that test how well students have learned the material. These tools also encourage students to extend their learning into different scenarios and higher levels of understanding and thinking. The following assessment tools appear in every chapter of *Wiley Pathways Project Management:*

▲ *Summary Questions* help students summarize the chapter's main points by asking a series of multiple choice and true/false questions that emphasize student understanding of concepts and mastery of chapter content. Students should be able to answer all of the Summary Questions correctly before moving on.

▲ *Applying this Chapter Questions* drive home key ideas by asking students to synthesize and apply chapter concepts to new, real-life situations and scenarios. Asks student to practice using the material they have learned in contrived situations that help reinforce their understanding, and may throw light on important considerations, advantages, or drawbacks to a specific methodology.

▲ *You Try It Questions* are designed to extend students' thinking, and so are ideal for discussion, writing assignments, or for use as case studies. Using an open-ended format and sometimes based on Web sources, they encourage students to draw conclusions using chapter material applied to real-world situations, which fosters both mastery and independent learning.

▲ *Post-test* should be taken after students have completed the chapter. It includes all of the questions in the pre-test, so that students can see how their learning has progressed and improved.

Instructor and Student Package

Wiley Pathways Project Management is available with the following teaching and learning supplements. All supplements are available online at the text's Book Companion Web site, located at www.wiley.com/college/portny.

▲ **Instructor's Resource Guide.** Provides the following aids and supplements for teaching an Introduction to Project Management course:

- *Sample syllabus.* A convenient template that instructors may use for creating their own course syllabi.
- *Teaching suggestions.* For each chapter, these include a chapter summary, learning objectives, definitions of key terms, lecture notes, answers to select text question sets, and at least 3 suggestions for classroom activities, such as ideas for speakers to invite, videos to show, and other projects.

▲ **PowerPoints.** Key information is summarized in 15 to 20 PowerPoints per chapter. Instructors may use these in class or choose to share them with students for class presentations or to provide additional study support.

▲ **Test Bank.** One test per chapter, as well as a mid-term, and two finals: one cumulative, one non-cumulative. Each includes true/false, multiple choice, and open-ended questions. Answers and page references are provided for the true/false and multiple choice questions, and page references for the open-ended questions. Available in Microsoft Word and computerized formats.

ACKNOWLEDGMENTS

Taken together, the content, pedagogy, and assessment elements of *Wiley Pathways Project Management* offer the career-oriented student the most important aspects of project management as well as ways to develop the skills and capabilities that current and future employers seek in the individuals they hire and promote. Instructors will appreciate its practical focus, conciseness, and real-world emphasis. We would like to thank the reviewers for their feedback and suggestions during the text's development. Their advice on how to shape *Wiley Pathways Project Management* into a solid learning tool that meets both their needs and those of their busy students is deeply appreciated.

BRIEF CONTENTS

CONTENTS

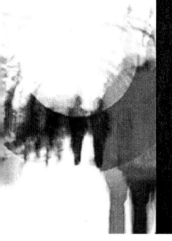

1

DEFINING PROJECT MANAGEMENT TODAY
Guiding People, Resources, and Processes to Successful Completion

Starting Point

Go to www.wiley.com/college/portny to assess your knowledge of the basics of project management.
Determine where you need to concentrate your effort.

What You'll Learn in This Chapter

- ▲ The range of projects in today's workplace
- ▲ Three essential elements of any project
- ▲ The contrasts between project management and general management
- ▲ The responsibilities of project managers
- ▲ Roles of key people associated with projects
- ▲ The challenges of project management
- ▲ Four types of projects based on product and process change
- ▲ On-site and off-site project management

After Studying This Chapter, You'll Be Able To

- ▲ Understand the foundational knowledge of project roles, responsibilities, types, and terms in order to manage projects
- ▲ Differentiate among the roles of project managers, functional managers, functional employees, upper management, and project champions
- ▲ Propose solutions to common project management challenges
- ▲ Compare projects based on product and process change they involve

INTRODUCTION

Dynamic companies organize their employees and resources around projects, which are managed by project managers. Project managers' careful balancing of outcomes, schedules, and resources often determines whether a project is a success. Although project management is considerably different from general management, typical roles and responsibilities exist for the people involved in projects. The challenges of project management—most notably the high expectations from upper management combined with little or no hierarchical authority—are intense, but savvy, thoughtful project managers can impact the entire direction of an organization. Projects fall into four general categories, regardless of industry. Thanks to technology, project managers can manage people and resources anywhere in the world.

1.1 Understanding Project Management

Successful organizations create projects that produce desired results in established time frames with assigned resources. As a result, businesses are increasingly driven to find individuals who can excel in this project-oriented environment.

People wanting to move ahead in their careers appear to be getting the message. Growing numbers of people at all levels in organizations are looking for ways to get a better handle on their projects. A *Fortune* magazine article recently identified "project manager" as the number-one career option. What the article didn't say is that the majority of people who are becoming project managers aren't doing so by choice. Instead, project management is often an unexpected but required progression in their chosen career paths.

Successful project managers need targeted skills and techniques so they can steer projects to successful completion.

1.1.1 Defining Projects

A **project** is a temporary endeavor undertaken to create a unique product or service. It is specific, timely, usually multidisciplinary, and always conflict ridden. Projects also vary greatly.

▲ **Projects may be large or small.** Installing a new subway system, which may cost more than $1 billion and take 10 to 15 years to complete, is a project, and so is preparing a report of monthly sales figures, which may take one day to complete.

▲ **Projects may involve many persons or just one.** Training all 10,000 members of an organization's staff in a new affirmative-action policy is a project, as is rearranging the furniture and equipment in an office.

▲ **Projects may be planned formally or informally.** Many projects are included in an organization's annual plan and require formal approval of all work to be performed, all personnel assignments, and all resource expenditures. Other projects are assigned to workers in the course of a conversation, with no mention of budget or additional staff.

▲ **Projects may be tracked formally or informally.** For some projects, all hours spent are faithfully recorded on time sheets and all dollars expended are separately identified in the organization's financial system. For others, no record of hours spent is ever kept and expenditures are just considered as part of the organization's operating budget.

▲ **Projects may be performed for external or internal clients and customers.** Repairing a piece of equipment that your company sold to a customer is a project. Writing an article for your organization's internal newsletter is also a project.

▲ **Projects may be defined by a legal contract or an informal agreement.** A signed contract between a builder and a customer to construct a house defines a project; a promise made to install a new software package on a colleague's computer similarly defines a project.

In the workplace, the following two terms are often confused with a project:

1. A **process** is a series of steps by which a particular job function is routinely performed. A company's annual budgeting process or the procedure a manager goes through to procure new office equipment are examples of processes. A process is *not* a one-time activity that achieves a specific result; instead, a process defines how a particular job is to be done *every* time it's done. Processes, such as the activities performed to buy needed materials, are often included as parts of projects.

2. A **program** is work performed toward achieving a long-range goal. A health-awareness program and an employee-morale program are examples. A program never completely achieves its goal (for example, the public will never be totally aware of all health issues). Instead, one or more projects may be performed to accomplish specific results that are related to the program's goal (such as conducting a workshop on how to minimize the risk of heart disease). In this case, a program is comprised of a series of projects.

1.1.2 Defining Project Management

Project management is the process of guiding a project from its beginning through its performance to its closure. Project management includes the following three basic operations, or activities:

1. **Planning** includes specifying results to be achieved, determining schedules, and estimating resources required. Chapter 4 deals with project planning in detail.

FOR EXAMPLE

The Power of Projects

For Daimler-Chrysler, team-based product development programs that integrate product design, engineering, manufacturing, and marketing have not only improved its products, but they've also allowed significant reductions in time-to-market. By organizing employees in project-based groups, Daimler-Chrysler cut almost 18 months from its new product development timeline and produced several new car lines (notably the LH sedans, Neon, and Viper models) that have sold well and received high-quality ratings. In addition to the value of good design, the economic value of the time saved is immense—faster design saves labor and overhead costs, as well as encourages earlier sales and return on the investment (in Daimler-Chrysler's case amounting to hundreds of millions of dollars).

---

2. **Organizing** includes defining people's roles and responsibilities. See Sections 1.4 and 4.2.

3. **Controlling** includes reconfirming people's expected performance, monitoring actions and results, addressing problems encountered, and sharing information with interested people. The chapters in Part IV deal with these responsibilities.

1.1.3 Why Projects and Project Management?

The reason that more organizations and businesses are organizing their operations around projects and assigning project managers to specific goals is simple. Projects attach the responsibility and authority for achieving an organizational goal on an individual or small group when the job does not clearly fall within the definition of routine work.

SELF-CHECK

1. What are the three main activities of project management? *Planning Organizing Control*
2. Which of the following is a project? *All*
   (a) conducting a 5-phase lab test based on FDA guidelines
   (b) sending out late-payment form letters by the 15th of each month
   (c) creating a new log for incoming packages
   (d) encouraging employees to invest in the company's 401(k) program

1.2 Defining Project Success

No matter the specific characteristics of a project, the same three core elements are essential.

1. **Outcome:** a project has at least one goal (and often several goals) of creating a specific product (a new car) or result (10 percent reduction in the number of negative customer service surveys).
2. **Schedule:** project work begins and ends on specific, established dates.
3. **Resources:** projects require amounts of people, funds, equipment, facilities, and information.

Figure 1-1 illustrates that each of the three core elements affects the other two. Expanding desired outcomes may require more time (a later end date, for example) or more resources (additional staff). Moving up the end date may necessitate paring down the results to be accomplished or increasing project expenditures (exceeding the established budgets) by paying overtime to project staff.

The performance of the project—and the effectiveness of the project manager—is measured by the degree to which these goals are achieved. Specifically,

▲ **Outcome:** does the project meet the agreed-upon specifications to the satisfaction of the customer?
▲ **Schedule:** is the project on time or early?
▲ **Resources:** is the project within or under budget?

Figure 1-1

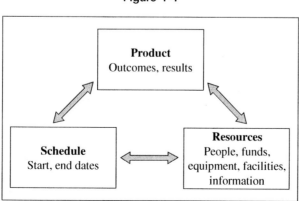

The three essential elements of any project.

Acting in response to the three essentials, a project team works to achieve the desired results. The type of information a project manager needs to plan and manage a project is the same, although the ease and the time required to develop it may differ. The more thoroughly a project manager plans and manages a project, the more likely the project will be deemed a success.

When project information is determined accurately and completely and shared effectively, project managers dramatically increase their chances of project success. When pieces of this information are vague, missing, or not shared effectively, the chances of success are reduced.

1.2.1 Meeting Specifications

A client sets the expectations of a project's outcomes; this makes each project unique. The success of outcome-related goals—meeting specifications—is set primarily by the customer or client. For the purposes of this book, the **client** can be someone or some organization outside the company performing the project or someone or some organization within the company performing the project.

Some management theorists insist that quality is a separate and distinct goal of the project along with time, cost, and specifications. However, this book considers quality an inherent part of the project specifications, not separable from them.

1.2.2 Factoring in Uncertainty

If this were a predictable world, no project would ever go awry. Managing projects would be relatively simple, requiring only careful planning. However, this is an uncertain world, filled with chance events and uncertainty. The best-made plans often go awry. Uncertainty ensures that projects travel a rough road.

FOR EXAMPLE

Balancing Outcomes, Schedules, and Resources

When a construction project—such as building a new suburban home by May 1—falls behind schedule due to bad weather, the contractor, acting as project manager, can get the project back on schedule by adding resources to the project. In the case of building a home, additional resources mean more labor and/or additional equipment. If the budget cannot be raised to cover the additional resources, the contractor may have to negotiate with the client for a later delivery date. If neither cost nor schedule can be negotiated, the contractor may have to swallow the added costs (or pay a penalty for late delivery) and accept lower profits.

All projects are carried out under conditions of uncertainty. Well-tested software routines may not perform properly when integrated with other well-tested routines. A chemical compound may destroy cancer cells in a test tube—and even in the bodies of test animals—but may kill the host as well as the cancer. As a result, project managers spend a great deal of time adapting to unpredicted change.

SELF-CHECK

1. Your manufacturing team is responsible for producing 500 office chairs every week. Which of the three core elements of a project are these chairs?
2. Of the three core elements of a project, *resources* refers to which of the following?

    (a) funds

    (b) facilities

    (c) people

    (d) all of the above
3. In most cases, the client or customer ultimately determines whether a project meets specifications and can be considered a success. True or false?

1.3 Comparing Project Management and General Management

Project management differs from general management largely because projects differ from "nonprojects." For example:

▲ **Each project is unique.** Project managers must be creative and flexible, and have the ability to adjust rapidly to changes. When managing nonprojects, the general manager tries to "manage by exception." In other words, for nonprojects, almost everything is routine and is handled routinely by subordinates. The manager deals only with the exceptions. For the project manager, almost everything is an exception.

▲ **Projects have a higher potential for conflict than nonprojects.** Project managers must have special skills in conflict resolution.

▲ **Project success is absolutely dependent on detailed planning.** The project plan is the immediate source of the project's budget, schedule, control, and evaluation. Detailed planning is critically important. Project planning is discussed in Section 4.1.

▲ **Project budgets and schedules are constructed differently from standard, nonproject budgets and schedules.** Budgets for nonprojects are primarily modifications of budgets for the same activity in the previous quarter or year. By contrast, project budgets are newly created for each project and often cover several periods in the future. A project budget is derived directly from the project plan that calls for specific activities. These activities require resources, and such resources are the heart of the project budget. Similarly, the project schedule is also derived from the project plan.

▲ **Projects are accomplished in unique ways.** In a nonproject manufacturing line, for example, the sequence in which various things are done is set when the production line is designed. The sequence of activities usually is not altered when new models are produced. On the other hand, each project has a schedule of its own. Previous projects with deliverables similar to the one at hand may provide a rough template for the current project, but its schedule is set by the project's unique plan and by the date on which the project is due for delivery to the client.

▲ **Projects are often multidisciplinary.** The routine work of most organizations takes place within a well-defined structure of divisions,

---

FOR EXAMPLE

Win-Win Negotiating and Ink-Jet Printers

Win-win negotiating is a valuable skill for any manager, but for the project manager it is almost essential to job success. Win-win negotiation involves taking a creative, collaborative approach to solving problems. For example, in a product development project for a new ink-jet printer, the design engineer working on the project suggests adding more memory to the printer so it can print faster. The project manager initially opposes this suggestion, feeling that the added memory will make the printer too costly. After comparing the proposed product with the competition and discussing their concerns, the design engineer and project manager agree that they need to search for another alternative (sometimes referred to as the "third alternative") that will increase the printer's speed without increasing its costs. A couple of days later, the design engineer identifies a new ink that can simultaneously increase the printer's speed and actually lower its total and operating costs.

departments, sections, and similar subdivisions. The typical project cannot thrive under such restrictions. Most projects need technical knowledge, information, and special skills from various departments to be successful. Section 4.6 discusses the multidisciplinary nature of projects.

▲ **Projects often don't fit into traditional managerial hierarchy.** A reasonably well-defined managerial hierarchy still exists in general management; subordinates report to superiors and the lines of authority are clear. In project management, this is rarely the case. The project manager may be relatively low in the hierarchical chain of command and still have a high level of responsibility for completing a project successfully. Responsibility without the authority of rank or position is so common in project management that it is the rule, not the exception.

SELF-CHECK

1. Projects typically combine professionals from similar disciplines while nonprojects require individuals from various disciplines and departments to work together. True or false?
2. Where do project budgets and schedules typically come from?
3. Nonproject work is largely about routine processes and responses, while project work can be described by which of the following?

   (a) it is uncontrollable and random

   (b) it requires unique solutions to exceptional situations

   (c) it is based on previous, successful examples

   (d) it requires a highly analytical manager

1.4 Defining Project Roles

Various individuals and groups are often involved in a single project. The following people typically play critical roles in a project's success:

▲ **Project manager:** the person ultimately responsible for the successful completion of the project.
▲ **Functional managers:** the team members' direct-line supervisors.

▲ **Functional employees** or **project team members:** people responsible for successfully performing individual project activities.

▲ **Upper management:** people in charge of the organization's major business units.

1.4.1 Considering the Project Manager's Role

Project managers are responsible for all aspects of the project. This doesn't mean they have to do everything themselves, but it does mean that project managers must see that everything gets done satisfactorily.

Project managers are specifically responsible for the following:

▲ Describing objectives, schedule, and resource budgets.

▲ Ensuring a clear, feasible project plan for how everyone will reach performance targets.

▲ Creating and sustaining a focused and committed team.

▲ Selecting or creating a team's operating practices and procedures.

▲ Managing the accomplishment of objectives, within time and budget targets.

▲ Monitoring performance against plans and dealing with any problems that arise.

▲ Resolving priority, work approach, or interpersonal conflicts.

▲ Controlling project changes.

▲ Reporting on project activities.

▲ Keeping clients informed and committed.

▲ Contributing to team members' performance appraisals.

Some companies use the terms *project director* or *project leader,* rather than *project manager.* Check with the expectations of the specific organization, but usually *project manager* and *project director* describe the same position. Project leaders, however, often do not have traditional management responsibilities (budgeting, employee evaluations, and so on) but are responsible for stimulating a shared vision and creating positive interpersonal relationships. But again, check with the specific organization for its expectation of *project leaders*—this may be its term for *project manager.*

The project manager's job is challenging. He or she must coordinate technically specialized professionals—who often have limited experience working together—to help them achieve a common goal. The project manager's own work experience is often technical in nature, yet his or her success requires a keen ability to identify and resolve sensitive organizational and interpersonal issues. Attitude and approach are critical to having the greatest chances for success.

1.4.2 Considering the Functional Manager's Role

Functional managers are responsible for orchestrating their staffs' assignments among different projects, as well as providing the resources to allow their staffs to perform their assignments in accordance with the highest standards of technical excellence.

Specifically, functional managers are responsible for the following:

▲ Developing or approving plans that specify the type, timing, and amount of resources needed to do tasks in their area of specialty.

▲ Ensuring team members are available to perform their assigned tasks when needed and for the amount of time promised.

▲ Providing technical expertise and guidance to help team members solve problems related to their project assignments.

▲ Providing the equipment and facilities for a person to do his or her work.

▲ Helping people maintain their technical skills and knowledge.

▲ Ensuring consistent methodological approaches on all projects throughout the organization dealing with a particular area.

▲ Completing team members' performance appraisals.

▲ Recognizing performance with salary increases, promotions, and job assignments.

▲ Approving team members' requests for annual leave, administrative leave, training, and other activities that will take time away from the job.

1.4.3 Considering the Functional Employee's Role

Functional employees—also known as project team members—must satisfy the requests of both their functional managers and their project manager. Team member responsibilities are related to project assignments and can include the following:

▲ Ensuring specific tasks are performed in accordance with the highest standards of technical excellence.

▲ Performing assignments on time and within budget.

▲ Maintaining special skills and knowledge as needed to complete work.

In addition, team members are responsible for working with and supporting other team members' project efforts. Such help may entail the following:

▲ Considering the effect an action might have on other team members' tasks.

▲ Identifying situations and problems that might affect team members' tasks.

▲ Keeping team members informed of progress, accomplishments, and any problems.

FOR EXAMPLE

Multiple Project Roles and Software Development

Fifteen years ago, a single, exceptionally talented individual was often responsible for researching, developing, writing, and testing a new software program. With today's marketplace demands for high-quality, reasonably priced, quick-to-market software, small development teams with numerous and overlapping roles have become the norm. Although every project is unique, software development teams typically consist of a client (or project sponsor), a project manager, multiple Subject Matter Experts (SMEs), an instructional designer (who brings educational expertise to the project), writers, graphic artist, programmers, audio and video producers, and quality assurance reviewers, in addition to business office administrators, marketing support, manufacturer, and distribution liaisons.

1.4.4 Considering the Role of Executives and Upper Management

Upper management creates the organizational environment; oversees the development and use of operating policies, procedures, and practices; and funds and encourages the development of required information systems.

More specifically, executives are responsible for the following:

▲ Setting policies and procedures for addressing resource priorities and conflicts.
▲ Creating and maintaining labor and financial information systems.
▲ Providing facilities and equipment to support the performance of project work.
▲ Defining the limits of managers' decision-making authority.

Before a project begins its life cycle, the parent organization typically must select or approve it for funding. Committees of upper managers usually go through a selection process to ensure that several conditions are considered before committing to undertake any project. These conditions vary widely from firm to firm, but several conditions are common, such as the following:

▲ Is the project potentially profitable?
▲ Does it have a chance of meeting our return-on-investment target?
▲ Does the company have, or can it easily acquire, the knowledge and skills to carry out the project successfully?
▲ Does the project involve building competencies that are considered consistent with our company's strategic plan?

Although the selection process is usually complete *before* a project manager is appointed to a project, the project manager needs to know exactly why the organization selected the specific project because this sheds considerable light on what the project (and hence the project manager) is expected to accomplish, from senior management's point of view.

The project may have been selected because it appeared to be profitable, or was a way of entering a new area of business, or a way of building a reputation of competency with a new client or in a new market. The knowledge of the reason for the project's selection can be very helpful to the project manager by indicating senior management's goals for the project, which will point to the desirability of some trade-offs and the undesirability of others.

SELF-CHECK

1. Project managers are typically responsible for which of the following?
    (a) determining whether a project is profitable
    (b) ensuring team members are available to work on the project
    (c) defending the rationale for the project
    (d) sustaining the focus and vision of the project team
2. Maintaining project participants' technical skills is most commonly the responsibility of which of the following?
    (a) functional employees and functional managers
    (b) functional managers and project managers
    (c) functional employees and upper management
    (d) project managers and functional employees
3. Upper management can impact projects by doing which of the following?
    (a) hiring only the best functional employees
    (b) evaluating employees and project managers rigorously
    (c) funding the purchase of a critical piece of equipment
    (d) monitoring the schedule and budget of the project

1.5 The Project Manager as a Planning Agent

The rules for performance in traditional organizations have historically been quite simple: A boss makes assignments; employees carry them out. Questioning an assignment was a sign of insubordination or incompetence.

The rules for most successful companies and organizations have changed. Today, the following is more likely:

▲ Your boss generates ideas; you must assess what it takes to implement them.

▲ Your boss tells you what he or she wants to achieve and the constraints for doing it. You must check to be sure the project meets the real need and then translate general expectations into specific results.

▲ You must determine the work to be done, schedules that can be met, and the resources required.

▲ You stay on top of the work performed and identify issues and concerns as they arise.

In many ways, the process doesn't make sense any other way. If a boss does all the detailed project planning, who creates visions and strategies? And a boss's assertion that something is possible doesn't automatically mean that it is. Knowledgeable, technical experts must get involved in developing the plans. The project manager has an opportunity to understand the expectations and proposed approaches and to raise any questions.

The hard part, though, is that most bosses, when assigning a project, don't remind project managers that they need to clarify the assignment, assess its feasibility, and so on. In fact, sometimes project managers are specifically directed *not* to spend time on further planning and analysis, but to start work at once in order to have any chance of meeting the aggressive time frames set.

Successful project managers must take the initiative for planning and controlling projects, whether or not they're asked to do this. Bosses want project managers to successfully complete the assigned project (even though it may, at times, feel like this isn't the case to harried project managers). Approaching a project assignment as a planning agent—giving the situation careful thought, questioning all assumptions, and developing strategies to meet goals—gives the project manager the greatest chance to meet expectations.

SELF-CHECK

1. Careful assessment and planning are critical to successful project management. Unfortunately, which of the following situations often occurs?

   (a) Upper management usually does the planning and then hands off plans to project managers.

> **(b)** Upper management rarely asks project managers to assess and plan prior to beginning a project.
>
> **(c)** Upper management usually demands extensive plans from project managers.
>
> **(d)** None of the above
>
> 2. For project managers to function as planning agents, project managers must do which of the following?
>
> **(a)** appropriately question all project assumptions
>
> **(b)** must be empowered by their bosses to analyze the project
>
> **(c)** determine the work to be done and the resources required
>
> **(d)** all of the above

1.6 Identifying Project Champions

A **project champion** is a person in a high position in the organization who strongly supports a project. Project champions are not necessarily part of a project team (see Section 1.4), although sometimes they are.

A project champion does the following:

▲ Advocates for a project in disputes, planning meetings, and review sessions.

▲ Takes necessary actions to help ensure a project is successfully completed.

▲ Has sufficient power and authority to help resolve conflicts over resources, schedules, and technical issues.

▲ Is willing to have his or her name cited as a strong supporter of the project.

Sometimes the best champion is one whose support is never called into service. Just knowing that this person supports a project helps others appreciate its importance and encourages others to work diligently to ensure its success.

If a project doesn't have a natural champion (for example, the executive who originally suggested the idea for the project), savvy project managers work hard to recruit one. Find people who can reap benefits from the project and who have sufficient power and influence to encourage serious, ongoing organizational commitment to the project. Explain to this person why it's in his or her best interest for the project to succeed and how specifically his or her help is necessary.

FOR EXAMPLE

Champion for Change

Prior to becoming President and CEO of book and magazine publisher Meredith Corporation (www.meredith.com), Stephen Lacy served as project champion for several projects for the organization in addition to holding various upper management positions. For example, in response to mid-western employees' requests to interact with top East and West Coast creative talent, Lacy supported the efforts of a small team of employees to develop and reserve corporate funding for an ongoing series of seminars that host outstanding writers, designers, and artists from across the United States on Meredith's Des Moines, Iowa, campus.

SELF-CHECK

1. Project champions can be official members of a project team. True or false?
2. Project champions develop naturally from a project; they cannot be effectively recruited or assigned. True or false?
3. Project champions may be called upon to do which of the following?

   (a) fund controversial projects

   (b) recommend project manager candidates

   (c) advocate for projects during planning meetings

   (d) publicize projects

1.7 Meeting the Demands of Project Management

Project management can be richly rewarding work and is often a critical step in an employee's progression from employee to higher levels of supervision and management. However, it is not easy work. Some of the most significant challenges of project management include the following:

▲ **High responsibility, little authority.** Unlike their general management counterparts, project managers have responsibility for accomplishing a project, but generally little or no legitimate authority to command the required resources from the existing functional departments. The project manager must be skilled at negotiation, creative problem-solving, and compromise to obtain these resources.

▲ **Project overload.** Because projects are, by definition, temporary, many project managers find themselves assigned to multiple projects at any one given time. Many project managers are asked to accept a new project in addition to—not in lieu of—existing assignments. Upper management often assumes that project managers will handle the difficulties. Also, when conflicts arise over a person's need to spend time on his or her different assignments, guidelines or procedures to resolve them might not exist or might be inadequate.

▲ **Team members often have never worked together before.** Many project teams are composed of people who haven't worked together before—in fact, some may not even know each other. These unfamiliar relationships may slow the project down because team members might have different operating and communicating styles, might use different procedures for performing the same type of activity, and might not have had the time to develop a sense of mutual respect and trust for each other. The project manager must do everything in his or her capability to quickly form flexible, open, and trust-based working relationships between team members (see Section 10.2).

▲ **No direct authority.** For most projects, the project manager and team members have no direct authority over each other. Therefore, common rewards such as salary increases, superior performance appraisals, and job promotions are not available to encourage top performance. And a project manager can't settle conflicts over time commitments or technical direction with one, unilateral decision. For the project manager, negotiation, discussion facilitation, and listening skills are essential.

▲ **Client demands.** In addition to being responsible for the success of the project to his or her superiors, a project manager is also responsible to the client. Clients are motivated to stay in close touch with a project they have commissioned. Because clients support the project, they feel they have a right to intercede with suggestions (requests, alterations, demands). Cost, schedule, and performance changes are the most common outcomes of client intercession, and the costs of these changes often exceed the client's expectations.

▲ **High communications demands.** A major part of any project manager's job is to keep senior management up to date on the state of the project. In particular, the project manager needs to keep management informed of any problems affecting the project—or any problem likely to affect the project in the future. A golden rule for project managers is, "Never let the boss be surprised!" Violating this rule can cost the project manager credibility, trust, and possibly his or her job. Project managers must

FOR EXAMPLE

Persuasion: An Essential Project Manager Skill

According to author and consultant Jay Conger, successful project managers must be skillful at persuading others if they want to meet the demands of project management in today's workplace. In his article for the *Harvard Business Review*, Conger breaks down the skill of persuading others into four essential elements: (1) effective persuaders must be credible to those they are trying to persuade; (2) they must find goals held in common with those being persuaded; (3) they must use "vivid" language and compelling evidence; (4) they must connect with the emotions of those they are trying to persuade.

inform senior management about problems in order to assist in its solution. Doing this in a timely, honest, and proactive fashion builds trust between the project manager and senior managers—and between the project manager and the project team.

SELF-CHECK

1. The "high responsibility, little authority" challenge of project management means which of the following?

   (a) Project managers are highly responsible for project expectations but have little authority to make assignments.

   (b) Project managers are highly responsible for results but have little authority to enforce decisions.

   (c) Project managers are highly responsible for team cohesiveness but have little authority to reward team members.

   (d) none of the above

2. In the rapid-prototyping division of a circuit board manufacturer, Bruno typically manages five small projects with intermittent deadlines. When his boss assigns him an additional large project with a deadline in the next month, Bruno is likely to experience which of the following?

   (a) shifting responsibility

   (b) scope creep

   (c) project manifestation

   (d) project overload

1.8 Classifying Projects

Most organizations and companies fund a mix of projects, spread appropriately across various areas of interest, with the hope of making diverse, significant contributions to the organization's goals (and financial interests).

One way to describe many of the projects (particularly product/service development projects) is in terms of the extent of product and process changes. Wheelwright and Clark (1992) suggest a model called the **aggregate project plan**, or **portfolio project plan**, which summarizes the various types of projects an organization engages in. Four categories of projects exist, based on the extent that a project requires product change and process change:

1. **Derivative projects.** These are projects with objectives or deliverables that are only incrementally different in both product and process from existing offerings. They are often meant to replace current offerings or add an extension to current offerings (e.g., lower priced version, upscale version).

2. **Platform projects.** The planned outputs of these projects represent major departures from existing offerings in terms of either the product/service itself or the process used to make and deliver it, or both. As such, they become "platforms" for the next generation of organizational offerings, such as a new model of automobile or a new type of insurance plan. If successful, platform projects eventually form the basis for future derivative projects.

3. **Breakthrough projects.** Breakthrough projects typically involve a newer technology than platform projects. It may be a "disruptive" technology that is known to the industry or something proprietary that the organization has been developing over time. Examples include the use of fiber-optic

FOR EXAMPLE

P&G Makes Way for the Web

With Tide®, Ivory®, Crest®, and Cover Girl®, Procter & Gamble (www.pg.com) has some of the best-known and best-selling brands in the world. Rather than relying on more than 100 years of popular products, P&G relies on a portfolio of projects to expand existing brands and products and research new lines. For example, P&G's roster of recent projects includes derivative projects (new berry-inspired shades of lipstick), platform projects (Olay® cosmetic products for every part of the body, not just the face), breakthrough projects (TideBuzz®, which uses detergent and electrostatic pulses to fight stains), and R&D projects (disposable diapers with rash-preventing ingredients in the absorbent lining).

cables for data transmission, cash-balance pension plans, and hybrid gasoline-electric automobiles.

4. **R&D projects.** These projects are "blue-sky," visionary endeavors, oriented toward using newly developed technologies or existing technologies in a new manner. They may also be for acquiring new knowledge or developing new technologies themselves.

SELF-CHECK

1. A project that uses cutting-edge technology is best defined as which of the following?

   (a) platform project

   (b) blue-sky project

   (c) R&D project

   (d) breakthrough project

2. A portfolio approach to projects ranks an organization's projects based on profitability. True or false?

3. A project that builds on established projects with only incremental differences and updates is best described as what type of project?

1.9 Managing Projects Off-site and On-site

More and more often, project teams are geographically dispersed. Many projects are international, and team members may be on different continents. For example, most aircraft engines are still designed in the United States while most engine construction occurs in Asia.

Geographically dispersed projects are referred to as **virtual projects**—possibly because so much of the communication is conducted by e-mail, through Web sites, by telephone or video conferencing, and by other high-technology methods.

Although long-distance project management is commonplace and no longer prohibitively expensive, it is beset with special problems. Written and voice-only communication (and even in video conferencing when the camera is not correctly aimed) does not allow communicators to see one another. In such cases, facial expression, vocal tone, and body language—all important tools in delivering a message—are not communicated between the parties. Two-way, real-time communication is the most effective way to transmit information or instructions. For virtual projects to succeed, communication between project manager and project team must be frequent, open, and two-way.

FOR EXAMPLE

An Innovative Approach

A sales manager for a national chain of automobile parts was assigned the task of training all sales representatives in his company in a new order entry process. The company had several hundred sales representatives located throughout the country, and he was to have the training completed within one month. In the past, the manager had delivered company training in instructor-led, on-site programs. After some preliminary consideration, though, he was convinced that it would take at least three months to design and present to all the sales representatives around the country using an instructor-led program. He was ready to tell his boss that the task was impossible when a colleague suggested presenting the training through his company's intranet. Using this new strategy, he completed the project ahead of schedule and at a considerable savings to the company.

SELF-CHECK

1. Locating a project manager off-site usually:
   (a) boosts productivity and collaboration.
   (b) only works for high-tech projects.
   (c) requires the project manager to take extra care communicating with team members.
   (d) all of the above
2. One of the greatest challenges of managing a virtual project is which of the following?
   (a) the lack of real-time, two-way communication
   (b) the fact that team members cannot be closely monitored
   (c) the financial demands of new technology to make such projects possible
   (d) the accessibility of managers

SUMMARY

In today's project-based job market, project managers provide the critical services of planning, organizing, and controlling the progress and success of medium- to large-size initiatives for organizations. General management with its hierarchy and rigid-reporting structure bears little resemblance to project management, where project participants have distinct roles and responsibilities and project managers must develop a host of specialized skills. Many organizations engage in a range of projects, while some project managers find themselves, with the aid of technology, orchestrating complex projects with resources and team members located all over the world.

KEY TERMS

Aggregate project plan	A summary of the various types of projects an organization engages in. Also known as portfolio project plan.
Breakthrough projects	Projects involving newer technology that may disrupt the status quo in an industry or marketplace.
Client	The entity for whom the project is being done; can be someone or some organization outside or within the company performing the project.
Controlling	Project-management responsibility that includes reconfirming people's expected performance, monitoring actions and results, addressing problems encountered, and sharing information with interested persons.
Derivative projects	Projects with objectives or deliverables that are only incrementally different in both product and process from existing offerings.
Functional employees	Individuals within projects who must satisfy the requests of both their functional managers and their project manager; also known as project team members.
Functional managers	Individuals in an organization or company who are responsible for orchestrating their staffs' assignments among different projects, as well as providing the resources to allow their staffs to perform their assignments in accordance with the highest standards of technical excellence.

Organizing	Project management responsibility that includes defining people's roles and responsibilities.
Outcome	A project-specific goal related to creating a specific product, service, or result.
Planning	Project-management responsibility that includes specifying results to be achieved, determining schedules, and estimating resources required.
Platform projects	Projects that represent major departures from existing offerings in terms of either the product or service itself or the process used to make and deliver it.
Portfolio project plan	See aggregate project plan.
Process	A series of steps by which a particular job function is routinely performed.
Program	Work (often multiple projects) performed toward achieving a long-range goal.
Project	A temporary endeavor undertaken to create a unique product or service.
Project champion	A person in a high position in the organization who strongly supports a project.
Project management	The process of guiding a project from its beginning through its performance to its closure. Project management requires planning, organizing, and controlling.
Project managers	Individuals responsible for seeing that all aspects of projects are completed satisfactorily.
Project team members	See functional employees.
R&D projects	Projects that are visionary and use newly developed technologies or existing technologies in a new manner.
Resources	The amount of people, funds, equipment, facilities, and information needed for a project.
Schedule	Plan that lists specific, established dates for work to begin and end.
Upper management	The people in charge of the organization's major business units.
Virtual projects	Geographically dispersed projects that can be managed through e-mail, Web sites, and other high-technology methods.

ASSESS YOUR UNDERSTANDING

Go to www.wiley.com/college/portny to assess your knowledge of the basics of projects and project management.
Measure your learning by comparing pre-test and post-test results.

Summary Questions

1. What is an example of a project, process, and program that you might find in the new product development department at a software development firm?

2. A project:
   (a) is a temporary arrangement undertaken to achieve a specific goal.
   (b) is limited by three elements: outcome, resources, and schedule.
   (c) can include people from various departments and specialties.
   (d) is all of the above.

3. Poor project managers end up spending much of their time negotiating with other departments and individuals to ensure their projects have adequate resources. True or false?

4. What are the four major roles associated with any project?

5. What are the two key differences between derivative, platform, breakthrough, and R&D projects?

6. How do the roles and responsibilities of a project manager directly contribute to the challenges of project management?

Applying This Chapter

1. In your job as an assistant manager at a fast food restaurant, you are frequently responsible for training new hourly workers to operate all the facility's food preparation equipment. How could you expand your experience and expertise in training new activities into a process, a project, and perhaps even a program?

2. As project manager for an electronics manufacturer, you are supposed to design a new, low-cost MP3 player in three months' time working with a team of three technicians. Because outcome, schedule, and resources are all interrelated, what are some options you might consider if you suddenly lose two of your technicians?

3. The major road paving project is three months behind schedule and nearly $1 million over budget. Given traditional roles and responsibilities,

how might a project manager, a functional manager, a functional employee, and a member of upper management appropriately respond to the situation?

4. Marissa's boss returns from an upper management off-site meeting and assigns the following public relations project to her: Marissa will project manage a team of writers, designers, and computer programmers in developing an anti-smoking Web site targeting teenagers. The Web site should use state-of-the-art online technology, be highly interactive, and be able to go live in six weeks. This is Marissa's first project management assignment, but past Web site projects that she's been part of have taken between 12 and 18 weeks to go live and didn't use extensive technology. How can Marissa approach this challenging project as a planning agent?

5. For the last year, you have project managed an initiative to gather and test crop samples from a fertilizer testing site located two miles south of your office. Your next project will resemble more of a virtual project, with you managing the gathering and testing of crop samples by regional teams located at four sites spread across the Unites States. How might your project management style need to adjust to meet this change?

6. Few products that manufacturers introduce as innovations truly count as such. Review the New Product section of a manufacturer's Web site or promotional materials. (If you don't have a manufacturer you want to review, visit the New Products page for Glade Air Freshening products at www.glade.com/new.aspx.) Considering the definitions of the four types of projects outlined in Section 1.8, which products are derivative, platform, breakthrough, or R&D projects?

YOU TRY IT

Process, Project, or Program?

Review your current resumé—if you don't yet have a resumé, begin drafting a list of responsibilities and achievements at each of your jobs, beginning with the most recent and working back. Carefully consider each position you list on your resumé and determine whether each responsibility or task involved work on a process, project, or program (refer to Section 1.1 for definitions). You don't need to add your identifications to your resumé, but prepare yourself for future job interviews by becoming able to quickly highlight an example of a difficult or important process you mastered, a project you participated on, a project (or portion of a project) that you led or managed, and a larger program that you contributed to in some way.

Project Management Trio: Outcome, Schedule, Resources

Try thinking of your next class project in terms of outcome, schedule, and resources. For your project to be successful, you need to have a clear sense of each element. For example, do you know the expected outcome for the assignment? What about the schedule—not only the final due date, but do you also know what deadlines you need to hit to consistently work toward the final date? Have you identified all your resources? What people, information sources, equipment, facilities,

and funds (if any) do you have access to to complete the project?

Your Champions

List several projects you've lead or worked on in the last two years. Your project may come from a variety of places—your job, volunteer organizations, community groups, church, family, or hobbies and interests. These projects could be large and formal (reorganizing your company's accounts payable department) or small and informal (planning and executing a friend's surprise birthday party). Review your proejct list and consider whether each project had a project champion (see Section 1.6). What specifically did each person do to champion your project? Is there anyone you've listed who might be worth considering to champion a project for you in the future? In what ways can you continue being in contact with these potential champions?

Your Challenges, Your Solutions

Select a project from your past that you led. Review the list of common project-management challenges in Section 1.7. Which of these challenges did you encounter while you led your project? The solutions that worked for you and your projects in the past are likely to be useful for future projects. What did you do to successfully meet the challenge(s)?

Handstar Inc. was created by two college roommates to develop software applications for handheld computing devices. In four years, it has grown to ten employees with annual sales approaching $1.5 million. Handstar's original product was an expense report application that allowed users to record expenses on their handheld computer and then import these expenses into a spreadsheet that then created an expense report in one of five standard formats.

Based on the success of its first product, Handstar subsequently developed three additional software products: a program for tracking and measuring the performance of investment portfolios, a calendar program, and a program that allowed users to download their e-mail messages from PCs and read them on handheld computers.

The two founders of Handstar have recently become concerned about the competitiveness of the firm's offerings, particularly since none of them has been updated since their initial launch. Therefore, they asked the directors of product development and marketing to work together to prepare a list of potential projects for updating Handstar's current offerings as well as to develop ideas for additional offerings. The directors were also asked to estimate the development costs of the various projects, product revenues, and the likelihood that Handstar could retain or obtain a leadership position for the given product. Also, with the continuing popularity and growth of Internet-based businesses, the founders asked the directors to evaluate the extent to which the products made use of the Internet.

The product development and marketing directors identified three projects related to updating Handstar's existing products. The first project would integrate Handstar's current calendar program with its e-mail program. Integrating these two applications into a single program would provide a number of benefits to users, such as allowing them to automatically enter the dates of meetings into the calendar based on the content of an e-mail message. The directors estimated that this project would require 1250 hours of software development time. Revenues in the first year of the product's launch were estimated to be $750,000. However, because the directors expected that a large percentage of the users would likely upgrade to this new product soon after its introduction, they projected that annual sales would decline by 10 percent annually in subsequent years. The directors speculated that Handstar was moderately likely to obtain a leadership position in e-mail/calendar programs if this project was undertaken and felt this program made moderate use of the Internet.

The second project related to updating the expense report program. The directors estimated that this project would require 400 hours of development time. Sales were estimated to be $250,000 in the first year and to increase 5 percent annually in subsequent years. The directors speculated that completing this project would almost certainly maintain Handstar's leadership position in the expense report category, although it made little use of the Internet.

The last product enhancement project related to enhancing the existing portfolio tracking program. This project would require 750 hours of development time and would generate first-year sales of $500,000. Sales were projected to increase 5 percent annually in subsequent years. The directors felt this project would have a high probability of maintaining Handstar's leadership position in this category and the product would make moderate use of the Internet.

The directors also identified three opportunities for new products. One project was the development of a spreadsheet program that could share files with spreadsheet programs written for PCs. Developing this product would require 2500 hours of development time. First-year sales were estimated to be $1 million with an annual growth rate of 10 percent. While this product did not make use of the Internet, the directors felt that Handstar had a moderate chance of obtaining a leadership position in this product category.

The second new product opportunity identified was a Web browser. Developing this product would require 1875 development hours. First-year sales were estimated to be $2.5 million with an annual growth rate of 15 percent. Although this application made extensive use of the Internet, the directors felt that there was a very low probability that Handstar could obtain a leadership position in this product category.

The final product opportunity identified was a trip planner program that would work in conjunction with a PC connected to the Web to download travel instructions to the user's handheld computer. This product would require 6250 hours of development time. First-year sales were projected to be $1.3 million with an annual growth rate of 5 percent. Like the Web browser program, the directors felt that there was a low probability that Handstar could obtain a leadership position in this category, although the program would make extensive use of the Internet.

In evaluating the projects, the founders believed it was reasonable to assume each product had a three-year life. They also felt that a discount rate of 12 per-

cent fairly reflected the company's cost of capital. An analysis of payroll records indicated that the cost of software developers is $52 per hour including salary and fringe benefits. Currently there are four software developers on staff, and each works 2500 hours per year.

Questions

1. Which projects would you recommend for Handstar?

2. Assume the founders weigh a project's revenue-generating capabilities as twice as important as both obtaining/retaining a leadership position and making use of the Internet. Knowing this preference, which projects do you recommend Handstar pursue?

3. In your opinion, is hiring an additional software development engineer justified?

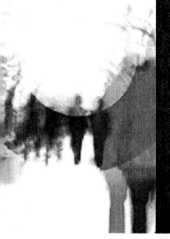

2
IDENTIFYING PROJECT NEEDS AND SOLUTIONS
Establishing Project Details and Direction

Starting Point

Go to www.wiley.com/college/portny to assess your knowledge of the basics of project needs and solutions.
Determine where you need to concentrate your effort.

What You'll Learn in This Chapter

▲ Three elements of a project definition—background, scope, and strategy
▲ Techniques to address and analyze project needs
▲ Basic project strategies
▲ Characteristics of strong project objectives
▲ Two common project boundaries: limitations and needs
▲ Two types of project unknowns
▲ Elements of a Statement of Work
▲ Advantages and disadvantages of project-management software
▲ Two types of project-management software

After Studying This Chapter, You'll Be Able To

▲ Evaluate, draft, and develop project definitions
▲ Evaluate project need statements
▲ Select project strategies
▲ Evaluate the clarity and specificity of project objectives
▲ Draft and develop project objectives
▲ Incorporate limitations into a project plan
▲ Respond effectively to project unknowns
▲ Draft and develop Statements of Work for projects
▲ Select project-management software

INTRODUCTION

Before planning projects, project managers need to clearly define several aspects of projects, including project needs, strategy, and objectives. Limitations and needs act as boundaries for projects, while unknowns need to be anticipated, evaluated, and planned for. Before beginning work on a project, many project managers draft an initial Statement of Work to define project goals and expectations for themselves and their teams. Project-management software can help project managers define projects, but like all technology, software cannot replace good planning and analysis.

2.1 Defining Projects

It would be nice if, when given an assignment, project managers were told both the specific project outcomes they should achieve (see Section 1.2) and the needs that the project is designed to address. Unfortunately, project managers are not always involved in the project selection process. Instead, project managers are often just told what to produce (the outcomes), not why it's to be done (the needs). Often, the project manager must take the initiative to figure out what the real needs are.

Understanding the situation and thought processes that led to a project helps ensure that the project addresses the true needs for which the project is intended. The needs that a project addresses may not be obvious from looking at the project itself. Suppose, for example, that an organization decides to sponsor a blood drive. Is this project being undertaken to address the shortage of blood in the local hospital or to improve the organization's image in the local community?

To understand a project's purpose and its needs, project managers need to know the following:

▲ **Background:** *why* people authorized the project.
▲ **Scope:** the description of the deliverables, or *what work* will be performed.
▲ **Strategy:** *how* project team members will approach the major work of the project. See Section 2.2.

After project managers clearly understand these needs, they can do the following, as necessary:

▲ Frame all project activities to be sure the true desired results can be accomplished.
▲ Monitor performance to ensure that the real needs are being met.
▲ Realize when the project as assigned isn't the best way to meet the real need and suggest the project be modified or canceled.

2.1.1 Identifying Project Needs

The following questions can help project managers understand and define the needs of a project:

▲ **What needs do people want the project to address?** At this point, project managers don't need to worry whether the project actually can address these needs or whether the project is the best way to address the needs. Project managers just need to identify the hopes and expectations that led up to the project.

▲ **Are the identified needs the real hopes and expectations that people have for the project?** Determining people's real thoughts and feelings can be difficult. Sometimes people don't want to share their thoughts or feelings; sometimes they don't know how to express them clearly.

Although many organizations skip this step, a cost-benefit analysis can be very helpful in determining how to proceed with a project. A **cost-benefit analysis** is a formal identification and assessment of all the benefits that are anticipated from a project plus all of the costs for performing the project. The cost-benefit analysis documents the particular results that people were counting on when they made the decision to proceed with a project. It is, therefore, an important source of information about the real needs a project is supposed to address.

2.1.2 Confirming That a Project Addresses Identified Needs

While needs may be thoroughly documented, project managers may have more difficulty determining with confidence whether the project can successfully address those needs.

To ensure that people's true expectations are identified, project managers should

▲ Encourage people to speak at length about their needs and expectations.

▲ Listen carefully for anything that isn't clear or for any contradictions.

▲ Encourage a person to clarify anything that's vague.

▲ Try to confirm information from two or more sources.

On occasion, extensive research is devoted to determining the chances that a project will successfully address a particular need. For example, someone associated with the project may order a formal **feasibility study** to investigate and document the likelihood of a project being successful.

Other times, however, projects are the results of brainstorming sessions or someone's creative vision. In this case, project managers may have less confidence that their projects can accomplish what is expected. Project managers

---

FOR EXAMPLE

Learn a Project's Back Story

After her boss returned from an upper management, product brainstorming retreat, a project manager was assigned a product development project. Because her company had an outstanding market research department, the project manager assumed that upper management had selected the new project based on recommendations from the research department in an effort to increase sales in the coming year. While reasonable, these assumptions turned out to be wrong after the project manager began asking her boss specific, thoughtful questions. The project was actually based on a single conversation between the company's president and a friend who asked whether the company made a product similar to another industry leader. Rather than admit that his company didn't, the president promised to provide his friend with the requested product. When the project manager learned the origins of her assignment, she realized that the project's true measure of success would be how the president's friend reacted to the new product—not a sales increase from introducing the new product. The project manager requested comprehensive market research into consumer interest in the product before proceeding with product development.

---

shouldn't necessarily reject a project at this point (and in reality, few project managers have the power to reject projects). Instead, project managers should aggressively investigate and try to determine the chances for success and how, if at all, they can increase these chances.

If project managers feel the risk of project failure is too great, they must share this information with the key decision makers and explain why they recommend not proceeding with the project. See the discussion of risk management in Section 13.1 for more information.

2.1.3 Determining How Important a Project Is to an Organization

The importance an organization places on a project directly influences the chances for the project's success. For example, when conflicting demands for scarce resources arise, resources are usually given to the project that the organization feels will provide the greatest benefit.

To determine the importance of a project to the larger organization,

▲ **Investigate how the project relates to the organization's top priorities.**
Consult the following sources to learn about an organization's top priorities:

▲ **Long-range plan:** a formal report that identifies an organization's overall direction, specific performance targets, and individual initiatives for the next one to five years.

▲ **Annual budget:** a detailed list of the categories and individual initiatives on which all organization funds will be spent during the year.

▲ **Capital appropriations plan:** an itemized list of all expenditures over an established minimum amount planned for facilities and equipment purchases, renovations, and repairs during the year.

▲ **Managers' annual performance objectives:** specific tasks and desired accomplishments that will be considered when conducting each manager's annual performance appraisal.

▲ **Examine the organization's relationship with outside clients.** Determine whether specific commitments related to the project's completion have been made to external customers.

▲ **Seek information from all possible sources.** Getting this type of information is rarely easy. The information can be sensitive, sometimes contradictory, and often discussed verbally (not in writing). Speak to two or more people from the same area to confirm information shared. Different people have different styles of communication as well as different perceptions of the same situation.

SELF-CHECK

1. To truly understand a project's purpose, you need to know what three things? *Background, Scope, Strategy*

2. After you identify the needs people expect a project to address, the next critical step is to do which of the following?

   ✓(a) Verify whether the project can possibly meet the identified needs.

   (b) Confirm whether the identified needs are the real expectations for the project.

   (c) Discuss the needs and expectations with your boss.

   (d) Find out which individual or department originally suggested the project.

3. What four common organizational documents can help you confirm that a project's identified needs are appropriate?

↳ *Long range plan, annual budget, Capital appropriations plan, + Managers annual performance objectives.*

2.2 Laying the Groundwork for Project Work

Projects are complex endeavors. Soon after defining the specifics of projects, project managers should examine two critical elements that influence and inspire all the work related to the project: strategies and objectives.

2.2.1 Considering Project Strategy

Project strategy is the general approach project managers plan to take to perform the work necessary to achieve a project's outcomes. A strategy isn't a detailed list of activities to be performed. That list is derived from a project Work Breakdown Structure, which is described in Section 4.3.

Examples of project strategy include the following:

▲ XYZ Corp. will buy the needed supplies from an outside vendor.
▲ ABC Inc. will conduct training in a series of instructor-led sessions.

When selecting a strategy,

▲ Consider the organization's usual approaches for handling similar projects.
▲ Where possible, choose a strategy with the least risks, uncertainties, and uncontrollables. You don't just want a strategy that might work; you want one with the greatest chance of working.
▲ For riskier projects, consider developing one or more backup strategies, in case a primary strategy runs into problems.

2.2.2 Establishing Project Objectives

In contrast to strategies, **objectives** are results to be achieved through the performance of a project. Objectives may include the creation of products and services or the impact realized through the application of these products and services. Objectives need to consider project risks and uncertainty (see Section 13.1). Clear, specific objectives are extremely useful, but project managers must also be able to update and refine objectives as a project progresses.

Project objectives are clear and specific. They include the following:

▲ **Statement:** a brief narrative description of what is to be achieved.
▲ **Measures:** one or more indicators used to assess achievement.
▲ **Performance targets:** the value of each measure that defines success.

For example, Table 2-1 shows the project objectives related to reformatting a department's monthly sales report.

Table 2-1: An Illustration of a Project Objective

Statement	Measures	Performance Targets
Create a revised report that summarizes monthly sales activity.	Content	Report must include the following data for each product line: • Total number of items sold • Total sales revenue • Total returns
	Schedule	Report must be operational by August 31.
	Budget	Development expenditures are not to exceed $40,000.
	Approvals	New report format must be approved by • Vice president of sales • Regional sales manager • District sales manager • Sales representatives

As Table 2-1 illustrates, clear and specific performance targets are essential and incredibly helpful. Some upper managers and project managers try to avoid setting specific performance targets for a measure by establishing a range within which performance will be deemed successful. This is just avoiding the issue. The more clear and specific project objectives are, the greater the chance the project team members will be able to achieve them.

Keep the following in mind to develop clear project objectives:

▲ **Less is more.** Be brief when describing an objective. If a project plan takes an entire page to describe a single objective, most people won't read it. And, even if they do, the chances are that the objective isn't as clear as it could be.

▲ **Avoid technical jargon or acronyms.** The workplace abounds with technical terms and acronyms. Each industry (telecommunications, finance, pharmaceuticals, and insurance, to name just a few) has its own vocabulary, as does each company within an industry. Within companies, different departments (such as accounting, legal, and information services) have their own jargon. It's not unusual today that the same TLA (three-letter acronym) can mean two or more different things in the same organization.

To make matters worse, people often don't ask if they aren't familiar with a term because they fear that doing so makes them appear to be ignorant or less qualified. The best bet is not to use acronyms at all; just use the words themselves. If an acronym is essential, define it the first time it appears on a page.

▲ **Create SMART objectives.** A SMART objective is:

    ▲ *Specific*: define the objective clearly, in detail, with no room for misinterpretation.

    ▲ *Measurable*: specify the measures or indicators used to determine whether the objective is met.

    ▲ *Aggressive*: set objectives that are challenging and that encourage people to stretch beyond their comfort zones.

    ▲ *Realistic*: set objectives that the project team believes it can achieve.

    ▲ *Time-sensitive*: include the date by which the objective will be achieved.

▲ **Make the objectives controllable.** If a project manager and project team don't believe they can influence whether they'll achieve an objective, they won't commit to achieving it—and they may not even try to achieve it. In that case, it becomes a wish instead of an objective.

▲ **Be sure all relevant parties agree on a project's objectives.** When upper management or clients evaluating the project buy in to a project's objectives, the project manager can feel confident that achieving the objectives constitutes true project success. When supporters buy in to a project's objectives, the project has the greatest chance that people will work their hardest to achieve the objectives.

FOR EXAMPLE

Specific Objective for SSP Project

The Scientific Services Program (www.intrex.net/ssp/index.html), or SSP, contracts consultants and analysts for the U.S. Department of Defense and other government agencies. For a recent neural network project, SSP published a detailed Statement of Work (see Section 2.5) that included the following specific project objective: to develop a precise form of a neural network and to determine, in a hybrid scheme with some conventional pattern recognition algorithms, the usefulness of the neural network. The tools for efficient computer use to accomplish this task must also be developed and specified.

SELF-CHECK

1. Project strategies include detailed ways you'll go about completing a project. True or false?

2. Strategies are general ways you go about doing things, while objectives are:

    (a) results to be achieved through the project.

    (b) clear and specific.

    (c) measurable.

    (d) all of the above.

3. In a SMART objective, the M stands for which of the following?

    (a) macro-level

    (b) managerial

    (c) measurable

    (d) meaningful

2.3 Defining Project Boundaries

Project managers may wish they could operate in a world where all things are possible—that is, where they can do anything they want to achieve the desired results. Clients, upper management, and the organization, on the other hand, want to believe that project managers can achieve everything asked of them with minimal or no cost. Of course, neither situation is true.

Defining the restrictions, or boundaries, on how project managers can approach projects helps to introduce reality in plans and helps clarify expectations. Boundaries on project managers include the following:

▲ **Needs:** Requirements the project manager determines must be met in order to achieve project success. See Section 2.1.1.

▲ **Limitations:** Restrictions that others place on the results, time frames, resources, and ways a project team can approach its tasks.

2.3.1 Identifying Limitations

When defining limitations, project managers must determine what's in the minds of others who will influence or be affected by the project. At this point, project managers need not concern themselves with whether they can overcome their limitations—they just want to identify them.

The following list shows the several types of limitations that exist:

▲ **Results:** the products and impact of the project. For example, a new semiconductor must use 15 percent less silicon during the manufacturing process.

▲ **Time frames:** the date by which certain results must be produced. For example, a project must be done by June 30. The project manager doesn't know yet whether the project can finish by June 30; she just knows that someone else expects it done by then.

▲ **Resources:** the type, amount, and availability dates. Resources are everything necessary to perform project work, including people, funds, equipment, raw materials, facilities, information, and so on.

▲ **Activity performance:** the strategies and approaches for performing different tasks. For example, a project manager is told that he must use the organization's printing department to reproduce the new user's manuals he's developing. He doesn't yet know what the manual will look like, how long it will be, the number of copies he needs, or when the company needs them. Therefore, he can't know whether the organization's printing department is capable of satisfactorily reproducing the manuals. But he does know that, at this point, someone in the organization expects that the printing department can handle the order and that he'll have them do the work.

Be careful of a vague limitation. Not only does a vague limitation provide poor guidance for how to proceed to satisfy that limitation, but it can also be demoralizing for everyone who has to deal with it.

For example, consider the following schedule limitation: ·

▲ **Vague:** "Finish this project as soon as possible." All work has to be done as soon as possible, so this statement really tells the project manager nothing. With this limitation, the project manager may fear that upper management will suddenly demand the project's final results.

▲ **Specific:** "Finish this project by close of business, November 30."

Or, consider the following resource limitation:

▲ **Vague:** "You can have an analyst part-time in May." How heavily can the project manager count on this analyst? From the analyst's point of view, how can she juggle all of the assignments given to her in the same time period if she has no idea how long each one will take?

▲ **Specific:** "You can have an analyst four hours per day for the first two weeks in May." If people can't be specific when they introduce a constraint, the project manager can't be sure that he can honor their request. The longer the limitation setter waits to be specific, the more likely that the project manager won't be able to adhere to the constraint while successfully completing the project.

FOR EXAMPLE

Project Boundaries for U.S. Department of Energy Contractors

Laboratory contractors responsible for projects involving receiving, analyzing, storing, and performing tests on radioactive samples on behalf of the Department of Energy Offices at the Hanford Nuclear Site near Richland, Washington (www.hanford.gov), work under clearly detailed project boundaries. For example, a recent Statement of Work notes that "analysis of all samples shall be performed by an ASPC trained and qualified workforce in accordance with approved procedures, using appropriate test and handling equipment," The Statement of Work goes on to state that contractor "shall perform all work in accordance with existing laws, applicable permits and good practice consistent with safety and quality in the laboratory. A nuclear materials safeguard and security program shall be developed, approved by the Department of Energy and implemented."

2.3.2 Determining Project Limitations

Determining limitations is a fact-finding mission, so the project manager's job is to identify and examine all possible sources of information. After project managers know what people expect, they can set about determining how (or if) they can meet those expectations.

To determine project limitations,

▲ **Consult the project's audiences and stakeholders.** Check with upper management about limitations regarding desired outcomes; check with team members about limitations concerning work approach and resources.

▲ **Review relevant written materials.** Long-range plans, annual budgets and capital-appropriations plans, cost-benefit analyses, feasibility studies, reports of related projects, minutes of meetings, and individuals' performance objectives can all offer useful information.

▲ **Note the source of any identified limitation.** Confirming a limitation from different sources increases the project manager's confidence in its accuracy. Resolve conflicting opinions about a limitation as soon as possible.

2.3.3 Incorporating Limitations into a Project Plan

A project plan can reflect limitations in two ways:

1. **Incorporate the limitations directly into the plan.** For example, if a key driver says Marta has to finish a project by September 30, she may choose to set September 30 as the project's completion date. Of course, because September 30 is the outside limit, she may also choose to set a completion date of August 31. In this case, the limitation influences the target but isn't equivalent to it.

2. **Identify any project risks that exist because of a particular limitation.** For example, if Marta feels a target completion date is unusually aggressive, the risk of missing that date may be significant. She can develop plans to minimize and manage the risk throughout the project. See Chapter 13 for more information on how to assess and plan for risks and uncertainties.

SELF-CHECK

1. Project needs and limitations help set which of the following?
   (a) the objectives of the project
   (b) the boundaries of the project
   (c) the audience of the project
   (d) the predetermined factors of the project

2. When encountering limitations early in a project, a project manager should do which of the following?
   (a) identify the limitations as clearly as possible
   (b) redefine the project based on the limitations
   (c) try to minimize the limitations
   (d) none of these

3. A project manager can identify project limitations by doing which of the following?
   (a) reviewing past projects and consulting the assigning manager
   (b) reviewing financial statements and consulting the project's champion
   (c) reviewing relevant written materials and consulting the project's audience
   (d) reviewing annual reports and consulting with other project managers

2.4 Dealing with Unknowns

As project managers proceed through the planning process, most identify issues or questions that may affect their projects' performance. Unfortunately, just identifying these issues or questions doesn't help address them.

Identifying and dealing effectively with unknowns can dramatically increase a project manager's chances for success.

Unknown information can fall into two categories:

1. A **known unknown:** information that you don't have but someone else does.
2. An **unknown unknown:** information that you don't have because it doesn't yet exist.

Project managers deal with known unknowns by finding out who has the information and determining what the information is. Project managers deal with unknown unknowns either by developing contingency plans to be followed when they find out the information or by trying to influence the value of the information.

For every issue project managers identify, they must decide what assumptions they need to build into their plans. Plan actions can make assumptions become reality. Consider the following examples:

▲ **Example 1**
   ▲ **Issue:** How much money will you get to perform your project?
   ▲ **Approach:** Assume you'll get $50,000 for your project. Plan out your project to spend up to but no more than $50,000. Develop detailed information to demonstrate why it's important that you receive a project budget of $50,000 and share that information with key decision makers.

▲ **Example 2**
   ▲ **Issue:** When will you get authorization to start work on your project?
   ▲ **Approach:** Assume you'll receive authorization to start work on August 1. Plan your project work so that no activities start before August 1. Explain to key people why it's important that your project start on August 1 and work with them to facilitate your project's approval by that date.

Project managers must consider project assumptions when they develop their projects' risk management plan (see Section 13.4).

In addition to helping project managers identify activities that they know they have to perform, developing a work breakdown structure (see Section 4.3) also helps identify unknowns that may cause problems on the project. As project managers think through the work required to complete projects, they often identify some considerations that affect how or whether they can perform one or more activities in the project.

FOR EXAMPLE

Dealing with a Known Unknown

A project manager in the public relations department of a large research hospital was tasked with conducting a satisfaction survey of recent heart bypass patients. Planning the project, the project manager determined that the first task was to select a sample of former patients to interview over the phone with a scripted survey. The project manager didn't know whether an up-to-date list of the hospital's recent bypass patients existed within the organization's records or if he needed to create a list. According to the project manager's estimates, if the list already existed, selecting a sample to survey would take about one week. If a list didn't exist, he'd have to create one, and selecting the sample would take about four weeks. Whether the list exists was a known unknown—the project manager didn't know but someone else did. He dealt with the unknown by calling people in Records Managements to see whether such a list existed.

SELF-CHECK

1. The best way to deal with unknowns is to be ready to respond to anything. True or false?

2. An example of an unknown unknown might be which of the following?

   (a) how much money the previous project manager spent on contract labor

   (b) how many days a worker will be sick next quarter

   (c) how hurricanes in the Gulf of Mexico affect the price of oil

   (d) how many units your top competitor sold last year

2.5 Developing a Statement of Work

A **Statement of Work** (often referred to as an SOW) is written confirmation of what a project will produce and the terms and conditions under which the project team will perform the work. Both the people who requested the project and the project team, through the process of negotiation and discussion, should agree to all terms in the Statement of Work before actual project work is started.

2.5.1 Identifying Components of Statements of Work

A Statement of Work typically includes the following information:

▲ **Purpose:** how and why the project came to be, the scope of the project, and the general approach to be followed.

▲ **Objectives:** specific outcomes the project will produce.

▲ **Constraints:** restrictions that will limit what's achieved, how and when the project team can do it, and for what cost.

▲ **Assumptions:** statements about uncertain information the project manager is taking as fact while conceiving, planning, and performing the project.

Many successful project managers think of Statements of Work as binding agreements.

▲ Project managers and their teams commit to producing certain results, and the projects' requesters commit to considering the project to be 100 percent successful if the team produces certain results.

▲ Project managers and their teams identify all restrictions regarding how they'll be allowed to approach project work and what they need to support the work. The project requesters agree there are no restrictions other than the ones identified and that they'll provide support as requested.

Of course, no project manager can possibly predict the future. However, a Statement of Work represents a project manager's project commitments, based upon what he or she knows today and expects to be true in the future. If and when situations change, the project manager must assess the impact of the changes

FOR EXAMPLE

A Specialized Statement of Work

A sediment management project along the Lower Fox River in Wisconsin for the Department of Natural Resources (www.dnr.state.wi.us) required a Statement of Work with several special sections in order to outline the project's purpose, objects, constraints, and assumptions. Some project-specific details included a brief description of removal actions and expectations, a list of clean-up objectives, and a basic process and timeline for removal implementation. Project-specific resources identified in the document include contractors, construction oversight, dredging specialists, water-treatment experts, and sampling services. (Review the complete Statement of Work at http://www.dnr.state.wi.us/org/water/wm/FoxRiver/sites/56_57sowfinal.html.)

Figure 2-1

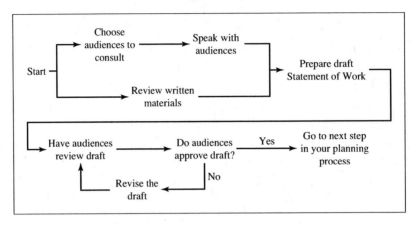

Developing a Statement of Work.

on the Statement of Work and propose any corresponding changes to the project. The project's requesters always have the option of accepting proposed changes, allowing the project to continue as originally defined, or canceling the project.

2.5.2 Developing a Statement of Work

Figure 2-1 illustrates a systematic approach for preparing a Statement of Work. As the figure suggests, the systematic steps help determine and document a project's purpose, objectives, constraints, and assumptions.

To develop a Statement of Work,

1. Identify audiences and stakeholders, the people who are looking for the results of the project or will be needed to support the project.
2. Meet with some or all of those people in the project's audience and find out what they think is desirable and feasible to achieve.
3. While working on Steps 1 and 2, review all written materials related to the project.
4. Combine the information from personal meetings and materials review to prepare a draft Statement of Work.
5. Have the people with whom you met in Step 2 review your draft Statement of Work and ask them to formally approve it (that is, to approve it in writing).
6. If the people agree with the information in the draft Statement of Work and formally commit to support it, move on to the next step in your planning process.
7. If some or all the people give you comments and suggestions about the draft, incorporate those suggestions into a revised draft Statement

of Work and ask the people to review and approve the revised document.

8. Continue until you obtain all necessary approvals.

On occasion, one or more reviewers won't approve a project manager's draft Statement of Work, even after several revisions. If this happens and the project manager believes that she's done all she can to respond to suggestions and concerns, the project manager needs to ask herself, "Am I willing to proceed without their support?"

If the answer is no, find someone at a higher level in the organization who can help resolve the issue. This may be a good time to seek help from a project champion (see Section 1.6). If the answer is yes, do the following:

1. Make a written record of attempts to get approval and the reasons why approval wasn't given.
2. Record the lack of approval within the risk management plan (see Section 13.4).
3. Move on to the next step in the planning process.

2.5.3 Comparing Statements of Work to Other Project Documents

Organizations may use a number of other documents that address issues similar to those in the Statement of Work. These documents are often excellent sources of information when preparing a project plan, but project managers need to carefully note how these documents differ from Statements of Work.

▲ **Market requirements document:** A formal request for a product to be developed or modified. The market requirements document, typically prepared by a member of the organization's sales and marketing group, may lead to the creation of a project. However, in its original form, it reflects only the desires of the person seeking a particular outcome and doesn't reflect any assessment of whether it's possible to meet the request or a commitment to meet it.

▲ **Business requirements document:** A description of the business needs to be addressed by a requested product, service, or system.

▲ **Project request:** A written request for the performance of a project by a group within the organization. The project request indicates a desire for a project, rather than a mutual agreement and commitment to perform it.

▲ **Project charter:** A document issued by upper management that spells out the project manager's authority to coordinate personnel in the performance of a project.

▲ **Project profile:** Highlights of key information about a project. Sometimes called a project summary or a project abstract.

▲ **Work order:** A written description of work to be performed by people or groups within an organization in support of a project. The signed work order focuses on work to be performed instead of on overall project outcomes to be achieved.

▲ **Contract:** A legal agreement for goods to be procured or services to be rendered from an external vendor or contractor. On occasion, the term *Statement of Work* is used to refer to the part of a contract that describes the goods and services to be procured from an outside source.

SELF-CHECK

1. A Statement of Work presents a commitment on the part of which of the following?

   (a) project managers and functional managers

   (b) upper management and project teams

   (c) project managers and their teams

   (d) project teams and clients

2. In a Statement of Work, information about uncertain information that the project manager is taking into account when planning and performing the project is covered in which of the following?

   (a) objectives

   (b) purpose

   (c) constraints

   (d) assumptions

3. When preparing a Statement of Work, you should first draft the statement and then share your draft with key audience members for the project. True or false?

4. A work order differs from a Statement of Work in the following way:

   (a) A work order is nonbinding, while a Statement of Work is a commitment from all involved in the project.

   (b) A work order focuses on specific work to be performed, while a Statement of Work covers the overall project outcomes to be achieved.

   (c) A work order is typically approved by upper management, while a Statement of Work rarely is.

   (d) All of the above

2.6 Using Software to Manage a Project

Project management entails using systems and procedures to help people work together to achieve common goals. A major part of project management is information—getting it, storing it, analyzing it, and sharing it. However, the key to successful project management is using information to guide and encourage people's performance.

Technological advances provide easier and more affordable ways to handle information. Computer software allows project managers to enter, store, and analyze information and to present the results in professional formats. Computer modeling software can effectively simulate the effects of project uncertainty and risk. E-mail allows project managers to communicate in writing with people in remote locations, at all hours of the day.

However, technology alone can't encourage focused and committed team performance. In fact, excessive reliance on today's technology can actually result in poor morale, confused and disorganized team members, and lower overall performance. Successful project management requires using the technology for those jobs where it is appropriate. Remember, the project manager should manage the software, rather than the software manage the project.

2.6.1 Using Computer Software Effectively

The software available today to help plan and control projects looks so good that project managers may be tempted to believe that using it is all that's required to ensure a project's success.

Software can help with data entry, data analysis, data storage, and report generating activities. Software can help in the following ways:

▲ **Storing and retrieving important project information.**
▲ **Analyzing and updating information.**
▲ **Simulating and testing budget and schedule uncertainty.**
▲ **Preparing presentations and reports describing the information and the results of the analyses.**

Computer software, however, cannot do the following:

▲ **Ensure that information entered is appropriately defined, timely, and accurate.** In most instances, information to support project planning or control is recorded by people and then entered into a computer. Most software can be programmed to check for correct formatting and internal consistency, but the software can't ensure the quality and integrity of the data. For example, Ray is using a computer program to maintain records of the labor hours that team members charge to his project.

Ray can program the computer to reject hours that are inadvertently charged to an invalid project code. However, he can't program the computer to recognize that hours are charged to a wrong project that also happens to have a valid code.

▲ **Make decisions.** Software can help project managers determine objectively what would happen if they chose a number of different possible courses of action. However, software can't effectively take into account all the associated objective and subjective considerations associated with each course of action. A human project manager must weigh options in order to decide which plan of action to pursue.

▲ **Create and sustain interpersonal relationships.** Despite people's fascination with chat rooms, e-mail, and other types of computer-aided communication, computers don't foster close, trusting relationships between people. If anything, technology makes it more difficult to get to know others because it removes the ability to see facial expressions and body language.

2.6.2 Choosing Software

Project-management software comes in two types:

1. **Stand-alone, specialty software:** separate packages that perform one or two functions very well and that can support project planning and performance.
2. **Integrated project-management software:** a single package that incorporates limited portions of the capabilities of several specialty packages to support a wider array of project planning and performance activities.

Each type of software offers benefits and drawbacks.

Stand-alone Specialty Software

Stand-alone, specialty software (such as word-processing, presentation, spreadsheet, database, accounting, and scheduling programs) is designed to perform one or two functions very well. As they have evolved, however, they've been expanded to include additional capabilities that support their primary functions: word-processing packages now possess some spreadsheet, graphics, and database capabilities; spreadsheet packages now have some business-graphics and word-processing capabilities; and database packages now have some spreadsheet and word-processing capabilities.

In general, specialty packages offer powerful capability in their area of specialty, but they are likely to encourage piecemeal approaches to project planning and control, which may result in omitting certain key steps. For example, a project manager could use a business graphics package to draw a Gantt chart (see Section 6.6) from any data. However, he has confidence that a production schedule is feasible only if he considers the impact of activity interdependencies when he develops the data—something that a business graphics package doesn't do.

One additional caution: Stand-alone specialty software isn't easily integrated. A project manager can, for example, depict a project's schedule on a Gantt chart with a graphics package and display personnel hours over the duration of each task in a spreadsheet. However, if one of team member is unexpectedly out sick for a week, the project manager has to make separate changes to each program to reflect a revised allocation of the person's hours in the spreadsheet and change the Gantt chart in the graphics package to reflect new activity start and/or end dates.

Integrated Project-management Software

Integrated project-management software combines database, spreadsheet, graphics, and word-processing capabilities to support many of the activities that are normally associated with planning and performing a project. The most popular example of an integrated package is Microsoft Project, although more than 100 such packages of all shapes and sizes are on the market today. Many organizations also have in-house versions of integrated project-management software.

A typical integrated project-management package allows users to do the following:

▲ Create a hierarchical list of project activities and their components.

▲ Define and store key information about projects, activities, and resources.

▲ Define activity interdependencies. See Chapter 6 for more information on activity interdependencies.

▲ Develop schedules by considering activity durations, activity interdependencies, and resource requirements and availability.

▲ Display a schedule in Gantt chart (see Section 6.6) and other table formats.

▲ Assign people to work on project activities for specific levels of effort at certain times.

▲ Schedule other resources to be used on project activities at specified times.

▲ Determine overall project budget.

▲ Simulate uncertainty (see Section 13.1) by seeing how alterations to a project's budget, schedule, and deliverables impact the entire project.

▲ Monitor the dates on which activities start, end, or reach milestones.

▲ Monitor person-hours and resource costs incurred.

▲ Present planning and tracking information in a wide array of graphs and tables.

When selecting an integrated project-management package, consider the following:

▲ Choose a package that supports the type of reports and reporting required within the larger organizations.

▲ Choose a package that team members will actually use. It doesn't help to have a package with state-of-the-art analysis and reporting capabilities if no one takes the time to learn how to use it.

▲ Thoroughly examine the software that's available and used within the organization already. All other things being equal, it makes sense to choose an existing package because others most likely will have experience with it.

FOR EXAMPLE

Software Is Not Enough

Recognizing the size, complexity, and importance of a project, upper management at a small office furniture retailer hired a person with extensive experience with a popular project-management software package to prepare the project plan. The expert worked intensely, coming in before others arrived and leaving after they were gone. After three months, he presented a plan with thousands of activities, detailed schedules, and resource assignments. Unfortunately, from the start, the plan was a disaster: Major areas of work had been omitted, responsibilities had been assigned to inappropriate people, and schedules failed to take into account other commitments and organization activities. The expert had consulted no one on the project team during the entire development process, and people were incensed that a stranger new to the organization would presume to tell them how to do their work. The project team threatened to resign en masse. Management took action in short order, firing the expert and trashing the plan. Not only had they wasted three months of time and effort, but they also still had no viable project plan. The message was clear—the use of project-management software cannot save a project burdened by bad planning.

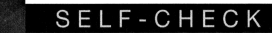

SELF-CHECK

1. Which of the following statements about project-management software is true?

   (a) The right software can cut project management time by 25 percent or more.

   (b) Stand-alone specialty software supports a wide array of project planning activities.

   (c) Software is effective only when the entered information is appropriately defined and accurate.

   (d) Proprietary software is superior to general market software.

2. Even with the latest project-management software, the project manager must do which of the following?

   (a) weigh options in order to make the best decisions

   (b) calculate lead times

   (c) draft work-flow diagrams

   (d) all of the above

SUMMARY

A project is defined when the project manager knows the project's needs, strategies, objectives, and limitations. Unknown factors will always be part of managing projects, but savvy project managers can seek out answers to unknowns and make assumptions for others. A Statement of Work is an early project document that outlines the purpose, objectives, constraints, and assumptions that will guide a project from start to finish. Project-management software can aid managers in making better decisions, but it cannot replace quality analysis, thoughtful questions, and real-world problem-solving.

KEY TERMS

Annual budget	Detailed list of the categories and individual initiatives on which all organization funds will be spent during the year.
Assumptions	Statements about uncertain information the project manager is taking as fact while conceiving, planning, and performing the project; part of the Statement of Work.

Capital appropriations plan	Itemized list of all expenditures over an established minimum amount planned for facilities and equipment purchases, renovations, and repairs during the year.
Constraints	Restrictions that others place on the results, time frames, resources, and ways a project team can approach its tasks; part of the Statement of Work.
Cost-benefit analysis	Formal identification and assessment of all the benefits that are anticipated from a project plus all of the costs for performing project.
Feasibility study	Formal investigation and documentation of the likelihood of a project being successful.
Known unknown	Information that you don't have but someone else does.
Limitations	Restrictions that others place on the results, time frames, resources, and ways a project team can approach its tasks; also known as constraints.
Long-range plan	Formal report that identifies an organization's overall direction, specific performance targets, and individual initiatives for the next one to five years.
Managers' annual performance objectives	Specific tasks and desired accomplishments that will be considered when conducting each manager's annual performance appraisal.
Measures	One or more indicators project managers use to assess achievement.
Needs	Requirements the project manager determines must be met in order to achieve project success.
Objectives	Results to be achieved through the performance of a project; part of the Statement of Work.
Performance targets	The value of each measure that defines success in a project objective.
Project strategy	The general approach project managers plan to take to perform the work necessary to achieve a project's outcomes.
Purpose	How and why a project came to be, the scope of the project, and the general approach to be followed; part of the Statement of Work.

Statement	A brief narrative description in a project objective that notes what is to be achieved.
Statement of Work (SOW)	Written confirmation of what a project will produce and the terms and conditions under which the project team will perform the work.
Unknown unknown	Information that you don't have because it doesn't yet exist.

ASSESS YOUR UNDERSTANDING

Go to www.wiley.com/college/portny to assess your knowledge of the basics of project needs and solutions.
Measure your learning by comparing pre-test and post-test results.

Summary Questions

1. Although every project is unique, which sequence of activities makes the most sense early in a project?
   (a) Select strategies, confirm needs, draft objectives, identify the audience
   (b) Identify the audience, confirm needs, select strategies, draft objectives
   (c) Confirm needs, draft objectives, identify the audience, select strategies
   (d) Identify the audience, draft objectives, confirm needs, select strategies
2. For a project to have a better chance of success, project unknowns should be anticipated and addressed in the Statement of Work. True or false?
3. The project objective "to increase sales of handheld organizers by 10 percent to consumers age 18 to 24 by May 1 of next year" is a SMART objective. True or false?

Applying This Chapter

1. Ronan's latest project assignment came directly from the CEO of his mid-size investment firm: to develop a plan that markets money-market savings accounts to lower-income workers. The CEO told Ronan that the firm needs to extend its market share and lower-income workers need investment options. Ronan wonders whether this is the complete story behind the project. What are some appropriate things he can do find out more about the project's needs?
2. One of the objectives for a software development project is "to encourage multiple daily DMPs and make our software package the best in the business." In what ways is this a poor project objective?
3. You are given the project limitation that your new assignment is now your top priority. How is this a vague limitation? How could this limitation become more specific?
4. As project manager of a new team that's developing an online shopping site for a traditional department store, you've been asked to calculate how much your team will spend on user testing in the next 12 months.

Your team has never conducted user testing, so this is an unknown. But is this a known unknown or an unknown unknown? How might you respond effectively to this unknown?

5. You are given a 10-page markets requirement document by your boss and told you should let it guide the management of your next project. Although a markets requirement document can be useful, in what ways is it different from a Statement of Work?

6. Carefully read through an entire Statement of Work for a project. If you don't have a Statement of Work for a current or past work project, ask your manager or other project managers if they have an example. Or, review online the Statement of Work from the U.S. Geological Survey's Web site for a coastal lands project in South Florida (sofia.usgs.gov/projects/scopesofwork03/coastalgrads.html). Does the Statement of Work include the four essential types of information: purpose, objectives, constraints, and assumptions? What other special sections does the Statement of Work include? What questions would you have about managing the project if you had to work from the Statement of Work?

YOU TRY IT

Confirming Project Needs

Knowing the needs of a project is critical—and so is confirming that the identified needs are legitimate. Consider the needs associated with writing a research paper for a class. Why are research papers necessary? If possible, ask the professor why a research paper is necessary. What does he or she hope you'll gain from writing a paper? Ask another instructor (or an upperclassman or parent) why he or she thinks research papers are important. Then consult the syllabus and textbook for the course. What do these resources say about the importance of writing research papers? You will probably find a range of responses for why research papers are necessary. What are the similarities and the differences in responses? Which responses make the most sense to you?

Aligning Your Project with Your Organization's Priorities

Consider how a project you're currently working on—at your job, in school, in your personal life—matches the larger organization's priorities. Look first at common corporate documents (long-range plans, annual budgets, and so on) and see where your project fits in. If your project isn't specifically identified in any of these documents, can you help others understand how your project will support other initiatives that are included in the long-range plan, your manager's performance objectives, and so on? Ask people to consider what would happen if you didn't perform your project. If they honestly feel it would make no difference, explore ways to modify your project so that it will make a difference.

What's Your Objective?

Write at least one objective for taking this project-management class. What one specific result do you want to achieve? If you can think of multiple objectives, goals, or results you have for taking the class, write these down as well. Now, compare your statement(s) to the five objective-writing tips in Section 2.2.2. Is your statement simple and to the point? Does it avoid technical jargon? Is it a SMART objective? Is it controllable? Do all relevant parties agree with the objective?

Know Your Limitations

Limitations aren't negative or positive; they're just neutral facts that affect your project. For example, what if you were hosting a Super Bowl party next month. What are your limitations? What specific results are you expecting to achieve? What results are your guests expecting to achieve? What is your time frame? What resources do you have available to help you host the party? Remember that resources include money, people, information, facitilities, equipment, and raw materials. What expectations (i.e., activity performance) are in place about how the party will happen? Your understanding of each of the preceding limitations makes a major impact on your final product—your party.

United Screen Printers (USP) produces a wide range of decals for displaying promotional messages on fleet vehicles (including delivery vans, eighteen-wheelers, and aircraft). Its decals range from flat-color designs to full-color photographic reproductions.

Although it is one of the oldest forms of printing, screen printing is superior to most of the more modern approaches because it permits making heavier deposits of ink onto a surface, resulting in more vibrant and longer-lasting finishes. Screen printing works by blocking out areas on a silk screen so that ink passes through only the unblocked areas to make an impression on the vinyl decal.

Many in the industry believe that the economics of fleet graphics makes them an extremely attractive form of advertising and should lead to their continued penetration of a largely untapped market. One industry source estimated that the cost of fleet graphics works out to be $2.84 per 1 million visual impressions. Given the highly cost-effective nature of using fleet graphics as a form of advertising, it is speculated that organizations will increasingly exploit this form of advertising. In addition, as organizations become better aware of this advertising medium, it is likely they will want to change their message more frequently. According to managers at USP, this could be one of the major factors apparently driving the competition to focus more on short lead times and prices, and less on decal durability.

USP is about to begin its annual evaluation of proposed projects. Six top projects have been defined as follows.

1. Purchase a new large press

There is currently a three-and-a-half to four-week backlog in the screen printing department. The result of this is that USP's total lead time is 4 to 6 weeks in comparison to an industry average lead time of 3.5 to 4 weeks. In a typical month, USP ships 13 percent of its orders early, 38 percent on-time, and 49 percent late. It has been estimated that 75 percent of the backlog is waiting for press 6, the largest press in the shop. Furthermore, press 6 is in dire need of replacement parts, but USP has been unable thus far to locate a source for these parts. Given the problem of finding replacement parts and the fact that the press is somewhat outdated, this project calls for purchasing a new large press for $160,000. Based on estimates that a new large press could process jobs 50 percent to 100 percent faster than press 6, it is calculated that the payback period for a new large press would be one year.

2. Build new headquarters

USP's CEO fervently believes that the company needs to have a strong corporate identity. He therefore purchased land and had plans drawn up for the construction of a new corporate headquarters. Analysis of the new headquarters indicated that although it would improve operating efficiencies, the savings generated would not pay for the new building (estimated to cost $4 million). Many of the board members viewed the project as too risky since it increases the company's debt as a percent of capital from almost zero to 50 percent.

3. Pursue ISO 9000 certification

This proposal also comes from USP's CEO. ISO 9000 is a set of standards that provides customers with some assurance that a supplier follows accepted business practices. In some industries obtaining ISO 9000 certification is essential, such as in industries that export to Europe and the domestic automobile industry. It was less clear what competitive advantage pursuing ISO 9000 would provide USP at this time. On the other hand, the process alone would help it document and perhaps improve its processes. The cost of this initiative was estimated to be $250,000 to $300,000 and would take one year to complete.

4. Develop formal procedure for mixing inks

This proposal comes from USP's plant manager. At present, mixing inks is a highly specialized skill that consumes 2 to 3 hours of the team leader's time each day. This project would focus on developing ink formulas to make the task of mixing inks more routine, and less specialized and subjective. The team leader is paid

$25,000 annually. The cost of pursuing this project is estimated to be $10,000.

5. Purchase and install equipment to produce four-color positives in-house

The lead time to have positives made by an outside supplier is typically one week and costs $1500 to $6000. According to this proposal, the cost of purchasing the equipment to produce four-color positives in-house would be approximately $150,000, plus $25,000 for installation and training. The variable costs of producing positives in-house are estimated to be $375 per job. If produced in-house, the lead time for the four-color positives would be approximately an hour-and-a-half.

6. Purchase ink-jet printers

An alternative to purchasing a new screen printing press is to add capacity based on newer technology. Given the ink-jet's production rate, six ink-jet printers at a cost of $140,000 would be needed to provide the equivalent capacity of a new large screen printing press. The major disadvantage of the ink-jet printers is that, compared to the screen printing process, the outdoor durability is more limited. In general, ink-jet printers are more economical for small orders, while screen printing presses are more economical for large orders.

USP currently has annual sales of approximately $7 million. It typically allocates up to 10 percent of sales to the preceding types of projects.

Questions

1. What criteria would you recommend USP use in selecting its projects this year?
2. What projects would you recommend USP fund this year? Are there any types of projects you would recommend USP pursue that were not proposed?
3. What are the boundaries and limitations associated with each project?
4. What additional information would you still need to write Statements of Work for each project? Where might you seek out this information?

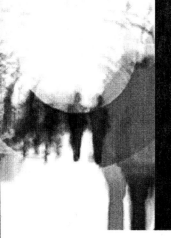

3

ORGANIZING PROJECTS
Managing Projects within Various Types of Organizations

Starting Point

Go to www.wiley.com/college/portny to assess your knowledge of the basics of project organization.

Determine where you need to concentrate your effort.

What You'll Learn in This Chapter

▲ Three main forms of organizational structure: central, functional, matrix
▲ Strengths and weaknesses of various organizational structures
▲ Trends and customization in organizational structures

After Studying This Chapter, You'll Be Able To

▲ Choose the best organizational structures—including central, functional, and matrix structures—for various situations
▲ Evaluate the type and effectiveness of various organizational structures
▲ Design and manage projects that best suit a company's organizational structures

INTRODUCTION

Companies have a variety of organizational structures with divisions, departments, and layers of managerial power, but organizational structures are variations of a few established forms. Traditional project organization structures include central and functional organization, while matrix organization (developed in the 1960s and '70s, elevated to high prominence in the 1980s and '90s) combines characteristics of central and functional organization. Understanding organizational structures—and how projects fit within them—gives project managers insights into managing projects more effectively and efficiently.

3.1 Exploring Traditional Project Organization Structures

In the traditional work environment, a supervisor gives work assignments, completes performance appraisals, approves salary increases, and authorizes promotions. However, increasing numbers of organizations are moving away from this traditional structure toward one in which people other than functional managers also direct work assignments. This new set of working relationships supports faster and more effective response to the diverse array of projects that today's successful organizations typically performs.

Working successfully in these new project-oriented organizations requires that project managers and project team members recognize the different people who define and influence the work environment, understand their unique roles, and know how to work with these people to create the greatest chances for successfully completing projects.

Over the years, projects have evolved from organizational afterthoughts to major vehicles for conducting current business and developing future capabilities. The approaches for organizing and managing projects have evolved from centralized and functional structures to matrix structures.

3.1.1 Working within Centrally Organized Structures

The traditional model for handling projects within an organization, the **centrally organized structure,** is illustrated in Figure 3-1. In this structure—sometimes referred to as pure project organization, individual units are established to handle all work in particular specialty areas, such as human resources, training, or information systems.

In a centralized structure, each unit reports to a manager at the corporate level, and any needs that arise in the organization for projects in a particular specialty area are submitted to the appropriate organizational unit. For example, if the emergency care department at mid-size hospital size needs a new invoice-

Figure 3-1

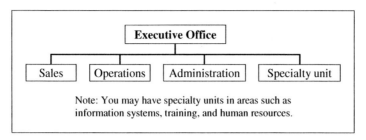

A centralized structure for administering projects.

monitoring system, the information systems department is asked to develop it, not someone within the emergency care department.

This form of organization is also referred to as a *fixed-group structure* because the specialty areas are established parts of the organization. People proficient in the technical skills and knowledge required to perform typical projects are permanently assigned to the group.

Working on projects within centralized structures offers the following benefits:

▲ **Centralized control over project selection:** all project requests are submitted to the manager of a group. The manager then chooses which projects to perform, based upon the relative benefits to the organization, other priority factors that may be identified, and the amount of time staff has available to do the required work.

▲ **One set of management procedures and reporting systems for all projects:** a consistent set of management procedures can be established to guide essential group processes, such as change management, conflict resolution, decision making, and project-progress reviews. Information systems needed to support these processes can be developed to support consistent planning and management of all projects performed by the group.

▲ **Established working relationships among people on a project team:** projects assigned to a group are performed by combinations of the people employed within a specific unit or division. Therefore, over time, team members become familiar with each person's skills, knowledge, and operating style. Managers come to know which people they can count on to honor their promises and commitments.

▲ **Clearly established lines of authority to more easily set priorities and resolve conflicts:** all project assignments are made or approved by the director of a specialty area. Therefore, choices for how to resolve conflicting demands can be made by one person.

▲ **Clear authority that increases pressure for people to honor their commitments:** the specialty area's manager completes the performance appraisals for the unit's staff. Therefore, how team members complete their project assignments can be directly reflected in their performance appraisals.

▲ **Clearly defined career path for people in the unit:** promotions and increased job responsibilities depend upon successful performance on project assignments. This further reinforces the chances that people will successfully complete their project tasks.

However, working in a centralized structure also presents the following challenges:

▲ **Slow response time to project requests:** groups throughout the organization are often competing against each other for the services of a specialty area with a fixed number of staff. The size of the staff may cause certain projects to be delayed. In fact, the very process of having to justify performing one project rather than others submitted from all over the organization may take a significant amount of time.

▲ **Difficult to manage the peaks and valleys in staff workloads:** because people are assigned full time to be in a specialty group, managers often

---

FOR EXAMPLE

Central Organization for Large Projects

Central organization can be very appropriate and efficient for some projects—the construction of a football stadium or shopping mall, for example. After land has been acquired and a design approved, a contractor can assign a project manager and a team of construction specialists to the project. Each specialist (electrical, mechanical, parking, landscaping, and so on) works from the architectural drawings and develops a set of plans for a specific aspect of the project. In the meantime, the project manager (or designated project scheduler) can arrange for timely delivery of large equipment and materials that various specialists may need. The project manager (or a project hiring manager) can hire a suitable number of local construction workers with the appropriate skills. In a well-managed project, supplies, equipment, and workers arrive when they are needed and everyone does his or her work. The project manager is, in effect, the CEO of the project. When the project is completed, the project manager and the specialists return to their parent firm and await their next jobs.

end up looking for project work to keep their staff busy for close to 100 percent of their time. Unfortunately, project requests don't always come in a smooth stream, and the requests received might not require the services of people who are available at a particular time.

▲ **People's lack of familiarity with areas that request their area's services:** people in specialty units are hired for their technical proficiency with the types of projects the unit normally performs. However, these people often have limited experience with the business areas requesting their services. As an example, a person from an information services group assigned to develop a repair parts inventory-control system may have extensive experience with inventory control systems but little or no experience with the repair parts operation in the organization.

3.1.2 Working within Functionally Organized Structures

The **functionally organized structure** was developed to be more responsive to the needs of different organizational areas. In the functional structure, separate units addressing the same specialty are established in the organization's different functional groups, as illustrated in Figure 3-2.

For example, an insurance provider may have three separate information services units assigned to its sales, operations, and administrative departments. Each specialty unit would respond only to the requests of the functional group in which it's located.

The functional structure is also known as a *fixed-group structure* because the specialty units are permanent parts of the organization. As such, functional structures offer many of the advantages of centralized structures (see Section 3.1.1), in addition to the following:

Figure 3-2

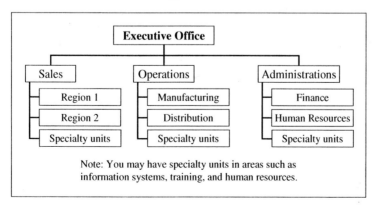

A functional structure for administering projects.

▲ **People in a specialty unit have a better understanding of the functional area they support.** Because each specialty unit only addresses the needs of one functional group, the unit can be staffed with people who are both technically proficient in the unit's area of expertise and experienced in the functional group's operations.

▲ **Organizational units don't have to compete with one another to get the support of their specialty groups.** A specialty unit addresses only the needs of the functional group in which it's located. This reduces the competitiveness and tension that arise when groups compete for scarce resources from the same pool. This leads to consistent and appropriate task assignment based on expertise and training with each functional area.

▲ **Functional groups are often very adept at technical problem-solving with the group.**

However, functional structures also raise the following concerns:

▲ **There is a possibility that different work procedures and reporting systems will be used to guide projects in the same specialty area.** Because each functional group has its own specialty units, each of those specialty units can set up to use its own systems and procedures.

▲ **It could be more difficult to make major investments in equipment and facilities needed to support a unit's technical work.** Suppose an organization's sales and marketing group and operations group both had their own publications units. Suppose further that both units wanted to buy a new document printer and sorter that cost $100,000. Both groups had $75,000 in their budgets that they can spend on such a machine, and each estimates it has work to keep the machine busy about 60 percent of the time. Neither group by itself has a sufficient workload to justify the purchase or sufficient funds to make it happen. However, the two units working together would have both sufficient need and sufficient funds to buy one machine.

▲ **There is a chance for overlap or duplication among projects in the same specialty area performed for different organizational groups.** Because groups in the same specialty area are located in different parts of the organization, the groups are not required to tell each other what they're working on or when they get similar or overlapping project requests. In fact, sometimes one group undertakes a project similar to one being handled by another unit because it wants to retain technical and administrative control. Unfortunately, this often results in duplicate or wasted effort.

1. One benefit of centrally organized structures is that:

   (a) a single worker can experience a wide range of projects.

   (b) managers often struggle to deal with the ups and downs of staff workloads.

   (c) project teams are based on established relationships and roles.

   (d) specialty groups have to compete less.

2. Within functionally organized structures, separate units, teams, divisions, or departments each have their own specialty services. True or false?

3. The chance for overlap and duplication of effort is more likely within which of the following?

   (a) A traditionally organized organization

   (b) A centrally organized organization

   (c) A status-organized organization

   (d) A functionally organized organization

4. As a project manager within a functionally organized company, which of the following is a challenge you are likely to face?

   (a) Funding major equipment or facilities purchases

   (b) Keeping your team busy

   (c) Responding quickly to upper management

   (d) All of the above

3.2 Choosing Matrix Organization

With increasing frequency, projects in today's organizations involve and affect many functional areas. Successful performance requires that these different areas work in concert to produce results that address people's individual and collective needs.

In an attempt to capture the advantages of both centrally and functionally organized projects (as well as to avoid the problems associated with each type), a new type of project organization—more accurately, a combination of the two previous types—was developed. **Matrix organization** was devised to enable a quick and efficient response to projects that must be performed under today's dynamic business conditions.

Figure 3-3

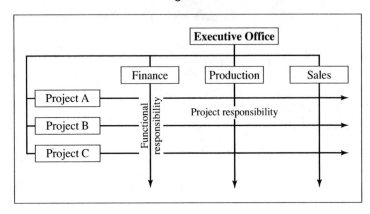

A matrix organizational structure for administering projects.

For example, at a small medical supply manufacturer, each of three project managers has a team of four workers. Each project manager reports to the Vice President of Projects who coordinates the activities of all the projects. At a given time the various projects may or may not be related, but they all demand the parent company's resources. The use of resources as well as the projects themselves must be coordinated. A matrix approach enables the company to organize the interaction between projects and the parent organization by using the major advantages of both central/pure (upper management still has a say in how projects are accomplished) and functional (project teams can have workers that duplicate expertise and knowledge) projects.

Figure 3-3 illustrates a matrix management environment in which people from different parts of the organization are assigned to work on projects as they are created. The project manager and team members may be assigned to the project for less than or equal to 100 percent of their time.

Matrix management offers numerous benefits, including the following:

▲ **Teams can be assembled rapidly.** Companies utilizing a matrix organization have a larger resource pool from which to choose project teams; these companies don't have to wait for a few select people to finish their current assignments before they can start on a project. Additionally, this approach reduces the need to have to go through the time-consuming process of hiring someone new from the outside.

▲ **Scarce expertise can be applied to different projects as needed.** Often, a project may require a small amount of effort from a person with highly specialized knowledge or skills. One project might not provide full-time employment for this person, but he or she can be supported by working part time on several projects.

▲ **Getting buy-in from team members' functional units is easier.** Units that have to work on a project or will be affected by its outcome are more likely to support the project if they're confident that the project team hears their concerns and issues.

▲ **Consistent systems and procedures can be used for projects of the same type.** In a matrix environment, a single functional group sets procedures for how work in its specialty area will be done. Because this group lends its staff to work on different projects throughout the organization, members of the group perform their work in accordance with the technical standards and approaches that their functional group has established.

For all its potential benefits, the matrix environment also introduces some new challenges that must be successfully addressed.

▲ **Team members respond to two different managers.** The team member's functional manager coordinates his or her assignments to different projects, completes the person's performance appraisal, and approves requests for leave. The project manager coordinates project work assignments and project team support.

▲ **Team members working on multiple projects might have to address competing demands for their time.** Each team member has at least two people giving him or her direction—a project manager and a functional manager. In addition, if the team member is working on more than one project, he or she could have more than one project manager. Some of these people who have some claim to the team member's time might be at similar levels in the organization's hierarchy, which makes it even more difficult to resolve conflicting demands for the person's time.

▲ **Team members may not be familiar with each other's styles and knowledge.** Because team members might not have worked extensively together before, they could require some time to build trusting relationships and become comfortable with each other's work styles and behaviors.

▲ **Potential lack of focus on project team and its goals, as opposed to each person's individual assignment.** Team members often represent their functional areas on different project teams and perform tasks associated with those areas. A procurement specialist from the purchasing department might, for example, be responsible for buying equipment and supplies for all projects on which he or she is a team member. In such a case, the specialist might become less concerned that a project's overall goals are met and more concerned that goods and services are bought on time and in accordance with the organization's procurement policies.

FOR EXAMPLE

Canon

Canon (www.canon.com) might be known for its cameras and copiers, but the company is also a world-class innovator in optical research. Ongoing optics research projects (carried out by the Canon Academy of Technology) overlap and affect numerous Canon product lines, including not only cameras and copiers but also binoculars, medical-imaging devices, and semiconductor photolithography equipment. Technology workers at Canon may simultaneously report to management in both a product group and a research group.

▲ **Multiple work processes and reporting systems might be used by different team members.** Team members will be familiar with the systems and processes used in their functional units. They'll have to be encouraged to develop common procedures and systems that all team members can use for their specific projects.

SELF-CHECK

1. Which of the following is NOT a benefit of a matrix organization?

   (a) The interdependency of various groups makes getting buy-in from a functional unit easier.

   (b) Clear authority makes it easy to monitor and control workers' performances.

   (c) Teams can be assembled and reconfigured fairly easily.

   (d) Expertise for one project can easily be applied to another project.

2. Although matrix organizations potentially allow team members to experience a wide range of projects, which of the following is a challenge for the project manager?

   (a) Developing team member expertise

   (b) Interacting effectively with differently skilled groups

   (c) Getting team members with multiple projects to pay attention to his or her project

   (d) All of the above

3.3 Mixed Organizational Systems

Central, functional, and matrix project organizations exist side by side in some companies (see Figure 3-4). In reality, organizational systems are never quite as neatly defined as they appear in the figure. Matrix or functional projects may be organized, become very successful, and expand into centrally organized longer-term business groups or departments.

The ability of companies to organize projects to fit their needs has resulted in a variety of **mixed organizations,** or hybrid organizations.

Figure 3-4

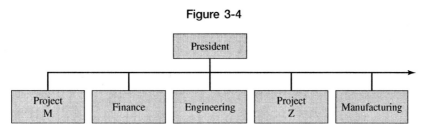

A mixed-organization structure.

FOR EXAMPLE

Integrated Care Management at Central Carolina Hospital

Central Carolina Hospital in North Carolina (www.centralcarolinahosp.com) is a mid-size regional hospital that introduced an Integrated Care Management program to combine aspects of various types of organizational structures. The hospital's team-oriented approach for patient care combines the processes and talents of the Surgical Intensive Care Unit and Patient Care Services. In Integrated Care Management, clinical professionals and case managers collaborate on surgery cases, using processes and tools developed in collaboration. Although the two groups share tools for patient assessment, transition, and discharge, the arrangement allows multiple opportunities for decision making, assigns clear responsibility for various decisions, and permits discussion of alternative treatments.

As hybridization increases, though, companies risk increasing the level of conflict within and between projects because of duplication, overlapping authority, and increased friction between project and functional management.

FOR EXAMPLE

NASA

From a business standpoint, the National Aeronautics and Space Administration, NASA (www.nasa.gov), is much more than shuttle launches and satellites. Overall, NASA is best described as a mixed organizational system; it's a complex partnership of government-sponsored groups and private research companies. The agency has literally dozens of overlapping yet distinct projects and divisions. Some projects are more centrally organized (the Mars Rover project), while others are more functionally organized (the Aeronautics Research Mission Directorate, which focuses on cutting-edge, fundamental research in traditional aeronautical disciplines for all NASA projects). Still other projects (such as NASA's numerous research grants and partnerships) use a more matrix-like organization, with top science workers reporting to both functional groups in their private-sector employers and central project managers at NASA.

SELF-CHECK

1. Mixed organizational structures are rare in today's market-driven workplaces. True or false?

2. Hybridization of organizational structures carries some potential risks, including which of the following?

    (a) Overlapping authority

    (b) Duplication of effort

    (c) Confusion regarding priorities

    (d) All of the above

SUMMARY

Organizational structures—including central, functional, and matrix organizations—each offer positives and negatives in creating environments for projects to occur. When project managers know the type of organization they are working in, they can tailor the way they manage their projects to capitalize on the strengths of a specific organizational structure and avoid its weaknesses. Truthfully, many of today's fast-paced organizations defy simple categorization and can be considered mixed organizations with characteristics of central, functional, and matrix organizations.

KEY TERMS

Centrally organized structure	Traditional organizing structure for handling projects within an organization; individual units are established to handle all work in particular specialty areas; also known as a *fixed-group organization*.
Functionally organized structure	Organizing structure in which separate units addressing the same specialty are established in the organization's different functional groups.
Matrix organization	Combination organization of both centrally and functionally organized projects, devised to enable a quick and efficient response to projects that must be performed under today's dynamic business conditions.
Mixed organization	Central, functional, and matrix project organizations exist side by side in a company; also known as *hybrid organizations*.

ASSESS YOUR UNDERSTANDING

Go to www.wiley.com/college/portny to assess your knowledge of the basics of project organization.

Measure your learning by comparing pre-test and post-test results.

Summary Questions

1. The technicians at a biochemical research firm are members of a laboratory team as well as topic-specific teams that focus on specific aspects of biochemical research (such as chemotherapy, blood-related, genetic, and so on). What sort of organizational structure is this?
2. For the project manager, which organizational structure typically offers clearly established lines of authority, making conflict resolution easier?
3. Which type of organizational structure typically results in a worker reporting to two (or more) managers?

Applying This Chapter

1. At a pharmaceutical firm, researchers are assigned to "clusters" of diseases (mental health conditions, auto-immune diseases, neurological diseases) rather than to a specific drug research project. What might be some of the benefits of organizing the firm's research efforts in this manner?
2. You're project managing (also known as executive producing) the developing and filming of the pilot for a new syndicated talk show. Although traditional and less flexible, why would more centrally organized structures be appropriate for this project?

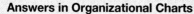

Answers in Organizational Charts

Spend some time with the organizational chart for your company or a company you're interested in working for. You can also review the organizational chart for your school or check out the organizational chart for Mitsubitshi's Heavy Industries division (www.mhi-pt.co.jp/injec_e/outline/chart.htm). How would you describe the organization in place? Who reports to whom? Is the company organized centrally, functionally, in a matrix fashion, or as some mixed form? How might a new product design project fit into the organization?

Choose Your Organizational Structures

You are project manager of a two-year-long effort to identify and offer solutions to common academic challenges faced by first-year college students at public colleges and universities. Some colleges and universities in your state are more centrally organized and others are more functionally organized. How might you need to manage the project while working with the centrally organized schools? What aspects of the project should work equally well in either type of school?

Servant to Two Masters

One of the most common frustrations for workers within matrix organizations is the fact that a functional manager often coordinates assignments to various projects, while a project manager coordinates the actual work done on the project team. Can you think of similar instances in your school, family, or personal life? In what ways did you feel like you were a servant to two masters? What, if anything, did you do to manage the situation? How might your actions and/or solutions apply to work-related situations?

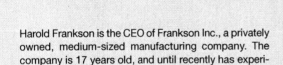

CASE STUDY: Frankson Inc.

Harold Frankson is the CEO of Frankson Inc., a privately owned, medium-sized manufacturing company. The company is 17 years old, and until recently has experienced rapid growth. Mr. Frankson credits the Asian economy with the company's recent problems.

Six months ago Mr. Frankson hired Elizabeth Baresak as the director of corporate planning for the company. After reviewing the company's financial statement and performance records for the last few years, Ms. Baresak came to the conclusion that the Asian economy was not the real problem impacting Frankson's recent performance. Ms. Baresak felt that the Frankson Company's products were out of date and the company had not done a good job of responding to its market. She found examples of the company not moving quickly enough when faced with a market threat or an opportunity.

Ms. Baresak met with Mr. Frankson, told him her conclusions, and added that she believed that the strong functional organization of the company impeded the kind of action required to fix projects. Accordingly, she recommended that Mr. Frankson create a new position, Projects and Programs Officer, to use and promote project-management principles and techniques at Frankson. The PPO would also act as a project manager for several current critical projects.

Mr. Frankson was pleased that Ms. Baresak found something that he could fix, but he did not care much for her solution. He believed that his functional department managers were capable, professional people who should be able to work together efficiently and effectively. He thought that he should work with his management team to provide them with the direction they needed—what to do, when to do it, and who should do it. He would then put the functional manager most closely related to the problem in charge of the group. He was sure that if he gave them a directed push, the projects would get rolling.

After this explanation by Mr. Frankson, Ms. Baresak is more convinced than ever that a separate, non-functional project manager is necessary for the company.

Questions

1. In what ways is Ms. Baresak correct? In what ways is Mr. Frankson correct?
2. If you were Ms. Baresak, how would you sell your idea to Mr. Frankson?
3. Are there other organizational ideas worth considering?
4. If a new position is created, what other changes would you recommend making?

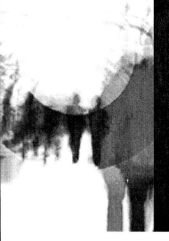

4

PLANNING PROJECTS
Preparing, Executing, and Completing Successful Projects

Starting Point

Go to www.wiley.com/college/portny to assess your knowledge of the basics of project planning.
Determine where you need to concentrate your effort.

What You'll Learn in This Chapter

▲ Five phases of the project life cycle
▲ Project planning activities associated with each life cycle phase
▲ S-shaped and J-shaped project life cycle curves
▲ Project audience and stakeholder roles
▲ Differences between drivers and supporters
▲ Work Breakdown Structures
▲ Linear Responsibility Charts
▲ Type of project responsibilities
▲ Characteristics of multidisciplinary teams
▲ Reasons for project failures—and ways to avoid failures

After Studying This Chapter, You'll Be Able To

▲ Propose, develop, and execute project planning activities appropriate to each project life cycle phase
▲ Evaluate and enhance existing project audiences
▲ Assemble project audiences and stakeholders and prepare them for project responsibilities
▲ Analyze, evaluate, create, and present Work Breakdown Structures
▲ Analyze, evaluate, and create Linear Responsibility Charts
▲ Recommend solutions to improve interactions of multidisciplinary project teams
▲ Assess potential project pitfalls and formulate appropriate solutions

INTRODUCTION

All projects change over time, so project managers have different planning responsibilities that match each phase of a project's life. To successfully launch a project,
everyone associated with the project must understand the roles and responsibilities
of project teams and stakeholders. Two planning tools can be critical to project
success: The Work Breakdown Structure summarizes all the work that needs to
happen in a project, while the Linear Responsibility Chart breaks down who is
responsible for each piece of work. Members of project teams today often have
varied backgrounds; project managers might need to make special efforts to build
relationships between team members. Although some projects fail, savvy project
managers can identify common pitfalls early on and then work to rectify problems.

4.1 Planning a Project Based on Life Cycle Phases

All organisms have a life cycle. They are born, grow, wane, and die. This is true
for all living things, as well as organizations, companies, and projects. A project's
life cycle measures project completion as a function of either time (schedule) or
resources (budget). Figure 4-1 suggests that every project passes through the
following five phases:

1. **Conceive phase:** an idea is born.
2. **Define phase:** a plan is developed.
3. **Start phase:** a team is formed.
4. **Perform phase:** the work is done.
5. **Close phase:** the project is ended.

Figure 4-1

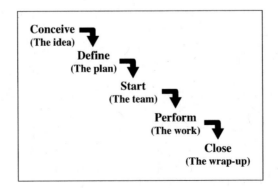

Under the guidance of a project manager,
projects move through five life phases.

For small projects, this entire process can take a few days. For larger projects, it could take many years. No matter how simple or complex the project is, however, the process is the same.

4.1.1 The Conceive Phase: Starting with an Idea

All projects begin with an idea. Perhaps a client identifies a need to be addressed, maybe someone in upper management thinks of a new market to explore, or maybe a project manager thinks of a way to refine a process within his or her organization. When an idea is formed, the project enters the conceive (or concept) phase.

Sometimes the concept phase is handled informally; for a small project it might consist of just a discussion and a verbal agreement. In other instances, especially for larger projects, proceeding with a project requires a formal review and decision.

Consider the following two questions to decide whether to move ahead with a project:

1. **Can the project be done?** Is the project technically feasible? Are the required resources available?
2. **Should the project be done?** Are the expected benefits worth the expected costs?

If the answer to both questions is "yes," a project is ready to proceed to the define phase (Section 4.1.2) and for development of its project plan. If the

FOR EXAMPLE

Revising Project Expectations

Maurice is in charge of the publications department at a health insurance provider. He's just received a request from his boss that requires his department to print 20,000 pages of marketing materials every ten minutes (2000 pages per minute). Maurice checks with his staff and confirms that the company's document reproducing equipment has a top speed of 500 pages per minute. Maurice then checks with his suppliers and finds that the fastest document reproducing equipment available has a top speed of 1000 pages per minute. Maurice's other option is to send the job to a third-party printer (at a higher cost) to meet the requested printing rate. Knowing what he knows, Maurice asks his boss whether she'll consider changing the request: Can the company upgrade its equipment to produce marketing materials at a rate of 20,000 pages every 20 minutes and keep the work in-house?

answer to either question is a definite "no," under no circumstances should the project move on. Someone involved with the project must consider whether to redefine the project and make it feasible and desirable. If feasibility isn't possible, the project should be canceled. Doing anything else guarantees wasted resources, lost opportunities, and frustrated staff.

Sometimes project managers quickly decide that meeting a project request is impossible or that the potential benefits aren't worth the costs to achieve them. Rather than jumping to conclusions, project managers should check with the people who developed or approved the request. They might know something the project manager doesn't.

For example, Byron works as a project manager in the facilities department of a 120-worker office. He feels that the only way to complete a company move in a one-week time period is to have all 3 members of his facilities staff work 12 hours a day from Monday through Sunday. However, Byron's boss turned him down the last five times he asked to authorize overtime for the facilities staff. Byron concludes that it's impossible to complete the move in one week—but he's basing this conclusion on past experience. The only way Byron can find out whether his boss will authorize overtime for this project is to ask.

Most often, project managers cannot be positive that projects are or aren't feasible and cost-beneficial; they can only be reasonably sure and use a variety of techniques. Savvy project managers can do the following:

▲ Consider carefully what is known and plan for uncertainty (see Section 2.4).
▲ Identify and plan for project risks (see Section 13.2).
▲ Conduct a cost-benefit analysis (see Section 2.1).

4.1.2 The Define Phase: Establishing the Plan

After project managers know what they hope to accomplish and believe it's possible, they need detailed plans to describe how the project team will make it happen.

A project plan includes the following elements:

▲ An overview of the reasons for the project (see Section 2.1).
▲ A detailed description of results to be produced (see Section 2.2).
▲ A listing of all work to be performed (see Section 4.3), including predecessors and successors.
▲ The roles all team members will play (see Section 4.2).
▲ A detailed project schedule (see Section 6.4).
▲ Budgets for required personnel, funds, equipment, facilities, and information (see Chapter 5).

▲ Assumptions (see Section 7.1).

▲ Identified risks and possible responses (see Section 13.2).

Plans should always be in writing. A written plan helps the project manager clarify details and reduce the chances of forgetting something. A plan for a small project can be a few lines on a single sheet; plans for large projects can run hundreds of pages. Any plan should be reviewed and approved in writing before beginning work on the project. For a small effort, approval might only need a brief email and someone's initials; large plans might include contracts and formal signing procedures.

The success of a project depends on how clear and accurate the plan is and whether people believe they can achieve it. Considering past experience helps to ensure reality, while involving people in the development helps to encourage their belief in and commitment to achieving it. Often the pressure to get results fast encourages people to skip over the planning and get right to the doing. This can create a lot of immediate activity but can also create significant chances for waste and mistakes.

4.1.3 The Start Phase: Getting Ready, Getting Set

Preparing to begin project work requires a variety of tasks. Project managers (often with the guidance or input of their managers or upper management) do the following:

▲ **Assign people to all project roles.** This includes identifying individuals who'll perform the different project assignments and negotiating agreements to assure the assigned people will be available to work on the project team (see Sections 9.1 and 9.2).

▲ **Give and explain tasks to all team members.** Project managers describe to each team member the work that he or she is to produce and how team members will coordinate their efforts (see Section 10.1).

▲ **Define how the team will perform the tasks necessary to complete assigned work.** Project managers and/or project teams decide how they will handle routine communications, make different project decisions, and resolve conflicts (see Section 10.2).

▲ **Set up necessary financial, personnel, and tracking systems.** Project managers and/or project teams decide which systems and accounts they will use to track the schedule, personnel information, and financial expenditures.

▲ **Announce the project to the organization.** Project managers let people know that the project exists, what it will produce, and when it will begin and end. This announcement is often connected to a launch meeting, in which project stakeholders come together for an initial overview of the project and its goals.

Sometimes project managers don't join projects until the start phase. The first task for these project managers is to revisit the thinking that led people to decide the project was possible and desirable during the conceive phase. At the least, the project manager should become familiar with all existing information. If people overlooked important issues, the project managers must raise them now.

4.1.4 The Perform Phase: Go!

Finally, the core work of the project is performed. Performing the work entails the following:

▲ **Doing the tasks laid out in the plan.**

▲ **Continually comparing performance with plans.** The project team collects information on outcomes produced, schedule achievement, and resource expenditures; from this information, they identify deviations from the plan and formulate corrective action plans.

▲ **Fixing problems that arise.** The project manager and the project team change tasks, schedules, or resources to bring project performance back on track with the existing plan or negotiate agreed-upon changes to the existing project plan.

▲ **Keeping everyone informed.** The project manager and the project team tell people about scheduled achievements that are realized, problems encountered, and revisions to the established project plan (see Section 10.3).

4.1.5 The Close Phase: Stop!

Finishing assigned tasks is only part of bringing a project to a close. In addition, project managers and project team members must do the following:

▲ Secure clients' approvals of the final results.

▲ Close all project accounts.

▲ Help people move on to their next assignments.

▲ Hold a post-project evaluation (see Section 14.1) to recognize project achievements and discuss lessons learned that can be applied to the next project.

4.1.6 Appreciating Differences in Project Life Cycles

Management theorists used to believe that the S-shaped curve shown in Figure 4-2 represented the life cycle for all projects. Many projects—such as building a house—do follow this S-shaped curve toward completion. For example, a house-building project starts slowly with a lot of discussion and planning. Then

Figure 4-2

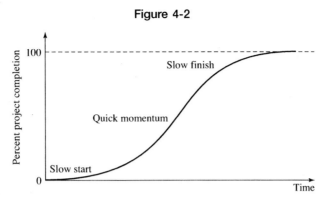

The S-shaped curve of a typical project life cycle.

construction begins and progress is rapid. When the house is built, but not finished inside, progress appears to slow down and it seemingly takes forever to paint everything, to finish all the trim, and to assemble and install the built-in appliances. Progress might seem slow-fast-slow.

While the S-shaped curve is typical of many projects, important exceptions exist. For example, baking a cake is a project that approaches completion in more of a J-shaped curved, as shown in Figure 4-3.

When baking a cake, the ingredients are mixed while the oven is preheated. The mixture is poured into a pan, inserted in the oven, and the baking process begins. Assume that the entire process, from assembling the ingredients to finished cake, requires about 45 minutes—15 minutes for assembling the materials and mixing, and 30 minutes for baking. At the end of 15 minutes, all you have to show for your effort is a goopy mixture. Even after 40 minutes, having baked for 25 minutes, the center of the cake is still goopy. Only in the final few minutes of the process does the goop in the middle become cake.

Figure 4-3

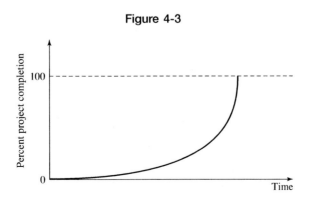

The J-shaped curve of alternative project life cycle.

Many projects are similar to baking a cake—the production of computer software and many chemical engineering projects, for instance. In these cases the project manager's job begins with great attention to having all the correct project resources at hand or guaranteed to be available when needed. After the "baking" process is underway—the integration of various sets of code or chemicals—one can usually not add missing ingredients. As the process continues, the project manager must concentrate on determining when the project is complete—baked in the case of cake, or a fully debugged program in the case of software.

SELF-CHECK

1. Which is the correct sequence of phases for a project life cycle?

   (a) define, conceive, start, perform, close

   (b) start, conceive, start, perform, close

   (c) conceive, define, start, perform, close

   (d) conceive, perform, close, define, start

2. During the conceive phase of a project, a major concern for the project manager is assigning responsibilities to team members. True or false?

3. During which project life phase does a project manager work on fixing problems that arise?

4. A project such as creating an online help desk service for your company probably follows which project life cycle model?

4.2 Filling Participants' Roles

Section 1.4 discusses the roles of various project team members, including the project manager, functional manager, functional employees, and upper management. In addition to the project teams, there are also **project audiences**—a person or group who will support, be affected by, or be interested in a project. See Section 9.1 for more on project audiences.

Project plans describe the roles project managers anticipate people will play and the amount of effort team members will have to invest. Typically, project plans identify these people by name, by title or position, or by the skills and knowledge they need.

At the start of a project, the project manager needs to confirm the identities of the people who'll work to support the project, either by verifying that the specific people included are still able to uphold their promised commitments or by recruiting and selecting new people to fill the remaining needs.

4.2.1 Confirming Team Members' Participation

Project managers need to contact all people identified in project plan and do the following:

▲ **Inform the team members that the project has been approved and when work will start.** Not all project plans are approved. Project managers rarely know in advance how long the approval process will take or how soon after approval a project will start. Project managers should inform team members of a project's approval and planned start date as soon as possible so that they can reserve the necessary time in their schedules to provide the support they promised.

▲ **Confirm that the team members are still able to support the project.** People's workloads and other commitments might change between the time the plan was prepared and the time it is approved. If a person is no longer able to provide the promised support, the project manager needs to recruit a replacement as soon as possible.

▲ **Reconfirm the work expected, including when the team members are to do it and the amount of time they are expected to spend.** The project manager needs to clarify with all persons the specific activities they will perform and the nature of the work they will do. Depending on the size and formality of the project, this might require anything from a quick email to a formal work-order agreement (see Section 4.2.2).

▲ **Explain what still needs to happen to develop the project team and start project work.** The project manager should tell all team members who else is on the team, introducing team members to each other if appropriate.

4.2.2 Drawing up Work-Order Agreements

A **work-order agreement** is a written description of work that a person agrees to perform on a project, the dates the person agrees to start and finish the work, and the number of hours the person agrees to spend on it.

A typical work-order agreement includes the following information:

▲ **Project identifiers:** basic details such as the project name, project number, activity name, and a Work Breakdown Structure code.

▲ **Work to be performed:** descriptions of the different activities and procedures to be done, as well as outputs to be produced.

▲ **Activity start date, end date, and number of hours to be spent:** this information reaffirms the importance of doing the work within the established schedule and budget, as well as the criteria to be used to assess a person's performance effort.

▲ **Written approvals:** the person who'll do the work, his or her supervisor, and the project manager should all sign the work-order agreement to increase the likelihood that everyone has read and understands the elements of the agreement.

If any of the preceding information is missing, project managers should do whatever they can to develop or find the information. The longer a project manager waits to specify any of these details, the greater the chances that people will not be able to provide the support hoped for.

4.2.3 Assuring That Others Are on Board

In addition to formal project team members, other people might play roles in a project's success but will not directly charge time to it. Such people might include drivers and supporters, described subsequently.

▲ **Drivers** are people who have some say in defining the results that a project is to achieve. These are the people for whom the project work is being performed.

▲ **Supporters** are people who help to perform project work. They include the people who authorize the resources for a project as well as those who work on it.

Project managers should contact all drivers and supporters and do the following:

▲ Inform them that the project has been approved and when work will start.

▲ Reaffirm what the project will produce.

▲ Clarify with identified drivers that the project's planned results still address their needs.

▲ Clarify with identified supporters exactly how they can help with the project.

▲ Develop specific plans for involving stakeholders throughout the project and keep them informed of progress.

In addition to drivers and supporters, **observers** are interested in a project but will not define what it should accomplish or directly support efforts. As observers are identified, project managers can choose individuals they wish to keep informed of progress and prepare a plan for how they'll do so. See Section 9.2 for more on drivers, supporters, and observers.

4.2.4 Recruiting People to Fill Project Positions

Many project plans identify proposed project team members by job title, position description, or skills and knowledge. Sometimes project managers have to find actual people to assume the specified roles, but often functional managers make these assignments. Project assignments can be made to people within the organization, outside the organization, or through contracts with external organizations to provide the necessary support. Negotiation is a key part of identifying and assigning people to project roles.

Preparing a written description of the activities is helpful for assigning people to project roles. This description can range from a simple memo for informal projects to a written job description for more formal ones.

Prepare a separate description of needs for each category of personnel to be recruited. At a minimum, include the following information in each description:

▲ Project name, number, and start date.

▲ Skills and knowledge that the person or people must have.

▲ Description and start and end dates of activities to be performed.

▲ Anticipated level of effort needed to perform the described work.

When planning to look inside the organization, project managers (often in conjunction with one or more functional managers) need to do the following:

▲ Identify potential candidates by working with human resources and/or area managers.

▲ Meet with candidates to discuss the project, describe the work expected, and assess candidate qualifications.

▲ Choose the best candidates and extend an offer for them to join the project team.

▲ Document the agreement of the work they'll do.

Although each organization operates differently, project managers should work with their organization's contracts office early on to obtain the support of external consultants. If external consultants are used, project managers should do the following:

▲ Provide the contracts office with a detailed description of the tasks to be performed, and the qualifications, skills, and knowledge that the consultants should have.

▲ Participate in the review of potential contractors and review any contracts before they're signed.

1. Which of the following statements is true about project audiences?

   (a) A project audience includes people who are affected by the project.

   (b) A project audience is the same thing as a project team.

   (c) A project audience should be clearly identified in the Statement of Work.

   (d) None of the above.

2. Project plans identify project audiences, so the project manager should proceed with making assignments as soon as a project launches. True or false?

3. Project managers can divide members of a project's audience into what three broad categories?

4. Which of the following is an appropriate activity for a project manager to confirm team member participation?

   (a) asking a team member to verify that she can give 10 hours a week to a project

   (b) informing the team member that the project has been approved by upper management

   (c) telling a team member who he or she will be working with on the project

   (d) all of the above

4.3 Using Work Breakdown Structures

Statements of Work (Section 2.5) offer only general descriptions of the actual work assignments for the project. Project managers need other documents to conduct the actual, day-to-day managing and working of projects.

In particular, the **Work Breakdown Structure**, or WBS, is an organized, detailed, and hierarchical representation of all work to be performed in a project. This section covers the creation and implementation of Work Breakdown Structures.

4.3.1 Thinking Hierarchically with Work Breakdown Structures

Project managers develop Work Breakdown Structures for large and small projects, but the hierarchical organization used to develop them is the same.

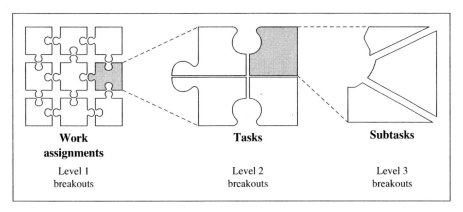

Thinking hierarchically to break down a project.

Figure 4-4 shows how a work assignment, like a jigsaw puzzle, can be broken down into increasingly more detailed levels.

Projects typically break down to levels of detail such as the following:

▲ Level 1: work assignment.
▲ Level 2: task.
▲ Level 3: subtask.
▲ Level 4: subsubtasks.

For example, if Tamara is planning to develop and present a new training program, a good first question is, "What major pieces of work have to be done for this project to be completed?" From this question, Tamara might identify that she needs to do the following:

▲ Determine the needs.
▲ Design the program.
▲ Develop the materials.
▲ Test the program.
▲ Present the program.

To further describe what needs to happen to meet each of these major items, Tamara can ask similarly, "What major pieces of work have to be done for X portion of the project to be completed?" For example, for "Determine the needs," Tamara might decide that the following must happen:

▲ Identify people who have an interest in the program.
▲ Interview some of these people.

▲ Review written materials that discuss needs for the program.

▲ Prepare a report of the needs the program will address.

Of course, project managers can (and often should) continue breaking down each item into increasingly more specific details. For example, when Tamara considers what major pieces of work have to be done to complete the goal "Interview some of these people," she might decide that she needs to do the following:

▲ Select the people to be interviewed.

▲ Prepare the questions to be asked during the interviews.

▲ Schedule the interviews.

▲ Conduct the interviews.

▲ Write up the results of the interviews.

Some people look at detailed Work Breakdown Structures and decide that they make projects more complex than they really are. (Looking at 100 tasks, all written out on paper, can be a little unnerving, not to mention 10,000 tasks.) The truth is, though, a project's complexity was there all the time; the Work Breakdown Structure just displays it. In fact, by clearly portraying all aspects of the work to be done, the Work Breakdown Structure actually simplifies the project.

4.3.2 Incorporating Conditional Activities in Work Breakdown Structures

Some activities, at first glance, seem impossible to include in a Work Breakdown Structure.

For example, a project plan might include an activity that could require an unknown number of repetitive cycles, such as obtaining approval of a report. In reality, the project managers will write a draft and submit it for review and approval. If the reviewers approve the draft, the project manager can proceed to the next activity (such as having the final version typed). If the reviewers don't approve the draft, the project manager must revise the report, incorporate comments, and resubmit it for a second review and approval. If it's now approved, the project manager can proceed to the next activity; if not, he or she must revise it again, and so on.

The revisions described in the preceding paragraph are a **conditional activity**, an activity that's performed only if certain conditions come to pass. Unfortunately, Work Breakdown Structures do not contain conditional activities. Project managers must plan to perform every activity that they include. Therefore, these conditional activities can be represented in a Work Breakdown Structure in the following two ways:

FOR EXAMPLE

Work Breakdown Structure Offers Greater Accuracy

Neal's boss asks him to estimate how long it will take to survey people to determine the characteristics for a new product under consideration for development. Based on some quick initial thinking, Neal figures he'll need to contact people in the office headquarters, in two regional activity centers, and from a sampling of current clients. Neal tells his boss that the project can be completed in one to six months, which is a rather useless response. (Neal figures that finishing any time before six months meets his promise; his boss figures, with some hard work, Neal will be done in one month, but in truth, Neal doesn't have a clue how long it will take.)

Developing a Work Breakdown Structure establishes a clearer picture of exactly what needs to happen and how long it takes. For instance, conducting a mail survey breaks down to five task activities:

▲ Selecting clients to survey: Neal figures it takes one week to select his sample if the sales department has a current listing of all company clients. He checks with them, and they do.

▲ Designing and printing a survey questionnaire: Neal gets lucky. A colleague tells him about a similar survey that was conducted of a different target population a year ago. Some extra questionnaires are available and appropriate for his project. Suddenly Neal does not need to allow any time or resources for designing and printing questionnaires.

▲ Sending out surveys and receiving returns: Neal consults with people who've done surveys before and finds out that for a response rate of 70 percent or greater he needs to plan on a three-phased approach: Mail out the first set of questionnaires and collect responses for four weeks. Then mail out a second set of questionnaires to nonrespondents and wait another four weeks. Finally, conduct phone follow-ups for two more weeks with the people who have still not responded.

▲ Entering and analyzing the data: Neal figures it takes about two weeks to enter and analyze the amount of data he anticipates receiving.

▲ Preparing the final report: Neal estimates two weeks to prepare the final report.

Neal's estimate of the time to complete the mail survey is 15 weeks. Because he has clarified the work to be done and how it will be completed, not only is he more specific, but he also has a higher confidence in his estimate.

1. Define a single activity, such as "Review/revise report" in the example above, and assign one duration to that activity in the Work Breakdown Structure. This approach means the project manager allows as many iterations as possible within the established time period.
2. List each iteration of the activity separately in the Work Breakdown Structure. As in the example above, assume the number of revisions that is likely to be required in order to receive approval and list each review/revision as a separate activity. This approach defines a separate milestone at the end of each iteration of the conditional activity, which allows more meaningful tracking of progress.

Of course, assuming that three reviews and two revisions will be required doesn't guarantee that a draft will be approved after the third review. If a draft is approved after the first review, the project can move on to the next activity. However, if the report still hasn't been approved after the third review, the project manager must continue to revise and resubmit until approval is obtained. At this point, the project managers must go back and re-assess the plan, determine the impact of the additional iterations, and see whether future activities need to be adjusted to keep the project on schedule and/or within budget.

4.3.3 Including Activities with No Obvious Break Points

Sometimes there is no apparent way to break down an activity into a specific time frame. And sometimes it just doesn't seem necessary. Even in these situations, project managers should divide the activity into smaller chunks just as a reminder to check periodically to ensure that the initial schedule and resource projections for the overall activity are still valid.

4.3.4 Planning Long-Term Projects

Long-term projects present a different challenge to Work Breakdown Structures. Often, the activities performed a year or more in the future depend on the results of work done between now and then. Even if project managers can accurately predict today the activities they will perform then, the further into the future you plan, the more likely that something will change and require plan modifications.

When developing a Work Breakdown Structure for a long-term project, do it in phases:

▲ Plan in detail (that is, down to activities that take two weeks or less to complete) for the first three months.
▲ Plan the remainder of the project in less detail, perhaps detailing the planned work in clusters of activities that take between one and two months to complete.

FOR EXAMPLE

Breaking down Waiting Time into Intervals

For one of his first projects, an engineer was assigned to design and build a piece of equipment. He ordered raw materials through his procurement office and was told that the material would be delivered in six months. He was told to notify the procurement office if he hadn't received the raw materials by the promised date. When he hadn't received raw materials after six months, he notified the procurement office. The procurement specialist learned that there had been a fire in the vendor's facilities five months earlier that had caused all production to stop. Production had just been resumed, and the vendor estimated the materials would ship in about five months. In essence, the engineer's Work Breakdown Structure had identified one activity: buy raw materials, with a single duration of six months. He argued that, after placing the order, nothing else was to happen until five and a half months passed, at which time work on his order would be started and the final materials would be delivered to him in two weeks. However, the engineer could have divided the waiting time into one-month intervals, and he could have called at the end of each month to see if anything had occurred which changed the projected delivery date. While checking wouldn't have prevented the fire, the engineer would have learned about it five months sooner and could have made other plans immediately.

▲ At the end of the first three months, revise the initial plan to detail the activities for the next three months in components that will take two weeks or less to complete.

▲ Modify any future activities as necessary, based on the results of the first three months' work.

▲ Continue revising the plan in this way throughout the project.

4.3.5 Developing Work Breakdown Structures

How a project manager develops Work Breakdown Structures depends upon how familiar he or she and the team are with the project, whether similar projects have been successfully performed in the past, and how many new methods and approaches will be used.

Choose one of the following two developmental approaches, depending upon the project's characteristics:

1. **Top down:** start at the top level and systematically develop increasing levels of detail for all activities. A top-down approach works well for projects that the project manager or team is familiar with. A top-down approach includes the following steps:

   (a) Specify all work assignments required for the entire project.

   (b) Determine all tasks required to complete each work assignment.

   (c) As necessary, specify the subtasks required to complete each task.

   (d) Continue in this way until the entire project is adequately detailed.

2. **Brainstorming:** generate, often as a project team, a list of activities that will have to be done and then group them into categories. A brainstorming approach works well for projects involving untested methods and approaches or for ones the project manager or team members have not done before. A brainstorming method includes the following steps:

   (a) On a single list, write any and all activities that have to be performed for the project. At this point, don't worry about overlap or level of detail.

   (b) Study the list and group the activities into a few major categories with common characteristics. These can become the project's work assignments.

   (c) If appropriate, group activities under a particular work assignment into a small number of tasks.

   (d) Consider each category created and use the top-down approach to determine any additional activities that might have been overlooked.

SELF-CHECK

1. What is the typical organization of a Work Breakdown Structure?
2. Conditional activities can be incorporated into Work Breakdown Structures by assuming a typical length of time for the activity based on experience in similar projects. True or false?
3. Work Breakdown Structures are inappropriate for long-term projects because project managers typically end up revising the Work Breakdown Structure during the months (or years) that the project involves. True or false?
4. What are the two main methods for developing the specific items within a Work Breakdown Structure?

Figure 4-5

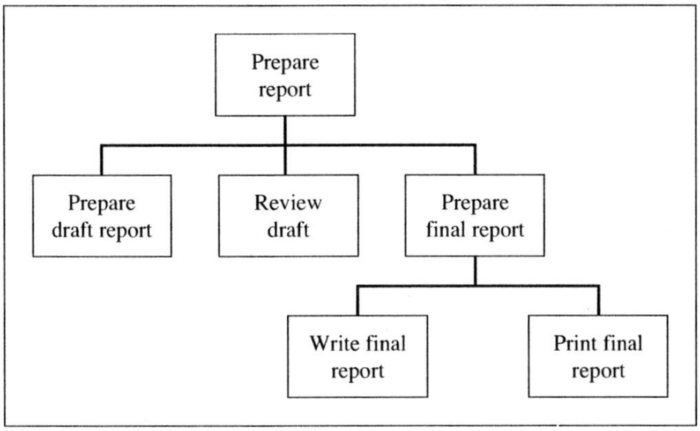

A Work Breakdown Structure as an organizational chart.

4.4 Displaying Work Breakdown Structures

Project managers can use several different formats to display Work Breakdown Structures.

4.4.1 The Organizational-Chart Format

Figure 4-5 shows how project managers can illustrate a Work Breakdown Structure in an **organizational-chart format.** This format effectively portrays an overview of the project and the hierarchical relationships of different work assignments (and perhaps tasks) at the highest levels. However, because this format requires a lot of space to draw, it's less effective for displaying large numbers of activities.

4.4.2 The Indented-Outline Format

The **indented-outline format** illustrated in Figure 4-6 is another way to display a Work Breakdown Structure. This format presents activities, tasks, and subtasks

Figure 4-6

Prepare report

1.0 Prepare draft report
2.0 Review draft report
3.0 Prepare final report
    3.1 Write final report
    3.0 Print final report

A Work Breakdown Structure as
an indented outline.

Figure 4-7

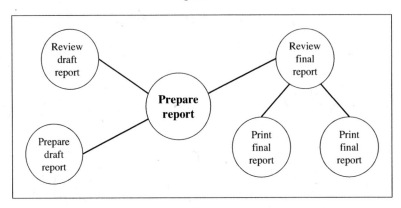

A Work Breakdown Structure as a bubble chart.

as a hierarchically organized list. It's easier to read and understand a complex Work Breakdown Structure with many activities if it's displayed in this format. Project-management software, such as Microsoft Project, can quickly create indented outlines.

Consider using a combination of the organizational-chart and indented-outline formats to explain a Work Breakdown Structure for a large project. Display the work assignments and possibly the tasks in the organizational-chart format and then portray the detailed breakout for every task in the indented-outline format.

4.4.3 The Bubble-Chart Format

The **bubble-chart format** illustrated in Figure 4-7 is particularly effective for supporting the brainstorming process. Project team members interpret the bubble chart as follows:

▲ The bubble in the center represents the entire project.
▲ Lines from the center bubble lead to work assignments.
▲ Lines from each work assignment lead to tasks related to that work assignment.

The freeform nature of the bubble chart makes it effective for easily recording thoughts generated in a brainstorming process. Project managers can also easily rearrange activities as they proceed with the analysis and planning.

However, bubble charts aren't usually effective for displaying Work Breakdown Structures to audiences and stakeholders who aren't familiar with a project. Use the bubble chart to develop a Work Breakdown Structure but transpose the chart into an organizational-chart or an indented-outline format to present it to others.

SELF-CHECK

1. Which presentation of a Work Breakdown Structure displays activities as specifically numbered items and subitems?

2. Which of the following is one downside of a bubble-chart presentation of a Work Breakdown Structure?

   (a) Bubble charts encourage brainstorming.

   (b) Bubble charts can be difficult for people new to the project to understand quickly.

   (c) Bubble charts require software to create effectively.

   (d) Bubble charts only work for projects with a limited number of observers.

4.5 Illustrating Work Relationships with Linear Responsibility Charts

Defining and sharing team roles and responsibilities up front can improve performance and help to identify and head off potential difficulties during a project. Figure 4-8 illustrates how these relationships can be described in a Linear Responsibility Chart.

A **Linear Responsibility Chart** is a matrix that depicts the role that each project team or stakeholder (see Section 4.2) plays in the performance of different project activities.

Figure 4-8

	Project Manager	Task Leader	Project Staffer A	Group Director	Purchasing
Design questionnaire	A	S, A	P		
Select respondents		P			
Conduct pretest		P	S		
Print questionnaires	A	P		A	A

P = Primary responsibility   S = Secondary responsibility   A = Approval

A Linear Responsibility Chart describes relationships.

Figure 4-8 illustrates a portion of a Linear Responsibility Chart for designing and conducting a customer needs survey. In a Linear Responsibility Chart, project roles are depicted in the following way:

▲ Project activities are listed in the left-hand column.
▲ Project stakeholders are identified in the top row.
▲ The role that each stakeholder plays with respect to each activity is specified in the intersections.

4.5.1 Assigning Responsibilities

Figure 4-8 also defines three roles that each stakeholder or team member can have with regard to project activities:

1. **Primary responsibility (P):** this individual has committed to ensure that the result for the specific activity is achieved.
2. **Secondary responsibility (S):** this individual(s) has committed to achieve some portion of the result for the specific activity.
3. **Approval (A):** this individual(s) is not actually doing work on the activity but will approve what has been done.

A Linear Responsibility Chart is a format. The project manager can define whatever roles he or she feels are appropriate for the project. For example, many project managers use the following roles:

▲ **Review (R):** these individuals will review and comment on the results of an activity, but their formal approval is not required.
▲ **Output (O):** these individuals will receive products from the activity or be affected by the project.
▲ **Input (I):** these individuals will provide input for the work performed on the activity.

4.5.2 Reading Linear Responsibility Charts

To read a Linear Responsibility Chart, consider the activity "Design questionnaire" in Figure 4-8. The chart suggests that three people will work together as follows:

1. Primary responsibility for the questionnaire's content, format, and layout rests with Project Staffer A. On this project, Project Staffer A reports to the task leader, who, in turn, reports to the project manager.
2. The task leader will perform selected parts of the questionnaire design under the general coordination of Staffer A. The task leader must approve

all aspects of the questionnaire design before work can proceed to the next step.

3. The project manager must approve the entire questionnaire, even though he or she isn't doing any of the actual design and layout.

Analyzing a Linear Responsibility Chart vertically by stakeholder and horizontally by activity helps project managers identify situations that might give rise to problems. After identifying these situations, the project manager can decide whether and how to address them. Table 4-1 presents some observations and potential issues related to the chart in Figure 4-8.

Table 4-1: Situations and Issues Suggested in the Linear Responsibility Chart in Figure 4-8

Situation	Possible Issues
The task leader is heavily committed.	The task leader will not have enough time to handle all these duties.
	The task leader is making all key decisions.
	What if the task leader leaves during the project?
The group director doesn't get involved until he or she is asked to approve the funds for printing the questionnaires.	The group director will slow down the approval process by asking questions about the purpose of the project, the use of the results, and so on.
The project manager has no direct responsibilities for individual project activities.	Will the project manager fully understand the substance and status of project work performed?
The task leader is the only person involved in selecting the respondents.	Do you want a key decision that can determine the value of the entire pre-test made with only one person's input?
The activity called "print questionnaires" requires three approvals.	Does anyone else have to approve the questionnaire before it can be used?
	Are too many people approving the questionnaire? Would it be acceptable to notify just one or two of these people?
	The activity might take longer than its estimate because this approval process is out of your control.

After identifying a possible issue, the project manager can choose how to deal with it. Possibilities include the following:

▲ **Ignore it.** For example, a project manager might decide that three approvals are necessary, even though the number is high.

▲ **Take simple steps to minimize the risk of a problem occurring.** For example, the project manager might ask the task leader to thoroughly document all important information in case he or she leaves the project unexpectedly.

▲ **Address it further in a formal risk management plan.** See Chapter 13 for a discussion of how to analyze and plan to manage project risks.

4.5.3 Developing Linear Responsibility Charts

Follow these steps to develop Linear Responsibility Charts:

1. Identify all people who'll participate in or support the project. See the discussion of audiences and stakeholders (Section 4.2).

2. Develop a complete list of activities to be performed on the project. See the discussion of Work Breakdown Structures (Section 4.4).

3. Consult with all team members and draft a Linear Responsibility Chart. If specific people haven't yet been identified for certain activities, consult with people who have done those types of activities before.

4. Ask all people with whom you spoke to review and approve your draft chart.

5. If some people don't approve the draft chart, incorporate their recommended changes into a second draft and again ask all people with whom you spoke to review and approve the chart.

6. Continue until all people approve the chart.

FOR EXAMPLE

Being Sure Everyone's on the Same Page

A project manager was preparing to start a large project. He asked each of the project's eight team members to prepare a chart that represented his or her understanding of everyone's roles and responsibilities. All the team members completed their charts in less than an hour, but when the project manager reviewed the results, he found that each chart portrayed a different view of what people's roles and responsibilities were. If people had tried to do their work without going through this exercise, they would have encountered frustration and conflict throughout the project.

4.5.4 Improving the Quality of Charts

Take the following steps to improve the quality of a Linear Responsibility Chart:

▲ **Develop a hierarchy of charts for larger projects.** Including 50 or more activities on the same Linear Responsibility Chart can be cumbersome. Consider developing a series of nested charts for larger projects. Prepare a high-level chart that identifies responsibilities for work assignments or tasks in a Work Breakdown Structure and then develop separate charts for individual work assignments or tasks in the main chart that detail responsibilities for associated lower-level activities. Figure 4-9 illustrates a simple example of a hierarchy of Linear Responsibility Charts.

▲ **Involve the entire team when developing a chart to ensure accuracy and buy-in.** It's unreasonable to expect the project manager to know exactly how experts and technical representatives from different groups should perform tasks in their areas of specialty. Further, people have a greater commitment to a plan if they participate in developing it.

Figure 4-9

Design and Conduct a Customer Needs Survey				
People / Activities	Project Manager	Team Leader A	Team Leader B	Team Leader C
Finalize requirements	A	P		
Design system	A		P	S
Test system	A	S	S	P

Finalize Requirements				
People / Activities	Team Leader A	Staffer A	Staffer B	Staffer C
Review literatrure	A	P	S	
Conduct focus groups	P	S		S
Prepare report	A	S	S	

A hierarchy of Linear Responsibility Charts.

▲ **Put the chart in writing.** People have to think about the issues addressed in the Linear Responsibility Chart as they plan and perform their project work. For example, before the Linear Responsibility Chart in Figure 4-8 was prepared, the task leader knew that he or she was primarily responsible for selecting respondents for pre-testing the questionnaire, and others knew that they were not involved in the activity but probably assumed that someone else was. Writing down this information in the table highlighted that the task leader was, in fact, the only one who would be involved in the activity.

▲ **Review and update the chart throughout the project.** The longer the project, the more likely that activities will be added or deleted, that people will leave the team, and that new people will join the team. Periodically reviewing and updating Linear Responsibility Charts enables the project manager to do the following:

▲ Assess whether the current assignments of roles and responsibilities are working out and, if not, where changes might be needed.

▲ Clarify the roles and responsibilities for new activities.

▲ Clarify the roles and responsibilities for people who join the team.

▲ Clarify how to handle the roles and responsibilities of someone who leaves the team.

Project managers can develop Linear Responsibility Charts at any time during a project. If a project manager joins a project and finds that no Linear Responsibility Chart exists, he or she should develop one. If the project is already underway, he or she can develop a chart to clarify the roles and responsibilities from the current point forward.

SELF-CHECK

1. What do R, O, and I responsibilities on a Linear Responsibility Chart typically stand for?
2. What are the three common types of responsibility to show in a Linear Responsibility Chart?

    (a) primary responsibility, secondary responsibility, and approval

    (b) sign off, sign on, and veto

    (c) functional responsibility, project responsibility, and approval

    (d) accountable, partially accountable, and observer

4.6 Working with Multidisciplinary Teams

Multidisciplinary teams (MTs) or transdisciplinary teams—work groups comprised of individuals from various department or divisions, with varying backgrounds and expertise—are a feature of many projects today.

4.6.1 Using Concurrent Engineering

Only 10 to 20 years ago, work on a new automobile design was most likely independent and sequential. Various groups involved in a design project did not work together:

For example, a product design group developed a design that seemed to meet the marketing group's specifications. This design was submitted to top management for approval, and possible redesign if needed. When the design was accepted, a prototype was constructed. The project was then transferred to the engineering group, who tested the prototype product for quality, reliability, and manufacturability, and who possibly altered the design to use less expensive materials. Any changes were submitted for management approval, at which time a new prototype was constructed and subjected to testing. After qualifying on all tests, the project moved to the manufacturing group, which proceeded to plan the actual steps required to manufacture the product in the most cost-effective way, given the machinery and equipment currently available. Again, changes were submitted for approval, often to speed up or improve the production process. If the project proceeded to the production stage, distribution channels had to be arranged, packaging designed and produced, marketing strategies developed, advertising campaigns developed, and the product shipped to the distribution centers for sale and delivery.

Conflicts between the various functional groups in these traditional arrangements were legend. Each group tried to optimize its contribution, which led to nonoptimization for the system. Additionally, the process was extremely time consuming and expensive—conditions not tolerable in today's competitive environment.

To solve the problem associated with traditional methods, many companies shifted to a process where two or more steps are carried out at the same time. **Concurrent engineering** (CE), also known as simultaneous engineering, saves time and costs when compared to traditional methods. (The word "engineering" here is used in its broadest sense, that is, the art of practically applying science.)

Concurrent engineering has been widely used for a great diversity of projects—everything from political campaigns to the design and construction of the space shuttle. Concurrent engineering has been generally adopted as the proper way to tackle problems that are multidisciplinary in nature.

FOR EXAMPLE

Concurrent Engineering and the PT Cruiser

U.S. automobile manufacturers usually take about three years to modify a car or truck for the Japanese market, but DaimlerChrysler used CE to make its PT Cruiser ready for sale in Japan four months after it was introduced in the United States.

The use of multidisciplinary teams and concurrent engineering in product development and planning is not without its difficulties. Successfully involving transfunctional teams in project planning requires that project managers impose some structure (such as Work Breakdown Structures, Linear Responsibility Charts, and other aids) on the planning process. A common solution is simply to define the group's responsibility as being the development of a detailed plan to accomplish whatever is established as the project objective.

If the members of a multidisciplinary team are problem-oriented, concurrent engineering works very well. Research shows that when problem-oriented people with different backgrounds enter conflicts about how to deal with a problem, they often produce very creative solutions—and without damage to project quality, cost, or schedule. For some highly effective teams, conflict can become a favored style of problem solving. But when team members are both

FOR EXAMPLE

Multidisciplinary Success at Thermos

Monte Peterson, CEO of Thermos (now a subsidiary of Nippon Sanso, Inc.), formed a flexible interdisciplinary team with representatives from marketing, manufacturing, engineering, and finance to develop the company's recently introduced electric outdoor grill. The interdisciplinary approach was used primarily to reduce the time required to complete the project. By including manufacturing representatives in the design process from the beginning, the team avoided some costly mistakes later on. Initially, for instance, the designers opted for tapered legs on the grill. However, after manufacturing explained at an early meeting that tapered legs would have to be custom made, the design engineers changed the design to straight legs. Under previous work organizations, manufacturing would not have known about the problem with the tapered legs until the design was completed. The grill went on to win four design awards in its first year.

argumentative and oriented to their own discipline, concurrent engineering is no improvement on any other method of problem solving.

4.6.2 Interface Coordination and Integration Management

Using multidisciplinary teams can raise serious problems for project managers. Sizable, complex projects with inputs from several different departments or groups often require project managers to coordinate the work of different functional groups interacting as team members. The following are strategies for organizing multidisciplinary teams:

▲ **Interface coordination:** the process of managing the way groups work together.

▲ **Integration management:** coordinating the work of groups and the timing of their interactions.

Members of multidisciplinary teams come from different functional areas and often are not used to dealing with one another directly. For the most part, they have no established dependencies on each other and being co-members of a team is not sufficient to cause them to associate—unless the team has a mission that makes it important for the members to develop relationships.

One approach to the problem of interface coordination is to introduce the structure of the project to the team as a graphical map. For example, Figure 4-10 graphically maps interfaces for the design of a silicon chip.

SELF-CHECK

1. A multidisciplinary team created to deal with a dated computer network has a better chance for success if it focuses on exploring the latest network technologies rather than focusing on the problems with the current network. True or false?

2. Which of the following is a reason concurrent engineering is much more prevalent in today's companies?

    (a) Concurrent engineering costs companies less than traditional engineering methods.

    (b) Products and services need to reach market more quickly for companies to be competitive.

    (c) Collaboration is easier during concurrent engineering than with traditional engineering methods.

    (d) All of the above.

Figure 4-10

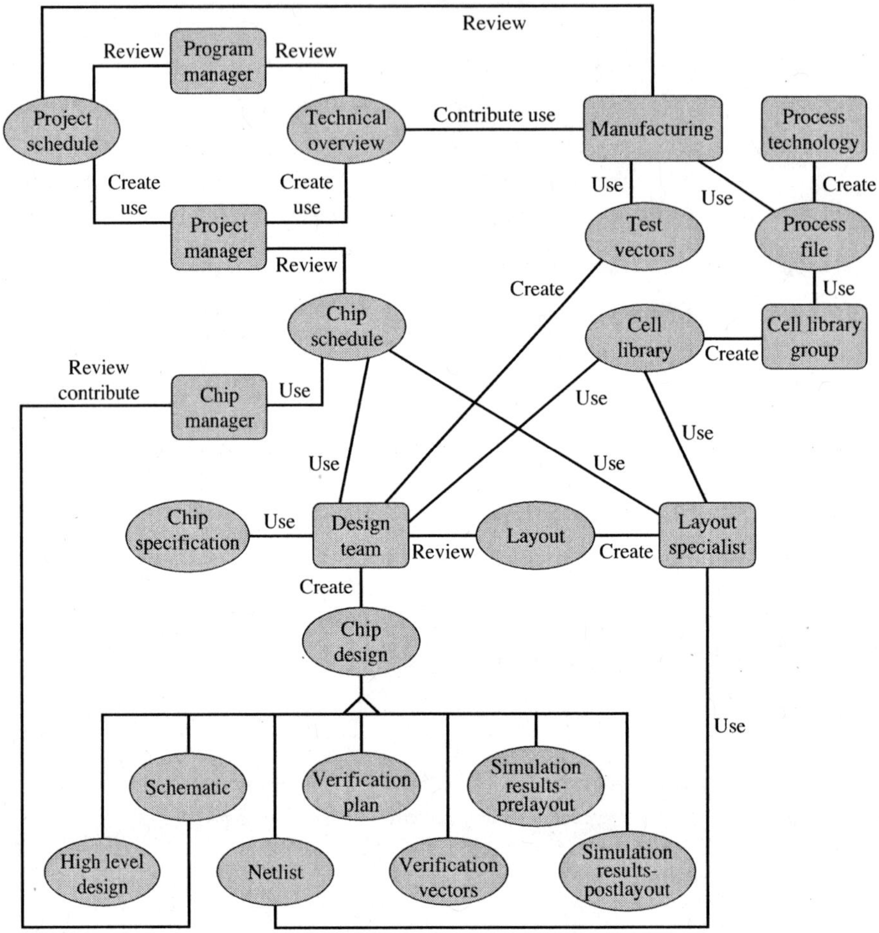

A map of the interfacing required to produce a microchip. Bailetti et al., 1994.

4.7 Examining Why Plans and Projects Fail

While many projects succeed, many fail. Although no exact formula for project success exists, the project plan and the actions of project managers during the initial planning phases of projects hold many critical elements for project success.

4.7.1 Anticipating Common Mistakes

The short-term pressures of project-management duties might encourage project managers to act today in ways that cause pain tomorrow. The following are common mistakes that project managers make during the planning phases of projects:

▲ **Jumping directly from the conceive phase to the perform phase.** When projects are on short time schedules, some project managers think that jumping in and starting the work will save time. However, this is rarely the case because the project manager hasn't yet defined what activities need to be done. In the end, the project often takes even more time to complete because the team must redo work that was inappropriately executed. Variations on this mistake include the following:

  ▲ **This project has been done many times before, so why do I have to plan it out again?** Even though projects are often similar to ones done in the past, some things are always different. Perhaps the current project involves working with new people, using a new piece of equipment, or operating under a different schedule. Project managers need to take the time at the start of project to be sure the established plan suits the current situation.

  ▲ **This project is so different from what's been done before, so what good is trying to plan?** This is a lot like driving through an area where you've never been and deciding that a road map is useless. Project managers must take time to plan for a new project because no one has taken this particular path before. While initial plans will likely have to be revised during a project, the project manager and project team need to have a clear statement of the intended plan.

▲ **Omitting the start phase completely.** Time pressure often leads project managers to assume that the start phase is a waste of time. However, a project team needs to take time to define its procedures and relationships before jumping in to the actual project work. See Chapter 10 for more information on important team-related activities during the start phase.

▲ **Jumping right into the work upon joining a project at its start phase.** Many project managers join projects during the start phase and assume the work before their arrival (during the conceive and define phases) needs no additional review or consideration. Reviewing work from the conceive and define phases allows project managers to do the following:

  ▲ See if they can identify any issues that might have been overlooked.

  ▲ Understand the reasoning behind the plan and decide if they feel the plan is achievable.

▲ **Only partially completing the close phase.** Because of scarce resources and short deadlines, project managers often move to another project quickly. Although new projects are always more challenging than wrapping up old ones, many project managers never really know how successful their projects were. Project managers need to take the time to ensure that all tasks are completed to the client's satisfaction. And if project managers don't take positive steps to determine and reflect lessons learned from a project in the performance of future ones, they are liable to make the same mistakes over and over again. See Sections 14.1 and 14.3 for more end-of-project activities.

4.7.2 Responding to Reality

In a perfect world, project managers would perform all work in one phase of a project before moving on to the next one. The real world, of course, isn't perfect, and project success often requires a flexible approach to project life cycles. For example,

▲ **Project managers sometimes have to work on two (or more) phases at the same time in order to meet established deadlines.** Working on the next phase before completing an earlier one increases the risk that tasks might have to be redone—which could cause missed deadlines and more expenses later on. Still, some situations require this approach. If a project manager must choose this approach, he or she needs to alert people to the risks and associated costs (see Section 13.1).

▲ **Project managers often learn by doing.** Even when project managers do their best to assess feasibility and develop detailed plans, many find out that they can't achieve what they thought could be done. In these cases, project managers need to go back to the earlier phases of their projects and rethink them in light of the new information learned.

▲ **Sometimes, things change.** A project manager's assessments of feasibility and relative benefits might be sound, and his or her plan detailed and realistic. During the project, however, certain key people the project manager was counting on left the organization. Or a new technology emerged that was more appropriate to use in the project. Ignoring these occurrences can seriously jeopardize a project's success; responding to these occurrences almost always adds time to a project.

4.7.3 Detecting Potential Pitfalls Early

A project succeeds when it accomplishes the desired outcomes on time and within budget. When success isn't achieved, time and again the same reasons are to blame. Recognizing and anticipating the following situations increases the likelihood of a successful project.

The following are common causes of project failure—and some solutions:

▲ **Not involving all key project stakeholders.** Instead, identify people who affect a project's success and involve them in a timely and effective way (see Section 4.2).

> ## FOR EXAMPLE
>
> **www.reformingprojectmanagement.com**
>
> Featuring project-management success (and horror) stories, *Reforming Project Management* (RPM) offers news, analysis, commentary, and more. Originally a print magazine, the publication's free Weblog component at www.reformingprojectmanagement.com is updated daily with stories, responses, and links. Although architecture, engineering, and construction projects are the focus, experienced project managers and writers in information technology, publishing, and product development frequently participate in online discussions and submit original essays.

▲ **Vague objectives.** Instead, create detailed performance targets and milestones to determine whether the project achieves its desired results (see Section 2.1).

▲ **Vague or nonexistent role and responsibility definitions.** Establish a clear distinction between how different people on the same project team will work together to perform their tasks (see Section 4.2).

▲ **Incomplete and inaccurate schedules and resource needs.** Identify all activities, set realistic estimates of task durations, consider task interdependencies, identify needed skills, and estimate person-hours in sufficient detail.

▲ **Not identifying and sharing key project assumptions.** Recognize that information one person considers true might not be. Investigate the rationale behind all assumptions (see Sections 2.4 and 2.5).

▲ **Not writing down key information.** Share important information and reach agreements verbally. Get things confirmed in writing.

▲ **Inaccurate and late progress monitoring.** Record personnel and financial expenditures and track dates on which activities start and end (see Section 11.2). Share this information with team members in a timely manner (see Section 12.2).

▲ **Not holding people accountable for performance.** Have rewards and consequences for meeting or missing project commitments (see Section 10.3).

▲ **Not anticipating and planning for risks and uncertainties.** Attempt to identify what could go wrong and develop contingency plans for anticipated problems (see Section 2.4). Always share information about unanticipated occurrences.

▲ **Poor team communications.** Share important information with all team members in a timely fashion (see Section 12.2).

▲ **Weak team leadership.** Clearly articulate the project vision and elicit people's commitments to achieve the desired results. Attempt to sustain individuals' motivation throughout the project (see Section 8.3).

▲ **Inconsistent upper-management support.** Make sure assigned people stay with the project, resolve time and resource conflicts, and use adequate systems and procedures to support project planning and control (see Section 1.4).

▲ **Lack of commitment by all team members to the project's success.** Make a personal commitment to achieve the promises made in the plan—and encourage the rest of the team to do the same (see Sections 1.4 and 10.3).

SELF-CHECK

1. Which of the following is a common mistake that project managers make in planning and executing projects?

   (a) spending too much time and resources on close phase activities

   (b) skipping start phase activities due to time

   (c) avoiding define phase activities because of the political challenges associated with this phase

   (d) differentiating what makes a new project unique from previous projects

2. A project manager joining at the start phase of a project should take time to analyze and evaluate the activities conducted during which other phases of the project?

SUMMARY

Project managers can increase a project's chance for success by planning and guiding based on understanding specific project life cycle phases. Getting the right people on board the project team and aligning the right project stakeholders provide critical resources and support during the course of the project. Developing a Work Breakdown Structure helps project managers organize all the activities necessary to complete the project. Project managers can use a Linear Responsibility Chart to further clarify who is responsible for various project aspects and in what sequence. Multidisciplinary teams are standard in many of today's organizations and require special consideration on the part of project managers in terms of using concurrent engineering and interface coordination techniques. Project failure can be traced to several basic mistakes. By identifying these pitfalls early on, project managers can respond effectively to situations and redirect projects toward success.

KEY TERMS

Bubble-chart format	A format for displaying a Work Breakdown Structure that presents activities, tasks, and subtasks as linked circles.
Concurrent engineering (CE)	Work processes in which two or more steps are carried out at the same time to save time and costs.
Conditional activity	A work activity that's performed only if certain conditions come to pass.
Drivers	People in a project who have some say in defining the results that a project is to achieve; the people for whom the project work is being performed.
Indented-outline format	A format for displaying a Work Breakdown Structure that presents activities, tasks, and subtasks as a hierarchically organized list.
Integration management	Coordinating the work of groups and the timing of their interactions.
Interface coordination	The process of managing the way groups work together.
Linear Responsibility Chart (LRC)	A matrix that depicts the role that each project team and stakeholder plays in the performance of different project activities.
Multidisciplinary teams (MTs)	Work groups comprised of individuals from various departments or divisions, with varying backgrounds and expertise; also known as transdisciplinary teams.
Observers	People who are interested in a project but will not define what the project should accomplish or directly support efforts.
Organizational-chart format	A format for displaying a Work Breakdown Structure that portrays an overview

	of the project and the hierarchical relationships of different work assignments (and perhaps tasks) at the highest levels.
Project audience	A person or group who will support, be affected by, or be interested in a project.
Project plans	Formal plans that describe the roles project managers anticipate people will play and the amount of effort team members will have to invest.
Supporters	People in a project who help to perform project work, including the people who authorize the resources for a project as well as those who work on it.
Work Breakdown Structure (WBS)	An organized, detailed, and hierarchical representation of all work to be performed in a project.
Work-order agreement	A written description of work that a person agrees to perform on a project, the dates the person agrees to start and finish the work, and the number of hours the person agrees to spend on it.

ASSESS YOUR UNDERSTANDING

Go to www.wiley.com/college/portny to assess your knowledge of the basics of project planning.

Measure your learning by comparing pre-test and post-test results.

Summary Questions

1. Creating a Work Breakdown Structure is a task to undertake during a project's define phase. True or false?

2. Forging relationships in new multidisciplinary teams requires planning from the project manager during which of the following project phases?

    (a) perform phase

    (b) define phase

    (c) conceive phase

    (d) start phase

3. A project manager must confirm each team member can participate on a project prior to creating a Work Breakdown Structure. True or false?

4. Multidisciplinary teams include people with various backgrounds and expertise, but all the team members function primarily as supporters of the project. True or false?

5. Which of the following might be an appropriate project manager task during the start phase?

    (a) interview upper management to determine the feasibility of the project and its goals

    (b) convert the Work Breakdown Structure from an indented outline to a bubble chart so the entire team can easily add their input

    (c) report on the progress of the project in various forms, as suits the needs of each aspect of the project's audience

    (d) brainstorm with the team a list of project responsibilities and activities

6. Although many real-world projects don't strictly follow the project life cycle model, project managers can do which of the following?

    (a) tactfully introduce upper management and their teams to the project life cycle model

    (b) establish an incentive-based system to encourage their teams to adhere to the project life cycle model

    (c) carefully work on activities related to two or more phases at the same time

    (d) none of the above

Applying This Chapter

1. The U.S. government releases new guidelines for fire-safety ratings for outdoor materials, and you work at a company that produces tents, tarps, and sleeping bags. You've just been assigned a project in which you will lead a team of chemical engineers to test the flame-retardant properties of all the company's products against the new guidelines in one month's time. What is an example of one critical task you as project manager need to plan and perform for each phase of the project's life cycle?

2. Mitch is planning a high-school graduation party for his younger brother Dan. Because Mitch lives 10 hours away from his brother, Mitch knows he needs to involve others in the party planning. Dan has supplied him with a list of family and friends he'd like to invite, and Mitch figures he can use the list to assign clear party-planning roles to each person. What are the next four or five party planning steps that Mitch needs to do?

3. You want to create a Work Breakdown Structure for a year-long project you've recently been assigned to. Your boss says that Work Breakdown Structures are a waste of time because long projects change many times over the course of the project. You counter that a Work Breakdown Structure is critical to figuring out the sequence of what needs to happen in the project. What are some things you can do as project manager to make Work Breakdown Structures work for your year-long project?

4. As the head chef at a new restaurant, you are leading the development of the entire menu, from appetizers to desserts. Your project stakeholders include the restaurant's owners, cooks, servers, food service workers, and diners, among others. You want to display the project Work Breakdown in the restaurant's kitchen area. Which display format will you use— organizational chart, indented outline, or bubble chart? Why?

5. Leah, a new project manager, has spent two weeks creating a Linear Responsibility Chart based on her analysis of all her project's documents, including a detailed Work Breakdown Structure. However, when she shared the Linear Responsibility Chart with her team, several members scoffed at the chart, even though everyone reviewed and agreed to the Work Breakdown Structure. What are some things Leah could do to increase buy-in for the chart?

6. Simon's team of chemical engineers was an already established group before he joined their latest project, the development of a new chlorine-free bleach, as project manager. The team has successfully developed new cleaning products in the past, and the project is two months behind

schedule. Simon recommends the team begin product testing in the lab as soon as possible to get the project back on schedule. Why is Simon's project-management decision potentially risky?

7. Recall an everyday project you led or managed that didn't go so well. Perhaps it's a paper that you didn't complete on deadline or a party you hosted that no one enjoyed. Which of the common mistakes in Section 4.7.1 did you experience? Which of the strategies to avoid these pitfalls (Section 4.7.3) might have helped your project be more successful?

YOU TRY IT

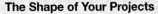

The Shape of Your Projects

Write down a list of five or six projects you've worked on in the last year. Projects could be large or small, formal or casual, work- or school-related, or personal. Review the definitions of S-shaped and J-shaped projects (Section 4.1.6) and consider your list of recent projects. Which projects followed more of an S-shaped life cycle? Which follows more of a J-shaped life cycle? How was work different during your S-shaped projects versus your J-shaped projects? During which type of project did you need to work harder at the beginning? The middle? The end? Or did you have to work consistently throughout the project?

Work Order Evaluation

Many companies have established templates or forms for work orders related to project responsibilities. If possible, evaluate your company's standard work order template. Some companies call this document a work for hire agreement, a freelance contract, or an outsourcing agreement. Ask your manager if you have questions, or review the official online work order for Air Brite (www.revitalizedtrailers.com/airbrite_workorder.asp), a service that polishes and restores vintage AirStream trailers. Does the work order cover the requirements outlined in Section 4.2.2? Revise the document to include critical details and expectations.

Choose Your Development Method

In general the development of Work Breakdown Structures follows two approaches—top-down and brainstorming (see Section 4.3.5). Think of an upcoming project or come up with a hypothetical project you'd like to take on at work or school. Which development method do you choose for your project? Why? Draft a Work Breakdown Structure for your project using your selected method.

Pick Your Presentation

For your next project, organize and display the Work Breakdown Structure for yourself and others. Draw or write out your Work Breakdown Structure. Post it in a location where you and any of the project's stakeholders can see it.

Linear Responsibility Chart

Use the steps outlined in Section 4.5.3 to create a Linear Responsibility Chart that summarizes the activities, stakeholders, and responsibilities for the project of spring cleaning your entire home. What tasks do you need to include? Who are the project's stakeholders—and what are their responsibilities? Where are the conflicts in your Linear Responsibility Chart—for example, unnecessary overlap of responsibility or overreliance on managerial approval (in this case, probably from the homeowner)?

Other Roles in Linear Responsibility Charts

As indicated in Section 4.5.1, Linear Responsibility Charts often categorize stakeholder responsibilities as primary responsibility, secondary responsibility, and approval or review, output, and input. What other categories of responsibility might be appropriate for projects you've managed or would like to manage? Create and describe a set of categories you'd find useful in managing a project.

Going Concurrent

Write down the steps involved in an everyday project (perhaps getting ready in the morning, preparing a family meal, or cleaning the bathroom top to bottom). Develop a concurrent engineering plan for the project in which some steps happen at the same time. Can you reduce the time the project requires? What additional resources (tools, people, money) do you need to execute the project with concurrent engineering?

CASE STUDY: St. Dismas Medical Center

St. Dismas Medical Center, an urban, nonprofit, 450-bed rehabilitation hospital, began to see a significant decline in admissions. St. Dismas's mission focuses on inpatient and outpatient rehabilitation of the severely injured and catastrophically ill. While the patient census varied from month to month, it appeared to the St. Dismas Board of Trustees that the inpatient population was slowly but steadily declining. The hospital's market researchers reported that fewer people were being severely injured due to the popularity of seat belts and bicycle/motorcycle helmets. In order to plan for the future of the organization, the Board and the CEO, Fred Splient, M.D., called for a major strategic planning effort to take place.

The outcome of the strategic planning retreat was that the Medical Center determined it needed to focus its efforts around two major strategic initiatives. The first, a short-run initiative, was to be more cost-effective in the delivery of inpatient care. The second, a long-run strategy, was to develop new programs and services that would capitalize on the existing, highly competent rehabilitation therapy staff and St. Dismas's excellent reputation in the region.

At the time of the retreat, Fred Splient's parents were living with him and his family. Fred was an active member of the "sandwich generation." His parents were aging and developing many problems common to the geriatric populace. Their increased medical needs were beginning to wear on Fred and his family. It crossed Fred's mind that life might be more pleasant if the hospital Board approved an expansion of the Medical Center's campus to include an assisted living facility.

Fred had his Business Development team prepare a rough estimate of the potential return on investment of an assisted living facility. He asked the team to identify different options for facility construction and the associated costs. The team also did a complete competitive analysis and examined the options for services to be offered based on St. Dismas's potential population base. The Business Development team visited several facilities across the country. The team also interviewed companies that could oversee the design, building, and operation of the facility for St. Dismas. The development team produced a preliminary business plan based on the rec-

ommended structure for the facility, estimated capital expenditure needs, estimated income from operation of the facility, as well as projected revenues to other Medical Center programs resulting from the facility's population.

Two months later, the plan for an assisted living facility was presented at a Board of Trustees meeting. The new facility would be set up as a for-profit subsidiary of the Medical Center so that it could generate a profit and not be subjected to the strict guidelines of the hospital's accrediting agencies. As a subsidiary organization, however, the Board would still have control.

The chosen facility design was a freestanding apartment-like facility with a sheltered connection to the Hospital for access to the kitchen and hospital services. The facility would have 100 units with 15 to 30 of the units classified as "heavy-assisted" and built to code to house the physically and medically disabled. The rest of the units would be "light-assisted," larger apartments. The population would be approximately 110 to 150 residents, with most being single occupants rather than couples.

The light-assisted apartments could hold residents who required only minor medical and social interventions. The residents of the heavy-assisted section would have more medical needs and would require assistance getting around. The Business Development team recommended this type of programming model because many assisted living facilities were erected across the country, but few had a medical focus and offered the types of services that St. Dismas could offer—physical and occupational therapy programs and behavior management programs, to name a few.

The Board was assured that the facility would meet the strategic initiative of growing business. The business plan projected an immediate increase in the number of referrals to the outpatient therapy programs. Another projected deliverable of the project was to enable St. Dismas to strengthen its focus on reimbursable preventive and wellness programs for the healthier geriatric population. The project's longer term goal was to increase the census in the hospital's inpatient units by having a location where people could age in place until they were in need of hospitalization, and then such a facility would be right next door.

115

Depending on the exact size of the apartments, their equipment, and the actual ratio of heavy- to light-assisted units, Fred estimated that the entire project would cost between $8.5 million and $11 million for the facility construction. That estimate included the cost of land, furnishings, and a sheltered connection to the hospital. When up and running, it was estimated that the net income would range between $9000 and $12,000 per unit per year. The team estimated the net cash flow for the entire project to be around $1.5 million per year.

Fred requested the Board to approve the concept and allow his team to prepare a more detailed plan for the Board to approve. The Board conducted several executive sessions, and in a month's time they voted to approve the concept. They approved the architectural-construction-management firm recommended by the team, and they requested Splient to proceed with developing a complete project plan. The Board appointed two Board members to sit on Fred's planning group.

A few weeks later, Dr. Splient gathered his executive team together and presented the project mission, scope, and goals. He reported that the Board had approved a small budget to finance the planning process. The Board also stated that they would like a plan that would allow the facility to open in 12 months' time. The CEO and executive team were now confident that they were ready to launch the project to plan, build, and open an assisted living facility at St. Dismas.

A few days later, Fred decided that it was time to set up the team that would take responsibility for what he called the ALF project. He quickly decided to include the following staff at the launch meeting:

▲ Chief Financial Officer (CFO).
▲ Vice President of Business Development and Marketing.
▲ Rehab Services Medical Director.
▲ Construction Project Manager for capital facilities projects.
▲ Chief Operations Officer (COO) for nursing, facilities, food services, and housekeeping.
▲ Director of Information Services.
▲ Director of Support Services (central supply, purchasing, and security).
▲ Two members of the Board of Trustees, one with construction experience.

Even though the department directors from Support Services and Information Services would not be involved until later, Fred decided to include them from the beginning. Fred knew some members of his team had a tendency to become obstacles to progress if they felt left out.

Fred named the group the ALF Project Steering Committee and held the first meeting. Fred presented his vision for the facility. He told the group that he personally would be managing this project. He led a discussion of all the major steps that must be included in the project plan, and asked each team member to identify the areas for which they would accept responsibility. The hospital's Construction Project Manager took responsibility for the construction of the facility, and the COO volunteered to oversee the building design, as well as define the needs for food services, housekeeping, staffing, and policy and procedure development. The CFO agreed to develop the budgets for each area of the project as well as the operating budget for the facility. The CFO also agreed to create the payroll and accounting systems necessary to operate the facility.

The Director of IS accepted responsibility to define and set up all the telecommunications and information system needs of the facility. The VP of Business Development agreed to create a preliminary marketing plan and a communication package for the community and hospital staff. In addition, she discussed organizing a major ground-breaking event. The Medical Director said that he would design an assessment tool for determining residents' levels of medical needs upon moving in to the facility. He felt this was the first step in defining what clinical services should be offered to residents. Fred told the team that he would develop the management structure for the new facility and work with in-house counsel to identify all governmental regulations as well as all industry standards that pertain to an assisted living facility and govern the facility's practices. Splient gave the team two months to come back with their detailed action plans for their areas of responsibility.

Questions

1. Define project deliverables.
2. Define project constraints and assumptions.
3. Develop a preliminary action plan.
4. Is Dr. Splient a good choice for project manager?

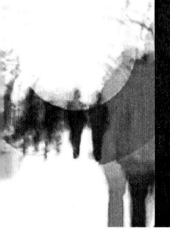

5

BUDGETING PROJECTS
Planning and Estimating Project Costs

Starting Point

Go to www.wiley.com/college/portny to assess your knowledge of the basics of project budgets.
Determine where you need to concentrate your effort.

What You'll Learn in This Chapter

▲ Differences between project budgets and annual budgets
▲ Budgeting methodologies
▲ Direct and indirect costs
▲ Stages of developing budgets
▲ Strategies to improve cost estimates
▲ Reasons that budgets estimate change
▲ Ways to minimize budget uncertainty

After Studying This Chapter, You'll Be Able To

▲ Evaluate budgets and cost estimates
▲ Produce accurate budget and cost estimates
▲ Categorize typical budget costs
▲ Propose ways to improve estimates and respond to budget uncertainty

INTRODUCTION ·

Although project managers are often responsible for producing project budget estimates, accountants and upper management often have different budget-related expectations. Project managers can create budgets by working from upper management's recommendations (top-down) or by gathering budget estimates at the task level (bottom-up). Whatever the chosen method, being able to accurately estimate costs is a critical project manager responsibility. Various tools and strategies can help project managers improve the accuracy of budget estimates, but successful project managers also develop strategic responses to budget changes and revisions.

5.1 Examining Methods of Budgeting

In addition to planning the technical aspects of project plans (how the work will get done and by whom), project managers also need to spend time on another important element of planning—establishing a project **budget**, the financial plans for allocating organization resources to project activities.

Project managers must develop budgets in order to obtain the resources needed to accomplish project objectives. Often, project managers (in conjunction with their functional managers) are required to prepare project budgets in order to receive the go-ahead from top management to proceed with projects.

But budgets also serve another purpose—they tie projects to an organization's aims and objectives through organizational policy.

Section 4.1 describes the project planning process as a series of phases, each with a detailed series of activities. Only when the overall project plan is divided and subdivided into smaller and smaller pieces—most likely by means of a Work Breakdown Structure (see Section 4.4)—can the project finally be sequenced,

FOR EXAMPLE

Budgeting at NASA

NASA's recent Mars Pathfinder-Rover mission included a new NASA policy—to achieve a set of limited exploration opportunities on Mars at an extremely limited cost. In 1976, NASA's two Viking-Mars Lander missions cost $3 billion to develop. In 1997, however, the Pathfinder-Rover mission cost only $175 million to develop, a 94 percent reduction. The difference was the change in both budgeting practices and organizational policy. In the 1970s, NASA had a design-to-performance orientation; today, the organization has more of a design-to-cost orientation.

assigned, scheduled, and budgeted. Hence, the project budget is nothing more than the project plan, based on the Work Breakdown Structure, expressed in monetary terms.

Once the budget is developed, it acts as a tool for upper management to monitor and guide the project. Project managers must collect and report appropriate data in a timely manner throughout the project or the value of the budget to identify current financial problems or anticipate upcoming ones is lost. Project managers need to work closely with their organization's finance departments to create collection and reporting systems for financial information because late reporting, inaccurate reporting, or reporting to the wrong person negates the main purpose of a budget. (For example, the store managers of a large electronics retailer were supposed to receive quarterly results for the purpose of correcting problems at their specific locations in the following quarter. The results took four months to reach the store managers, which completely negated the value of even having a budgeting-reporting system.)

5.1.1 Understanding the Challenges of Project Budgets

Developing project budgets is typically more difficult than developing regular departmental budgeting, which usually follow the formula: "the same as last year plus X percent."

By contrast, projects are unique activities. Project budgets, such as the budget for developing and testing a control system for a computer network, do not have tradition to guide them. Of course, there might be similar past projects that can serve as a budgetary model, but these are rough guides at best. Forecasting a budget for a multiyear project such as a large product or service development project is even more hazardous because the unknowns can escalate quickly with changes in technology, materials, and even the findings of the project up to that point.

Organizational tradition impacts project budgeting, particularly in decisions about how overhead and other indirect costs are charged against the project. Every firm has its own accounting idiosyncrasies; project managers cannot expect their accounting departments to make special allowances for their individual projects. Although accounting will·charge normal expenditures against a particular activity's account number, as identified in the Work Breakdown Structure, unexpected overhead charges, indirect expenses, and usage or price variances might suddenly appear when the project manager least expects it, and probably at the worst possible time. Project managers must simply take the time to become completely familiar with their organization's accounting systems, as painful as that might be.

In the process of gaining this familiarity, the project manager is likely to discover that costs can be viewed from three different perspectives:

▲ **Project managers:** project managers recognize a cost after a commitment is made to pay someone for resources or services, for example when a machine part is ordered. Because project managers must manage projects, they need to set up budget-related systems that allow them to track the project's commitments rather than the processing of invoices.

▲ **Accountants:** accountants recognize an expense when an invoice is received and the cost is actually incurred—not, as most people believe, when the invoice is paid.

▲ **Controllers:** controllers perceive an expense when the check for the invoice is mailed. Controllers are concerned with managing an organization's cash flow.

Project managers also need to understand that accountants live in a linear world. When a project activity has an $8000 charge and runs over a four-month period, the accounting department (or worse, their software) simply spreads the $8000 evenly over the time period, resulting in a $2000 allocation per month. If expenditures for this activity are planned to be $5000, $1000, $1000, and $1000, the project manager should not be surprised when the organization's controller storms into the project office after the first month screaming about the unanticipated and unacceptable cash flow demands of the project.

The following sections cover some of the most common methods of budgeting for projects.

5.1.2 Focusing on Cost per Unit

Budgeting is simply the process of forecasting what resources a project will require, what quantities of each resource will be needed, when the resource will be needed, and how much it will cost. For example, Tables 5-1 and 5-2 depict two methods of displaying the direct costs involved in making a corporate training video.

▲ **Table 5-1** shows the cost per unit of usage (cost/hour) of seven different personnel categories and one facility. Note that the facility does not charge by the hour but has a flat rate charge.

▲ **Table 5-2** shows the resource categories and amounts used for each activity required to make the tape. The resource costs shown become part of the budget for producing the tape. Overhead charges may be added to these direct charges.

Many companies employ experienced estimators who can forecast resource usage and cost-per-unit with amazingly small errors. For instance, a bricklayer can usually estimate within 1 or 2 percent the number of bricks required to construct a brick wall of given dimensions. In many fields, the methods of cost estimation are well documented based on the experience of estimators gathered over many years. The cost of a building or house is usually estimated by the square

Table 5-1: Resource Cost per Unit for Producing a Training Video

ID	Resource Name	Max. Units	Std Rate	Ovt. Rate	Cost/ Use	Accrue At
1	Scriptwriter	1	$25.00/hr	$40.00/hr	$0.00	Prorated
2	Producer	1	$45.00/hr	$60.00/hr	$0.00	Prorated
3	Client	0.2	$0.00/hr	$0.00/hr	$0.00	Prorated
4	Secretary	1	$10.00/hr	$20.00/hr	$0.00	Prorated
5	Editor	1	$25.00/hr	$45.00/hr	$0.00	Prorated
6	Production staff	1	$20.00/hr	$35.00/hr	$0.00	Prorated
7	Editing staff	1	$20.00/hr	$35.00/hr	$0.00	Prorated
8	Editing room	1	$0.00/hr	$0.00/hr	$250.00	Start

Table 5-2: Budget by Resource for Producing a Training Video

ID	Task Name	Resource	Work Hours	Cost	Task Duration
1	Project approval	Total	0 hr	$0.00	0 days
2	Scriptwriting	Total	112 hr	$2800.00	14 days
		Scriptwriter	112 hr	$2800.00	
3	Schedule shoots	Total	240 hr	$5400.00	15 days
4	Begin scheduling	Total	0 hr	$0.00	0 days
5	Propose shoots	Total	120 hr	$2800.00	5 days
		Scriptwriter	40 hr	$1000.00	
		Producer	40 hr	$1800.00	
		Client	40 hr	$0.00	
6	Hire secretary	Total	40 hr	$1800.00	5 days
		Producer	40 hr	$1800.00	
7	Schedule shoots	Total	80 hr	$800.00	10 days
		Secretary	80 hr	$800.00	
8	Scheduling comp	Total	0 hr	$0.00	0 days

(Continued)

Table 5-2: (*continued*)

ID	Task Name	Resource	Work Hours	Cost	Task Duration
9	Script approval	Total	80 hr	$1800.00	5 days
		Producer	40 hr	$1800.00	
		Client	40 hr	$1800.00	
10	Revise script	Total	80 hr	$2800.00	5 days
		Scriptwriter	40 hr	$1000.00	
		Producer	40 hr	$1800.00	
11	Shooting	Total	160 hr	$3600.00	10 days
		Editor	80 hr	$2000.00	
		Production staff	80 hr	$1600.00	
12	Editing	Total	168 hr	$2770.00	7 days
		Editor	56 hr	$1400.00	
		Editing staff	56 hr	$1120.00	
		Editing room	56 hr	$250.00	
13	Final approval	Total	160 hr	$3050.00	5 days
		Producer	40 hr	$1800.00	
		Client	40 hr	$0.00	
		Editor	40 hr	$1000.00	
		Editing room	40 hr	$250.00	
14	Deliver video to client	Total	0 hr	$0.00	0 days

feet of floor area multiplied by an appropriate dollar value per square foot and then adjusted for any unusual factors.

5.1.3 Top-Down Budgeting

Top-down budgeting is based on the collective judgments and experiences of top and middle managers concerning similar past projects. These managers estimate the overall project cost by estimating the costs of the major tasks. These estimates are then given to the next lower level of managers to split up among the tasks under their control, and so on until all the work is budgeted.

On the surface, top-down budgeting offers several advantages, including the following:

▲ Overall budget costs can be estimated quite accurately, though individual elements might be in substantial error.

▲ Errors in funding small tasks need not be individually identified because the overall budget allows for exceptions.

▲ Small but important tasks (which are sometimes unintentionally over-looked during the planning stages) do not usually cause serious budgetary problems. The experience and judgment of top management are presumed to include all such elements in the overall estimate.

Unfortunately, top-down budgeting allows budgets to be controlled by people who play little role in designing and doing the actual work required by the project. This can and often does cause problems, as Section 5.2.3 discusses.

5.1.4 Bottom-Up Budgeting

In **bottom-up budgeting**, the Work Breakdown Structure (see Section 4.4) or action plan identifies the elemental tasks, whose resource requirements are estimated by those responsible for executing them (for example, programmer hours in a software project are estimated by the programmers themselves). These resources, such as labor and materials, are then converted to costs and combined to determine an overall direct cost for the project (see Section 5.2.1). The accounting department or finance department then adds, according to organizational policy, indirect costs (such as general administrative costs), a reserve fund for contingencies and emergencies, and a profit figure to arrive at a final project budget.

Bottom-up budgeting offers the following benefits:

▲ Bottom-up budgets typically result in more accurate estimates (although they run the risk of overlooking some small but costly tasks).

▲ When combined with a participative management philosophy, bottom-up budgets can lead to better morale, greater acceptance of the resulting budget, and heightened commitment by the project team.

▲ Bottom-up budgeting can serve as a good managerial training technique for aspiring project and general managers.

Unfortunately, true bottom-up budgeting is rare. Upper level managers are often reluctant to let workers develop budgets, fearing the natural tendency to overstate costs, and fearing complaints if the budget must later be reduced to meet organizational resource limitations. Moreover, a budget is upper management's primary tool for control of a project, and they are reluctant to let others set the control limits.

Ideally, organizations can employ both forms of developing budgets. Both forms of budgeting have advantages, and the use of one does not preclude the use of the other. Making a single budget by combining the two requires the organization to set up a specific system to negotiate differences. Section 5.2.2 discusses such a system. The only disadvantage of this approach is that it requires some extra time and trouble—a small price to pay for the advantages.

SELF-CHECK

1. A budget ties a project to the organization's aims and objectives. True or false?

2. At MIMA Corp., teams are assigned projects and produce budget estimates based on the work tasks they identify. Upper management also produces budget estimates based on past projects and overall company goals. The two budgets are then debated and reconciled in a committee of senior managers and team members. Which of the following methods of budgeting a project does this process describe?

   (a) a preference for top-down budgeting

   (b) a combination of bottom-down budgeting and estimating

   (c) a combination of top-down and bottom-up budgeting

   (d) an avoidance of bottom-up budgeting

3. To a project manager, a budget is a commitment to pay someone for a product or service, but for a controller a budget is which of the following?

   (a) an expense when the check for the invoice is mailed

   (b) an expense when the invoice is received by the company

   (c) an expense when an outside party provides a good or service

   (d) an expense when the check clears and money is transferred

5.2 Cost Estimating

All project resources cost money. In a world of limited resources, everyone is constantly deciding how to get the most return for his or her investment. Therefore, estimating a project's costs is important to project managers for several reasons:

▲ Project managers can assess anticipated benefits, with respect to anticipated costs, to see whether the project makes sense.

▲ Project managers can see whether they can get the funds necessary to support the project.

▲ Project managers can establish criteria as they monitor ongoing performance to help ensure they have sufficient funds to complete the project.

Project managers might not personally be involved with all steps in the development of a project budget. If a project manager joins a project after some initial planning has been done, he or she should be sure to review the plans and resolve any questions and issues.

5.2.1 Identifying Different Types of Project Costs

A project budget is typically developed in stages, from an initial rough estimate to a detailed budget estimate through to a completed, approved project budget. On occasion, project managers might even revise an approved budget while the project is in progress to reflect changes in planned work and results.

Budgets take into account the following types of costs:

▲ **Direct costs** are expenditures for resources that are used solely to perform project activities. Direct costs include salaries paid to the people who work on the project; materials, supplies, and equipment bought for the project; travel to perform project work; and subcontracts for services performed for the project.

▲ **Indirect costs** are expenditures that are incurred to support project activities but that aren't tracked individually. Indirect costs fall into two subcategories:

　▲ **Overhead costs:** expenditures for resources used to perform project activities but which are difficult to subdivide and allocate directly. Examples include employee benefits, office space rent, supplies, and the rental or purchase of furniture, fixtures, or equipment used to support work on the project.

　▲ **General and administrative costs:** expenditures that keep the organization operational (if the organization didn't exist, the project can't happen). Examples include salaries of finance department employees and top management, as well as fees for accounting and legal services.

Consider the project of designing, developing, and producing a company brochure. Direct costs for this project might include:

▲ **Labor:** salaries paid for the hours spent working on the brochure.

▲ **Materials:** the special paper stock on which the brochure is copied.

▲ **Travel:** the costs for the miles driven to investigate different firms that can design the brochure cover.
▲ **Subcontract:** the services of an outside company that will design the cover art for the brochure.

Indirect costs for the brochure project might include:

▲ **Employee benefits:** the cost of health insurance and retirement contributions earned in addition to salary while working on the brochure.
▲ **Rent:** the cost of the office space used while developing the copy for the brochure.
▲ **Equipment:** the computer and printer used use to compose the copy for the brochure.
▲ **Management and administrative salaries:** a portion of the salaries of upper managers and staff who perform the administrative duties necessary to keep the larger organization functioning.

5.2.2 Developing Project Budgets

The project manager should develop project budgets in the following stages:

1. **Rough order-of-magnitude (ROM) estimate:** an initial estimate of costs that's based on a general sense of the type of work the project will likely entail. This estimate is also known as a ballpark estimate. Sometimes this estimate is more a statement of what someone is willing to spend rather than what the project will really cost. Typically, project managers don't detail this estimate by lowest-level project activity because the estimate is prepared in a short amount of time, before the needed project activities have completely been identified. Whether or not people choose to accept

---

FOR EXAMPLE

Indirect versus Direct Costs

Ted realizes that he needs an office to work on his project activities and he knows that office space costs money. However, Ted's organization has an annual lease for office space that requires 12 monthly installments be paid to the landlord. The office space is broken into many individual offices and work areas, and people are performing numerous projects in these offices at any one time. Unfortunately, Ted has no clear record of the portion of each month's rent check that goes to pay for the office space he uses to work on his project. Ted's office space is an indirect project cost.

it, initial budget estimates included in annual plans and long-range plans are typically rough order-of-magnitude estimates.

2. **Detailed budget estimate:** an itemization of the estimated costs for each project activity. Project managers prepare this estimate by developing a detailed Work Breakdown Structure (see Section 4.4) and estimating the costs associated with all lowest-level activities.

3. **Completed, approved project budget:** a detailed project budget that essential people approve and agree to support.

As Section 4.1 explains, projects move through five phases as they evolve from idea to reality: conceive, define, start, perform, and close. Project managers should perform the following budget-development activities during each phase:

1. **Conceive phase:** develop a rough order-of-magnitude estimate. Rather than an actual estimate of costs, this estimate often represents an amount that can't be exceeded if a project is to have an acceptable return for the investment. A project manager's confidence in this estimate is usually low because it isn't based on detailed analyses of the activities to be performed.

2. **Define phase:** develop detailed budget estimates during the definition phase, after specifying the required project activities. Project managers should get their detailed budgets approved before leaving this phase.

3. **Start phase:** review approved budgets in the start phase while identifying the people who will be working on the project and start to develop formal agreements for the use of equipment, facilities, vendors, and other resources. Get any required budget changes approved before moving to the perform phase.

4. **Perform phase:** monitor project activities and related occurrences throughout the phases to determine when budget revisions are necessary. Develop budget revisions and get them approved as soon as possible.

5. **Close phase:** identify situations that could require changes to the approved project budget. Obtain approved, revised budget, as needed.

5.2.3 Developing Project Costs

During the define phase, project managers develop detailed project budget estimates by using bottom-up and top-down budgeting (see Sections 5.1.3 and 5.1.4).

For bottom-up budget estimates, do the following:

1. Consider each lowest-level activity in turn.
2. Determine direct labor costs for each activity by multiplying the number of hours each person will work on the activity by the person's hourly salary. Direct labor costs can be estimated by the following:

▲ Using the salary of each person on the project.

▲ Using the average salary for people with a particular job title, in a certain department, and so on.

3. Estimate the direct costs for materials, equipment, travel, contractual services, and other resources for each activity.

4. Determine the indirect costs that will be allocated to each activity. Estimate indirect costs as a fraction of the planned direct labor costs for the activity. In general, an organization's finance department determines this fraction annually by doing the following:

▲ Estimating organization direct labor costs for the coming year.

▲ Estimating organization indirect costs for the coming year.

▲ Dividing the estimated indirect costs by the estimated direct labor costs. Some organizations express this indirect cost rate as a percentage that's determined by multiplying the fraction by 100.

Choosing the appropriate method to estimate indirect costs requires a project manager to weigh the potential accuracy of the estimate against the effort needed to develop it. The following two sections cover two approaches for estimating indirect costs.

Using One Rate for Overhead Costs, Another Rate for General and Administrative Costs

For this method:

▲ The finance department determines the overhead rate by calculating the ratio of all projected overhead costs to all projected direct salaries.

▲ The finance department determines the general and administrative rate by calculating the ratio of all projected general and administrative costs to the sum of all projected direct salaries, overhead costs, and other direct costs.

▲ The project manager determines the overhead costs associated with an activity by multiplying the direct salaries for that activity by the overhead rate.

▲ The project manager determines the general and administrative costs associated with an activity by multiplying the sum of direct salaries, calculated overhead costs, and other direct costs for the activity by the general and administrative rate.

Using One Indirect Cost Rate for All Overhead, General, and Administrative Costs

For this method:

▲ The finance department determines the combined indirect cost rate by calculating the ratio of all projected overhead costs to all projected direct salaries.

> ## FOR EXAMPLE
>
> ### Actual Costs and Cost Estimates
>
> George needs the services of a graphic artist to design overheads for a presentation. The head of the graphics department estimates the person will have to spend 100 hours on the project. If George knows Harry (with a salary rate of $30/hour) will be assigned to the activity, he can estimate the direct labor costs to be $3000 ($30 × 100 hours). However, if the director doesn't know whom she will assign to the project, George must ask for (or calculate himself) the average salary for a graphic artist in his organization in order to estimate the direct labor costs. To ensure the estimate's accuracy, George and the graphic department need to be sure the salary data they use closely mirror the needs and expectations of the current project. (For example, there's no sense including high-end jobs where advanced illustrating skills were required in the estimate if George's project only requires someone skilled at page layout.)

▲ The project manager determines the indirect costs associated with an activity by multiplying the direct salaries for that activity by the indirect cost rate.

Some organizations develop weighted labor rates, which combine hourly salary and associated indirect costs. For example, suppose Naomi's salary is $30/hour, and the organization's indirect cost rate is 0.5. Naomi's weighted labor rate would be $45/hour (equal to $30 + [0.5 × $30]).

5.2.4 Reviewing Budget Estimates

Table 5-3 illustrates the presentation of a budget estimate. The table lists cost estimates related to designing and producing a company brochure. The following are some of the assumptions about the project and the budget:

▲ The project manager estimates he'll spend 200 person-hours on the project and a teammate (Mary) will spend 100 person-hours.

▲ The project manager's salary rate is $45/hour and Mary's is $25/hour.

▲ The project manager will have to buy stationery on which to copy the brochures; estimated cost is $1000.

▲ The project manager estimates $300 in travel costs to visit vendors and suppliers.

▲ The project manager expects to pay an external company $5000 to do the artwork for the brochure.

▲ The organization has developed a combined indirect cost rate of 60 percent.

Table 5-3: Project Budget for Designing and Producing a Company Brochure

Cost Category	Cost	Total
Direct Labor		
Project Manager: 200 hours @ $45/hour	$9000	
Mary: 100 hours @ $25/hour	$2500	
Total Direct Labor		$11,500
Indirect Costs @ 60 percent		$6900
Other Direct Costs		
Materials	$1000	
Travel	$300	
Subcontract	$5000	
Total Other Direct Costs		$6300
TOTAL PROJECT COSTS		$24,700

Top-down budgeting encourages project managers to consider the relative emphases they contemplate placing on the different aspects of the project. As an example, suppose a project manager plans to develop a new piece of equipment. The project manager develops a bottom-up cost estimate that suggests the project will cost $100,000, broken out as follows for each of the major work assignments:

▲ Design ($60,000)
▲ Development ($15,000)
▲ Testing ($5000)
▲ Production ($20,000)

However, experience with similar projects suggests that approximately 40 percent of the total budget for this type of project should be spent on design, rather than the 60 percent that has been estimated. In essence, it appears that the project manager has planned a design phase for a $150,000 project rather than for a $100,000 project.

The project manager has two choices: He or she can either reexamine the activities included under design to see whether he or she can devise an alternative strategy, or he or she can request an additional $50,000 for the project. Whatever the project manager does, he or she shouldn't just arbitrarily change the numbers without a strategy for how to perform the necessary work for the new figures.

Sometimes organizations approve projects that are forecast to lose money when fully costed and sometimes even when only direct costed. Such decisions by upper management are not necessarily foolish because there could be other, more important reasons for proceeding with a project, such as the following:

▲ Acquiring knowledge about a new technology.

▲ Getting the organization's "foot in the door."

▲ Obtaining the parts, services, or maintenance portion of the work.

▲ Allowing an organization to bid on more lucrative, follow-up contracts.

▲ Improving the organization's competitive position.

▲ Broadening a project or service line.

Of course, such projects are expected to lose money in the short term only and over the longer term will bring extra profits to the organization.

SELF-CHECK

1. You hire a part-time technical writer for your team's upcoming project. The tech writer is contracted only to work on the project for 40 hours total. What type of cost is the writer's salary?

2. During the conceive phase of a project, the project manager should develop a budget that's which of the following?

   (a) a detailed listing of cost associated with each task

   (b) a rough order-of-magnitude estimate

   (c) a list of activities and costs for upper management approval

   (d) a lump-sum estimate of total project costs

3. To create a bottom-up budget estimate, the project manager needs to consider which of the following?

   (a) direct labor costs, direct non-labor costs, and indirect costs

   (b) indirect costs only

   (c) overhead costs, facilities costs, and material costs

   (d) team estimates, upper management recommendations, and ROM estimates

5.3 Improving Cost Estimates

Project managers have a number of ways to improve the process of cost estimating. These range from better formalization of the process, using forms and other simple procedures, to more sophisticated quantitative techniques involving learning curves and tracking signals.

5.3.1 Using Forms

Project managers can use simple forms, such as the one shown in Figure 5-1, to obtain more accurate estimates, not only of direct costs, but also about resources—when the resource is needed, how many are needed, who should be contacted, and if the resource will be available when needed.

Project managers can collect the necessary information for each task on an individual form and then combine it into a single summary report for the project as a whole.

FOR EXAMPLE

The Learning Rate in Action

A firm wins a contract to supply 25 units of a complex electronic device to a customer. Although the firm can produce the device, it has never produced one as complex as the one ordered by the customer. Based on the firm's experience, it estimates that if it were to build many such devices it would take about four hours of direct labor per unit produced. With this estimate, and the wage and benefit rates the firm is paying, the project manager can derive an estimate of the direct labor cost to complete the contract. Unfortunately, the estimate is inaccurate because the project manager is underestimating the labor costs to produce the initial units that will take much longer than four hours each. Likewise, if the firm builds a prototype of the device and records the direct labor hours, which might run as high as 10 hours for this device, this estimate applied to the contract of 25 units would give a result that is much too high. If the electronic device required 10 hours to produce the first unit, and the firm followed a typical 80 percent learning curve, then the second unit would require 8 hours (.80 × 10 hours) to produce. Continuing this calculation out further, the fourth unit would require 6.4 hours, the eighth unit 5.12 hours, and so on. Of course, after a certain number of repetitions, say 100 or 200, the time per unit levels out and little further improvement occurs.

Figure 5-1

Project name_____
Date_____
Task number_____

RESOURCES NEEDED

Resources	Person to Contact	How Many/ Much Needed	When Needed	Check (√) If Available
People: Managers, Supervisors				
Professional & Technical				
Nontechnical				
Money				
Materials: Facilities				
Equipment				
Tools				
Power				
Space				
Special Services: Research & Test				
Typing/clerical				
Reproduction				
Others				

An example form for gathering data on project resource needs.

5.3.2 Using Learning Curves

One reason that cost estimates are often inaccurate is based on the learning exhibited by humans when they repeat a task. In general, research shows unit performance (how long it takes to make a product, for example) improves by a fixed percent each time the total production quantity doubles. More specifically, each time the output doubles, the worker hours per unit decrease by a fixed percentage of their previous value.

This percentage, called the **learning rate,** is typically between 70 and 95 percent. The higher values are for more mechanical tasks, while the lower values are for more mental tasks such as solving problems. A common rate in manufacturing is 80 percent.

The use of learning curves in project management has increased greatly in recent years. The impact of learning rate and learning curves can be incorporated into spreadsheets developed by the project manager or an outside resource to help prepare the budget for a project.

5.3.3 Using Tracking Signals

Project managers spend much time estimating—activity costs and durations, among many other things. Two types of errors in these estimates are most common.

▲ **Random errors.** Errors are random when there is a roughly equal chance that estimates are above or below the true value of a variable and the average size of the error is approximately equal for over- and underestimates. Random errors cancel out, which means that if we add them up the sum will approach zero.

▲ **Systematic errors.** If the chance of either over- or underestimates is not about equal or the size of over- or underestimates is not approximately equal, the estimates are said to be **biased.** Errors caused by bias do not cancel out.

Calculating a number called the **tracking signal** can reveal whether estimates have a systematic bias in cost and other estimates and whether the bias is positive or negative. Knowing whether estimates are biased can help project managers make future estimates.

Many project-management software packages can analyze estimates and collected data and determine whether an estimate is biased. After project managers know that an estimate was positively or negatively biased, they can adjust future estimates accordingly.

5.3.4 Considering Other Factors

Studies consistently show that between 60 and 85 percent of projects fail to meet their time, cost, and/or performance objectives. While the variety of problems that

> ### FOR EXAMPLE
>
> **Resource Pricing Resource**
>
> The Bureau of Labor Statistics in the U.S. Department of Commerce publishes price data, "inflators," and "deflators" for a wide range of commodities, machinery, equipment, and personnel specializations. This resource is a good place to begin estimating resource prices more accurately. Visit the Bureau of Labor Statistics website at www.bls.gov.

can plague project cost estimates seems to be unlimited, some problems occur with high frequency. The following are some of the most common problems and some solutions:

▲ **Changes in resource prices.** The most common managerial approach to this problem is to increase all cost estimates by some fixed percentage. A better approach, however, is to identify each input that has a significant impact on the costs and to estimate the rate of price change for each one.

▲ **Not factoring in adequate allowances for waste and spoilage in estimated costs.** Similar to dealing with changes in resource prices, the best approach is to determine the individual rates of waste and spoilage for each task rather than to use some fixed percentage.

▲ **Not adding an allowance for increased personnel costs due to loss and replacement of skilled project team members.** Not only do new members go through a learning period, which increases the time and cost of the relevant tasks, but professional salaries also usually increase faster than the general average. Thus, it might cost substantially more to replace a team member with a newcomer who has about the same level of experience. Additionally, as workers are hired, either for additional capacity or to replace those who leave, they require training in the project environment before they become productive. This training is informal on-the-job training conducted by their coworkers who must take time from their own project tasks, thus resulting in ever more reduced capacity as more workers are hired.

▲ **Overly optimistic estimates.** Sometimes in the excitement to get a project approved, to win a bid, or to respond to pressure from upper management, project cost estimators give a more optimistic picture than reality warrants. Inevitably, the estimate understates the cost. When the project is finally executed, the actual costs then result in a project that misses its profit goals, or worse, fails to make a profit at all.

▲ **Organizational climate factors.** If the penalty for overestimating costs is much more severe than underestimating, almost all costs will be underestimated—and vice versa. Identifying and responding to organizational climate factors is difficult and requires ongoing discussions between project estimators and upper management.

▲ **Plain bad luck.** Sometimes something that is indestructible breaks. Or something that is impenetrable leaks. Wise project managers include allowances for these **unexpected contingencies.** A common contingency to include in budgeting is a **management reserve,** a designated amount of time and money to account for parts of the project that cannot be predicted, such as major disruptions in the project caused by serious weather conditions or an accident. Project managers should take into consideration as many known influences as can be predicted, and those that cannot be predicted must then simply be allowed for.

▲ **Arbitrary cuts to estimates.** A serious source of inaccurate estimates of time and cost is the all too common practice of some managers arbitrarily cutting carefully prepared time and cost estimates. Managers rationalize their actions with statements such as, "I know they built a lot of slop in these estimates," or, "I want to give them a more challenging target to shoot at." This is not effective management. It is not even good common sense. Cost and time estimates should be made by the people who designed the work and are responsible for doing it. Upper management, project managers, and team members will always have different estimates of resource needs and task durations, but managerially dictated arbitrary cuts in budgets and schedules almost always lead to projects that are late and over budget.

FOR EXAMPLE

Organizational Demands Lead to Inaccurate Estimates

A major manufacturer of airplane landing gear parts wondered why the firm was no longer successful, over several years, in winning competitive bids. An investigation was conducted and revealed that three years earlier the firm was late on a major delivery to an important customer and paid a huge penalty as well as being threatened with the loss of future business. The reason the firm was late was because an insufficient number of expensive, hard-to-obtain parts were purchased for the project and more could not be obtained without a long delay. The purchasing manager was demoted and replaced by his assistant. The assistant's solution to this problem was to include a 10 percent allowance for additional, hard-to-obtain parts in every cost proposal. This resulted in every proposal from the firm being significantly higher than their competitors' proposals in this narrow-margin business.

SELF-CHECK

1. Use of a tracking signal to evaluate your estimate reveals that you consistently overestimate costs by an average of 15 percent. Your overestimates can be considered which of the following?

   (a) random error

   (b) systematic error

   (c) direct-cost error

   (d) systemic error

2. To determine the accuracy of an estimate over time, you need to take into account which of the following?

   (a) allowances for waste and spillage

   (b) estimator errors

   (c) the tracking signal and learning curve

   (d) the learning rate and learning curve

3. Vince's new product development team estimated costs for new team member training, but his project is still over-budget. One possible reason might be which of the following?

   (a) Vince didn't take into account the time established team members would be required to help train new team members.

   (b) Vince didn't accurately estimate price resource costs based on established national averages.

   (c) Vince didn't factor in adequate waste and spillage in his estimated costs, and downtime due to training that can be counted as a waste.

   (d) all of the above

5.4 Dealing with Budget Uncertainty

In spite of the care and effort project managers and project teams expend to create accurate and fair budgets, budgets are only estimates made under conditions of uncertainty. Because projects are unique, risk pervades all elements of the project, particularly the project's goals of performance, schedule, and budget.

The following section discusses the issue of budget uncertainty. See Chapter 13 for more about the related topic of risk and risk management.

5.4.1 Re-estimating Project Budgets

For project managers, the uncertainty of the budget can be illustrated like the shaded portion of the top graph in Figure 5-2. In the top graph, the actual project costs might be either higher or lower than the estimates the project manager has derived.

As a project unfolds, cost uncertainty decreases as the project moves toward completion. Project managers often make new forecasts about project completion time and cost at fixed points in a project's life cycle or at special milestones. The middle and bottom graphs in Figure 5-2 illustrate this. At time t_1 on the middle graph, the cost to date is known and another estimate is made of the cost to complete the project. This process is repeated at t_2 in the bottom graph of Figure 5-2.

The reasons for cost uncertainty in projects are many: Prices might escalate, different resources might be required, the project might take a different amount of time than expected thereby impacting overhead and indirect costs, and so on. Section 5.3 discusses ways to improve cost estimates and anticipate such uncertainty, but change is a fact of life, including life on the project, and change invariably alters previous budget estimates.

5.4.2 Identifying Causes for Change

Three basic causes create change in projects, and thus introduce budget uncertainty:

▲ **Cost estimator errors.** Some changes are due to errors the cost estimator made about how to achieve the tasks identified in the project plan.

FOR EXAMPLE

Budget Checklists at NIAID

Many organizations provide specific procedures for project managers to evaluate the accuracy of their project budgets. For example, the National Institute of Allergy and Infectious Diseases (www.niaid.nih.gov) provides a checklist of questions for leaders of proposed research projects to run through prior to submitting a project proposal to the organization. While some items on the checklist are NIAID-specific concerns, many of the budget-related recommendations are applicable to non-NIAID projects of various sizes and/or durations. For instance, the questions, "Did I consider the equipment and materials that I already have on hand?" and "Have I considered other options rather than purchasing expensive equipment?" seem applicable to the estimation (and re-estimation) process of almost any project. See www.niaid.nih.gov/ncn/grants/charts for NIAID checklists and recommendations.

Figure 5-2

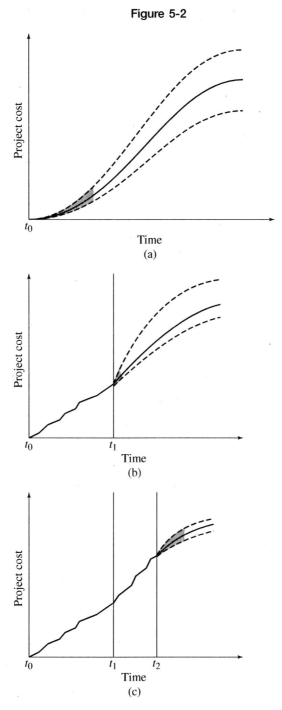

(a)

(b)

(c)

Estimates of project costs at a project's start and two
times later in the project.

Such changes are due to technological uncertainty. Examples include a building's foundation needing to be reinforced because of a fault in the ground that wasn't identified beforehand or a new innovation allowing a project task to be completed more easily than was anticipated.

▲ **New learning.** Other changes result because the project team or client learns more about the nature of the performance goal of the project or the setting in which a product is to be used. Examples include a medical team revealing plans to use a device in the field as well as in the hospital or chemists finding another application of the granulated bed process if it is altered to include additional minerals.

▲ **Mandated change.** Perhaps a new law is passed, a trade association sets a new standard, or a governmental regulatory agency adopts a new policy. These changes alter the previous rules of conduct under which the project had been operating—usually to the detriment of the budget.

5.4.3 Responding to Changes

Project managers can handle change in various ways. The least preferred way is simply to accept a negative change and take a loss on the project. The best approach is to prepare for change ahead of time by including provisions in the original plan or contracting for such changes.

A relatively easy change to handle is the change that results from an increased specification by the client, yet even this kind of change is often mishandled by organizations. The best practice for dealing with this kind of change is to include in the contract a formal **change control procedure,** a statement that allows for renegotiation of price and schedule for client-ordered changes in performance.

More difficult changes are those resulting from misunderstood assumptions, technological uncertainty, and mandates. Assumptions and some technological uncertainties are most easily handled by carefully listing all the assumptions, including those regarding technology, in the contract (see Section 2.5). Project managers should state that if the assumptions fail to hold, the contract will have to be renegotiated.

Mandates are the most difficult to accommodate because they can affect anything about the project and usually come without warning. The shorter the project duration, however, the less likely an unexpected mandate will impact the project. Thus, when contracting for a project of extended duration, it is best to divide it into shorter segments and contract for only one segment at a time. Of course, this strategy also allows the client to reconsider whether it wants to complete the full project, as well as gives the competition an opportunity to steal the remainder of the project from the initial supplier. Nevertheless, if a client wants to cancel a contract and is locked into a long-term agreement, the project will not have a happy ending anyway. At least with shorter segments, the client might be willing to finish a segment before dropping the project. In any event, if the client is pleased with a supplier's performance on one segment of the contract, it is unlikely that a competitor has the experience and cost efficiencies that the initial supplier has gained.

5.4.4 Revising Budgets

As changes impact a project's costs, the budget for the remainder of the project will certainly have to be revised. Project managers have three ways to revise a budget during the course of a project, each depending on the nature of the changes that have been experienced:

1. If the changes are confined to early elements of the project and are not seen to impact the rest of the project, then the new budget can be estimated as the old budget plus the changes from the early elements.
2. If something systemic has changed that impacts the costs of the rest of the project tasks (such as a higher rate of inflation), the new budget estimate will be the accumulated costs to date plus the previous estimates of the rest of the budget multiplied by some correction factor for the systemic change. The Bureau of Labor Statistics is an excellent source for historical data that can aid project managers in estimating an appropriate correction factor.
3. If there might be some individual changes now perceived to impact specific elements of the remaining project tasks, the new budget estimate will then be the actual costs to date plus the expected costs for the remaining project tasks.

Generally, both systematic and individual changes in the project should be revised in all three ways at once.

SELF-CHECK

1. Which of the following are the main causes of budget change on projects?

   (a) new learning, misunderstood assumptions, and escalating costs

   (b) change control procedures, mandated change, and learning rates

   (c) cost estimator error, new learning, and mandated change

   (d) none of the above

2. A formal change control procedure allows the organization to renegotiate with the client on future projects if project costs differ drastically from estimates. True or false?

SUMMARY

Although budgets mean different things to project managers, accountants, and upper management, project budgets tie project activities to the financial plans of organizations. Budgets can be handed down by upper management, estimated by workers based on experience, or a combination of these two extremes. However budgets are created, the process of estimating direct and indirect costs requires careful development and review by project managers. Project managers can improve the accuracy of cost estimates using various tools, including forms, learning curves, tracking signals, and other factors. While project budgets will always have an element of uncertainty, project managers can prepare for common types of change and revise budgets accordingly.

KEY TERMS

Approved project budget	A detailed project budget that essential people agree to support.
Biased	In estimating, when either the chance of over- or underestimates is not about equal or the size of over- or underestimates is not approximately equal.
Bottom-up budgeting	Financial estimating process in which a Work Breakdown Structure or action plan identifies elemental tasks, which are then converted to costs and combined to determine an overall direct cost for the project.
Budget	The financial plans for allocating organization resources to project activities.
Change control procedure	A statement within a project contract that allows for renegotiation of price and schedule for client-ordered changes in performance.
Detailed budget estimate	An itemization of the estimated costs for each project activity. Prepared by a project manager based on a Work Breakdown Structure.
Direct costs	Expenditures for resources that are used solely to perform project activities.
General and administrative costs	Indirect costs that keep the organization operational.
Indirect costs	Expenditures that are incurred to support project activities but that aren't tracked individually.

Learning rate	The percentage at which unit performance improves each time the total production quantity doubles.
Management reserve	A designated amount of time and money to account for parts of the project that cannot be predicted, such as major disruptions in the project caused by serious weather conditions or an accident.
Overhead costs	Indirect costs associated with resources used to perform project activities, but which are difficult to subdivide and allocate directly.
Rough order-of-magnitude (ROM) estimate	An initial estimate of costs that is based on a general sense of the type of work the project will likely entail; also known as a ballpark estimate.
Top-down budgeting	Financial estimating process in which top and middle managers estimate the overall project cost by estimating the costs of the major tasks.
Tracking signal	A number project managers can calculate to reveal whether cost estimates have a systematic bias in cost and whether the bias is positive or negative.
Unexpected contingency	Budget allowance for surprising, unplanned incidents.

ASSESS YOUR UNDERSTANDING

Go to www.wiley.com/college/portny to assess your knowledge of the basics of project budgets.
Measure your learning by comparing pre-test and post-test results.

Summary Questions

1. Direct costs and indirect costs can be figured:
   (a) on a cost-deferred basis.
   (b) on a cost-analysis basis.
   (c) on a cost-per-quarter basis.
   (d) on a cost-per-unit basis.
2. Considering the effects of the learning rate on cost estimates would be most appropriate during a project's define phase. True or false?
3. Budget changes resulting from misunderstood assumptions can often be avoided by creating detailed Work Breakdown Structures. True or false?

Applying This Chapter

1. Your company is considering switching from a top-down budgeting process to a bottom-up process. As a project manager in the company's new product development group, you are in favor of being able to create budgets using a bottom-up method and have been asked to share the reasons for your preference at the next senior management planning meeting. What benefits of bottom-up budgeting will you highlight to senior management? How might you respond to upper management's concerns that bottom-up budgets are often more costly than top-down budgets?
2. To test a new product, you estimate that you'll need to hire two temporary lab specialists to run a specific test. One specialist's contract is $10,000 for 65 hours of work; the other is $12,500 for 80 hours of work. What is your estimated cost per unit for specialists on the project?
3. Mia's team is helping her put together a budget estimate for a proposed project. The team has been complaining that budget estimates are a waste of time because "the project costs what it costs." What are some things Mia can do or say to help her team appreciate the worth of estimating costs?
4. Bottom-up cost estimating determines a project will cost $35,000, while top-down estimating determines the same project will cost $10,000. What specifically can the project manager for the project do to help reconcile these two budget estimates?

5. The budget you've submitted for a new product development team you're leading has been criticized as being inaccurate and vague. However, you believe that upper management just doesn't want to fund the actual costs you believe are associated with the project. What are some things you can do as project manager to reconsider (and perhaps reaffirm or revise) the accuracy of your estimates?

6. Gregory's human resource team is supposed to produce a comprehensive website to attract and screen new hires. Gregory recently reviewed the project's budget and feels the project needs an additional $25,000 to respond to changes in the project. What might be an example of each of the categories of change (Section 5.4.2) that Gregory can cite to justify additional money for the project?

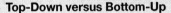

Top-Down versus Bottom-Up

Choose an everyday project (cleaning up a yard's worth of fall leaves, hosting a garage sale, or mailing out holiday cards, for example). Prepare a preliminary budget estimate using a top-down approach—assume you're the head of household and have the finances of your entire family in mind. Then prepare a preliminary budget estimate using a bottom-up approach—assume you're a child in the family who's been assigned the work of the project. How did the budgeting process seem different when working with each method? Did the processes produce different budget estimates?

Direct and Indirect Costs

New projects often require detailed budgets to get off the ground. Think of a work-related project that you'd like to introduce to your company—or to a company you'd like to work for some day. Maybe your new project is an employee retention committee with monthly events or a new product research team you'd like to create to investigate a new market or technology. Whatever the case, think big! Then brainstorm a list of cost categories associated with the project. Divide the costs into direct and indirect costs. Review Section 5.2.1 to see whether you've missed any cost categories.

What Does a Project Really Cost?

Consider a nonwork project that you'd like to lead (perhaps creating a new gardening club, chairing a fundraising event, or hosting a holiday party). Although these types of activities do not go through a formal budgeting process, as project leader/manager you need to have a clear sense of the direct and indirect costs of doing the project. Prepare a two-part budget—including direct and indirect costs as outlined in Section 5.2.1. Are there "costs" that extend beyond the dollars and cents associated with the project? Estimate a cost for each activity and include these estimates in the budget as well. Describe any unique methods you had to come up with to calculate unusual project costs.

Building More Accurate Budgets

Develop a comprehensive chronological list of steps for creating project budgets that combines the general plan outlined in Section 5.2.3 with the tools for improving estimates (Section 5.3) and the strategies for managing budget uncertainty (Section 5.4). Assume that you and your organization have adequate resources to utilize all the tools and techniques outlined in Sections 5.3 and 5.4. What sort of checks and tests did you add to the process?

CASE STUDY: General Sensor Company

Justin Jordan has been named project manager of the General Sensor Company's new sensor manufacturing process project. Sensors are extremely price sensitive. General has done a great deal of quantitative work to be able to accurately forecast changes in sales volume relative to changes in pricing.

The company president, Guy General, has faith in the model that the company uses. He insists that all projects affecting the manufacturing costs of sensors be run against the model to generate data to calculate the return on investment. The net result is that project managers, like Justin, are under a great deal of pressure to submit realistic budgets so go/no-go project decisions can be made quickly. Guy has canceled several projects that appeared marginal during their feasibility stages and recently fired a project manager for overestimating project costs on a new model sensor. The project was killed early in the design stages, and six months later a competitor introduced a similar sensor that proved to be highly successful.

Justin's dilemma is how to construct a budget that accurately reflects the costs of the proposed new process. Justin is an experienced executive and feels comfortable with his ability in estimating costs of projects. However, the recent firing of his colleague has made him a little gun-shy. Only one stage of the four-stage sensor manufacturing process is being changed. Justin has detailed cost information about the majority of the process. Unfortunately, the costs and tasks involved in the new modified process stage are unclear at this point. Justin also believes that the new modifications will cause some minor changes in the other three stages, but these potential changes have not yet been clearly identified. The stage being addressed by the project represents almost 50 percent of the manufacturing cost.

Questions

1. Under these circumstances, would Justin be wise to pursue a top-down or a bottom-up budgeting approach? Why?
2. What factors are most relevant in terms of creating a budget in this situation?

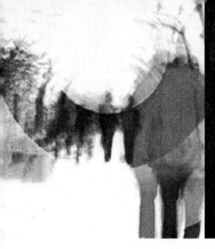

6

ESTABLISHING PROJECT SCHEDULES
Sequencing Activities and Events

Starting Point

Go to www.wiley.com/college/portny to assess your knowledge of the basics of project schedules.
Determine where you need to concentrate your effort.

What You'll Learn in This Chapter

▲ Network diagram elements and formats
▲ Paths, slack time, and critical dates on network diagrams
▲ Activity relationships
▲ Schedule modifications
▲ Time-saving strategies
▲ Activity duration estimates
▲ Three formats for presenting schedules
▲ Network diagram innovations

After Studying This Chapter, You'll Be Able To

▲ Create network diagrams that accurately illustrate activities and schedules
▲ Calculate and evaluate critical dates offered by network diagrams
▲ Build activity relationships into network diagrams
▲ Analyze network diagrams for opportunities to reduce required time
▲ Reformulate diagrams to reduce required time
▲ Create project schedules in various formats

INTRODUCTION

Network diagrams enable project managers to graphically represent, analyze, evaluate, and make critical adjustments to project schedules. Although network diagram formats vary, they all focus on activities, events, and time spans to determine critical paths and start and finish dates. By establishing relationships between project activities, reconsidering these relationships, and accurately estimating activity duration, project managers can develop project schedules that meet (and often beat) time expectations. Project managers tailor their choice of presentation formats to fit the audience they're communicating with; there are a range of presentation formats and charts based on network diagrams to choose from.

6.1 Exploring Schedule Possibilities with Diagrams

Project assignments always have deadlines. Even if the project manager is not exactly sure what the project is to accomplish, he or she probably knows when it has to be finished.

Project managers often feel like they don't have enough time to complete a project. But the truth is, when project assignments are first received, project managers usually don't know how long a project will actually take to complete. First reactions are often based more on fear and anxiety than on facts, especially for project managers trying to juggle multiple responsibilities and deadlines.

The total time required to perform a group of activities depends on the following:

▲ **Duration:** how long each individual activity will take.
▲ **Sequence:** the order in which the activities will be performed.

FOR EXAMPLE

The Importance of Duration and Sequence

Jan is assigned a project consisting of 10 activities that each require one week to complete. How long will it take her to complete the project? Unfortunately, there's not enough information to know for sure at this point. Jan's project could be finished in one week, if she can perform all the activities at the same time and she has sufficient resources. Or her project could take 10 weeks, if she has to do the activities one at a time in sequential order. Or her project could take between one and ten weeks if she has to do some of the activities in sequence. A project manager must know both the duration and sequence of Jan's activities in order to create any plan involving Jan.

6.1.1 Drawing Network Diagrams

Every day, people consider in their heads how long an activity takes and what needs to be completed before what. They develop schedules for small projects, such as cleaning the house or shopping for groceries. However, for projects with more than 15 to 20 activities that can be performed at the same time (for example, launching a new Web site or upgrading a piece of software), project managers need a method to guide their analysis.

A **network diagram** is a flow chart that illustrates the order in which activities need to be performed in a project. The network diagram can be considered the project's test laboratory: It gives the project manager a chance to try out different project strategies before actually performing the work.

Network diagrams include three elements:

1. **Event:** a significant occurrence in the life of the project; sometimes called a milestone or a deliverable. Events take no time and consume no resources; they occur instantaneously. Think of them as signposts that signify the project has reached a certain point in its trip completion. Events mark the start or finish of an activity or a group of activities. Examples of events are "draft report approved" and "design begun."

2. **Activity:** work required to move from one event to the next in a project. Activities take time and consume resources; they're described by action verbs. Examples of activities are "design report format" and "identify needs for new product."

   (a) Events and activities are sometimes confused. For example, a newspaper might call the presidential inaugural ball "the premier social event of the season." But in project-management terms, an inaugural ball is an activity rather than an event, because it takes time and lots of resources to produce.

   (b) Activities can have other activities that come before them (predecessors) and activities that come after (successors). See Section 6.2.4.

3. **Span time:** the actual calendar time required to complete an activity; also called duration or elapsed time. The amount of work effort required, people's availability, and whether two or more people can work on an activity at the same time all affect the activity's span time. Capacity (for example, a computer's processing speed and the pages per minute that a copier can print) and availability of non-personnel resources also affect span time.

   (a) Understanding the basis of span time helps project managers figure out ways to reduce it, if necessary. For example, suppose Mitch has to test a software package he just purchased. He estimates that he has to run the package for 24 hours on a computer to do a complete test. If he's allowed to use the computer for only six hours in any one day, the span time for his software test is four days. If he wanted to cut the span time for the software test in half, doubling the number of people assigned to the activity won't do it—but getting approval to use the computer for 12 hours a day will.

(b) Different units of time are used to describe two related but different activity characteristics. Span time describes duration; work effort is the number of hours a person would have to work on the activity to complete it. Suppose four people had to work full-time at the same time for five days to complete an activity. The activity's span time is five days. The work effort required is 20 person-days (four people multiplied by five days).

(c) Pure delay can also add to an activity's span time. Suppose Rupert's boss has to approve a report Rupert wrote. Rupert puts the report in his boss's inbox and it sits there for four days and seven hours. His boss then removes it, reads it for one hour, and signs it. The activity's span time is five days; the work effort invested is one hour.

6.1.2 Considering Network Diagram Options

Project managers can draw network diagrams in either of two formats:

1. **Activity-on-the-arrow:** also referred to as activity-on-the-node, the classical approach, or the traditional approach.
2. **Activity-in-the-box:** also referred to as activity-in-the-node or precedence diagramming.

These two formats are interchangeable; nothing can be represented in one that can't also be represented in the other. The only difference between the two formats is the symbols used to represent the three elements.

Project managers also frequently use the following terms to refer to flow-charts of project activities:

▲ **Precedence diagram:** another term for a network diagram in the activity-in-the-box format.

▲ **Dependency diagram:** another term for a network diagram in either format.

▲ **CPM charts:** CPM stands for Critical Path Method. This method of diagramming projects was developed independently by DuPont de Nemours, Inc. in the 1950s. CPM uses deterministic (or certain) estimates but includes both time and cost estimates to allow time/cost trade-offs to be used.

▲ **PERT chart:** refers to a network diagram in the activity-on-the-arrow format. PERT is an acronym that stands for program evaluation and review technique. PERT was created in the 1950s to plan the Polaris weapon system's design and development. PERT is an analytical technique that allows project managers to assign optimistic, pessimistic, and most likely estimates for an activity's span time, when they don't expect that repeated performances of the activity will take the same time. Project managers use probabilities to determine the likelihood that individual activity span times and overall project duration will fall within specified limits.

▲ **Gantt chart:** Gantt charts are another popular, often easier-to-read method for illustrating schedules (see Section 6.6.2).

When writing about the history of project management, differentiating between CPM and PERT is important and interesting. When managing projects, the distinction is merely fussy. Both CPM and PERT methods identify a critical path of tasks that cannot be delayed without delaying the project. Both methods identify activities with slack (or float) that can be somewhat delayed without extending the time required to complete the project. While CPM and PERT use slightly different ways of drawing the network of activities, anything that can be done with PERT can be done with CPM and vice versa.

Using the Activity-on-the-Arrow Diagramming Approach

The activity-on-the-arrow approach uses distinct symbols to describe each of the three elements of the diagram:

1. A circle represents an event.
2. A line with an arrowhead represents an activity.
3. The letter "t" represents span time.

Every activity starts from and ends in an event. Figure 6-1 presents a simple example. When someone reaches Event A (represented by the circle on the left), he's allowed to perform Activity 1 (represented by the arrow). It is estimated that Activity 1 will take two weeks to complete (described in the caption beneath the

Figure 6-1

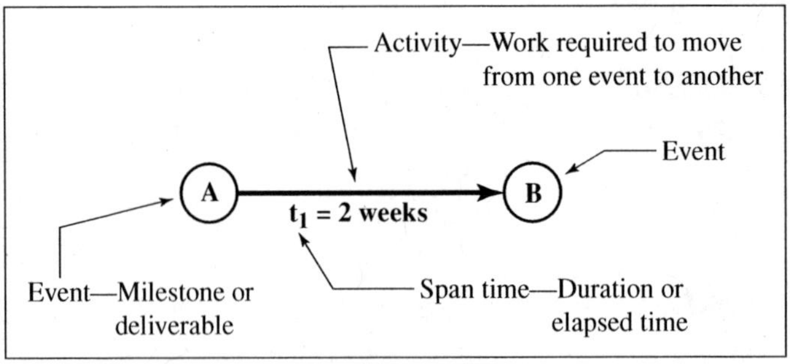

The three symbols used in an activity-on-the-arrow network diagram.

arrow). Upon completing Activity 1, the team member reaches Event B (represented by the circle on the right). The length of the arrow representing an activity can be proportional to the activity's span time but does not have to be.

Occasionally, a fourth symbol is used in this diagramming scheme: A **dummy activity** is an activity with 0 span time that's used to represent a required dependency between events. For example, Bill and Susan both have to approve a system's design before their project manager can consider the overall design complete and proceed to implement it. The project manager can represent this in a network diagram by defining two separate events, "Bill's approval received" and "Susan's approval received," and having a dummy activity start from each one and end in the "Overall system design completed" event.

Using the Activity-in-the-Box Diagramming Approach

The activity-in-the-box approach uses only two symbols to describe the three elements of the diagram:

1. A box represents both an event and an activity. A box's span time indicates whether it represents an event or an activity. If the span time is 0, it's an event. In addition, the boxes representing events are sometimes highlighted by making their lines bold, double, and so forth.
2. The letter "t" represents span time.

Figure 6-2 shows a simple activity-in-the-box diagram. When someone reaches Event A (represented by the box on the left), she's allowed to perform Activity 1 (represented by the box in the middle). Upon completing Activity 1, she reaches Event B (represented by the box on the right). The arrows only indicate the direction of workflow. Figure 6-2 uses the activity-in-the-box approach to represent both events and activities. In this approach, however, the use of events is optional; one activity can lead directly to another, with no event in between.

Figure 6-2

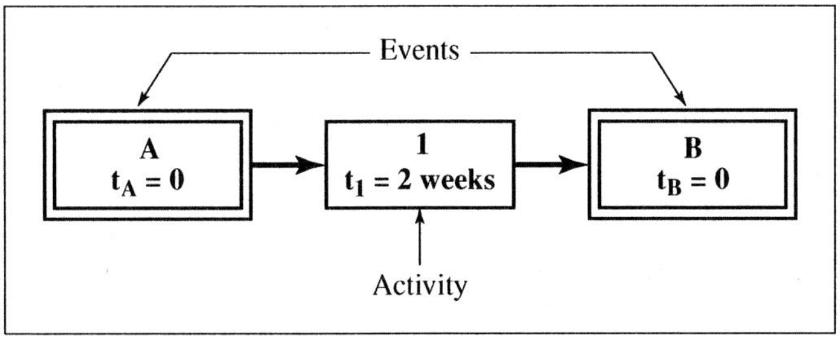

The two symbols used in an activity-in-the-box network diagram.

6.1.3 Choosing Network Diagram Formats

Although the diagramming formats are interchangeable, project managers should consider the following when choosing which approach to use:

▲ **The activity-on-the-arrow approach represents each element with a unique symbol.** This is especially helpful when just learning network diagrams because confusing activities and events is less likely.

▲ **The activity-in-the-box approach allows a project manager to draw out an entire project without defining any events.** This approach often takes less time and space to draw because events are only defined if needed.

▲ **The more commonly used integrated project-management software packages use the activity-in-the-box approach.**

The rest of the chapter uses the activity-in-the-box approach.

SELF-CHECK

1. A project manager must know an activity's duration and importance in order to include the activity in a network diagram. True or false?

2. In a network diagram, a milestone or an event is the same as which of the following?

    (a) an activity

    (b) a duration

    (c) an objective

    (d) a deliverable

3. What are the three main elements of network diagrams?

4. A diagram that utilizes only two symbols and allows project managers to draw the diagram without defining events is what kind of diagram?

6.2 Analyzing Network Diagrams

Project managers can learn a great deal by carefully examining network diagrams. This section covers the rules and key insights for understanding, evaluating, and creating network diagrams accurately and effectively.

6.2.1 Following Two Rules

Use the following two rules to draw and interpret network diagrams. After understanding these rules, analyzing diagrams is fairly straightforward.

▲ **Rule 1:** after someone finishes an activity or reaches an event; she or he can proceed to the next activity or event, as indicated by the arrow(s) leaving from that activity or event.

▲ **Rule 2:** to be able to start an activity or reach an event, someone must complete all activities and reach all events from which arrows entering that activity or event emanate.

Figure 6-3 shows a network diagram drawn in the activity-in-the-box format. Rule 1 says that after starting a project (that is, when the event called "Start" is reached), someone can work on Activities 1 or 3. That means someone can do Activity 1, Activity 3, or both Activities 1 and 3. In other words, they're independent of one another.

The diagram in Figure 6-3 also means someone can choose to do neither of the activities. Rule 1 is an "allowing" relationship, not a "forcing" relationship. It says that a project team member *can,* if he or she chooses, work on the activities to which the arrows from the event called "Start" lead; it doesn't say that he or she *must* work on any of them. Of course, if no one works on any of the activities, the project will be in a state of delay. That, however, is the project team's choice.

Figure 6-3

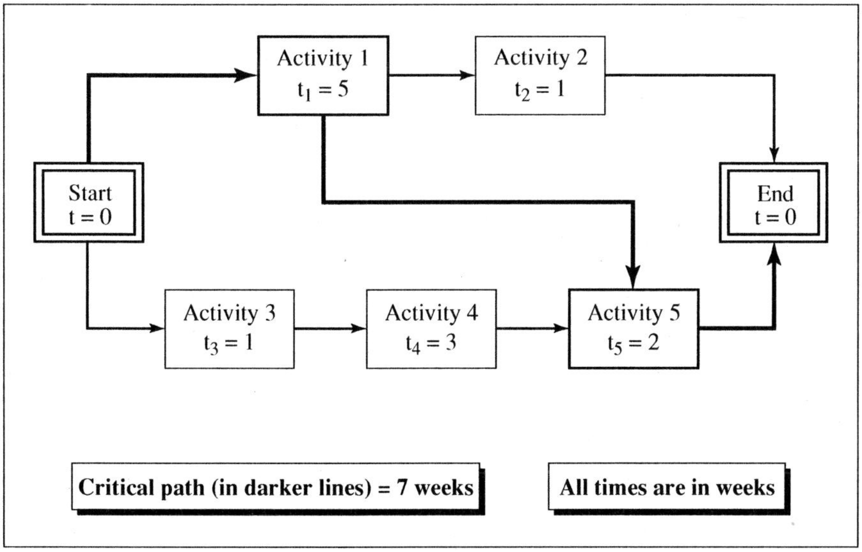

Example of a network diagram.

FOR EXAMPLE

Diagrams as Road Trips

One way to think of a project is to imagine it as a trip that several friends will take. Each person has his or her own car and will travel a different route to arrive at the final destination. During the trip, two or more of the routes will cross at certain places. Everyone agrees that all people who are scheduled to pass through a common point must arrive at that point before anyone can proceed on to the next leg of his or her journey. The trip is over when everyone reaches the final destination. No one would want to undertake a trip this complex without first planning it out on a map. Planning allows travelers to determine how long the entire trip will take, identify potential difficulties, and consider alternate routes to get to the final destination quickly. A network diagram is the roadmap for a project. The legs of each person's journey are the activities that project team members will perform, and milestones signify the start or end of the legs. A path is any sequence of activities that is performed during the project.

Rule 2 says that someone can start working on Activity 2 as soon as Activity 1 is completed because the arrow from Activity 1 is the only one leading into Activity 2. Rule 2 is a "forcing" relationship. If arrows from three activities entered Activity 2, the diagram doesn't indicate that someone can start working on Activity 2 by completing any one of the three activities that he or she chooses; the activities from which all three arrows emanate must be completed before starting to work on Activity 2.

Network diagrams help project managers determine the following information and figure out what schedules are possible:

▲ **Critical path:** a sequence of activities in a project that takes the longest time to complete.

▲ **Noncritical path:** a sequence of activities that can be delayed by some amount, while still allowing the overall project to finish in the shortest possible time.

▲ **Slack time:** the maximum amount of time that someone can delay an activity and still finish the project in the shortest possible time.

▲ **Earliest start date:** the earliest date that someone can possibly start an activity.

▲ **Earliest finish date:** the earliest date that someone can possibly finish an activity.

▲ **Latest start date:** the latest date that someone can start an activity and still finish the project in the shortest possible time.

▲ **Latest finish date:** the latest date someone can finish an activity and still finish the project in the shortest possible time.

The length of a project's critical path defines how long the project will take to complete. If project managers want to get projects done in less time, they need to consider ways to shorten the time to complete the critical path. Project managers must monitor critical-path activities closely during project performance because any delays in critical-path activities will delay final project completion.

Of course, a project can have two or more critical paths at the same time. In fact, every path in a project can be critical if they all take the same amount of time to complete. This is a high-risk situation because a delay in any activity will immediately cause the final completion of the project to be delayed.

Critical paths can change as a project unfolds. Sometimes activities on the critical path are finished so early that the total time to complete the path becomes less than that required to complete one or more other paths. It's also possible that activities on a path that's initially noncritical are sufficiently delayed that the time to complete the path exceeds that of the current critical path.

6.2.2 Determining Critical Paths, Noncritical Paths, and Earliest Start and Finish Dates

A project manager's first step in analyzing a project's network diagram is to start at the beginning of the project and see how fast the activities can be completed along each path of the project until reaching the project's finish. This start-to-finish analysis is called the **forward pass.**

A forward pass through the diagram shown in Figure 6-3 would go as follows: Rule 1 says someone can consider working on Activities 1 or 3 as soon as the project starts (that is, as soon as someone reaches the event called "Start"). First consider the upper path comprised of Activities 1 and 2:

▲ The earliest someone can start Activity 1 is the moment the project starts.

▲ The earliest someone can finish Activity 1 is the end of week 5 (add Activity 1's estimated span time of five weeks to its earliest start time, which is the start of the project).

▲ Rule 2 says the earliest someone can start Activity 2 is the beginning of week 6, since the arrow from Activity 1 is the only one entering Activity 2.

▲ The earliest someone can finish Activity 2 is the end of week 6.

So far, so good. Now consider the path at the bottom of the diagram, comprised of Activities 3, 4, and 5.

▲ The earliest someone can start Activity 3 is the moment the project starts.

▲ The earliest someone can finish Activity 3 is the end of week 1.

▲ The earliest someone can start Activity 4 is the beginning of week 2.

▲ The earliest someone can finish Activity 4 is the end of week 4.

Something a little different emerges here. According to Rule 2, the two arrows entering Activity 5 indicate someone can't start Activity 5 until both Activity 1 and Activity 4 are complete. Even though Activity 4 can be finished by the end of week 4, Activity 1 can't be completed until the end of week 5. Therefore, the earliest someone can start Activity 5 is the beginning of week 6.

This situation illustrates the following guideline:

If two or more activities lead to the same activity, the earliest date someone can start the activity is equal to the latest of the earliest finish dates for these activities.

In the example, the earliest finish dates for Activity 4 and Activity 1 are the ends of weeks 4 and 5, respectively. Therefore, the earliest date someone can start Activity 5 is the beginning of week 6. Therefore:

▲ The earliest someone can start Activity 5 is the beginning of week 6.

▲ The earliest someone can finish Activity 5 is the end of week 7.

▲ The earliest someone can finish Activity 2 is the end of week 6.

▲ Therefore, the earliest the entire project can be completed (reaching the event called "End") is the end of week 7.

The preceding analysis reveals the following information about a project:

▲ The length of the critical path is seven weeks, the shortest time in which the project can be completed. There is one critical path that takes seven weeks; it includes the event called "Start," Activity 1, Activity 5, and the event called "End."

▲ Activity 2, Activity 3, and Activity 4 are not on critical paths.

▲ The earliest dates someone can start and finish each activity in the project are summarized in Table 6-1.

6.2.3 Determining Slack Times and Earliest Start and Finish Dates

Determining critical paths and earliest start and finish dates (see Section 6.2.2) is only half of a project manager's responsibilities. Project managers also need to determine how much they can delay the activities along each path of a project

Table 6-1: Earliest Start and Finish Dates for Figure 6-3

Activity	Earliest Start Date	Earliest Finish Date
1	Beginning of week 1	End of week 5
2	Beginning of week 6	End of week 6
3	Beginning of week 1	End of week 1
4	Beginning of week 2	End of week 4
5	Beginning of week 6	End of week 7

and still finish the project at the earliest possible date. This finish-to-start analysis is called the **backward pass.**

The forward pass analysis in Section 6.2.2 reveals that the earliest date someone can reach the event called "End" is the end of week 7. However, Rule 2 says someone can't reach the event called "End" until Activities 2 and 5 are both completed. Therefore, if a project is to be finished by the end of week 7, the latest someone can finish Activities 2 and 5 is the end of week 7. Again, consider the lower path comprised of Activities 3, 4, and 5.

▲ Someone must start Activity 5 by the beginning of week 6, at the latest, if Activity 5 is to be finished by the end of week 7.

▲ Rule 2 says someone can't start Activity 5 until Activity 1 and Activity 4 are finished. Therefore, someone must finish Activity 1 and Activity 4 by the end of week 5, at the latest.

▲ Hence, someone must start Activity 4 by the beginning of week 3, at the latest.

▲ Someone must finish Activity 3 before work can begin on Activity 4. Therefore, Activity 3 must be finished by the end of week 2, at the latest.

▲ Someone must start Activity 3 by the beginning of week 2, at the latest.

Finally, consider the upper path.

▲ Someone must start Activity 2 by the beginning of week 7, at the latest.

▲ No one can work on Activity 2 until Activity 1 is finished. Therefore, someone must finish Activity 1 by the end of week 6, at the latest.

So, Activity 1 must be finished by the end of week 5 to allow work on Activity 5 to start at the beginning of week 6 and by the end of week 6 to allow work on Activity 2 to start at the beginning of week 7. Finishing Activity 1 by the end of week 5 will satisfy both requirements. This situation illustrates the following guideline:

Table 6-2: Latest Start and Finish Dates for Figure 6-3

Activity	Latest Start Date	Latest Finish Date
1	Beginning of week 1	End of week 5
2	Beginning of week 7	End of week 7
3	Beginning of week 2	End of week 2
4	Beginning of week 3	End of week 5
5	Beginning of week 6	End of week 7

If two or more arrows leave from the same activity or event, the latest date by which someone must finish the activity or reach the event is the earliest of the latest dates by which someone must start the activities or reach the events to which these arrows lead.

In this example, the latest start dates for Activity 2 and Activity 5 are the beginning of week 7 and the beginning of week 6, respectively. Therefore, the latest date by which someone must finish Activity 1 is the end of week 5. The rest is straightforward: Someone must start Activity 1 by the beginning of week 1, at the latest.

The latest dates by which each activity must start and finish in the project are summarized in Table 6-2.

Sometimes, project managers feel bogged down in all the preceding calculations. To clarify things and make the whole process seem simpler, they can write the earliest and latest start dates and the earliest and latest finish dates at the top of each box, as shown in Figure 6-4.

Finally, project managers can determine the slack time associated with each activity in one of two ways:

1. Subtract the earliest possible start date from the latest allowable start date.
2. Subtract the earliest possible finish date from the latest allowable finish date.

Table 6-3 presents the slack times for each activity in the example. If an activity's slack time is 0, the activity is on a critical path.

Slack time is actually associated with a sequence of activities rather than with an individual activity. Table 6-3 indicates that both Activities 3 and 4, which are on the same path, have slack times of 1 week. However, if Activity 3 is delayed by a week, Activity 4 will have 0 slack time.

Figure 6-4

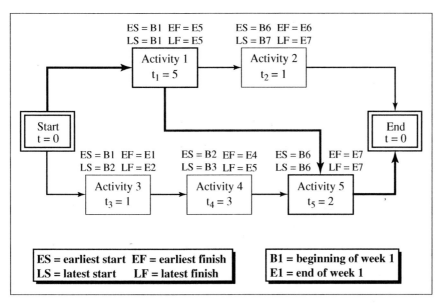

Example network diagram with earliest and latest start and finish dates written in.

6.2.4 Sequencing Activities on Diagrams

There is one final, critical element to creating network diagrams: In order to draw a project's network diagram, the project manager must decide the sequence in which a project's activities will be performed.

A **predecessor** to Activity 4 is an activity that must be completed before someone can work on Activity 4. An activity is an **immediate predecessor** to Activity 4 if someone doesn't have to perform any other activities between finishing it and starting on Activity 4.

Table 6-3: Slack times for Figure 6-3

Activity	Slack Time (Weeks)
1	0
2	1
3	1
4	1
5	0

FOR EXAMPLE

Goldratt's Critical Chain

In his book *Critical Chain* (1997), Eliyahu Goldratt further explores the notion of critical paths, applying his Theory of Constraints to the management of projects large and small. Goldratt recommends project managers think in terms of the critical chain, which, similar to the critical path, is the longest sequence of consecutively dependent tasks. Project managers should give activities on the critical chain the highest priority. For example, in order to ensure that resources are available when needed, project managers should contract all resources along the critical chain. Project managers should keep these resources updated on the status of the project and remind them periodically of when inputs will be needed. (Specifically, Goldratt suggests reminding these resources two weeks before the start of their work, then three days prior to their start, and finally the day before they start.) Because any delay of an activity on the critical chain can cause a delay of the entire project, it is important that a resource immediately switch to the task on the critical chain when needed.

Project managers should determine the immediate predecessors for every activity in a project based on the information available in the project's network diagram. Relationships between activities can be based on several considerations:

▲ **Required relationships:** relationships that must be observed if project work is to be successfully completed

▲ **Legal requirements:** federal, state, and local laws or regulations that require certain activities to be done before others. For example, a pharmaceutical company develops a new drug in the laboratory and has demonstrated its safety and effectiveness in clinical trials. They'd like to start producing and selling the drug immediately, but they can't. Federal law requires that the company first obtain Food and Drug Administration (FDA) approval of the drug before they can start to sell it.

▲ **Procedural requirements:** company policies and procedures that require certain activities to be done before others. For example, Bruce is developing a new piece of software for his organization. He finishes the design and wants to start programming the software. However, his organization follows a systems development methodology that requires an established management oversight committee to formally approve his design before he can start his development work.

▲ **Discretionary relationships:** relationships the project manager or project team chooses to establish between activities.

▲ **Logical relationships:** logical relationships involve choosing to do certain activities before others because it seems to make the most sense. For

Table 6-4: Immediate Predecessors

Work Breakdown Structure Code	Activity Description	Immediate Predecessors
1	(Include activity name)	None
2	(Include activity name)	1
3	(Include activity name)	None
4	(Include activity name)	3
5	(Include activity name)	1, 4

example, Janice is writing a report. Because much of Chapter 3 depends upon what she writes in Chapter 2, she decides to write Chapter 2 first. She could write Chapter 3 first or work on both at the same time, but that increases the chance that she'll have to rewrite some of Chapter 3 after she finishes Chapter 2.

▲ **Managerial choices:** these are arbitrary decisions to work on certain activities before others, perhaps because they are harder, more apt to have problems, and so on.

Project managers can decide upon the immediate predecessors for a project's activities in one of two ways:

1. **Front-to-back.**
   (a) Select the first activity or activities to be performed as soon as the project starts.
   (b) Consider one of these activities and decide which activity or activities will be performed as soon as the chosen activity is finished.
   (c) Continue in this way until all activities in the project have been considered.

2. **Back-to-front.**
   (a) Identify the last activity or activities to be performed before the project is over.
   (b) Choose one of these activities and decide which activities will be performed immediately before starting on the chosen activity.
   (c) Continue on in this manner until all activities in the project have been considered.

In either case, project managers should record a project's immediate predecessors in a simple table, as illustrated in Table 6-4.

Project managers determine precedence based on the nature and requirements of the activities, not on the resources they think will be available. Suppose Activities A and B can be performed at the same time but the project manager decides to assign the same person to do both activities. The project manager shouldn't make A the immediate predecessor for B because the person can work on only one activity at a time. If the project manager shows that the activities can be done at the same time, she can better evaluate the impact on the project were she unexpectedly told that she has another resource that can help out with this work. See Chapter 7 for more on allocating resources to projects.

SELF-CHECK

1. On a network diagram, you can only do which of the following?

   (a) proceed to another activity on the diagram if you finish the activity

   (b) proceed to another activity on the diagram if you complete all the activities entering that activity

   (c) proceed to another activity that is that linked by arrow to the completed activity

   (d) all of the above

2. The earliest finish date determines a project's critical path. True or false?

3. You exceed the slack time on a noncritical path. The noncritical path can now be described as what?

4. On the critical path, the earliest finish date equals which of the following?

   (b) earliest start date

   (c) latest finish date

   (d) latest start date

   (d) none of the above

5. Which of the following is not a required relationship to consider when sequencing activities for a project?

   (a) The U.S. government needs two months to review any research findings.

   (b) At your company, the Vice President of Sales must give final approval to any marketing plans after a marketing director has given the plan preliminary approval.

   (c) Your manager wants to you to do a trial run of any presentation for him prior to the actual presentation.

   (d) New products in your category are not permitted to be sold in your state without approval by a peer-review board.

6.3 Using Network Diagrams to Analyze a Simple Example

This section considers the project of preparing for a picnic to illustrate how project managers can use network diagrams to determine schedule possibilities and ways to meet people's expectations.

Here's the scenario: It's Thursday afternoon and two friends, Anthony and Brenda, decide to visit a local lake for a picnic the following afternoon. In an effort to get the most enjoyment possible from the picnic, Anthony and Brenda decide to plan this outing carefully by drawing and analyzing a network diagram.

Table 6-5 illustrates the seven activities that must be performed to prepare for the picnic and get to the lake.

In addition, Anthony and Brenda agree to observe the following constraints:

▲ Anthony and Brenda will start all activities at Anthony's house on Friday morning at 8:00 a.m.—they can't do anything before that time.

▲ All activities must be completed before the project can be considered done.

▲ Anthony and Brenda can't change who must do the different activities.

▲ The two lakes they're considering are in opposite directions from Anthony's house, so they must decide which lake to visit before beginning their drive.

First, Anthony and Brenda must decide the order in which they'll perform the various activities. (In other words, they need to determine the immediate

Table 6-5: Activities Required for a Picnic at the Lake

Activity ID	Activity Description	Who Will Do the Work	Duration (Minutes)
1	Load car	Anthony and Brenda	5
2	Get money from bank	Anthony	5
3	Make egg sandwiches	Brenda	10
4	Drive to lake	Anthony and Brenda	30
5	Decide which lake	Anthony and Brenda	2
6	Buy gasoline	Anthony	10
7	Boil eggs (for egg sandwiches)	Brenda	10

FOR EXAMPLE

The Effects of Parkinson's Law in Schedule Estimates

Project managers making time estimates need to take care to remember and incorporate Parkinson's Law in their time estimates. Essentially, **Parkinson's Law** states that work will expand to fill the amount of time allotted. For instance, Joe says an activity will take 40 hours to complete, although he knows he could finish the work in 28 hours. While he might be trying to deceive people with a bogus estimate, more likely he's added padding to account for potential mistakes and issues and to ensure that he doesn't have to work at 100 percent on the project. However, his estimate has major impact on the project because his task will likely grow to take the allotted 40 hours.

---

predecessors—see Section 6.2.4—for each activity.) The following dependencies are required:

▲ Brenda must boil the eggs before she can make the egg sandwiches.
▲ Anthony and Brenda must decide which lake to visit before they can start their drive.

How they do the rest of the activities is up to them. They might consider the following approach:

▲ Decide which lake to visit before doing anything else.
▲ As soon as they both decide on the lake, Anthony drives to the bank to get money.
▲ After Anthony gets money from the bank, he gets gasoline.
▲ As soon as they decide on the lake, Brenda starts to boil the eggs.
▲ As soon as the eggs are boiled, Brenda makes the sandwiches.
▲ As soon as Anthony gets back with the gas and Brenda is finished making the egg sandwiches, Anthony loads the car.
▲ They start the drive to the lake, right after the car is loaded.

Table 6-6 illustrates these predecessor relationships.

Based on the information in Table 6-6, a network diagram for the project can be drawn up, using the following steps:

Table 6-6: Predecessor Relationships for Your Picnic

Activity ID	Activity Description	Immediate Predecessors
1	Load car	3, 6
2	Get money from bank	5
3	Make egg sandwiches	7
4	Drive to lake	1
5	Decide which lake	None
6	Buy gasoline	2
7	Boil eggs (for egg sandwiches)	5

1. Start the project with a single event, "Start."
2. Next, find all activities that have no immediate predecessors (see Section 6.2.4). These activities can all be started as soon as the project begins.
   (a) In this case, Activity 5 is the only such activity.
3. Start creating a diagram by representing these relationships, as illustrated in Figure 6-5. Represent this activity in a box, and draw an arrow from the event called "Start" to this box.
4. Find all activities that have Activity 5 as an immediate predecessor.
   (a) Table 6-6 indicates there are two: Activities 2 and 7. Represent them in boxes and draw arrows from Activity 5 to these boxes.
5. Continue on in the same way.
   (a) According to Table 6-6, Activity 6 is the only activity that has Activity 2 as an immediate predecessor. Draw a box representing Activity 6 and draw an arrow from Activity 2 to Activity 6.

Figure 6-5

Starting a network diagram for a picnic project.

Figure 6-6

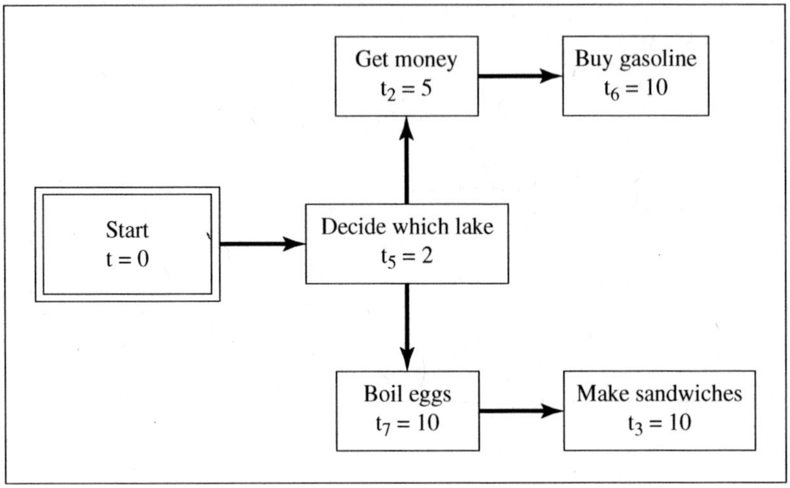

Continuing the picnic-at-the-lake network diagram.

(b) Table 6-6 shows further that Activity 3 is the only activity that has Activity 7 as an immediate predecessor. Draw a box representing Activity 3 and draw an arrow from Activity 7 to Activity 3. The diagram-in-progress is depicted in Figure 6-6.

(c) Activity 1 has both Activities 3 and 6 as immediate predecessors. Draw a box representing Activity 1 and draw arrows from Activity 3 to Activity 1 and from Activity 6 to Activity 1.

(d) The rest is pretty straightforward. Activity 4 is the only activity that has Activity 1 as its immediate predecessor. Therefore, draw a box representing Activity 4 and draw an arrow from Activity 1 to Activity 4.

(e) Finally, draw a box representing the event called "End" and draw an arrow from Activity 4 to the event. Figure 6-7 depicts the project's complete network diagram.

Now for the important questions. First, how long will it take to get to the lake for the picnic?

▲ The upper path, consisting of Activities 2 and 6, takes 15 minutes to complete.

▲ The lower path, consisting of Activities 7 and 3, takes 20 minutes to complete.

▲ Because the critical path is the longest path through the project, the path consisting of Activities 5, 7, 3, 1, and 4 is the critical path. It'll take 57 minutes to get to the lake, following the plan outlined in the network diagram.

Figure 6-7

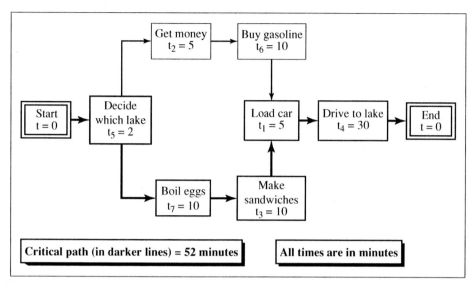

Completed picnic-at-the-lake network diagram in the activity-in-the-box format.

Now a second question: Can Anthony and Brenda delay any activities and still get to the lake in 57 minutes? If so, which ones?

▲ The upper path, consisting of Activities 2 and 6, is a noncritical path.

▲ The network diagram reveals that Activities 5, 7, 3, 1, and 4 are on the critical path and, therefore, can't be delayed at all if they want to get to the lake in 57 minutes.

▲ However, Activities 2 and 6 can be performed at the same time as Activities 7 and 3. Activities 7 and 3 will take 20 minutes to perform, while Activities 2 and 6 will take 15 minutes. Therefore, Activities 2 and 6 have a total slack time of 5 minutes.

Figure 6-8 illustrates the network diagram for this project drawn in the activity-on-the-arrow format (see Section 6.1.2). Event A is equivalent to "Start" and Event I is equivalent to "End" in Figure 6-7.

Note that the events at the start and end of each activity in Figure 6-8 haven't been named yet. Choose names that describe the point reached in the project. Where possible, a useful approach is to consider the activity that just been completed. For example, Event B, the end of Activity 5, "Decide which lake," could be named "Decision reached."

Figure 6-8

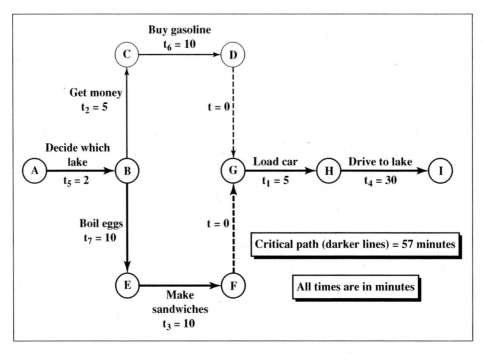

Completed picnic-at-the-lake network diagram in the activity-on-the-arrow format.

A **simple event** is one that represents the completion of a single activity. Defining simple events at the end of all activities in the activity-on-the-arrow format makes it easier to monitor and report on activity performance status. If Activity 1 has multiple predecessors, instead of having arrows representing each of the predecessors coming directly into the event from which Activity 1 leaves, do the following:

▲ Have each of the predecessors end in a simple event.
▲ Tie them all together into a single event using dummy activities.
▲ Have Activity 1 leave from that single event.

This technique is illustrated in Figure 6-8. Activity 6 "Buy gasoline" and Activity 3 "Make sandwiches" must be completed before Anthony and Brenda can load the car. Rather than have both activities lead directly into Event G, Activity 6 ends in Event D, "Gasoline purchased," and Activity 3 ends in Event F, "Sandwiches made." They can then draw dummy activities (see Section 6.1.2) from Events D and F into Event G, which could be defined as "Ready to load car."

SELF-CHECK

1. A good name for Event C, the end of Activity 2 ("Get money"), would be which of the following?

   (a) "money obtained"

   (b) "visit bank"

   (c) "money"

   (d) none of the above

2. Which of the following is one benefit of including a simple event in an activity-on-the-arrow diagram?

   (a) You can establish precedence of two concurrent activities.

   (b) You can more clearly monitor slack time.

   (c) You can have multiple preceding activities all tie together in a single event.

   (d) all of the above

6.4 Developing Project Schedules

Developing actual project schedules requires project managers to find a combination of activities, resources, and activity performance sequences that provides the greatest chance of meeting an audience's expectations with the least risk.

6.4.1 Laying Down Initial Schedules

Project managers can draft a first attempt at a project schedule by using the following steps.

1. Describe the project's objectives, constraints, and assumptions (see Section 2.4).
2. Detail the project's activities (see Section 4.4).
3. Identify immediate predecessors for all activities in the project (see Section 6.2.4).
4. Estimate span times for all activities in the project.
5. Identify any intermediate and final dates that must be met.
6. Identify all activities or events outside the project that affect the performance of project activities.

7. Draw the network diagram.

8. Analyze the project's network diagram to determine the identity and length of all critical paths and the slack times of noncritical paths.

If the completion date a project manager develops this way is acceptable to the project's audiences, the project manager is done with scheduling. However, if the audiences want the project to finish faster than the initial schedule allows, analyses are just beginning.

6.4.2 Avoiding the Pitfall of Backing in to Schedules

Project managers need to beware of developing schedules by backing in. **Backing in** is the process of starting at the end of a project and working back toward the beginning, identifying activities and estimating durations that eventually will add up to the amount of time the project has been given. Backing in might sound like a reasonable strategy, but using this approach substantially decreases the chances that the project will meet its schedule for the following reasons:

▲ Project managers might miss activities because their focus is more on meeting a time constraint than ensuring they identify all required work.

▲ The span time estimates are based on what project managers can allow activities to take, rather than what they actually require.

▲ The order in which project managers propose to perform activities might not be the most effective one.

6.4.3 Meeting an Established Time Constraint

If a project manager must find a way to complete a project in less time than the initial schedule allows, he or she can consider the following options for all critical path activities:

▲ **Recheck the original span time estimates.**
  ▲ Be sure the activity's work is clearly described.
  ▲ If past performance was used as a guide for developing the span times, recheck to be sure all aspects of the current situation are the same as the situation on which the time estimates are based.
  ▲ Ask other experts to review and validate estimates.
  ▲ Ask the people who'll actually be doing the work on these activities to review and validate the estimates.

▲ **Consider using more experienced personnel.** Sometimes more experienced personnel can get work done in less time. Of course, using more experienced people might cost more money. Also, many people within the organization probably want to use the organization's more experienced personnel, so they might not always be available.

▲ **Consider different strategies or technology for performing them.** For example, if the work was going to be done internally, a project manager might consider contracting it out. Or vice versa.

▲ **Consider removing activities from the critical path by doing them in parallel with one or more other critical path activities. Fast tracking** entails performing two or more activities at the same time to reduce the overall time to complete a project. While it's possible to get done faster with this approach, there's also more risk that portions of the work might have to be redone.

As project managers find ways to reduce the lengths of critical paths, they must monitor paths that aren't initially critical to ensure that they haven't become critical. If one or more has become critical, use these same approaches to reduce their length.

6.4.4 Reducing the Required Time

Consider applying some of the time-saving strategies in the preceding sections to the picnic project outlined in Section 6.3. For example, if arriving at the lake in 57 minutes is okay, analysis can be considered done. But suppose Anthony and Brenda want to get to the lake no later than 45 minutes after starting the project on Saturday morning. What changes can be made in the initial plan to save 12 minutes?

Anthony and Brenda might be tempted to change the estimated time for the drive from 30 minutes to 18 minutes, figuring that they'll just drive faster. Unfortunately, this won't work if the drive actually takes 30 minutes. Remember, a plan represents an approach that a project manager believes has a chance to work (though not necessarily one that's guaranteed). If Anthony and Brenda have to drive at speeds in excess of 100 miles per hour over dirt roads to reach the lake in 18 minutes, simply reducing drive time has no chance of working.

Performing Activities at the Same Time

Creative thinking is necessary to devise a plan that both saves time and has a chance of working. Here's a first thought:

▲ Assume there's an Automatic Teller Machine (ATM) next to the gas station. If Anthony pulls into a full-service gas island, he can get money from the ATM while the attendant fills up the car's gas tank.

▲ If Anthony follows this strategy, he can perform Activities 2 and 6 at the same time in a total of 10 minutes, instead of the 15 minutes indicated in Figure 6-7.

At first glance, it might seem that Anthony and Brenda can cut the total time down to 52 minutes by making this change. Look again. These two activities aren't on the critical path, so reducing the time it takes to complete them has no impact on the overall project schedule at all. (Remember, Anthony can't spend the extra five minutes at home helping Brenda make egg sandwiches; for this example, Anthony and Brenda agreed that they cannot swap jobs.) Anthony and Brenda must reduce the length of the critical path if they want to save time.

Here's another idea: Both Anthony and Brenda are in the car for the drive to the lake, but only one of them is driving while the other is just sitting. Anthony can volunteer to do the driving and Brenda can load the fixings for the sandwiches into the car and make the sandwiches during the drive to the lake. This takes a 10-minute activity off the critical path.

The question is, though, how much time does this change actually save? Examine the diagram in Figure 6-7 to figure out the answer as follows:

▲ The upper path comprised of Activities 2 and 6 takes 15 minutes, and the lower path comprised of Activities 7 and 3 takes 20 minutes. Because the lower path is the critical path, removing five minutes from the lower path saves five minutes in the overall time to complete the project. At this point, there are two critical paths, each taking 15 minutes.

▲ Taking an additional five minutes off the lower path doesn't save any more time for the overall project because the upper path still takes 15 minutes. It does, however, add five minutes of slack to the lower path.

Figure 6-9 reflects this change in the picnic project network diagram.

Anthony can now reconsider his earlier idea and get money at the ATM while an attendant fills up the car with gas. This now saves the project five minutes because the upper path is now critical. Finally, Anthony and Brenda can decide which lake to visit and load the car at the same time, which saves them an additional two minutes. The final 45-minute solution is illustrated in Figure 6-10.

Consider a situation where someone has to complete two or more activities before working on two or more new ones. Represent this in a diagram by defining an event that represents the completion of the two or more activities and drawing arrows from these activities to this event. Then draw arrows from this event to the other activities that can then be started.

This is illustrated in Figure 6-10. After completing the activities "Get money," "Buy gasoline," and "Boil eggs," Anthony can perform the activities "Load car" and "Decide which lake." Represent this by drawing arrows from each of the first three activities to a newly defined event, "Ready to load car," and arrows from that event to the activities "Load car" and "Decide which lake."

Figure 6-9

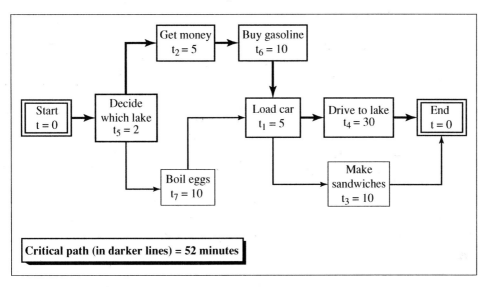

Making sandwiches while driving to the lake.

Figure 6-10

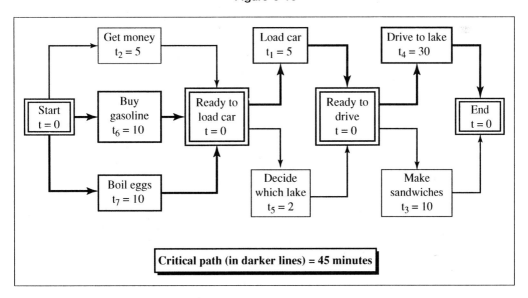

Arriving at the picnic at the lake in 45 minutes.

Considering the Prices to be Paid

Of course, analysis like this takes time. Project managers always pay the following prices in order to perform a group of activities faster:

▲ **Increased planning time:** project managers have to detail precisely all the activities and their interrelationships; they can't afford to make mistakes.

▲ **Increased risks:** the list of assumptions grows, and it becomes more likely that one or more of the assumptions will not come to pass.

For example, in the picnic-at-the-lake example, the following assumptions are necessary to travel to the lake in 45 minutes, rather than 57 minutes:

▲ Anthony can get right into a full-service island at the gas station when he pulls in at 8:00 a.m.

▲ Attendants are available to fill up the tank as soon as Anthony pulls into the full-service island.

▲ The ATM is available and working when Anthony pulls into the full-service island.

▲ Anthony and Brenda can load the car and make a decision together without getting into an argument that takes an hour to resolve.

▲ Brenda can make sandwiches while driving in the car without totally destroying the car's interior in the process.

However, after identifying assumptions, project managers can either take steps to increase the chances that they'll prove to be true or they can develop contingency plans, in case they don't come to pass.

For example, consider the assumption that Anthony can get right into a full-service island upon pulling into the gas station at a little after 8:00 a.m. on Saturday morning. First, Anthony can ask the gas station owner whether this assumption is reasonable. If he doesn't like the risk associated with the owner's answer, Anthony can decide to pay the attendant $100, guaranteeing that the full-service island will be available at 8 a.m. The lesson? Most uncertainty can be reduced for a price. A project manager's job is often determining how much the uncertainty can be reduced and what it will cost.

Devising Entirely New Strategy

The preceding plan makes it possible to reach the lake in 45 minutes. The plan is not guaranteed to work, but at least it has a chance of succeeding.

However, suppose Brenda tells Anthony she really needs to get to the lake in 10 minutes, instead of 45. How can they possibly reach the lake in 10 minutes when the drive to the lake takes 30 minutes by itself?

Without realizing it, many project managers change the criterion for project success from achieving a desired result, where it belongs, to performing a series of activities, where it doesn't. The success of the picnic-at-the-lake project is arriving at the lake for the picnic, not performing a predetermined set of activities. The seven activities as formulated are fine, as long as they allowed Anthony and Brenda to get to the lake within established constraints. But if the activities don't allow them to achieve success as it's now defined, they can consider changing the activities.

For example, Anthony does some checking and finds out that they can rent a helicopter for $500 per day, which can fly them to the lake in 10 minutes. Because Anthony and Brenda originally wanted to spend $10 on the picnic, it's clearly absurd to spend $500 to get to a $10 picnic. Thus, Anthony doesn't even tell Brenda about the possibility of renting the helicopter; he just reaffirms that it's impossible.

But what if Anthony knew the reason why Brenda wanted to get to the lake in 10 minutes? It turns out that if she can get to the lake in 10 minutes, she can make a $10,000 profit on a business deal. Is it worth it to spend $500 to make $10,000? Sure. But Anthony didn't know about the $10,000.

When developing schedule options, it's not the project manager's job to take away someone else's authority to make the schedule decision. Instead, project managers want to identify *all* possible options and their associated costs so that the decision maker can make an informed decision by considering all possibilities.

Subdividing Activities

Another way project managers can reduce the time to complete a sequence of activities is by subdividing one or more of the activities and performing some parts of them at the same time.

FOR EXAMPLE

Law of Diminishing Returns

Often adding more resources to an activity (more people, more money, more equipment) will speed up the activity, but only to a point. The Law of Diminishing Returns controls project yield against the amount of labor available. Suppose Kayla's IT networking project includes an activity that will take 40 hours for two network engineers to complete. If Kayla adds two additional network engineers to the activity, can they finish the work in 20 hours? Maybe. If Kayla adds 40 network engineers to the activity, can the activity get done in a few minutes? Not likely. The reason why is that not all activities are effort-driven; many are of fixed duration, which is a technical way of saying that it doesn't matter how many people jump in and help on an activity—the activity still takes a certain amount of time to complete.

Figure 6-11 illustrates how Brenda's friend can save seven minutes when boiling eggs and making egg sandwiches as she prepares for the picnic.

The following is an example of subdividing:

▲ **Divide the activity of boiling into two parts.**

   ▲ Prepare to boil eggs: Remove the pot from the cupboard, take the eggs out of the refrigerator, put the water and the eggs in the pot, put the pot on the stove, and turn on the heat—estimated span time of three minutes.

   ▲ Boil eggs in water: Allow the eggs to boil in a pot until they're hard—estimated span time of seven minutes.

▲ **Divide the activity of making the egg sandwiches into two parts.**

   ▲ Perform initial steps to make sandwiches: Take the bread, mayonnaise, lettuce, and tomatoes out of the refrigerator; take the wax paper in which you will wrap the sandwiches out of the drawer; put the bread on the wax paper; put the mayonnaise, lettuce, and tomatoes on the bread—estimated span time of seven minutes.

   ▲ Finish making sandwiches: Take the eggs out of the pot, shell them, slice them, put them on the bread, slice the sandwiches, and finish wrapping the sandwiches—estimated span time of three minutes.

Note that the total time for the original activity to boil the eggs is still 10 minutes (three minutes to prepare and seven minutes in the water) and the total time for the original activity to make the sandwiches is still 10 minutes (seven minutes for the initial steps and three minutes to finish up).

Figure 6-11

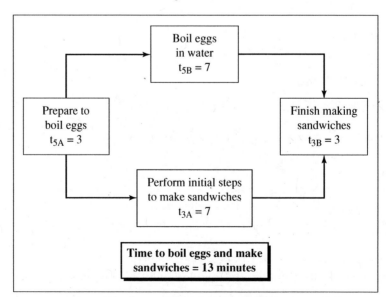

Reducing span time by subdividing an activity.

▲ **Perform the activities as illustrated in Figure 6-11.**

   ▲ Prepare to boil eggs.

   ▲ When preparations are done, simultaneously boil the eggs in water and perform the initial steps to make the sandwiches.

   ▲ When these two activities are both done, finish making the sandwiches.

By describing in more detail exactly how to perform these activities, Brenda can complete the two activities in 13 minutes instead of 20.

S E L F - C H E C K

1. While backing in a schedule has some risks, it's often the only way to determine whether all the required activities can occur in the given time. True or false?

2. While fast tracking offers the possibility of reducing the overall time to complete the project, it also introduces which of the following?

   (a) the risk that work won't get done on time

   (b) the cost of purchasing additional equipment and resources

   (c) the risk the work will have to be redone

   (d) the cost of additional planning time

3. Holly needs to reduce the required time for her project. Which strategies might be useful for her to consider?

   (a) delegating activities or combining activities

   (b) subdividing activities or performing activities at the same time

   (c) eliminating activities or prioritizing activities

   (d) enhancing activities or performing activities chronologically

6.5 Estimating Activity Duration

A **span time estimate** is a project manager's best sense of how long it'll actually take to perform an activity. It's not how long the project manager would like it to take or how long someone tells the project manager it must take, but how long the project manager really thinks it will take.

Estimation is not negotiating or bartering. Unrealistically short span time estimates can actually cause an activity to take longer than necessary because of the following:

▲ Not identifying the reasons why an activity will take a certain amount of time makes it difficult for the project manager to come up with strategies that could reduce the time.

▲ If people believe estimates are totally unrealistic, they won't even try to meet them.

6.5.1 Describing What Happens

When estimating an activity's span time, project managers should first describe the following components of the activity:

▲ **Work performed by people:** physical and mental activities people perform. Examples include writing a report, assembling a piece of equipment, and thinking of ideas for an ad campaign.

▲ **Work performed by nonhuman resources:** testing software on a computer and printing a report on a high-speed copy machine are examples.

▲ **Processes:** physical or chemical reactions. Concrete curing, paint drying, and chemical reactions in a laboratory are examples.

▲ **Time delays:** passage of time where no resource is performing any work. Time delays are typically due to the availability of resources. The need to reserve a conference room two weeks prior to holding a meeting is an example.

FOR EXAMPLE

Accurate Estimates versus Negotiation

Noel's boss asks him to complete a project in six months. He explores all possible alternative strategies and determines he can't complete the project in less than 12 months. After some back and forth negotiating, they agree that Noel will complete the project in nine months. If both Noel and his boss were being honest initially, he's just guaranteed the project's failure. Noel agreed to complete the project three months before it's possible. His boss agreed to accept the final product three months after he needs it. On the other hand, if both Noel and his boss weren't both being honest initially, they each learned something about the other. Noel learned that, whenever his boss gives him an end date, he should add 50 percent to it (nine months is 50 percent more than six months). Noel's boss learned that when Noel states the earliest date he can finish an assignment, he should subtract 25 percent from it (nine months is 25 percent less than 12 months). Unfortunately, at the worst, they've reached an agreement that defines a performance target that isn't acceptable to either party. At the best, they learned not to trust the information either provides.

6.5.2 Considering Resource Characteristics

The following types of resources might be needed to support project work:

▲ Personnel
▲ Equipment
▲ Facilities
▲ Raw materials
▲ Information
▲ Funds

For each resource needed to support or perform the activity's work, project managers need to determine the following:

▲ **Capacity:** productivity per unit time period.
▲ **Availability:** when on the calendar a resource will be available.

6.5.3 Finding Sources of Supporting Informaticn

After project managers clearly describe all aspects of an activity, they should consult the following information sources to develop span time estimates:

▲ Historical records of how long it took to perform similar activities in the past.
▲ People who've performed similar activities in the past.
▲ People who'll be working on the activities.
▲ Experts familiar with the type of activity, even if they haven't performed work exactly like it before.

6.5.4 Improving Activity Span Time Estimates

Project managers can practice the following to improve the accuracy of their span time estimates:

▲ Define activities clearly: Minimize the use of technical jargon and describe associated work processes fully.
▲ Subdivide activities until the estimate shows that the lowest-level activities will take two weeks or less.
▲ Define activity start and end points clearly.
▲ Minimize the use of fudge factors.

A **fudge factor** is an amount of time project managers add to an estimate of span time, "just to be safe." An example is adding an additional 50 percent to all initial time estimates. Fudge factors compromise planning for several reasons:

▲ Work tends to expand to fill the time allotted for it: If Bill can finish an activity in two weeks but uses a 50 percent fudge factor and indicates a span time of three weeks, the likelihood he'll finish in less than three weeks is almost zero.

▲ People use fudge factors as an excuse to avoid studying activities in sufficient depth to enable developing viable performance strategies.

▲ Others lose faith in the accuracy and feasibility of fudge-factor plans because they know the project manager is playing with numbers instead of thinking things through in detail.

No matter how hard project managers try, it's sometimes difficult to estimate how long an activity will take. Activities that haven't been done before, activities that will be performed far in the future, and activities with a history of unpredictability are examples. In these cases, do the following:

▲ Make the best estimate possible by following the approaches and guidelines outlined in Sections 6.5.1 through 6.5.3.

▲ Monitor closely as the project unfolds to identify anything that might cause the initial estimate to change.

▲ Reflect any changes in the project schedule as soon as possible.

SELF-CHECK

1. The length of an activity is impacted by which of the following?

    (a) the actual work performed by people

    (b) the time required for natural or chemical processes

    (c) the actual work performed by nonhuman resources

    (d) all of the above

2. Making accurate time estimates requires project managers to consider which of the following?

    (a) the availability and cost of each resource

    (b) the cost and necessity of each resource

    (c) the capacity and duration of each resource

    (d) none of the above

3. One way project manager Zoe can avoid including a fudge factor in her team's activity duration estimates is to review other project managers' data to see how long specific activities took on past projects. True or false?

6.6 Displaying Project Schedules

Network diagrams present information project managers will consider in developing schedules. This section covers several common ways to display project schedules.

6.6.1 Choosing Presentation Formats

Project managers can consider the following formats to present project schedules, after they select (or are assigned) actual dates for their projects:

▲ **Key-events report:** a table that lists events and the dates on which you plan to reach them.

▲ **Activities report:** a table that lists activities and the dates on which you plan to start and end them.

▲ **Gantt chart:** a graph illustrating on a time line when each activity will start, be performed, and end. See Section 6.6.2 for more on Gantt charts.

▲ **Combined milestone chart and Gantt chart:** a graph illustrating on a time line when activities will start, be performed, and end, as well as when selected events will be achieved.

The 45-minute schedule for the picnic-at-the-lake project detailed in Section 6.4 is presented in a key-events report, an activities report, and a Gantt chart in Figures 6-12, 6-13, and 6-14, respectively.

Consider the following when choosing the format to display a project schedule:

▲ A key-events report and an activities report are more effective for indicating specific dates.

▲ The Gantt chart provides a clearer picture of the relative lengths of activities and their overlap.

6.6.2 Displaying Project Schedules as Gantt Charts

Henry Gantt, a major figure in the scientific management movement of the early twentieth century, developed the Gantt chart around 1917. As noted in Section 6.6.1, a Gantt chart is a type of bar chart that displays project activities as bars measured against a horizontal time scale. It is the most popular way of exhibiting sets of related activities in the form of schedules.

The Gantt chart in Figure 6-15 shows the expected times for a project that extends over two and a half months. Although Gantt charts are easy to draw (most project-management software packages generate them in seconds),

Figure 6-12

Key Event	Person Responsible	Date Due (minutes after start)	Comments
Ready to load car	You and your friend	10	Critical path
Ready to drive	You and your friend	15	Critical path
End: arrived at lake	You and your friend	45	Critical path

> Note: This list includes several key events you have defined for your project. If you want to, you can choose to define and represent an event at the end of each activity.

The picnic-at-the-lake project as a key-events report.

understanding them can be more difficult, particularly when several tasks begin at the same time and have the same duration.

If one task is on the critical path and the others are not, it could be difficult to find the critical path on a Gantt chart. For instance, if activities have

Figure 6-13

Activity	Person Responsible	Start Date (minutes after start)	End Date (minutes after start)	Comment
1. Load car	You and your friend	10	15	Critical path
2. Get money	You	0	5	
3. Make egg sandwiches	Your friend	15	25	
4. Decide which lake	You and your friend	10	12	
5. Drive to lake	You and your friend	15	45	Critical path
6. Buy gasoline	You	0	10	Critical path
7. Boil eggs	Your friend	0	10	Critical path

The picnic-at-the-lake project as an activities report.

Figure 6-14

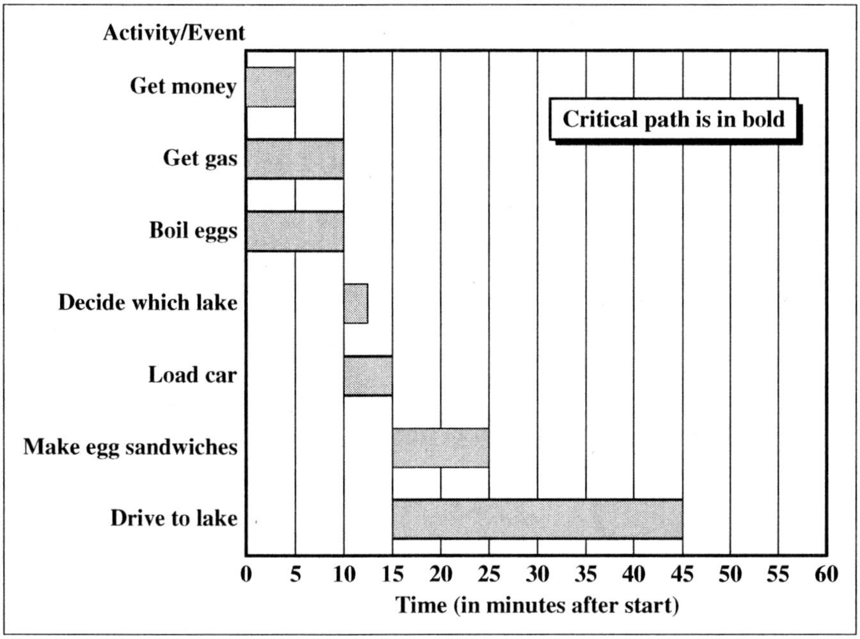

The picnic-at-the-lake project as a Gantt chart.

the same duration, it would not have been possible to tell which was predecessor to various tasks, just by looking at the chart. Most project-management software packages use arrows, bolded bar outlines, colored boxes, or some other visible means of marking the critical path on a Gantt chart, as in Figure 6-15.

Even with the aid of software, technical dependencies are harder to see on Gantt charts than on network diagrams. On network diagrams, technical dependencies are the focus of the model. As Figure 6-16 shows, information can easily be added to the chart to show such things as earliest start and finish dates and slack.

Gantt charts can be modified to show time and/or resource requirements. Figure 6-16 includes only time estimates to save space, but resource requirements could easily be added as well. Figure 6-16 shows a project that is partially complete (the project was started on April 21 and its progress is being measured as of June 6). Note that Activity 4 starts days late. It was scheduled to start at midday on May 17 but did not begin until May 19. Activity 4 finishes a week late. If nothing is done to correct the matter, and if nothing happens to increase the lateness, the project will finish about a week late.

Figure 6-15

WBS	Task	Estimate dur	Start	Finish	Late start	Late finish
1	a	10.67 days	01/14	01/28	01/14	01/28
2	b	12.17 days	01/28	02/15	01/28	02/15
3	c	12.33 days	02/15	03/03	02/18	03/07
4	d	6 days	02/15	02/23	02/15	02/23
5	e	14.33 days	02/15	03/07	02/17	03/09
6	f	9.33 days	03/03	03/16	03/07	03/20
7	g	10.33 days	02/23	03/09	02/23	03/09
8	h	7.83 days	03/09	03/20	03/09	03/20

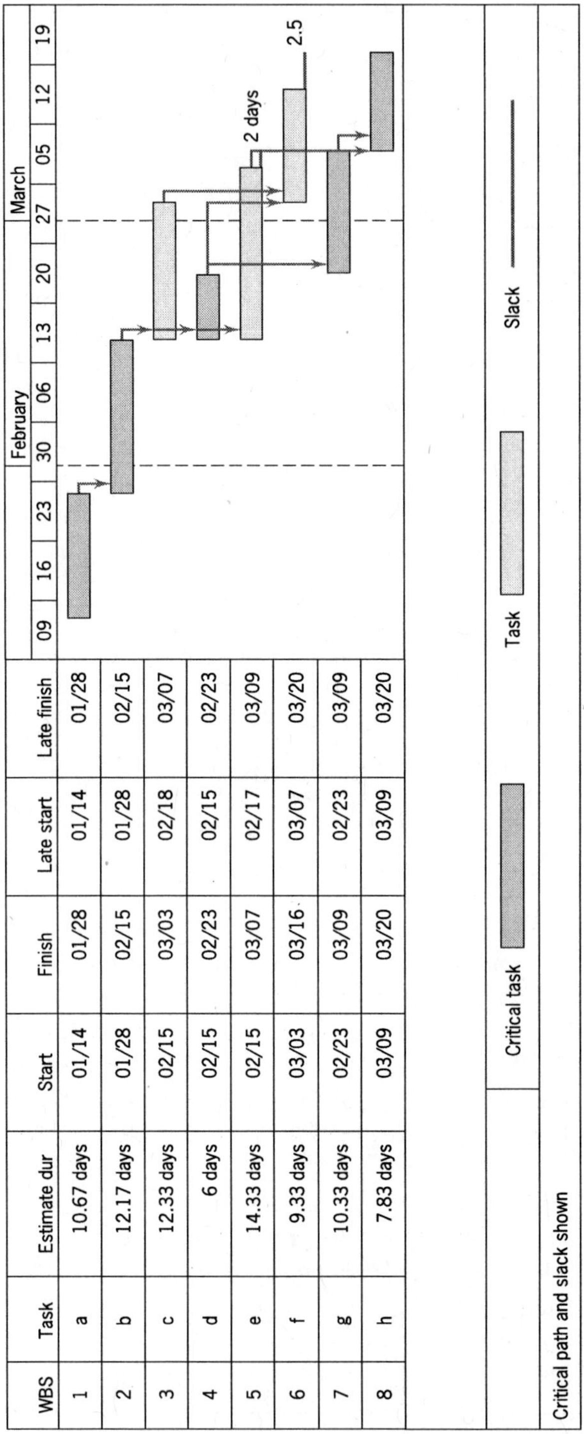

Critical path and slack shown

Critical task   Task   Slack

A Gantt chart with critical path, slack times, and other critical information.

Figure 6-16

Day Care Investigation

ID	Task Name	Actual Dur.	Baseline Dur.	Start	Finish	Baseline Start	Baseline Finish
1	Develop employee survey to assess need and desire	2 wks	2 wks	04/21	05/04	04/21	05/04
2	Send survey out to staff	0 days	0 days	05/04	05/04	05/04	05/04
3	Develop ad campaign to get staff to participate in survey	1.67 wks	1.67 wks	05/05	05/17	05/05	05/17
4	Surveys returned	2.33 wks	2.33 wks	05/19	06/05	05/17	06/01
5	Analyze results	0.2 wks	1.27 wks	06/09	06/19	06/02	06/12
6	Meet with YMCA to assess and verify proposal for service	2 wks	3 wks	04/21	05/04	04/21	05/11
7	Identify other centers in the area (usage, fee structure, etc.)	5.83 wks	5.83 wks	04/21	06/01	04/21	06/01
8	Cost/Benefit analysis	0 days	1.5 days	06/19	06/28	06/12	06/21
9	Go/No Go decision	0 wks	1.07 wks	06/28	07/06	06/21	06/29
10	If Go, develop implementation action plan	0 wks	3 wks	07/06	07/27	06/29	07/20

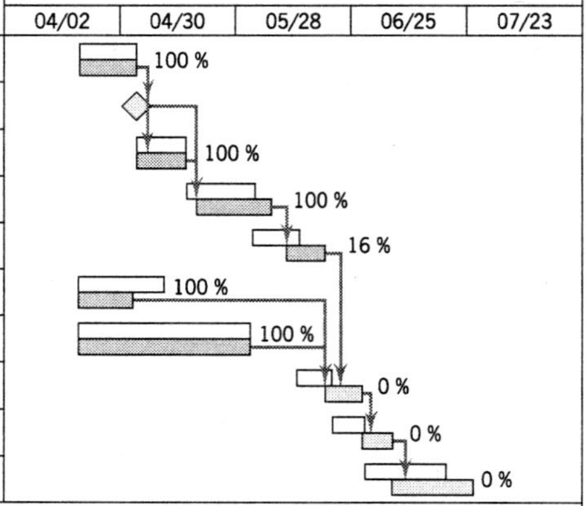

Timeline: 04/02 | 04/30 | 05/28 | 06/25 | 07/23

Gantt progress percentages: Task 1 — 100 %; Task 3 — 100 %; Task 4 — 100 %; Task 5 — 16 %; Task 6 — 100 %; Task 7 — 100 %; Task 8 — 0 %; Task 9 — 0 %; Task 10 — 0 %

Legend:
- Task
- Progress
- Baseline task
- Completed milestone
- Milestone

Project start date: 04/21
Project current date: 10/04

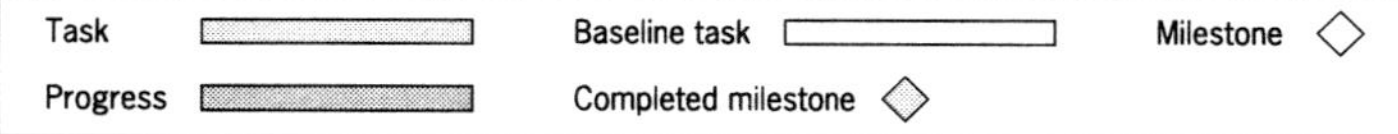

Progress shown

A Gantt chart that incorporates resource requirements.

Project-management software makes it easy to use Gantt charts or network diagrams to view critical tasks and paths of projects. Project managers can even experiment with adjustments to the project—play "what if" with the project schedule, immediately observing results of the experiments on the screen. At times the project manager might question an estimate of task duration submitted by a member of the project team. The project manager can easily enter alternate time estimates and instantly see the impact on project duration.

The major advantages of Gantt charts are that they are easy to read and they can be updated easily. Anyone interested in the project can read a Gantt chart with little or no training—and with little or no technical knowledge of the project. These advantages are also the chart's weakness: Gantt charts are deceptive in their apparent simplicity. An intimate knowledge of the project's technology is required to interpret beyond a simplistic level what appears on the chart or to alter the project's course.

Project managers must be cautious about publicly displaying Gantt charts that include activity slack, or latest start and finish times. Some members of the project team might be tempted to procrastinate and tackle the work based on latest start and finish times. If done, this makes a critical path out of a noncritical path and becomes an immediate source of headaches for the project manager, who, among other things, loses the ability to reschedule the resources used by tasks that once had slack. Senior managers have even been known to view activity slack as an invitation to shorten an entire project's due date.

At base, Gantt charts are excellent devices to aid in monitoring projects and communicate information to others. Gantt charts, however, are not adequate replacements for network diagrams. They are complementary scheduling and

FOR EXAMPLE

Customizing Gantt Charts

Project managers can add a great deal of information to Gantt charts without making them difficult to read. A construction firm adds special symbols to activities that are slowed or stopped because of stormy weather. They use other symbols to indicate late deliveries from vendors, the failure of local government to issue building permits promptly, and other reasons why tasks might be delayed. Milestone symbols are added to the charts—with different shading or color to differentiate between "scheduled" and "completed" milestones. Project-management software is limited only by the project manager's imagination in what can be shown on a network diagram, Gantt chart, or project plan.

Figure 6-17

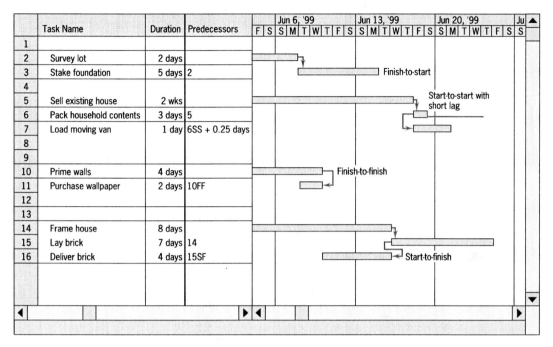

Precedence diagramming conventions.

control devices. PERT/CPM networks are often used as complements to Gantt charts.

6.6.3 Precedence Diagramming

In recent years several extensions of network diagrams and charts have been developed. At times these extensions are quite sophisticated and specific to a company or industry. (Elihu Goldratt's Critical Chain is a scheduling method using network diagrams that combines project scheduling with resource allocation. See Section 7.5.)

One problem with PERT/CPM networks is that it is difficult to show lead/lag relationships between activities. If someone were building a sidewalk from the back door to a patio, for example, there would be a task named "Pour concrete," and the next task would have to be "Wait for concrete to harden." "Remove concrete forms" or "Score concrete joints" might follow this. The "wait" activity requires no resource except time (perhaps one day if the weather is pleasant). Rather than create an activity called "Wait," precedence diagramming allows the planner to build in an equivalent lag. The

"Remove forms" task cannot start until one day after the "Pour concrete" task has ended.

With precedence diagramming, activities may be linked in the following ways:

▲ **Finish-to-start linkage.** This is the most common linkage and applies to situations when the preceding task must be completed before the successive task can be started. Figure 6-17 shows precedence diagramming for the construction of a new house; here the lot must be surveyed before the foundation can be staked out.

▲ **Start-to-start linkage.** The start-to-start linkage is commonly used to start two or more activities at the same time. Thus, this linkage is used in cases where the start of one activity depends on the start of its preceding activity. In Figure 6-17, this is exemplified in the situation where the start of the moving van loading activity can begin shortly after the start of the pack household contents activity. Clearly, loading the moving van can be started before the final box of household contents is packed.

▲ **Finish-to-finish linkage.** The finish-to-finish linkage is used in situations where it is desirable for two or more activities to finish at the same time. In Figure 6-17, this is illustrated by the activities priming the walls and purchasing the wallpaper. Since it is desirable to hang the wallpaper right

FOR EXAMPLE

Graphical Evaluation and Review Technique (GERT)

GERT combines structures such as flowgraphs, probabilistic networks, and decision trees. The result is a complex but powerful scheduling method. The major difference between traditional PERT/CPM and GERT is that GERT can allow a wide range of statistical distributions for estimates of activity duration. GERT also allows loops back to earlier events, as in the case of rework on manufactured parts, whereas loops are not allowed in PERT/CPM. Further, GERT allows probabilistic branching from a node. This is applicable, for example, when quality control rejects some percent of output, accepts some percent for rework, and unconditionally accepts the rest. GERT is a valuable addition when it is required, but there is often a simpler and cheaper, if somewhat less effective, way to deal with such problems.

after the walls are primed, it is appropriate to complete priming the walls and purchasing the wallpaper at the same time.

▲ **Start-to-finish linkage.** The start-to-finish linkage is used to ensure that a particular activity finishes based on the preceding activity's start time. This type of relationship is common in the delivery of materials. Referring to Figure 6-17, the delivery of bricks is scheduled to coincide with the start of the brick-laying task. By using the start-to-finish linkage, the brick-laying operation drives the brick-delivery task. Had a finish-to-start linkage been used from deliver brick to lay brick, then the delivery of the bricks would have controlled the brick-laying task and not vice versa.

SELF-CHECK

1. Which of the following statements is not true of Gantt charts?

   (a) Although Gantt charts are easy to read, it can be difficult to determine the critical path without additional information.

   (b) Technical dependencies require additional notation to become apparent on Gantt charts.

   (c) Gantt charts highlight specific start and finish dates effectively.

   (d) Gantt charts can be modified extensively to suit a project's specific needs.

2. On a construction project, the delivery of shingles should drive the schedule, rather than the beginning of the activity "shingling a roof." In terms of precedence diagramming, what type of linkage does this scenario indicate?

SUMMARY

Project scheduling is a critical responsibility for most project managers. Graphical tools, including charts and diagrams, enable project managers to summarize and organize the various events, activities, and span times of project tasks. Several formats of network diagrams exist for project schedules, but all formats allow project team members to determine the critical path of a project, as well as its critical dates, including the earliest finish date. Project managers can utilize several activity arranging strategies to meet established time constraints. Key-events and activity reports, Gantt charts, and precedence diagramming are all ways to visually represent and share a project's schedule with others.

KEY TERMS

Activities report	A table that lists activities and the dates on which you plan to start and end them.
Activity	Work required to move from one event to the next in a project.
Activity-in-the-box	A type of network diagram; also referred to as activity-in-the-node or precedence diagramming.
Activity-on-the-arrow	A type of network diagram; also referred to as the classical or traditional approach.
Availability	When on the calendar a resource will be available.
Backing in	The schedule process of starting the end of a project and working back toward the beginning, identifying activities as you go and estimating durations that eventually will add up to the amount of time the project has been given.
Backward pass	Finish-to-start analysis by a project manager to determine critical paths and earliest start and finish dates.
Capacity	Productivity per unit time period.
Critical path	A sequence of activities in a project that takes the longest time to complete.
Critical path method (CPM) charts	A network diagram that uses deterministic, certain estimates but includes both time and cost estimates to allow time/cost trade-offs to be used.
Dependency diagram	Another term for a network diagram in either activity-on-the-arrow or activity-in-the-box format.
Discretionary relationships	Relationships the project manager or project team chooses to establish between activities.
Dummy activity	An activity with 0 span time that's used to represent a required dependency between events.
Duration	How long each individual activity will take in a project.
Earliest finish date	The earliest date that someone can possibly finish an activity.
Earliest start date	The earliest date that someone can possibly start an activity.
Event	A significant occurrence in the life of the project; also called a milestone or a deliverable. Events

take no time and consume no resources; they occur instantaneously.

Fast tracking	Schedule process in which you perform two or more activities at the same time to reduce the overall time to complete a project.
Forward pass	Start-to-finish analysis by a project manager at the beginning of the project to see how fast the activities can be completed.
Fudge factor	An amount of time project managers add to an estimate of span time just to be safe.
Gantt chart	A graph illustrating on a time line when each activity will start, be performed, and end.
Graphical evaluation and review technique (GERT)	A network diagram technique that combines structures such as flowgraphs, probabilistic networks, and decision trees, creating a complex schedule.
Immediate predecessor	Term given to an activity that, upon completion, can allow someone to start on the following activity.
Key-events report	A table that lists events and the dates on which you plan to reach them.
Latest finish date	The latest date someone can finish an activity and still finish the project in the shortest possible time.
Latest start date	The latest date that someone can start an activity and still finish the project in the shortest possible time.
Legal requirements	Federal, state, and local laws or regulations that require certain project activities to be done before others.
Logical relationships	Choosing to do certain activities before others because it seems to make the most sense.
Managerial choices	Arbitrary decisions to work on certain activities before others.
Network diagram	A flowchart that illustrates the order in which activities need to be performed in a project.
Noncritical path	A sequence of activities that can be delayed by some amount while still allowing the overall project to finish in the shortest possible time.
Parkinson's Law	States that work will expand to fill the amount of time allotted.

Precedence diagram   Another term for a network diagram in the activity-in-the-box format.

Predecessor   An activity that must be completed before someone can work on another activity.

Procedural requirements   Company policies and procedures that require certain project activities to be done before others.

Program evaluation and review technique (PERT) chart   A network diagram in the activity-on-the-arrow format that allows project managers to assign optimistic, pessimistic, and most likely estimates for an activity's span time.

Required relationships   Relationships between project activities that must be observed if project work is to be successfully completed.

Sequence   The order in which the activities will be performed in a project.

Simple event   One that represents the completion of a single activity.

Slack time   The maximum amount of time that someone can delay an activity and still finish the project in the shortest possible time.

Span time   The actual calendar time required to complete an activity; also called duration or elapsed time.

Span time estimate   A project manager's best sense of how long it'll actually take to perform an activity.

ASSESS YOUR UNDERSTANDING

Go to www.wiley.com/college/portny to assess your knowledge of the basics of project schedules.

Measure your learning by comparing pre-test and post-test results.

Summary Questions

1. When creating a project schedule, what is the most appropriate sequence for the following activities?
    (a) detailing project activities, identifying immediate predecessors for each activity, and drawing the network diagram
    (b) identifying immediate predecessors for each activity, describing project objectives, and drawing the network diagram
    (c) detailing project activities, drawing the network diagram, and identifying final dates that must be met
    (d) any of the above

2. Although project scheduling work often yields a shorter overall amount of time required to do project activities, the process always increases planning time and risks. True or false?

3. The legal requirement that the government must approve a drug before your company can sell in drugstores would most likely be considered what type of linkage in a precedence diagram?

4. In back-to-front analysis of a schedule, you identify the last activity or activities to be performed before the project is over, but in backing out a schedule, you do which of the following?
    (a) estimate the schedule based on data
    (b) determine the schedule based on an assumed final end date
    (c) add up slack time to determine the critical path
    (d) none of the above

Applying This Chapter

1. Suggest an example of an activity and an event for each of the following projects: developing a new line of herbal hair care products, opening a gift shop at a popular tourist attraction, launching a new corporate Web site.

2. You're managing your first project—the creation of a company brochure for trade shows, announcing a new line of pet toys. Your team is small

Figure 6-18

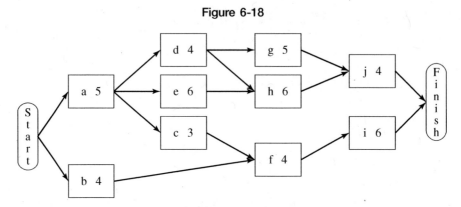

An example of a network diagram.

(one designer, one writer), as is your organization. What form of network diagram should you choose for your project and why?

3. Evaluate the above network diagram (Figure 6-18). In each box, the letter on the left is the name of the activity and the number on the right indicates the activity duration in days. Use the forward and backward pass to figure out earliest start time, earliest finish time, latest start time, and latest finish time at each activity.

   What is the critical path in the diagramin in Figure 6-18? What is the duration of the critical path? Check your work against Figure 6-19.

4. You're planning to manage the remodeling of your kitchen. You'll be organizing the schedules and efforts of a plumber, an electrician, tile installer, and a carpenter. (In the remodeling/home improvement industry, this is known as general contracting a project.) What is an example of a legal requirement, procedural requirement, logical relationship, and managerial choice that would affect the sequencing of activities in the project?

5. The PR and Marketing team that you lead at a small college just found out that you need to launch new-student admissions packages one month earlier than originally forecasted in order to attract top students. Your carefully scheduled plan that was supposed to take four months must now take three months. What are four things you and your team can consider doing in order to meet the newly established time constraint?

6. Jill's project schedule for a construction project simply states that it will take her team 29 days total to build a house—3 days to pour a building's foundation, 5 days to construct the building's frame, 4 days to side the

Figure 6-19

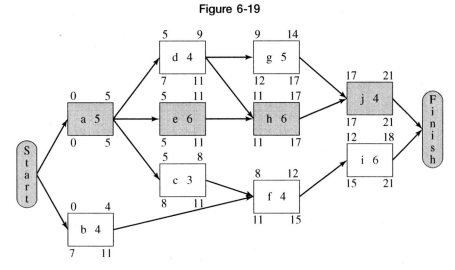

An example of a network diagram with critical path and all critical times identified.

structure, 2 days to roof the structure, and 15 days to complete interior finish work. Jill's boss has called Jill's estimates into question. What are some ways Jill can defend her time estimates?

7. Evaluate the following Gantt chart for a project (Figure 6-20).

Figure 6-20

WBS	Task	Duration	Predecessors	Month 1	Month 2	Month 3
1	a	10.67 days		a		
2	b	12.17 days	1	b		
3	c	12.33 days	2		c	
4	d	6 days	2		d	
5	e	14.33 days	2		e	
6	f	9.33 days	3, 4		f	
7	g	10.33 days	4		g	
8	h	7.83 days	5, 7			h

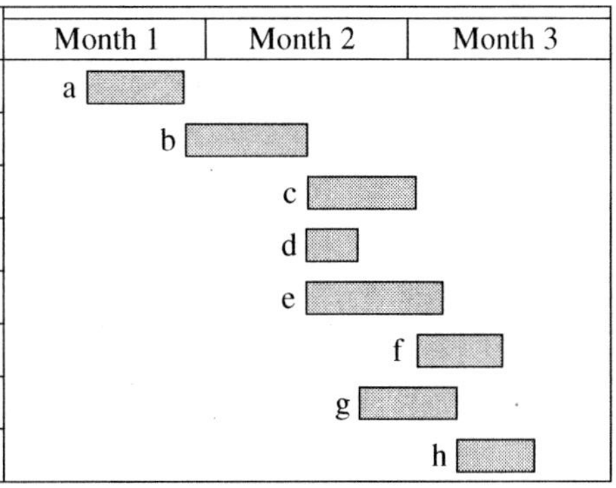

An example of a Gantt chart.

Why does task f overlap task e, but not tasks c and d? If c and d had been the same duration, would you still be able to determine the critical path for the project just by information in the Gantt chart?

8. For your first project—managing the rollout for a revised employee handbook for your human resources department—you want to develop and present a project schedule for project team members, your boss, and people in the company just generally interested in the project. In the interest of time, you can only select one schedule format. Which format would you pick?

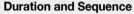

Duration and Sequence

Consider an everyday project with numerous steps or parts—cleaning the basement or decorating your home for the holidays. Brainstorm a list of activities that are required to complete this project. Review the list and estimate how long each specific task will take. You might need to further divide the tasks into subtasks if your events take several hours or days. Finally, put your tasks into chronological order. Be sure to identify tasks that can be done at any time in the project.

Diagramming a Project

Working with the same everyday project, create a graphic diagram using either an activity-on-the-arrow or activity-in-the box format. Work through the diagrams using the forward pass (Section 6.2.2) and the backward pass (Section 6.2.3) to determine the earliest start time, earliest finish time, latest start time, and latest finish time. What is the critical path of your project? Highlight the critical path on the diagram with special shading or a color.

Reducing Required Time

Working again with your everyday project, analyze your schedule of activities and see whether you can reduce the required time for the project by using any of the strategies in Section 6.4.4. What if you had a helper to work on the project with you? What activities could be performed at the same time? Which of your activities are just too big or too long? These activities are good candidates to subdivide into smaller tasks. Draw up a new diagram that illustrates your revised plan.

Thinking Outside the Box

Some of the time-reducing solutions discussed in the picnic-in-the-park scenario in Sections 6.3 and 6.4 might seem outlandish, but these are all examples of creative problem-solving solutions. Come up with a time-wasting problem in your life (a long daily commute to school/work, spending 20 minutes looking for things every morning in your disorganized house, or never having time to eat a home-cooked meal). Convert your problem into a time-saving project (devise a way to shorten my commute, generate a plan to reduce my morning prep time by 20 minutes, and so on). Brainstorm some out-of-the-box solutions that can save you time and write down a list of ideas. Don't worry about money or resources—just come up with things you can do differently to solve your time-related problem.

Reducing Required Time

Return one last time to your everyday project and prepare a report or chart to detail your project schedule and share your plans with others. Which format did you choose to illustrate your schedule? Why?

CASE STUDY: Springville

The city of Springville is building a new fire station. The city is expanding and is in need of a second fire station closer to the newer areas of the city to ensure shorter response times. The project manager and the project team have been selected for the project. The team is very interested in selecting the scheduling technique that will be used to follow the project through to completion.

The project manager, city manager, and chief of the fire department have set the following criteria for the process of selecting the scheduling technique:

easy to use, shows durations of tasks, shows milestones, can see the flow of work, can see the sequence of events, can depict which tasks can be undertaken at the same time, and can tell how far tasks are from completion. The city manager favors the Gantt chart, the chief likes PERT, and the project manager prefers CPM.

Question

1. If you were the project manager, which method would you use, and why?

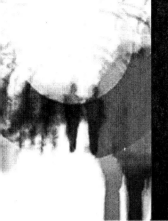

7

ESTIMATING AND ALLOCATING RESOURCES
Assigning People and Resources to Projects

Starting Point

Go to www.wiley.com/college/portny to assess your knowledge of the basics of project resources.
Determine where you need to concentrate your effort.

What You'll Learn in This Chapter

▲ Strategies for defining and allocating resources
▲ Skills Rosters
▲ Work effort estimates
▲ Factors that affect work estimates
▲ Ways to support work effort estimates
▲ Resource loading and overloading
▲ Resource leveling

After Studying This Chapter, You'll Be Able To

▲ Create Skills Rosters for a project's human resources
▲ Estimate work effort' required for a project
▲ Evaluate and support work estimates
▲ Analyze and evaluate work commitments
▲ Plan resource assignments, including scarce resources, for an entire project

INTRODUCTION

All projects compete for limited human and physical resources; project managers work to effectively utilize available resources to ensure project success. For human resources, tools like Skills Rosters help project managers determine the specific abilities that are available for their projects. To appropriately assign a human resource, project managers must accurately estimate and support work efforts. Resources are frequently assigned to multiple projects, so project managers must take care to load—but not overload—resources. Overloaded resources require leveling, and truly scarce resources require project managers to do creative problem solving and to sometimes make difficult choices between tasks or projects.

7.1 Establishing Who, How Much, and When

We live in a world of limited resources and not enough time. There will always be more work to do than time and resources will allow. The project manager's job is to decide which tasks to pursue and to do everything possible to succeed in the selected activities.

Physical and human resources are granted to and used by projects in order to meet performance objectives. The amount of resources that can be allocated, of course, depends on the timing of the allocation as well as on the total supply of resources available for allocation. **Resource allocation** is how project managers allocate specific, limited resources to specific activities (or projects) when there are competing demands for the same limited resources.

Projects compete for the same resources in two different ways.

1. A resource is limited but is not consumed when used—for example, the services of a specific technical specialist. The problem here is which project gets to use the resource first and which must wait.
2. A resource is limited and is consumed when used—for example, a specific chemical reagent. In this case, the second project might have to wait until more of the reagent can be purchased and delivered. Time is another project resource that is limited and consumed.

In both cases, the project that must wait might suffer a schedule delay that makes it late.

Just as projects compete for resources, different activities of the same project might compete. For example, two or more concurrent activities might require the same personnel, equipment, or even work space. One activity will be given priority, and the others must wait.

Therefore, identifying and planning for the resources needed to perform is a critical task for project managers. Carefully considering and allocating resources enables project managers to do the following:

▲ Explain to those who'll have to support the project what they'll have to contribute.

▲ Ensure that the resources are available when they're needed.

▲ Develop more accurate and realistic schedules.

▲ Monitor resource expenditures to identify and address possible overruns.

Some organizations have systems and procedures that detail and track every resource used on every project performed, while others don't formally plan or track project resources at all. This information is invaluable to help project managers ensure project success, whether or not an organization requires project managers to consider it.

7.1.1 Planning Personnel Needs

A project's success rests on the project manager's ability to enlist the help of the right people to perform necessary work. Given the preference in today's workplace to structure projects around teams, project managers and functional managers must pay considerable attention to the human resources they select and develop within their projects.

Successful personnel planning within a project team requires a project manager and functional manager to do the following:

▲ Identify the skills and knowledge needed to perform a project's activities.

▲ Specify the people who'll work on each activity.

▲ Determine how much effort each resource will have to invest to complete his or her assignment.

▲ Determine when over the life of a task the resources will invest their time, if they work on the task less than full time.

7.1.2 Describing People's Skills and Knowledge

A **Skills Roster,** or Skills Inventory, illustrated in Figure 7-1, is a graphic format project managers can use to display the skills and knowledge of people who might work on a project.

The left-hand column in the Skills Roster identifies skill and knowledge areas, and the top row lists people's names. The intersection of the rows and columns shows each person's particular combination of skills, knowledge, and interests.

Figure 7-1 uses a popular method of symbols and descriptions to describe various skills and knowledge levels; these descriptions are explained below:

▲ **Primary capability:** the person is able to assume a lead role in an assignment requiring this skill or knowledge.

Figure 7-1

	Bill	Mary	Sue	Ed
Technical writing			●△	△
Legal research	△	△		●
Graphic design	●△		○	●△
Questionnaire design	○			△

● – Primary skill or knowledge   ○ – Secondary skill or knowledge   △ – Interest

Displaying people's skills, knowledge, and interests in a Skills Roster.

▲ **Secondary capability:** the person has some training or experience in the skill or knowledge area but should work under another person's guidance.

▲ **Interest:** the person would like to work on assignments involving this skill or knowledge.

For example, the Skills Roster in Figure 7-1 indicates that Sue is qualified to lead technical writing assignments and that she'd like to work on this type of assignment. Ed is qualified to lead legal research tasks, but he would prefer not to work on them. He would like to work on questionnaire design activities, but he has no skills or knowledge in this area.

At first glance, a project manager might figure that Ed would never be assigned to work on a questionnaire design activity because he has no relevant skills or knowledge. However, if the project manager were trying to find more people who can develop questionnaires, Ed would be a prime candidate. Because he wants to work on these types of assignments, he most likely would be willing to put in extra effort to learn the necessary capabilities.

In addition to serving as a guideline to help project managers request the appropriate people to work on project activities, a Skills Roster can reveal gaps and weaknesses in staff skills and knowledge that can guide the following:

▲ **Training:** the organization can develop or make available training to address the deficiencies.

▲ **Career development:** individuals develop skills and knowledge that are in short supply to increase their opportunities to assume greater responsibilities in the organization.

> ## FOR EXAMPLE
>
> ### Customized Skills Rosters
>
> Project managers can incorporate a variety of numerical and/or alphanumeric codes to describe a person's skill, knowledge, or interest level within Skills Rosters and Inventories. Many technology-based organizations list relative levels of skill, knowledge, or interest using a 1-to-5 numerical scale, where a rating of 1 indicates minimal skill or knowledge and a 5 indicates outstanding skill or knowledge. Some organizations use online tools to generate Skills Rosters for participants. For instance, St. John's Episcopal Church in Plymouth, Michigan, organizes all of its projects and programs via an online Skills Inventory. Visit www.stjohnsplymouth.org/aboutus/skills/skills.html to review St. John's online inventory.

▲ **Recruiting:** recruiters can look for candidates who have skills and knowledge in short supply in the organization in addition to the primary skills and knowledge needed for the primary jobs.

Because of their potential use in different areas of an organization, group managers and supervisors, training departments, and employee recruiting departments might already have Skills Rosters prepared for some or all staff. If a project manager decides to create a new Skills Roster, proceed as follows:

1. Develop a complete list of the skill and knowledge areas that might be required for anticipated project assignments.
2. Develop a list of all people who will be included in the Skills Roster.
3. Have the people on the list rate their proficiency in each skill and knowledge area, as well as their interest in working on assignments in each area.
4. Have each person's direct supervisor rate the person's skill, knowledge, and interest.
5. Compare the ratings made by the person and his or her supervisor and reconcile any differences.
6. Prepare a final version of the Skills Roster.

Comparing a team member's ratings of his or her skills, knowledge, and interests with those made by his or her supervisor can help project managers identify situations that could lead to future performance problems. The following are typical situations, associated problems, and possible solutions when ratings discrepancies arise:

▲ **A team member rates his or her skills and knowledge in an area higher than a supervisor rates them.**

   ▲ **Potential situation:** the team member might feel that the supervisor is unfairly choosing not to give him or her more challenging assignments with greater responsibility.

   ▲ **Possible solution:** the supervisor can give the team member a more challenging assignment and monitor performance closely. If all goes well, the supervisor's opinion of the team member's capabilities will improve. If the team member has problems with the assignment, he or she can work out a plan with the supervisor to develop any skills or knowledge that might be lacking.

▲ **A team member rates his or her skills and knowledge in an area lower than a supervisor rates them.**

   ▲ **Potential situation:** the team member checks with his or her supervisor about the smallest issues and decisions because the team member doesn't feel qualified to deal with them.

   ▲ **Possible solution:** the supervisor can explain to the team member initially why he or she feels the team member is qualified to handle an assignment. The supervisor can point out times when the team member handles issues correctly and why.

▲ **A team member has interests in areas that his or her boss doesn't know about.**

   ▲ **Potential situation:** the team member misses out on opportunities to work on assignments.

   ▲ **Possible solution:** the team member can frequently talk with his or her supervisor about interests and what makes him or her a good candidate for the assignments.

▲ **A boss thinks a team member has interests in areas where he or she doesn't.**

   ▲ **Potential situation:** a team member is repeatedly given assignments in which he or she has little or no interest, becoming bored and disinterested in work. Productivity suffers.

   ▲ **Possible solution:** the team member can discuss interests with his or her boss and ask whether he or she can do some work in a special-interest area, in addition to handling the normal assignments where the team member's special skills might be needed.

In a project environment, team members often work with people they don't know well or haven't spent much time with before. Project managers who make a special effort to learn about team members' skills, knowledge, and interests can make more appropriate use of special talents—and also improve morale and productivity.

SELF-CHECK

1. Multiple projects compete for resources; which of the following can be said of tasks and activities within a single project?

    (a) They do not compete for resources.

    (b) They can compete for resources.

    (c) They are interdependent of resources.

    (d) none of the above

2. Which of the following is an appropriate notation on a Skills Roster?

    (a) a numerical score from 1 to 5, with 1 being "minimal" and 5 being "outstanding"

    (b) primary capability, secondary capability, or interest

    (c) experience leading or being part of a team effort

    (d) all of the above

3. In addition to helping project managers assign resources, what other task can Skills Rosters be effectively used on?

7.2 Estimating Needed Commitment

Planning out personnel needs begins with identifying who the project needs and how much effort he or she will have to invest. Project managers can display this information in a **Human Resources Matrix**, which displays individual resources that will work on an activity and the work effort that each resource will invest in the activity. A Human Resources Matrix is illustrated in Figure 7-2.

Figure 7-2

Activity		Personnel (Person-hours)		
Work Breakdown Structure Code	Description	J. Jones	F. Smith	Analyst
2.1.1	Design questionnaire	32	0	24
2.1.2	Pilot questionnaire	0	40	60
2.2.1	Prepare instructions	40	24	10

Displaying personnel needs in a Human Resources Matrix.

Work effort or **person effort** is the actual time a person spends working on an activity. Work effort is expressed in units of person-hours, person-days, person-weeks, and so forth. Work effort is related to, but different from, span time or duration (see Section 6.1). Work effort is a measure of resource use; span time is a measure of time passage.

Consider the work effort required to complete "design questionnaire" in the Human Resources Matrix in Figure 7-2. According to the Matrix, this activity requires J. Jones for 32 person-hours and an unnamed analyst for 24 person-hours. This information alone, however, doesn't tell the span time of the activity. If both people can work on the activity at the same time, if they're both assigned 100 percent to the project to do their respective work, and if there are no other aspects of the task that will take additional time, the activity could be finished in four days. However, if either person is available for less than 100 percent time, if one or both has to work overtime, or if one person has to finish his or her work before the other can start, the span time would be different.

7.2.1 Describing Needed Personnel

A **lowest-level activity** is an activity in a Work Breakdown Structure that's not divided into further detail (see Section 4.4). Project managers need to identify all personnel that will have to work on each lowest-level activity in a project. Project managers can identify personnel by listing the following:

▲ **Name:** the name of the person who'll do the work.
▲ **Position description:** the position description or title of the person who'll eventually do the work.
▲ **Skills and knowledge:** the specific skills and knowledge that anyone assigned to the task will need to possess.

Early in the planning process, project managers should specify needed skills and knowledge, if possible, such as, "a person who can develop work process flowcharts" or, "a person who can use Microsoft PowerPoint." If project managers can identify the exact skills and knowledge that a person must have to do a particular task, they increase the chances that the proper person will be assigned.

On occasion, a position description or title such as "operations specialist" is used to identify needed resources. Doing this assumes that the position description or title accurately describes the skills and knowledge that anyone with the position description or title would have. Unfortunately, titles are often vague and position descriptions are frequently out of date. Therefore, this is a risky way for project managers to try to get the right person for the job.

Very often, project managers identify people they want on projects by name. The reason is simple: If a project manager has worked with someone before and this person did a good job, the project manager will want to work with that person again. Unfortunately, while this is great for the ego of the person whom everyone requests, it often reduces the chances that the project managers will get the best person for the project. People who develop reputations for excellence are often requested for more time than they have available. If the project manager doesn't specify the particular skills and knowledge needed, the manager who has to find a substitute for the person requested by name doesn't know what skills and knowledge the substitute should have.

7.2.2 Estimating Required Work Effort

For all lowest-level activities in a project, project managers should estimate the work effort that each person will need to invest to complete his or her assigned portion of the work. Project managers can develop work effort estimates as follows:

1. Describe in detail all work to be done when performing the activity. Include work directly and indirectly related to the activity. Examples of work directly related to an activity include writing a report, meeting with clients, performing a laboratory test, and designing a new logo. Examples of work indirectly related to an activity include receiving skills or knowledge training required to perform activity-related work and preparing periodic activity progress reports.

2. Consider history. Past history doesn't guarantee future performance. It does, however, provide a guideline for what's possible. Determine whether the activity or parts of the activity have been performed before. If they have, review written records to determine the work effort spent on the activity in the past. If written records weren't kept, consult with people who've done the activity before to determine their estimates of the work effort they spent. When using prior history to support the estimates of required work effort, be sure the work was performed as follows:

   (a) By people with qualifications and experience similar to those of the people anticipated for the project.

   (b) Using facilities, equipment, and technology that's similar to that planned for the project.

   (c) In a time frame similar to the one anticipated for the project activity.

3. Have the person who'll do the work participate in estimating the required work effort.

   (a) Having people participate in developing work effort estimates for the activities they'll perform provides two benefits: Their understanding of everything that goes into performing the activity is improved and their commitment to do the work for the estimated level of work effort is increased.

(b) When project managers know who'll be working on the activity at the time they're developing initial plans, they can have those people participate then. If people join the project team at the start of the project or during the project, project managers can have them review and comment on the plans that have been developed.

4. Consult with experts familiar with this type of activity, even if they haven't performed work exactly like it before. Experience and knowledge from all sources improve the accuracy of estimates.

7.2.3 Factoring in Productivity, Efficiency, and Availability

Having a team member assigned to a project full time doesn't mean that he or she will perform project work at peak productivity 40 hours per week for 52 weeks per year. Other personal and organizational activities will reduce the actual number of hours the team member is available to do project work.

Project managers need to consider each of the following factors when determining the number of hours that people will need to be assigned to a project to complete their work:

▲ **Productivity:** the results produced per unit of time that project team members spend working on the activity. Productivity is affected by the following:

  ▲ **Knowledge and skills:** the raw talent and capability a person has to perform a particular task.

  ▲ **Prior experience with similar tasks:** familiarity with the work required and the typical problems encountered for a particular task.

  ▲ **Sense of urgency:** the drive a member has to generate the desired results within established time frames. Urgency influences the focus and concentration on an activity.

  ▲ **Ability to switch back and forth among several tasks:** a team member's comfort moving to a second task as soon as a roadblock is encountered to avoid stewing about frustrations and, ultimately, wasting time.

  ▲ **The quality and setup of the physical environment:** proximity and arrangement of furniture and support equipment, as well as the availability and condition of equipment and resources that are used to perform the work.

▲ **Efficiency:** the proportion of time on the job that the project team spends on project work, as opposed to organizational tasks that aren't related to specific projects. Efficiency is affected by the following:

  ▲ **The time spent on non-project-specific professional activities:** these activities include attending general organization meetings, handling incidental requests on other issues, and reading technical journals and periodicals about project-related topics.

FOR EXAMPLE

Nonproject Activities in Today's Workplace

A recent study determined that, on average, a typical employee spends about four hours of an eight-hour work day working on preplanned project activities and work assignments. The interviewers in this study spoke with people in more than 100 organizations, with a wide range of job responsibilities. This means that the typical employee in this study was working at an efficiency of about 50 percent! Numerous organizations have done similar studies of their own operations and shared their findings. These organizations all found workers' efficiency to be about 75 percent. (Of course, organization-sponsored studies are biased. Employees want their organization to think they are spending most of their time working on planned project assignments, and the organization wants to believe this is the case.) Still, the organization-sponsored studies found that people spent about 25 percent of each day doing something other than preplanned, project-related activities.

▲ **The time spent on personal activities:** personal activities could include getting a drink of water, going to the restroom, organizing work areas, conducting personal business on the job, and talking about non-work-related topics with coworkers.

▲ **Availability:** the amount of time that project team members are at the job, as opposed to on leave. Availability is determined by organization policy. Project managers and functional managers determine potential availability by specifying the number of days each year staff can use for annual leave, sick leave, holiday leave, administrative leave, personal leave, mental health leave, and so on.

7.2.4 Supporting Estimates with Historical Data and Experience

How project managers reflect efficiency in their personnel planning depends on whether and how they track their team's work effort. Project managers don't have to factor in a separate measure for efficiency if they base estimates on historical data from a time-recording system and either of the following situations is true:

▲ The organization's time sheet has one or more categories to record time spent on non-project-specific work and team members report accurately by activity their actual time expenditures. If this is the case, the historical information represents the actual number of hours people recorded to do the activity in the past. These numbers reflect the actual time spent working on the activity in the past, and project managers can comfortably use these numbers to predict the number of hours needed to do the activity this time.

▲ The organization's time sheet has no category for recording time on non-project-specific work, but team members report accurately (by activity) the time spent on work-related activities, and they apportion in a consistent manner their project-specific work among the available project activities. The historical information again reflects the actual number of hours that people recorded to do the activity in the past. In this instance, the recorded hours will include some portion of time spent on non-project-specific work, as well as on the activity itself. However, if time-recording practices haven't changed, this information will suggest the number of hours recorded (for both project and nonspecific work) to do the activity this time.

On the other hand, project managers do have to consider factoring in a separate measure of efficiency if they base estimates on the personal opinions of people with experience performing similar activities or of the people who will be doing this activity.

FOR EXAMPLE

Efficiency versus Availability

Norma was convinced that she took efficiency into account when she estimated needed levels of resources for her projects. Her organization had performed an internal study and determined that each year, the typical employee spent about 25 percent of his or her time on sick leave, holiday leave, vacation leave, personal leave, and administrative leave. Therefore, she defined "full-time availability" to be 120 person hours each month, which was 75 percent of the approximately 160 person-hours an employee was potentially available to work during a month. (She derived her estimate of 160 person-hours potentially available by multiplying eight hours per day by five days a week by four weeks per month—admittedly, this is an approximation.) Unfortunately, the 120 person-hours Norma derived was the *total time* an employee was available each month, and people don't work at 100 percent efficiency for all the hours they are available. For a more accurate estimate, Norma should consider that a person has about 90 productive hours each month that can be spent on project work, considering that a person worked at 75 percent efficiency (160 hours ×.75 availability factor ×.75 efficiency factor = 90 productive hours).

If a project manager plans to be doing an activity him- or herself, the project manager can estimate the required work effort assuming 100 percent efficiency. But the project manager must take this estimate and modify it to reflect efficiency as follows:

▲ If team members will be recording time accurately on a time sheet that has one or more categories to record time spent on non-project-specific work, don't include an efficiency factor.

▲ If team members will be recording time accurately on a time sheet that has no categories to record time spent on non-project-specific work, include an efficiency factor.

For example, suppose Carl estimates he needs 30 person-hours to perform a task (if he could be 100 percent efficient), and his organization's time sheets have no categories for recording non-project-specific work. If Carl considers he'll actually be closer to 75 percent efficient, he should plan to charge 40 person-hours to his project to complete the task because 75 percent of 40 person-hours is 30 person-hours (the amount he said he really needed).

Additionally, the following time sheet practices cause the data collected to be inaccurate:

▲ Employees aren't allowed to record overtime spent.

▲ Employees fill out time sheets for the entire period several days before the period is over.

▲ Employees just copy the work effort estimates from the project plan onto their time sheet each period.

If any of these situations exist within an organization (and they're surprisingly common), project managers should not use data from time sheets to support their work effort estimates for projects.

Failing to consider efficiency when estimating and reviewing work effort invested can lead project managers to draw incorrect conclusions about people's performance.

For example, Elliot's boss assigns him a project on Monday morning and tells Elliot that it'll take about 40 person-hours to finish the project, but the boss really needs it completed by Friday, close of business. Elliot works intensely all week and finishes the task by Friday close of business. In the process, Elliot records on his time sheet that he spent 55 person-hours on the project. If Elliot's boss doesn't realize that his initial estimate of 40 person-hours was based upon Elliot working at 100 percent efficiency, he is likely to think Elliot took 15 hours longer to do the assignment than it should have. On the other hand, if Elliot's boss recognizes that 55 person-hours on the job translates into about 40 person-hours of work on specific project tasks, his boss will appreciate that Elliot

Table 7-1: Person-Hours Available for Project Work

	100% efficiency, 100% availability	75% efficiency, 100% availability	75% efficiency, 75% availability
1 person-day	8	6	4.5
1 person-week	40	30	22.5
1 person-month	173	130	97.5
1 person-year	2080	1560	1170

invested extra effort to meet the aggressive deadline. Although Elliot's performance is written on his time sheet in black and white, Elliot's boss can easily overlook the impact of efficiency and makes Elliot appear less capable—or the boss can correctly consider Elliot's efforts and decide Elliot is intensely dedicated.

The longer a person's involvement in an assignment, the more important it will be to consider efficiency and availability. Suppose Monique decides she has to spend one hour on an assignment. She can figure her availability is 100 percent and her efficiency is 100 percent, so she charges one hour to the project. If Monique needs to spend six hours on an assignment, she can still probably figure that her availability will be 100 percent, but she must consider that her efficiency will be 75 percent (or whatever planning figure she decides to use). Therefore, Monique should charge one workday (eight work hours) to the project to ensure she can spend the six hours working on the task.

Additionally, if a team member is scheduled to devote one month or more to an assignment, the project manager needs to recognize that the team member will likely take some leave days during that time. Even though project budgets don't typically include cost estimates for vacation or sick leave, project managers must recognize that being available for one person-month means that someone is really only available for about 97 hours of productive work, assuming 75 percent efficiency and 75 percent availability (2080 hours total in a year ÷ 12 months in a year ×.75 ×.75).

Table 7-1 outlines some basic guidelines for estimating personnel requirements for long-term projects. Of course, project managers need to develop their own planning figures based on their organization's efficiency and availability data and expectations.

7.2.5 Improving Work Effort Estimates

Project managers can practice the following to improve the accuracy of their work effort estimates:

▲ Define activities clearly. Minimize the use of technical jargon and describe associated work processes.

▲ Focus on the time required to *complete* an activity, not how long an activity takes; the difference can be subtle but profound.

▲ Subdivide activities until the estimate for lowest-level activities will take two person-weeks or less.

▲ Minimize the use of fudge factors (see Section 6.5.4).

▲ Look to tracking signals to help determine whether work effort estimates are accurate (see Section 5.3).

▲ Update work effort estimates when project personnel or task assignments change.

SELF-CHECK

1. George is estimating work effort for an upcoming project. He knows specifically what each project task entitles and how long these tasks have taken on past projects. What else can he do to accurately estimate work effort for the project?

2. Which of the following is not a concern related to using time sheets to support work effort estimates?

   (a) Time sheets are often filled out a week at time, leading to inaccuracies.

   (b) Time sheets are private employment information; you must have human resources approval to use this information.

   (c) Time sheets often don't allow employees to list non-project-specific work.

   (d) Time sheets often require employees to list only 40 hours of work, regardless of overtime commitments.

3. Accurate work effort estimates need to consider which of the following factors?

   (a) productivity, scarcity, and cost

   (b) training, speed, and skill set

   (c) efficiency, commitment, and redundancy

   (d) productivity, efficiency, and availability

7.3 Juggling Multiple Commitments

For the project manager, determining whether a team member is overcommitted is straightforward if the person works on only one activity at a time. However, if the team member is supposed to work on several activities that partially overlap during a particular time period, someone must decide when during each activity the team member will put in his or her hours to see whether multitasking is making him or her overcommitted. While team members have opinions about whether they are overcommitted, project managers often must get involved in these situations, as the following sections outline.

7.3.1 Preparing an Initial Commitment Analysis

Project managers can begin analyzing a resource's time by developing the following:

▲ A Human Resources Matrix (see Section 7.2).
▲ A Person Loading Graph or Person Loading Chart for each individual in the Human Resource Matrix.

For example, suppose Nicole plans to work on Tasks 1, 2, and 3 of a project. Table 7-2 depicts the person-hours estimated to be needed on each task (consider that efficiency has already been reflected in these estimates).

Figure 7-3 illustrates when Tasks 1, 2, and 3 are supposed to be performed. According to the Gantt chart, Nicole will perform Task 1 in weeks 1, 2, and 3; Task 2 in weeks 2 and 3; and Task 3 in weeks 3, 4, and 5.

The Gantt chart at the top of Figure 7-3 indicates that Task 1 will take three weeks, Task 2 will take two weeks, and Task 3 will take three weeks. Table 7-2 suggests Nicole will spend 60 person-hours (46 percent of the available time), 40 person-hours (31 percent of the available time), and 30 person-hours (23 percent of the available time) on Tasks 1, 2, and 3, respectively. Therefore, Nicole would have no problem completing her work on each one if she didn't have to work on them at the same time.

Table 7-2: Proposed Work Effort on Three Activities

Activity	Level of Effort (Person-Hours)
Task 1	60
Task 2	40
Task 3	30

Figure 7-3

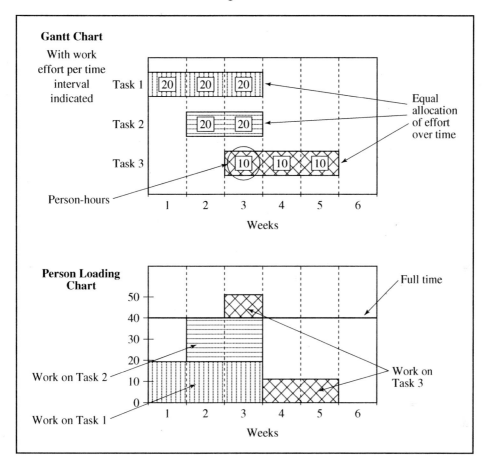

Planning to work on several activities over the same time period.

But Nicole's initial plan has her working on both Tasks 1 and 2 in week 2 and on all three tasks in week 3. Nicole has to make the following decision to see whether she can do her work on all three activities as they are currently scheduled: When over the life of each activity will Nicole put in her required time?

As a starting point, assume Nicole will spend her time evenly over the life of each task. That means she'll work 20 hours a week on Task 1 during weeks 1, 2, and 3; 20 hours a week on Task 2 during weeks 2 and 3; and 10 hours a week on Task 3 during weeks 3, 4, and 5. This initial allocation of work effort by task is illustrated on the Gantt chart at the top of Figure 7-3.

Nicole can determine the total effort she'll have to devote to the project each week by adding up the hours she'll spend on each task each week:

▲ In week 1, Nicole will work 20 person-hours on Task 1 for a total commitment to the project of 20 person-hours.

▲ In week 2, Nicole will work 20 person-hours on Task 1 and 20 person-hours on Task 2, for a total commitment to the project of 40 person-hours.

▲ In week 3, Nicole will work 20 person-hours on Task 1, 20 on Task 2 and 10 on Task 3, for a total commitment to the project of 50 person-hours.

▲ In weeks 4 and 5, Nicole will work 10 person-hours on Task 3, for a total commitment to the project of 10 person-hours each week.

These commitments are displayed in the "Person Loading Chart" of Figure 7-3.

A quick review reveals that this plan has Nicole working 10 hours of overtime in week 3. If everyone is comfortable with her putting in this overtime, this plan will work. If someone is not comfortable (Nicole herself, Nicole's functional manager, the project manager), an alternative strategy to reduce Nicole's week 3 commitments must be resolved.

7.3.2 Resolving Potential Resource Overloads

Project managers can consider the following strategies to avoid overcommitting resources:

▲ Allocate time unevenly over the duration of one or more activities.

▲ Take advantage of any slack time (Section 6.2.3) that might exist in assigned activities.

▲ Assign some of the work to someone else on the project.

▲ Have new people assigned to a project.

▲ Hire an external vendor or contractor to perform some of the work that was originally going to be done internally.

Suppose Nicole (working with her project manager) chooses to spend her hours unevenly over the duration of Task 1, as depicted in Table 7-3. Figure 7-4 illustrates how this choice removes the need for overtime in the third week.

Figure 7-5 illustrates how Nicole can remove the need for overtime in the third week by taking advantage of slack time that might be associated with

Table 7-3: Proposed Work Effort Each Week on Task 1

Time Period	Level of Effort (Person-Hours)
Week 1	30
Week 2	20
Week 3	10

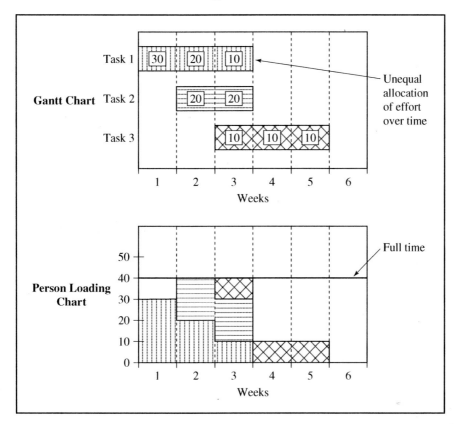

Eliminating a resource overload by changing the allocation of hours over the task life.

Task 3. If Task 3 had at least one week of slack time associated with it, Nicole can reduce her total work on the project in the third week to 40 person-hours by delaying both the start and end of Task 3 by one week.

Detailed allocations of work effort can be displayed by time period in a tabular format, as well as in a graphical format known as a **Person Loading Chart.** Figure 7-6 presents the information from the Person Loading Graph of Figure 7-3 in an individual Person Loading Chart. Most project-management software, including Microsoft Project, can quickly create Person Loading Charts based on supplied data.

Project managers often prepare a separate individual Person Loading Chart for each person on their project teams to plan when team members will work on various tasks. Figure 7-7 details the total hours that each person will spend on a project as a summary Person Loading Chart. The entries in the rows for weeks 1 through 5 are the same as those in the "Total" row of the individual Person Loading Chart in Figure 7-6.

Figure 7-5

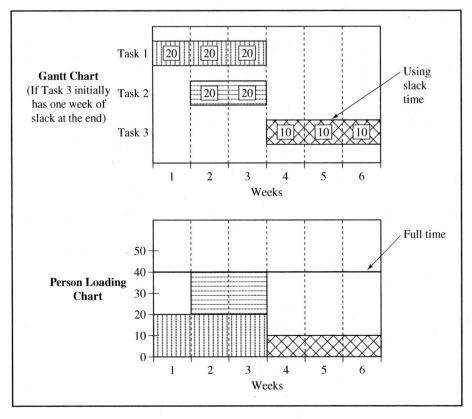

Eliminating a resource overload by changing the start and end dates of a task with slack time.

Figure 7-6

	Person-hours					
	Week 1	Week 2	Week 3	Week 4	Week 5	Total
Task 1	20	20	20			60
Task 2		20	20			40
Task 3			10	10	10	30
Total	20	40	50	10	10	130

Example of an individual Person Loading Chart.

Figure 7-7

	Person-hours					
	Week 1	Week 2	Week 3	Week 4	Week 5	Total
You	20	40	50	10	10	130
Bill	10	20	10	30	10	80
Mary	15	10	20	10	30	85
Total	45	70	80	50	50	295

A summary Person Loading Chart.

Summary Person Loading Charts help project managers do the following:

▲ Identify who might be available to share some of the load for people who are overcommitted.
▲ Determine the personnel budget for a project by multiplying the number of hours people will work on the project by their weighted labor rates. (See Section 5.2.3 for more on estimating indirect costs.)

7.3.3 Coordinating Assignments across Multiple Projects

Figure 7-8 illustrates a Person Loading Chart that presents the total hours committed for each person within a group during selected months. This chart is derived from the summary Person Loading Charts for the projects on which they'll be working.

FOR EXAMPLE

Making Better Resource Assignments with Business Engine

In response to employee complaints to project managers and upper management that project team members were consistently being overassigned to multiple projects, Business Engine Software Corporation of San Francisco (www.businessengine.com) developed a software system in which team members commit only to what they can handle. Functional managers coordinate with project managers to verify the estimated time and skills necessary for a project, but ultimately, the team member agrees (or disagrees) to sign on to a project. The software system proved so successful within Business Engine (it reports that in some cases product delivery cycles can be shortened by 25 percent to 50 percent) that the company now develops and services similar systems at dozens of top companies, including NASA, Boeing, Prudential, and Corning, as well as hundreds of small and mid-size organizations worldwide.

Figure 7-8

	Project A						Project B						Project C			
	Jan	Feb	Mar	Apr			Jan	Feb	Mar	Apr			Jan	Feb	Mar	Apr
You	50	(40)	20	30		You	30	(20)	40	35		You	50	(40)	30	45
John	20	80	50	40		Ann	40	30	35	25		Fran	40	30	35	30
Sue	30	20	30	35		Ted	70	50	35	40		Pat	20	60	50	30

	All Projects			
	Jan	Feb	Mar	Apr
You	130	(100)	90	110
Mike	90	120	70	86
⋮				

Using Person Loading Charts to plan a resource's time on several projects.

For example, as Figure 7-8 indicates, Nicole will be working on three projects in January, February, and March. In February, she's already committed to work on Projects A, B, and C for 40, 20, and 40 person-hours, respectively. If someone wants Nicole to devote 80 person-hours to Project D in February, there are several options. If Nicole assumes that she has a total of 160 person-hours available in the month, then she can devote 60 person-hours to Project D with no problem. However, she doesn't have the other 20 hours available that Project D would require. To meet the demands of Project D, Nicole can consider the following:

▲ Finding someone to assume 20 person-hours of work on Projects A, B, and C in February.

▲ Shifting her work on one or more of these projects to January or March.

▲ Working overtime.

Section 7.4 covers resource loading and leveling in detail.

7.3.4 Working in Everything Else

Project managers can plan for all other resources, such as equipment and facilities, the same way they plan for personnel. To do so, project managers need to develop the following:

▲ A resources matrix (for all non-personnel resources).

▲ Individual usage charts (for each non-personnel resource).

▲ A summary usage chart (for all non-personnel resources).

Figure 7-9 illustrates a resources matrix for non-personnel resources. The following information is displayed for every lowest-level activity in the project:

▲ The non-personnel resources needed to perform the activity: Examples include computers, copiers, and use of a test laboratory.

▲ The total amount of each resource that is needed.

Figure 7-9 suggests the project needs 40 hours of computer time and 32 hours of the test laboratory to design a device.

Project managers can estimate the amount of each resource needed by examining the nature of the task and the capacity of the resource. For example, a project manager could use the following steps to determine the amount of copier time needed to reproduce a report:

1. Estimate the number of report copies needed.
2. Estimate the number of pages per copy.
3. Specify the copier capacity in pages per minute.
4. Multiply the first two numbers together and then divide by the third number to determine the amount of copier time needed to reproduce reports.

Figure 7-10 illustrates a computer usage chart that displays when over the life of a task the project manager plans to use the computer required to support it. The chart suggests that the project needs 10 hours of computer time for Task 1 in weeks 1, 2, and 3, respectively.

Figure 7-9

Activity		Amount of Resource Required (Hours)		
Work Breakdown Structure Code	Description	Computer	Copier	Test Lab
1.2.1	Design layout	32	0	0
2.1.4	Prepare report	0	40	0
3.3.1	Design device	40	0	32

A resources matrix.

Figure 7-10

	Computer Time Required (Hours)					
	Week 1	Week 2	Week 3	Week 4	Week 5	Total
Task 1	10	10	10			30
Task 2		20	20			40
Task 3			10	20	30	60
Total	10	30	40	20	30	130

A computer usage chart.

SELF-CHECK

1. A Person Loading Chart can show which of the following?
   (a) the overlapping responsibilities of two or more resources
   (b) the availability of a specific resource compared to another resource
   (c) the cost of a specific resource on a per-hour basis
   (d) the overtime requirements of a resource to meet an expectation
2. Loading charts are appropriate for assessing the assignments of human resources but are not effective for assigning non-human resources. True or false?

7.4 Resource Loading and Leveling

From the first day on the job, project managers are concerned with resource loading. **Resource loading** refers to the amounts of specific resources that are scheduled for use on specific activities or projects at specific times. Resource loading usually takes the form of a list or table.

7.4.1 Loading Resources

Figure 7-11 is an action plan and Gantt chart (see Section 6.4) for the project of production of a videotape. Task names, durations, finish dates, and the resource requirements for each step in the process are shown in Figure 7-11. (Preceding activities—see Section 6.2.4—are not listed in the action plan, but they are illustrated on the Gantt chart.)

Based on the project plan, project managers can use project-management software to create **resource schedules**, such as Table 7-4, that list the availability

Figure 7-11

Producing a Videotape
A. J. Lucas

WBS	Task Name	Duration	Resource Names
1	Project approval	0 days	
2	Scriptwriting	14 days	Scriptwriter
3	Schedule shoots	15 days	
3.1	Begin scheduling	0 days	
3.2	Propose shoots	5 days	Producer, client, scriptwriter
3.3	Hire secretary	5 days	Producer
3.4	Scheduling shoots	10 days	Secretary
3.5	Scheduling complete	0 days	
4	Script approval	5 days	Client, producer
5	Revise script	5 days	Scriptwriter, producer
6	Shooting	10 days	Scriptwriter, production staff
7	Editing	7 days	Editor, editing staff, editing room
8	Final approval	5 days	Client, producer, editor, editing room
9	Deliver video to client	0 days	

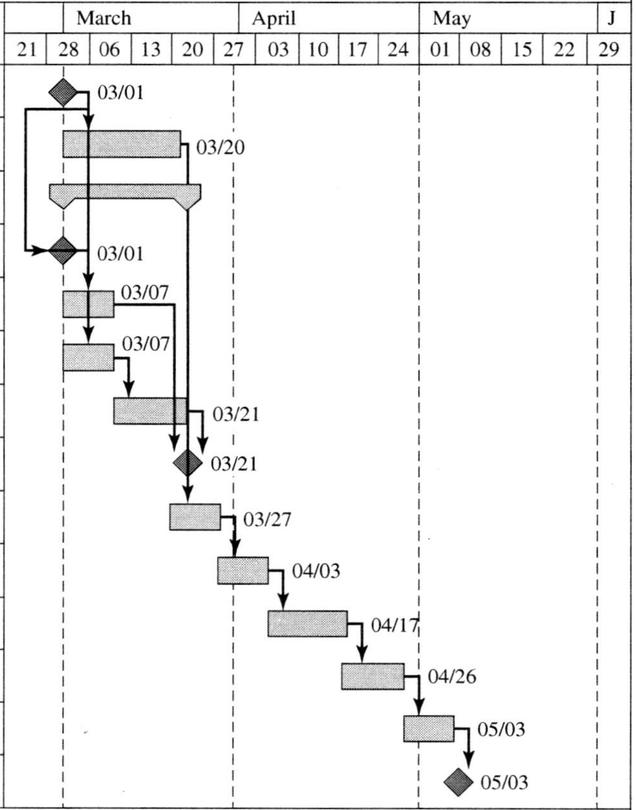

Start date: 03/01
Finish date: 05/03

Task   Milestone ◆   Summary

An action plan and Gantt chart for production of a videotape.

225

of all resources—including personnel and non-personnel resources, such as rooms and machinery. Resource schedules can list pay rates, typical work hours, and **exception dates** (dates the resource is on vacation or, in the case of a room, already booked for another project).

By creating the project resource schedule shown in Table 7-4, the project manager can tell that the client, whose input is required for several activities, will be on vacation between March 13 and March 26 and that the editing room is available for a limited amount of hours each work day. These critical pieces of information mean that the project schedule needs to be recalculated. Figure 7-12 shows a revised plan where the completion date has been extended from May 3 to May 17.

From the project plan, the new schedule, and the list of resources required, the project manager (using project management software) can produce a **resource loading chart**, such as Table 7-5, which lists the amounts of various specific resources that are scheduled for use on specific activities at specific times during the life of the project.

Table 7-5 reveals that in the first week of the project (March 1–4) the scriptwriter is overallocated and scheduled to work 72 hours. The producer's first week is also overallocated at 48 hours. Something must be done, as Section 7.4.2 discusses.

FOR EXAMPLE

A Charismatic VP

Gordon, the Vice President and Manager of a division of a chemical company, became aware that a number of projects he had assigned to his subordinates were not being completed on time. Some were finished late, and others were simply unfinished. Gordon was tireless, spending 60 to 80 hours per week at work. He was very well liked, and his people tried hard to please him. If he asked a subordinate if a task could be handled, invariably the answer was "yes." However, Gordon began to suspect that he was overcommitting his subordinates. He suggested this to his people, but most of them insisted that they could handle the work. Not entirely convinced, Gordon installed a project-oriented management system and initiated resource-loading reports for all personnel doing project work. The reports showed clearly that the division had an urgent need for additional staff engineers. As is typical of such cases, the individuals most overworked were the most experienced and most skilled people. Those engineers with spare time were the least skilled and, for the most part, recent hires. The untrained remained untrained. Gordon, however, altered work assignments and ordered that additional engineers be hired. Overscheduling was limited to 125 percent (50 hours per week) and was to remain at that level for a limited time only. A policy of partnering new engineers with experienced cohorts was instituted. Within six months, division projects were progressing reasonably on time.

Table 7-4: Resource Availability Calendars for Selected Resources for Videotape Production

Name	Standard Rate	Overtime Rate	Work
Scriptwriter	$25.00/hr	$40.00/hr	192 hr

RESOURCE CALENDAR (modified Standard)

Day	Hours
Monday	8:00 a.m.–12:00 p.m., 1:00 p.m.–6:00 p.m.
Tuesday	8:00 a.m.–12:00 p.m., 1:00 p.m.–6:00 p.m.
Wednesday	8:00 a.m.–12:00 p.m., 1:00 p.m.–6:00 p.m.
Thursday	8:00 a.m.–12:00 p.m., 1:00 p.m.–6:00 p.m.
Friday	8:00 a.m.–12:00 p.m., 1:00 p.m.–6:00 p.m.
Saturday	8:00 a.m.–12:00 p.m., 1:00 p.m.–6:00 p.m.
Sunday	Nonworking
Exceptions	None

Name	Standard Rate	Overtime Rate	Work
Producer	$45.00/hr	$60.00/hr	200 hr

RESOURCE CALENDAR (unmodified Standard)

Day	Hours
Monday	8:00 a.m.–12:00 p.m., 1:00 p.m.–5:00 p.m.
Tuesday	8:00 a.m.–12:00 p.m., 1:00 p.m.–5:00 p.m.
Wednesday	8:00 a.m.–12:00 p.m., 1:00 p.m.–5:00 p.m.
Thursday	8:00 a.m.–12:00 p.m., 1:00 p.m.–5:00 p.m.
Friday	8:00 a.m.–12:00 p.m., 1:00 p.m.–5:00 p.m.
Saturday	Nonworking
Sunday	Nonworking
Exceptions	None

Name	Standard Rate	Overtime Rate	Work
Client	$0.00/hr	$0.00/hr	120 hr

RESOURCE CALENDAR (modified Standard)

Day	Hours
Monday	8:00 a.m.–12:00 p.m., 1:00 p.m.–5:00 p.m.

Table 7-4: (Continued)

Tuesday	8:00 a.m.–12:00 p.m., 1:00 p.m.–5:00 p.m.	
Wednesday	8:00 a.m.–12:00 p.m., 1:00 p.m.–5:00 p.m.	
Thursday	8:00 a.m.–12:00 p.m., 1:00 p.m.–5:00 p.m.	
Friday	8:00 a.m.–12:00 p.m., 1:00 p.m.–5:00 p.m.	
Saturday	Nonworking	
Sunday	Nonworking	
Exceptions:	Date	Hours
	03/13–03/26	Nonworking
Name *Standard Rate*	*Overtime Rate*	*Work*
Editing room $0.00/hr	$0.00/hr	96 hr

RESOURCE CALENDAR (modified Standard)

Day		*Hours*	
Monday		9:30 a.m.–3:00 p.m.	
Tuesday		9:30 a.m.–3:00 p.m.	
Wednesday		9:30 a.m.–3:00 p.m.	
Thursday		9:30 a.m.–3:00 p.m.	
Friday		9:30 a.m.–3:00 p.m.	
Saturday		Nonworking	
Sunday		Nonworking	
Exceptions		None	

7.4.2 Leveling Resources

When project resources are **overallocated** (also known as overloaded), project managers often need to find ways to level the use of resources to ensure that a project can succeed in reality and not just on paper.

As Figure 7-12 shows, Tasks 2, 3.2, and 3.3 are all scheduled to start on March 1. The scriptwriter is required for the first two of the three items and the producer for the last two. The scriptwriter's calendar (Table 7-4) indicates that the scriptwriter can work a 54-hour week—six days per week at nine hours per day. The producer is available for a standard 40-hour week. The resource loading chart (Table 7-5) shows the tasks assigned to the scriptwriter

Figure 7-12

Revised start date: 03/01
Revised finish date: 05/17

Producing a Videotape

WBS	Task Name	Adj. Duration	Start	Finish	Late Start	Late Finish
1	Project approval	0 days	03/01	03/01	03/11	03/11
2	Scriptwriting	14 days	03/01	03/15	03/11	03/27
3	Schedule shoots	15 days	03/01	03/21	04/26	05/17
3.1	Begin scheduling	0 days	03/01	03/01	05/10	05/10
3.2	Propose shoots	6.5 days	03/01	03/07	05/10	05/17
3.3	Hire secretary	5 days	03/01	03/07	04/26	05/03
3.4	Schedule shoots	10 days	03/08	03/21	05/03	05/17
3.5	Scheduling complete	0 days	03/21	03/21	05/17	05/17
4	Script approval	10 days	03/15	03/31	03/27	04/03
5	Revise script	6.63 days	03/31	04/07	04/03	04/10
6	Shooting	10 days	04/10	04/21	04/10	04/24
7	Editing	10.06 days	04/24	05/08	04/24	05/08
8	Final approval	7.19 days	05/08	05/07	05/08	05/17
9	Deliver video to client	0 days	05/17	05/17	05/17	05/17

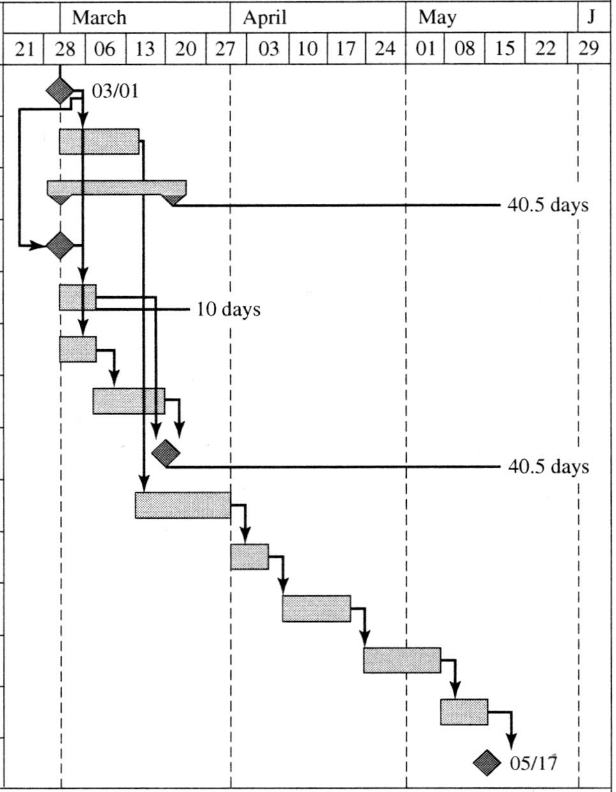

Slack shown

Task — Milestone — Slippage
Split — Slack — Summary

Adjusted for resource availability

Adjusted action plan and Gantt chart for producing a videotape.

Table 7-5: Resource Loading Chart for Videotape Production

Producing a Videotape Resource Loading
Standard
Overtime
March
April
May
Resource Name
Rate
Rate
Work
02/28
03/06
03/13
03/20
03/27
04/03
04/10
04/17
04/24
05/01
05/08
05/15

Scriptwriter $25.00/hr $40.00/hr 192 hrs 72h 58h 22h 10h 30h

Scriptwriting 112 hrs 36h 54h 22h

Propose shoots 40 hrs 36h 4h

Revise script 40 hrs 10h 30h

Producer $45.00/hr $60.00/hr 200 hrs 48h 32h 20h 20h 0h 40h 37.5h 2.5h

Propose shoots 40 hrs 24h 16h

Hire secretary 40 hrs 24h 16h

Table 7-5: *(Continued)*

Script approval 40 hrs 20h 20h

Revise script 40 hrs 0h 40h

Final approval 40 hrs 37.5h 2.5h

Client $0.00/hr $0.00/hr 120 hrs 24h 16h 40h 37.5h 2.5h

Propose shoots 40 hrs 24h 16h

Script approval 40 hrs 40h

Final approval 40 hrs 37.5h 2.5h

Secretary $10.00/hr $20.00/hr 80 hrs 24h 40h 16h

Schedule shoots 80 hrs 24h 40h 16h

Editor $25.00/hr $45.00/hr 176 hrs 40h 40h 40h 16h 37.5h 2.5h

Shooting 80 hrs 40h 40h

Editing 56 hrs 40h 16h

Final approval 40 hrs 37.5h 2.5h

Production staff $20.00/hr $35.00/hr 80 hrs 40h 40h

Shooting 80 hrs 40h 40h

Editing staff $20.00/hr $35.00/hr 56 hrs 40h 16h

Editing 56 hrs 40h 16h

Editing room $0.00/hr $0.00/hr 96 hrs 27.5h 27.5h 27.5h 13.5h

Editing 56 hrs 27.5h 27.5h 1h

Final approval 40 hrs 26.5h 13.5h

Overallocated resources bolded

and producer. Apparently both are expected to do two different jobs at the same time.

The scriptwriter's conflict must be reduced. Figure 7-13 illustrates the problem clearly by focusing only on the tasks for which the scriptwriter is scheduled.

Fortunately, Figure 7-13 also shows considerable slack in Task 3.2. Working manually or with project-management software, a project manager can focus on using available slack time (see Section 6.2.3) to level the resources so they do not

Figure 7-13

						March					April				May		
WBS	Task Name	Duration	Sch. Start	Sch. Finish		28	06	13	20	27	03	10	17	24	01	08	15
2	Scriptwriting	14 days	03/01	03/15					Scriptwriter								
3.2	Propose shoots	6.5 days	03/01	03/07				Producer, client, scriptwriter									
5	Revise script	6.63 days	03/31	04/07								Scriptwriter, producer					

Project start date: 03/01   Resource Overallocated: Scriptwriter
Project finish date: 05/17

Prior to resource leveling	Preleveled task		Preleveled milestone	
	Preleveled split	- - - - - -	Milestone	
	Task		Delay	
	Split	- - - - - -	Slack	
	Progress		Summary	

Resource overallocation for scriptwriter.

exceed their capacities. This strategy avoids extending project duration. Figure 7-14 shows the effect of resource leveling on the scriptwriter's workload. In this case the project duration is not affected because there is sufficient slack time associated with Task 3.2.

Figure 7-14 appears to report that the scriptwriter is still working overtime on Tasks 2 and 3.2. This is not the case. The scriptwriter's efforts are solely devoted to scriptwriting (Task 2), but the producer and the client are working on Task 3.2, so the task is shown as being underway. The new plan splits Task 3.2, and the scriptwriter begins work on the task on Wednesday, March 15, after work on Task 2 has been completed. The second part of Task 3.2 does not begin until all work on Task 2 is complete.

Sometimes resource allocation decisions are intended to avoid future problems rather than to cure present problems. For example, while the scriptwriter is no longer overallocated, the project manager can decide to add a second scriptwriter to Task 2. The project manager might also level the producer's apparent overallocation just to add some slack to the producer's schedule. Both of these additions can made to ensure that the project is not made late by a glitch in the producer's work or in the scriptwriting activity, which is on the project's critical path. The result of all these moves is seen in Figure 7-15. The project can be finished five days earlier than indicated in Figure 7-12.

Figure 7-14

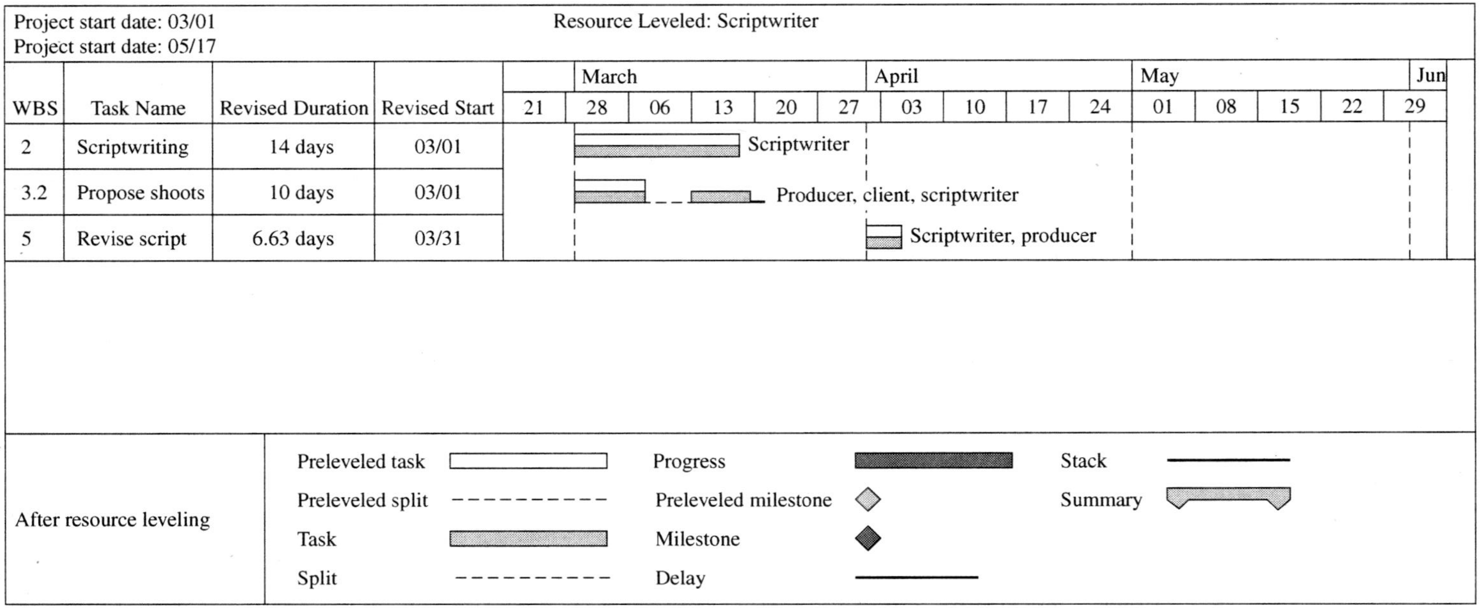

Project start date: 03/01
Project start date: 05/17
Resource Leveled: Scriptwriter
WBS
Task Name
Revised Duration
Revised Start
March
April
May
Jun
21
28
06
13
20
27
03
10
17
24
01
08
15
22
29
2
Scriptwriting
14 days
03/01
Scriptwriter
3.2
Propose shoots
10 days
03/01
Producer, client, scriptwriter
5
Revise script
6.63 days
03/31
Scriptwriter, producer
After resource leveling
Preleveled task
Preleveled split
Task
Split
Progress
Preleveled milestone
Milestone
Delay
Stack
Summary

Resource leveled for scriptwriter.

Figure 7-15

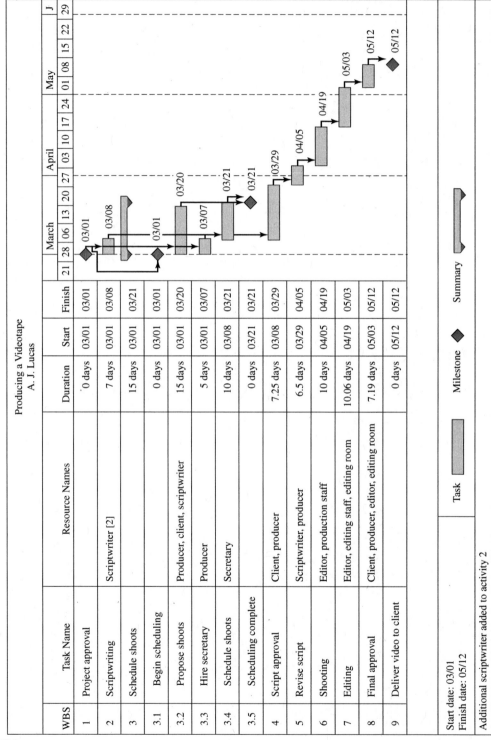

Producing a Videotape
A. J. Lucas

WBS	Task Name	Resource Names	Duration	Start	Finish
1	Project approval		0 days	03/01	03/01
2	Scriptwriting	Scriptwriter [2]	7 days	03/01	03/08
3	Schedule shoots		15 days	03/01	03/21
3.1	Begin scheduling		0 days	03/01	03/01
3.2	Propose shoots	Producer, client, scriptwriter	15 days	03/01	03/20
3.3	Hire secretary	Producer	5 days	03/01	03/07
3.4	Schedule shoots	Secretary	10 days	03/08	03/21
3.5	Scheduling complete		0 days	03/21	03/21
4	Script approval	Client, producer	7.25 days	03/08	03/29
5	Revise script	Scriptwriter, producer	6.5 days	03/29	04/05
6	Shooting	Editor, production staff	10 days	04/05	04/19
7	Editing	Editor, editing staff, editing room	10.06 days	04/19	05/03
8	Final approval	Client, producer, editor, editing room	7.19 days	05/03	05/12
9	Deliver video to client		0 days	05/12	05/12

Start date: 03/01
Finish date: 05/12

Task | Milestone ◆ | Summary

Additional scriptwriter added to activity 2

Final videotape project Gantt chart schedule, with two scriptwriters and producer leveled.

7.5 Allocating Scarce Resources

For the situation involving an overloaded scriptwriter in Section 7.4, the solution was simply to make use of available activity slack time. The project completion date was not altered because the task's slack time was large enough to swallow the added time.

Often, however, this strategy is not enough or is not possible, and project managers need to prioritize when allocating scarce resources to several tasks—which tasks should get the resources immediately and go first, and which could be delayed.

7.5.1 Establishing Priorities

Most solutions involving scarce resources start with network diagrams (such as PERT/CPM schedules; see Section 6.1). Each activity can be examined period by period and resource by resource. If the demand for a resource exceeds its supply, project managers can consider the tasks one by one and assign resources to the tasks according to some priority rule chosen by the organization or the project manager him- or herself. Tasks that receive resources under this rule proceed as originally scheduled. Tasks that do not get resources are delayed until ongoing tasks are completed and the required resources are freed up for use. If this increases the project duration, the change will be visible on the project's Gantt chart or network diagram.

Many possible rules exist for assigning preference to some activities over others when allocating scarce resources. Several of the most commonly used rules by project managers (and project-management software) include the following:

▲ **As soon as possible:** this is the standard rule in scheduling. Activities are scheduled to start on their earliest start dates (see Section 6.2.1), and resources are made available with that in mind.

▲ **As late as possible:** resources are made available so that activities start on their latest start dates whenever possible without increasing the project's duration. This might seem irrational, but it preserves the organization's resources and delays cash outflows as long as possible.

▲ **Shortest task duration first:** always consistent with technological precedences, shorter tasks are given priority over longer tasks. This rule maximizes the number of tasks that can be completed by a system in a given time period.

▲ **Minimum slack first:** tasks are supplied with resources in inverse order of their slacks. This rule usually minimizes the number of late activities.

▲ **Most critical followers:** the number of successors on the critical path(s) for each activity is counted. Activities with a higher number of critical successors take precedence. The rationale here is that such activities cause the greatest damage to project performance if they are late.

▲ **Most successors:** similar to the preceding rule except that *all* successors are counted.

FOR EXAMPLE

"Walts"—Truly Scarce Resources

In spite of project managers' complaints about the scarcity of resources, resource scarcity rarely apply to resources in general, but rather to one or two very specific resources. Authors Samuel Mantel, Jack Meredith, Scott Shafer, and Margaret Sutton refer to these specific resources as "Walts," a term derived from the name of an individual, Walter A., who was employed by a large insurance company for which the authors did project-management consulting work. Walt was a specialist in the laws affecting insurance policies for certain types of casualty losses in the firm's commercial lines of business—knowledge that was required when designing new policies. The firm had only one Walt, and while the firm was training others, such training takes years. Projects requiring Walt's input were scheduled around his availability. Other examples of projects with Walts include military combat missions scheduled around the availability of attack aircraft, construction projects scheduled around the availability of a piece of machinery, or a Broadway play scheduled around the availability of a star actress.

▲ **Most resources first:** the greater the use of a specific resource on a task, the higher the task's priority for the resource. This rule is based on the assumption that more important activities have a greater demand for scarce resources.

Organizations typically have additional rules for assigning scarce resources. For example, company policy could put favored customers' projects at the head of the resource line. Similar favoritism might be shown to projects that are considered highly valuable to the parent firm. (Some firms show favoritism to specific high-value activities within a project, but this rule makes little sense because all project activities must be completed to finish the project.)

Project-management researchers have conducted considerable research on the various prioritizing rules, and the minimum slack rule is usually the best or second best option to determine priority. It rarely performs poorly. If a high-slack task is not given resources in one period, its slack is automatically decreased and in the next period it has a better chance of receiving resources. The resource allocation is repeated periodically (hourly, daily, weekly, or monthly, etc.), depending on the time frame of the project's activities. If a task becomes critical, that is, all the slack is used up before the activity receives resources, the project will be delayed.

7.5.2 Allocating Scarce Resources to Several Projects

When the problem of allocating scarce resources is extended to situations involving several concurrent projects, the size and complexity of the problem increase—but the nature of the underlying problem remains the same.

There is a decided advantage if several projects are joined as a set. For example, a single project is composed of a set of first-level tasks connected in relationships of predecessors and successors. Each first-level task is composed of a set of second-level tasks, which are divided into third-level tasks, and so on. Project managers can take several projects and link them together with **dummy activities** (or pseudoactivities), which are activities that have duration but do not require any resources.

Similarly, a set of projects linked by dummy activities can become a sort of superproject. Project managers can use dummy activities to establish predecences between the projects they connect, and thus we can separate the projects in time. In the network diagram in Figure 7-16, each oval (or "node") represents a project, and the arrows connecting them are dummy activities. The temporal relationships between the projects are altered by varying the duration of the dummy activities.

The dummy activities in Figure 7-16 could represent technological relationships among the projects—often the case when individual projects are parts of an overall program. Additionally, dummy activities might separate projects according to planned delivery dates, or the separations might be completely arbitrary.

Figure 7-16

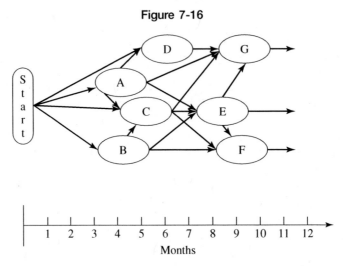

Multiple projects connected with dummy activities.

Project-management software is usually necessary to conduct resource loading and leveling for multiple interconnected project and superprojects. Project-management software typically offers leveling routines that enable project managers to examine the consequences of adopting different resource allocation priority rules or of adding more resources to the project.

Regardless of the way in which project managers prioritize projects, they still often must choose between alternative outcomes and different arrangements and durations of dummy activities.

Many measurable criteria are available to help project managers choose a priority rule. The following are the most common criteria:

▲ **Schedule slippage. Schedule slippage** simply measures the amount by which a project, or a set of projects, is delayed by application of a leveling rule (or by extending a dummy activity so that a project finishes later because it starts later). The project manager (and senior management) must trade off penalty costs and the possible displeasure of clients against the cost of adding resources, if that is possible, or by reducing the overallocation of scarce resources. Just as serious is the ripple effect that often occurs when a delay in one project causes a delay in others.

▲ **Resource utilization.** Resource utilization is important because making resources available is expensive. Project managers can seek to smooth out the peaks and valleys in resource usage, thereby minimizing the amount of resources needed. This technique is particularly important for expensive machine and human resources. On the other hand, efforts to control resource costs by setting system capacity as close as possible to the demand on the system are counterproductive when there is uncertainty in the system and the demand made on it.

▲ **In-process inventory.** The level of in-process inventory is a measure of how much unfinished work is in the system. Clients have little desire to pay for things they have not yet received—though partial prepayment is sometimes arranged by contract—and the organization carrying out projects might have large quantities of human and material resources invested in projects that have little value until the projects are complete. Minimizing this measure of effectiveness is a major function of the shortest-task-first rule for assigning resources.

Similar to assigning scarce resources within a single project, the minimum slack rule (see Section 7.5.1) is probably the best overall priority rule, according to research on the subject. The minimum slack rule gives the best combination of minimum project slippage, minimum resource idle time, and minimum in-process inventory. While first-come-first-served might be the client's idea of "fair," it is a poor priority rule when measured against almost any of the others. If the minimum slack rule produces ties among two or more projects (or activities), the shortest task rule seems to be the best tie-breaker.

SELF-CHECK

1. You consider the number of activities on a project's critical path to establish which tasks to prioritize. Which precedence rule are you using?

    (a) most resources first

    (b) as soon as possible

    (c) minimum slack time

    (d) most critical followers

2. Dummy activities can force project managers to establish precedence between tasks and project. True or false?

3. When establishing project/task prioritization, project managers frequently consider which of the following?

    (a) opportunity costs and in-process inventory

    (b) schedule slippage and quality control

    (c) resource utilization and in-process inventory

    (d) quality control and opportunity costs

SUMMARY

To accurately assign and manage the resources associated with a project, a project manager must first define the available resources; a Skills Roster can be an effective tool to more clearly identify human resources. Looking at the project plan, the project manager estimates the work effort associated with each task, verifying these estimates with historical information, team members' estimates, and expert opinions. Using a resource matrix and a loading chart, project managers can assign human and material resources to a project and determine if resources are over- or underloaded. Resources can be leveled by establishing precedences and priorities, which are difficult and important decisions that project managers must make.

KEY TERMS

Dummy activities	Activities on network diagrams that have duration but do not require any resources; also known as pseudoactivities.
Exception dates	Dates that a resource is unavailable.
Human Resources Matrix	A graphic display that project managers can use to show individual resources that will work on an activity and the work effort that each resource will invest in the activity.
Interest	On a Skills Roster, the "interest" descriptor indicates that the person would like to work on assignments involving this skill or knowledge.
Lowest-level activity	An activity in a Work Breakdown Structure that's not divided into further detail.
Person effort	See work effort.
Person Loading Chart	A graphic display that shows a detailed allocation of work effort by time period.
Primary capability	On a Skills Roster, the "primary capability" descriptor indicates that the person can assume a lead role in an assignment requiring this skill or knowledge.
Resource allocation	The process by which project managers assign specific, limited resources to specific activities (or projects) when there are competing demands for limited resources.
Resource loading	The amounts of specific resources that are scheduled for use on specific activities or projects at specific times.

Resource loading chart	A list that shows the amounts of various specific resources that are scheduled for use on specific activities at specific times during the life of the project.
Resource schedules	Tables that list the availability of all resources—including personnel and non-personnel resources. Resource schedules can list pay rates, typical work hours, and exception dates.
Schedule slippage	A measure of the amount by which a project, or a set of projects, is delayed by leveling a resource.
Secondary capability	On a Skills Roster, the "secondary capability" descriptor indicates that the person has some training or experience in the skill or knowledge area but should work under another person's guidance.
Skills Roster	A graphic format project managers can use to display the skills and knowledge of people who might work on a project; also known as a Skills Inventory.
Work effort	The actual time a person spends working on an activity, expressed in person-hours, person-days, or person-weeks; also known as person effort.

ASSESS YOUR UNDERSTANDING

Go to www.wiley.com/college/portny to assess your knowledge of the basics of project resources.
Measure your learning by comparing pre-test and post-test results.

Summary Questions

1. Skills Rosters help project managers do which of the following?
   (a) identify available resources to allocate in human resource assignments
   (b) identify available resources to allocate in equipment assignments
   (c) identify suitable resources to allocate in human resource assignments
   (d) identify suitable resources to allocate in equipment assignments
2. Although project managers make most of the decisions in allocating resources to projects, team members can help by doing which of the following?
   (a) identifying and rating skills in Skills Rosters
   (b) completing accurate, detailed time cards
   (c) both of the above
   (d) neither of the above
3. A Skills Roster and Person Loading Chart are necessary to load resources for a project. True or false?
4. Which of the following is an irresponsible response to a human resource that is overloaded for two weeks during a month-long project?
   (a) Pay the resource to work overtime.
   (b) Hire another resource to take on some or all of the work.
   (c) Adjust the sequence of tasks to level the resource's commitments.
   (d) none of the above

Applying This Chapter

1. All resources are limited, but some are consumed when used while others are not. What is an example of each type of resource when developing a new software product?
2. Jenna asked her team members to complete a Skills Roster at the start of a new project. One team member, Marissa, rates her skills as outstanding in several areas. Jenna disagrees with Marissa's ratings. What might Jenna do about the situation when making assignments for the new project?

3. For your drug-testing project, you estimate that each lab technician will need to commit 32 hours a week to the project. What does this figure translate to at 100 percent efficiency/100 percent availability, 75 percent efficiency/100 percent availability, and 75 percent efficiency/75 percent availability?

4. Tyrone is hosting a wedding anniversary party for his parents. Because the party is next weekend and he's done very little work ahead of time, he and his team (his brother and sister) need to be highly productive in the next week. What five factors can positively affect Tyrone's productivity? What might be a specific example of each factor?

5. You create Person Loading Charts for the three members of a research team you're managing for the next month. For this project, a full-time commitment is 40 hours a week. But you find that Team Member #1 is committed 40, 45, 60, and 30 hours per week; Team Member #2 is committed 40, 40, 20, and 20 hours per week; and Team Member #3 is committed 60, 40, 60, and 20 hours per week. Assuming your team members are similarly qualified, what are some options you have for resource leveling to avoid overcommitting resources?

6. For a development and launch of a new corporate Web site, what purposes might be served by using each of the following priority rules for allocating scarce resources—as late as possible, shortest task duration time, and minimum slack time?

7. John manages eight small projects with many of the same resources. He wants to link the projects with dummy activities to create a superproject. What reasons can he give his team members and upper management for using dummy activities?

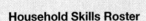
Household Skills Roster

Approach the care, cleaning, and maintenance of your home like a project by creating a Skills Roster. Ask each person you live with to list and rate his or her household skills (organizing, cleaning, straightening, washing clothes, and so on). If you don't live with another person, think back to a time when you did or choose another group activity. Prepare a Skills Roster that lists skills, people, and ratings. Use any of the ratings systems described in Section 7.1—or develop your own custom system.

Your Work Effort Estimate

For your next major school or work assignment (a big presentation, a lengthy paper, and so on), create an accurate work effort estimate before you begin the project. First identify the specific tasks and subtasks for the project. Consider how long it took you to do similar tasks on previous projects. Then ask for work effort estimates from anyone besides yourself involved in the project. Finally, ask an "expert" (a professor, a friend who's already done the assignment) how long he or she thinks it will take to complete each task. Combine all the data you've collected to create a revised work effort estimate.

Resource Matrix for Your Car

Select a non-person resource in your life that performs a variety of tasks. A car, computer, or cell phone are exam-

ples of limited resources. List as many tasks as possible that the resource is used for. Estimate the number of hours per week the resource is dedicated to each task. Prepare a resource grid/matrix (see Section 7.3.4 for an example) for the resource. Is the resource overcommitted? How would you load the resource with additional commitments? How would you level the resource?

Putting It All Together

Create a comprehensive resource allocation plan for a work, school, or personal project you have coming up. To create a resource allocation plan, you need to have a list of activities, identify immediate precedessors for each activity, know the duration of each activity, and know the resources required for each activity. If you don't have this information about your project, you can use the following information about a landscaping project or create similar data to work from:

First, draw a Gantt chart or network diagram based on the information. Next, assuming a five-day work week, find the critical path and calculate the project duration in days. Assuming that each resource is assigned 100 percent to each task, identify any resource constraints. If necessary, level the resources (no overtime, each resource can only work five days a week) and determine the new critical path and duration time. Finally, identify any alternative solutions that you can use to shorten the project duraction without overallocating a resource.

Activity	Immediate Predecessor	Activity Duration (days)	Resources Used
A		2	X, Y
B	A	2	X
C	A	3	X
D	B, C	4	X, Y
E	D	3	W, X
F	D	1	W, X, Y
G	E, F	2	X, Y

CASE STUDY: Charter Financial Bank

Charter Financial Bank operates three branches in a southeastern city. Ray Copper, Vice President of Information Technology at the bank, has recently been charged by the bank's president to develop a Web site to promote bank services, provide access to customer account information, and allow individuals to apply on-line for loans and credit cards.

Ray decided to assign this project to Rachel Smith, one of two directors in the information technology group. Since Charter Financial did not currently have a presence on the Web, Ray and Rachel agreed that an appropriate starting point for the project would be for the project team to benchmark existing Web sites in order to gain a better understanding of the state-of-the-art in this area. At the conclusion of their first meeting, Ray asked Rachel to prepare a rough estimate of how long this project would take and how much it would cost if it were pursued at a normal pace. Noting that the president appeared particularly anxious to launch the Web site, Ray also requested that Rachel prepare a time and budget estimate related to launching the Web site as quickly as possible.

During the first project team meeting, the team identified seven major tasks associated with the project. The first task was to benchmark existing Web sites. The team estimated that completing this task at normal pace would likely require 10 days at a cost of $15,000. However, the team estimated that this task could be completed in as few as seven days at a cost of $18,750 if the maximum allowable amount of overtime was used.

Once the benchmark study was completed, a project plan and project definition document would need to be prepared for top management approval. The team estimated that this task could be completed in five days at a cost of $3750 working at a normal pace or in three days at a cost of $4500.

When the project received the approval of top management, the Web site design could begin. The team estimated that Web site design would require 15 days at a cost of $45,000 using no overtime or 10 days at a cost of $58,500 using all allowable overtime.

After the Web site design was complete, three tasks could be carried out simultaneously: (1) developing the Web site's database, (2) developing and coding the actual Web pages, and (3) developing and coding the Web site's forms. The team estimated that database development would require 10 days and cost $9000 using no overtime, but could be completed in seven days at a cost of $11,250 using overtime. Likewise, the team estimated that developing and coding the Web pages would require 10 days and cost $15,000 using no overtime or could be reduced by two days at a total cost of $19,500. Developing the forms was to be subcontracted out and would take seven days at a cost of $8400. The organization that was to be used to create the forms does not provide an option for paying more for rush jobs.

Finally, once the database was developed, the Web pages coded, and the forms created, the entire Web site would need to be tested and debugged. The team estimated that this would require three days at a cost of $4500. Using overtime, the team estimated that the testing and debugging task could be reduced by a day at a total cost of $6750.

Questions

1. What is the cost of completing this project if no overtime is used? How long will it take to complete the project?

2. What is the shortest amount of time in which the project can be completed? What is the cost of completing the project in the shortest amount of time?

3. Suppose that the benchmarking study actually required 13 days as opposed to the 10 days originally estimated. What actions would you take to keep the project on a normal schedule?

4. Suppose the president wanted the Web site launched in 35 days. What actions would you take to meet this deadline? How much extra would it cost to complete the project in 35 days?

8

BEING AN EFFECTIVE PROJECT MANAGER
Leading Projects with Skill and Style

Starting Point

Go to www.wiley.com/college/portny to assess your knowledge of the basics of effective project management.
Determine where you need to concentrate your effort.

What You'll Learn in This Chapter

▲ Characteristics of successful project managers
▲ Code of ethics for project managers
▲ Management and leadership aspects of project-management jobs
▲ Types and importance of power
▲ Ways to maximize accountability
▲ Ways to minimize micromanagement
▲ Reasons projects get off-track—and techniques to get them back on

After Studying This Chapter, You'll Be Able To

▲ Evaluate actions and options in terms of a code of ethics
▲ Develop personal characteristics that suit project-management duties
▲ Create your personal base of power
▲ Formulate strategies to increase accountability within teams
▲ Build trusting employee–manager relationships
▲ Analyze and evaluate projects to determine whether they are on-track
▲ Propose strategies to get projects back on track

INTRODUCTION

Successful project management encompasses more than watching over schedules, budgets, and resource allocations. On a personal level, project managers need credibility, sensitivity, and strong ethics to effectively manage projects. The duties of project management require both traditional management skills and leadership, including a keen understanding of the nature and use of personal power. Project managers must balance between encouraging accountability from team members and minimizing micromanagement. While projects fall behind for various reasons, various techniques enable project managers to get their projects back on schedule and on budget.

8.1 Selecting a Project Manager

As Section 1.4.1 discusses, project managers are responsible for seeing that all aspects of the project are completely satisfactorily. Project managers are responsible for acquiring the human and material resources needed by the project. Project managers are also responsible for exercising leadership, putting out fires, and dealing with obstacles that impede the project's progress. Finally, the project manager is responsible for making the trade-offs between budget, schedule, and specifications that are needed to ensure project success. To be successful at meeting these responsibilities, the project manager must be skilled at negotiation, conflict resolution, and persuasion.

Selecting these important individuals can be a challenge for senior management. Many organizations simply select project managers by considering a list of employees (often technical specialists) who can be spared from their current jobs. Unfortunately, availability is only one of many necessary selection criteria. Other critical characteristics include the following:

▲ **Focused on finishing.** In many ways, the prospective project manager must be, in the language of salespeople, a "closer." Project managers must complete the tasks they are given. Hard workers are easy to find; what is rare is an individual who is driven to *finish* the job.

▲ **Credibility.** Project managers must be believable in two specific areas—technical matters and administrative matters.

    ▲ **Technical credibility.** Project managers are not expected to have expert knowledge of each of the technologies used in a project. The project manager should, however, be able to explain the current state of the project, its progress, and its problems to senior management. Additionally, the project manager should be able to interpret the wishes of management and the client to the project team.

    ▲ **Administrative credibility.** For management and the client to have faith in the viability of a project, reports, appraisals, audits, and evaluations must be timely and accurate. For the team, resources, personnel, and knowledge must be available when needed. For all parties, the project manager must be able to make the difficult trade-offs that allow the project to meet its objectives as well as possible. This requires mature judgment and considerable courage.

▲ **Sensitivity.** The project manager needs a finely tuned set of political antennae as well as an equally sensitive sensor of interpersonal conflict between team members, or between team members (including him- or herself) and other parties-at-interest to the project. Also needed are technical sensors that indicate when technical problems are being swept under the rug or when the project is about to fall behind its schedule.

▲ **Leadership.** A leader is someone who indicates to other individuals or groups the direction in which they should proceed. When complex projects are divided into a set of tasks and subtasks, project members tend to focus on their individual tasks, thereby ignoring the project as a whole. Only the project manager is in a position to keep team members working toward completion of the whole project rather than its parts. In practice, leaders keep their people energized, enthusiastic, well organized, and well informed. This, in turn, will keep the team well motivated. (Section 8.2 and Chapter 10 further discuss the leadership responsibilities of project managers.)

▲ **Ethics.** Project managers must have—and communicate—a strong sense of ethics. Because projects differ from one to another, there are few standard procedures that can be installed to ensure honest and ethical behavior from all project participants. The daily papers are filled with examples of kickbacks, bribery, cover-ups of mistakes, use of substandard materials, theft, fraud, and outright lies on project status and performance. Dishonesty on anyone's part should not be permitted in projects. The Project Management Institute (PMI) has developed a Code of Ethics for the profession (see Table 8-1).

Table 8-1: Code of Ethics for the Project Management Profession*

PREAMBLE: Project Management Professionals, in the pursuit of the profession, affect the quality of life for all people in our society. Therefore, it is vital that Project Management Professionals conduct their work in an ethical manner to earn and maintain the confidence of team members, colleagues, employees, employers, clients, and the public.
ARTICLE I: Project Management Professionals shall maintain high standards of personal and professional conduct and:
a. Accept responsibility for their actions.
b. Undertake projects and accept responsibility only if qualified by training or experience, or after full disclosure to their employers or clients of pertinent qualifications.

Table 8-1: *(Continued)*

c. Maintain their professional skills at the state of the art and recognize the importance of continued personal development and education.

d. Advance the integrity and prestige of the profession by practicing in a dignified manner.

e. Support this code and encourage colleagues and coworkers to act in accordance with this code.

f. Support the professional society by actively participating and encouraging colleagues and coworkers to participate.

g. Obey the laws of the country in which work is being performed.

ARTICLE II: Project Management Professionals shall, in their work:

a. Provide necessary project leadership to promote maximum productivity while striving to minimize cost.

b. Apply state of the art project management tools and techniques to ensure quality, cost, and time objectives, as set forth in the project plan, are met.

c. Treat fairly all project team members, colleagues, and coworkers, regardless of race, religion, sex, age, or national origin.

d. Protect project team members from physical and mental harm.

e. Provide suitable working conditions and opportunities for project team members.

f. Seek, accept, and offer honest criticism of work, and properly credit the contribution of others.

g. Assist project team members, colleagues, and coworkers in their professional development.

ARTICLE III: Project Management Professionals shall, in their relations with their employers and clients:

a. Act as faithful agents or trustees for their employers and clients in professional business matters.

b. Keep information on the business affairs or technical processes of an employer or client in confidence while employed, and later, until such information is properly released.

c. Inform their employers, clients, professional societies, or public agencies of which they are members or to which they may make any presentations, of any circumstances that could lead to a conflict of interest.

Table 8-1: *(Continued)*

d. Neither give nor accept, directly or indirectly, any gift, payment or service of more than nominal value to or from those having business relationships with their employers or clients.

e. Be honest and realistic in reporting project quality, cost, and time.

ARTICLE IV: Project Management Professionals shall, in fulfilling their responsibilities to the community:

a. Protect the safety, health, and welfare of the public and speak out against abuses in these areas affecting the public interest.

b. Seek and extend public knowledge and appreciation of the project management profession and its achievements.

*Source: Project Management Institute.

FOR EXAMPLE

A Question of Style

Many assume that research into the best managerial style for general management applies to project management as well. Recent studies, however, raise some questions about this assumption. While there is little doubt that the most effective overall style is participative, Aaron Shenhar of the Howe School of Technology Management (howe.stevens.edu) has added another dimension to style. Shenhar found that as a project's level of technological uncertainty went from "low tech" to "very high tech," the appropriate management style (while being fundamentally participative) went from "firm" to "highly flexible." In addition, he found that the complexity of the project, ranked from "simple" to "highly complex," called for styles varying from "informal" to "highly formal." The more complex a project, the more formal the style should be. In this context, flexibility applies primarily to the degree that new ideas and approaches are considered. Formality applies primarily to the degree to which the project operates in a structured environment. Thus, the more technically uncertain a project, the more flexible the style of management should be. When faced with technological uncertainty, project managers must be open to experimentation. In the same way, if a project is highly complex with many parts that must be combined with great care, the project manager cannot allow a haphazard approach by the project team.

SELF-CHECK

1. What two types of credibility should a project manager have?
2. All project managers have an ethical responsibility to which of the following?

   (a) themselves, their communities, their employees, and their clients

   (b) their schedules, budgets, and resources

   (c) their team members and their organizations

   (d) none of the above

8.2 Leading in a Project Environment

A project manager's success on a project depends on his or her ability to organize, coordinate, and support a diverse team working toward a common goal. Often, team members come from different areas of an organization, have different operating styles, and don't report to the project manager administratively. Successfully guiding such a group of people requires both vision and structure.

8.2.1 Practicing Both Management and Leadership

Management and leadership are two related but distinct sets of behaviors that project managers use while guiding and supporting people through the stages of projects. Management focuses on creating plans and assessing performance; leadership emphasizes defining a vision and taking actions to increase the chances that the vision becomes reality. Management focuses on systems, procedures, and information; leadership focuses on people. Management creates order and predictability; leadership helps people to address change.

Table 8-2 illustrates leadership and management approaches to support the key stages of a project. Project managers must practice both management and leadership to maximize the chances for achieving project success, as follows:

▲ In a project's planning stages, explore the "why" of the project (a leadership issue) to help elicit people's buy-in and commitment, as well as the "what," "when," and "how" (management issues).

▲ When preparing to begin project work, assign people to the team and explain their roles and responsibilities (management), and negotiate with functional managers and get team members' personal commitments that they'll perform their assignments to the best of their abilities (leadership).

▲ Throughout the project, track progress and deal with any problems as soon as they're encountered, and also encourage people to sustain their ongoing commitments to achieving project success.

Table 8-2: Comparison of Leadership and Management Approaches to Project Activities

Activity	Leadership	Management
Planning	Creating and sharing visions and strategies	Specifying objectives, schedules, and budget
Organizing	Eliciting commitments from team members	Assigning people to the team and defining their roles
Performing	Motivating team members	Monitoring and reporting on progress and dealing with problems

8.2.2 Developing Personal Power and Influence

Power is the ability to influence the actions of others. Establishing effective bases of power enhances a project manager's ability to lead a project and inspire cooperation from the project team and other key audiences and stakeholders.

People respond to a project manager's requests and directions for different reasons, as discussed below:

▲ **Rewards: reward power** is the power to get people to do what a project manager asks because they want the benefits that the project manager can give them (rewards). Examples of rewards include raises, bonuses, and recognition. Project managers rarely have this capability.

▲ **Punishments: punishment power** is the power to get people to do what a project manager asks because they don't want what the project manager can give them (punishments). Examples of punishments include poor performance appraisals and undesirable job assignments. Project managers rarely have this capability.

▲ **Position: position power** is the power to get project team members to take a project manager's requests more seriously because they feel that it's appropriate for the project manager to direct team members. Of course, project managers can lose this power if they behave inappropriately, but they have it initially.

▲ **What a project manager stands for:** people do what a project manager asks because they agree with what the project manager is trying to accomplish. They know that requests and actions are attempts to achieve the results that they also want to achieve.

▲ **Personality:** people listen to a project manager because they appreciate and respect who the project manager is, as reflected by his or her sensitivity, loyalty to others, sense of humor, or other characteristics.

▲ **Expertise:** people listen to a project manager because they respect the skills and knowledge that the project manager brings to the job. They'll listen because they believe that the project manager is probably right.

Project managers don't have to be the technical experts on projects to command the respect of team members. They do, however, need to be experts in the skills and knowledge that they're called upon to use on their projects. Specific project manager skills and knowledge include an ability to plan and control the project, an ability to encourage effective communication, an ability to encourage a positive and productive work environment, and an understanding of the political environment in the organization in which the project is being performed.

Being both the technical expert and the project manager on a project can work against the project manager. If the project manager isn't careful, he or she can inhibit others' willingness to accept responsibility and perform their work independently because of the following:

▲ They feel that their work will never be as good as the project manager's.
▲ The project manager keeps the challenging and important assignments for him- or herself because he or she likes the work and thinks that he or she can do the best job.
▲ The project manager resists approaches that differ from the ones he or she normally takes.
▲ The project manager tends to micromanage people to ensure that they're performing their assignments just as he or she would.

Of course, a project manager's technical expertise can be a significant asset if used correctly. Praise from a technically astute project manager for a job well done means a lot more than praise from someone who is less qualified to assess the work.

While many factors can contribute to a project manager's ability to influence people, in general, power over others can be one of the following:

▲ **Ascribed power:** someone gives the project manager the authority to reward and punish those whom he or she wants to influence.
▲ **Achieved power:** the project manager earns the respect and allegiance of those whom he or she wants to influence.

Achieved power is far more effective than ascribed power. People who act in response to ascribed power usually look to do the least necessary to get the rewards they want or to avoid the consequences they fear. On the other hand, people who are motivated by achieved power work to achieve the highest possible quality of results because they have decided that doing so is in their best interests.

Whether they recognize and acknowledge it, project managers have considerable opportunity to develop and use achieved power. Project managers can

> **FOR EXAMPLE**
>
> **Knowledge as Power**
>
> In his ongoing writing and research on the topic of power (including his book *Powershift*), author Alvin Toffler asserts that power has always existed between humans in three forms: violence, wealth, and knowledge. Throughout much of history, violence (usually in the form of punishment) was used by the few to negatively control the many. With the Industrial Revolution, wealth became a more appealing form of power because businesses and individuals withhold money or spend money to make things happen or not happen. Today, knowledge is emerging as the dominant and preferred form of power. Toffler calls knowledge the "third wave of power" and notes that it can be seen in the preference for modern nations to become information allies rather than military allies and in the growth of knowledge-based businesses (engineering, computer sciences, communications networks, and so on) rather than manufacturing and traditional industry.

choose how they want to influence people's behavior, or they can inadvertently influence their behavior. Either way, a project manager's actions will influence people's behavior.

8.2.3 Establishing Bases of Power

Project managers can take the following steps to increase their abilities to influence team members and others within the project environment:

▲ Determine what authority the project manager has over the people to be influenced. Typical types of authority include the ability to give salary increases, give promotions, complete performance appraisals, and assign people to future jobs.

▲ Find out who else has authority over the people to be influenced.

▲ Clarify the reasons why successfully completing the project is in the organization's interest, and then share those reasons with others.

▲ Get to know others and understand, appreciate, and acknowledge their special talents and strengths.

▲ Let others get to know your good side. A project manager's power to influence people is based on their perceptions of his or her character, abilities, and authority.

▲ Don't condemn or complain but do give feedback when necessary.

▲ Become proficient in the tasks to be performed.

A project manager's bases of power will diminish over time if he or she doesn't consistently reinforce them. Meeting with team members at the start of a project can help them to see and appreciate a project manager's style and recognize that the entire team is trying to accomplish similar goals. If the team doesn't have contact for the next six months, however, those initial positive impressions will fade, and a project manager's ability to influence people's commitment and performance will decrease as well. Project managers can use e-mails, Intranet sites, and other virtual team tools to ensure a project remains prominent in team members' minds.

SELF-CHECK

1. Management involves creating plans and assessing performance, while leadership focuses on which of the following?
   (a) defining a vision and taking action to increase the chances that the vision becomes reality
   (b) proposing plans and collaborating with others to refine plans
   (c) selecting human resources carefully and ensure the resources meet expectations
   (d) establishing a clear hierarchy of power and responsibility
2. Whenever her project falls behind schedule, Paula assigns mandatory weekend overtime to team members. Paula's approach involves which of the following?
   (a) reward power
   (b) punishment power
   (c) personality power
   (d) position power
3. Elsa worked for five years as a chemical engineer before being promoted to project manager. In her new position, Elsa can assign work to any other chemical engineer in her department. Is Elsa's power more achieved or ascribed?

8.3 Holding Others Accountable for Projects

Project success requires that project managers can count on the help promised to them by people throughout the organization. In matrix organizations, project managers often have no direct authority over team members—not to mention interested observers (see Section 4.2 for more on project roles).

The following sections cover ways project managers can increase the chances that people throughout their organizations live up to their commitments.

8.3.1 Involving People Who Really Have Authority

Project managers need to take the time to confirm with each team member's supervisor that the person can spend the necessary time to help on the project. Getting this agreement at the outset does the following:

▲ Reduces the chances that the person's supervisor will inadvertently assign work to the person that will make it impossible for him or her to work on the project in a timely manner.

▲ Establishes a relationship with the person's supervisor so that the project manager can ask for help if work isn't being done in a timely manner or can express appreciation when it is.

▲ Elicits a commitment to perform from someone who does have authority over the resources needed to do the work.

Project managers should also be sure to let team members know they want to bring the supervisor into the discussion and why; otherwise it might appear that the project manager is bringing in the supervisor because he or she doesn't trust the person.

8.3.2 Getting the Desired Results

The goals of a project are outlined early on, in the project plan. In order to meet these goals, the project manager needs help from multiple project team members. To get the most from project participants, project managers can use the following strategies:

▲ **Be specific.** Successful project managers make an effort to be specific with each team member regarding expected end results, time frames, and levels of effort. Often, when a person doesn't perform according to the project manager's expectations, it's because he or she misunderstood the desired results or time frame, or underestimated the effort needed to produce the results.

▲ **Get a commitment.** Team members must make specific promises to do project work; likewise, functional and upper managers must commit to the critical aspects of the project (the budget, schedule, resources, and so on). Project managers should beware of platitudes and generalities such as "I'll try" from team members or "I think your project is great" from functional and upper management.

▲ **Put it in writing.** After team members commit verbally to specific project duties, project managers should confirm these agreements in writing. Written confirmation clarifies the agreements reached and serves as a reminder of promises made. It also emphasizes the seriousness of the commitment. For some reason, people sometimes feel they can promise things verbally and it's okay if they don't honor their promises. But when it's in writing, it looks official.

▲ **Emphasize the urgency and importance of the assignment.** Project managers need to tell each team member where his or her work fits into the overall project plan. People will put in a greater effort if they know that it really makes a difference.

▲ **Tell others about a person's commitment.** This doesn't need to be a test of power between a project manager and team member; instead, the project manager simply tells others about the work the person has agreed to perform. The more people know about the work the person has promised to do, the greater the recognition he or she will get when the work is done (or not).

▲ **Act with authority.** After a team member commits to do some work on a project, that person gives the project manager the right to act as if he or she has authority over the team member. Project managers should never abuse their authority, but they make and enforce decisions based on this agreed-to power.

8.3.3 Monitoring Others' Work

Eliciting firm, specific commitments from team members is only part of the challenge for project managers. To actually achieve the goals of projects, project managers need to monitor activities and projects and follow up with team members. See Chapter 11 for more on controlling and monitoring all aspects of projects.

Following up might seem like busy work, but it is not. Following up on a regular basis with each project team member to gauge his or her progress reinforces the fact that an assignment is important and that the project manager fully expects the person to perform an activity in a promised time frame. Additionally, following up enables project managers to identify as soon as possible any problems that might arise.

To effectively monitor a project's follow-up activities, the project manager should do the following:

▲ Schedule a brief follow-up meeting a few days to a week prior to deadlines defined in the project plan.

▲ Check to see when each team member plans to start and finish the different parts of the task.

▲ Use any appropriate check-in method, including phone calls, drop-ins, in-person communication, or traditional scheduled meetings.

▲ Emphasize that the purpose of the follow-up activity is to see whether the team member has any questions or if there's anything the project manager can do to help with the assignment.

FOR EXAMPLE

Ladder of Accountability

As part of its ongoing commitment to organization development, the Human Resource department at the University of Victoria (www.uvic.ca) sees teams and projects as a critical aspect of life and productivity for the institution. The department offers a range of online resources, including the "ladder of accountability" philosophy, in which individual team members are highly accountable for the success of projects. The ladder of accountability is made of eight levels of accountability, ranging from "denial of the situation" to "implement solutions." Teams are encouraged to use a graphic representation of the ladder of accountability to examine their work-related issues and make effective individual and group choices about who is accountable for specific aspects of projects or decisions. For more on the University of Victoria's ladder of accountability and how to use the ladder in group decision-making processes, visit web.uvic.ca/hr/hrhandbook/organizdev/ladderofaccountability.pdf.

SELF-CHECK

1. Rhona's team members are often excited about her projects early on but tend to turn in low-quality work, which frustrates Rhona immensely. Which of the following is a technique that could help Rhona get higher quality work from her team members?

    (a) emphasizing the urgency of the project

    (b) setting up a system of punishments

    (c) being more specific in work assignments

    (d) none of the above

2. When making project assignments, you should involve a team member's functional manager in the process because doing so:

    (a) holds another person partially responsible for achieving an expectation.

    (b) helps establish a relationship with someone who has real authority over the resource.

    (c) ensures the team member is neither over- nor underloaded.

    (d) gives the team member a greater opportunity to self-define his or her responsibilities.

3. Unexpected weekly check-ins are an effective way to monitor a team member's performance throughout a project. True or false?

8.4 Handling Employee–Manager Problems

Micromanagement is one of the prime complaints employees have about their managers. **Micromanagement** is a person's excessive, inappropriate, and unnecessary involvement in the details of a task that he or she asks another person to perform. Whatever the reasons for micromanagement, it can lead to inefficient use of personal time and energy, as well as tension and low morale among staff.

8.4.1 The Reasons behind Micromanagement

Someone might micromanage for a variety of reasons. Following are several possible situations, along with suggestions for how to deal with them.

- ▲ **The person is interested in and enjoys the work.** Set up times to discuss interesting technical issues with the person.
- ▲ **The person is a technical expert and feels that he or she can do the job best.** Review technical work frequently with that person; give the person opportunities to share his or her technical insights. Encourage the micromanager to remember why he or she assigned the task to someone else in the first place.
- ▲ **The person might feel that he or she didn't explain the assignment clearly or that uncertainties might crop up.** Set up a schedule to discuss and review progress frequently so that the micromanager can promptly uncover any mistakes and help correct them.
- ▲ **The person is looking for ways to stay involved with the project and the team.** Set up scheduled times to discuss project activities. Provide the micromanager with periodic reports of project progress, and make a point to stop by and say hello periodically.
- ▲ **The person feels threatened because someone has more technical knowledge than he or she does.** When talking about the project in front of others, always give the micromanager credit for his or her guidance and insights. Share key technical information with the person on a regular basis.
- ▲ **The person doesn't have a clear understanding of how he or she should be spending his or her time.** Discuss with the person the roles he or she would like everyone else to assume on project activities. Explain how the person can provide useful support as others perform work on the project.
- ▲ **The person feels that he or she has to stay up on the work being done in case anyone else asks about it.** Discuss with the person what type of information he or she needs and how frequently he or she needs it. Develop a schedule to provide progress reports that include this information.

FOR EXAMPLE

The Difference between Interference and Interest

After his first year of graduate school, Stan worked during the summer for a manufacturer of electronic equipment. He was excited about the job because it was the first time he was regarded as a real member of a technical staff. On his first week, his boss stopped by his desk several times each day to discuss Stan's assigned project. By the end of the week, Stan was demoralized and depressed. Stan was convinced that his boss felt he didn't have the necessary skills to do a good job and that he was hanging over his shoulder to ensure that he didn't make any mistakes. However, as Stan got to know his boss better, he realized that he'd misread his boss's intentions. First, his boss was excited to have someone on staff who had been studying the latest developments in a technology that was important to the project. Rather than thinking that Stan was incapable, he wanted to learn from him. Second, the boss was a thoughtful and considerate person. He knew how daunting it could be for a young person to come into an established group and try to get to know everyone. He came around frequently to get to know Stan and to help him feel comfortable in the new environment. Stan's insecurities led him to believe that his boss's complimentary and considerate actions were meant as criticisms and expressions of distrust, when this was hardly the reality of the situation.

8.4.2 Helping Micromanagers Gain Confidence

For whatever reason, a boss might be micromanaging because he or she doesn't yet have full confidence in someone else's ability to perform. Rather than being angry or resentful, individuals feeling micromanaged can take the following steps to help the person develop that confidence:

▲ Don't be defensive or resentful when the person asks questions; doing so makes it appear as though you're hiding something and makes the person worry even more.

▲ Thank the micromanager for his or her interest, time, and technical guidance. Complaining about excessive oversight will strain work relationships, increase the person's fears and insecurities, and most likely cause the person to micromanage in even more detail. Make it clear to the micromanager that his or her input is valued and will be taken it into account, then try to develop a more acceptable working relationship.

▲ Work with the person to develop a scheme for sharing progress and accomplishments. Develop meaningful and frequent checkpoints. Frequent monitoring early in the project will reassure both parties that assignments are being successfully completed.

8.4.3 Working with a Micromanager

Individuals can reduce or even eliminate most micromanagement by improving communication and strengthening interpersonal relationships. Consider taking the following steps:

▲ **Don't assume.** Don't jump to conclusions. Examine the situation, get to know the person who's micromanaging, and try to understand his or her motivations. Expect to develop a working relationship in which both parties can be comfortable.

▲ **Listen.** Listen to the micromanager's questions and comments; see if patterns emerge. Try to understand the person's real interests and concerns.

▲ **Observe the person's behavior with others.** If the person also micromanages others, it's likely that the micromanagement stems from what he or she is feeling rather than from something you are or aren't doing. Try to figure out ways to address the person's real interests and concerns.

▲ **If at first you don't succeed, try, try again.** Draw conclusions and take steps to address the situation. If that approach doesn't work, reassess the situation and develop an alternative strategy.

SELF-CHECK

1. An effective way to handle a micromanaging boss who thinks he or she didn't explain an assignment clearly enough is to establish a schedule of check-ins and progress updates so the boss can promptly uncover any mistakes and help correct them. True or false?

2. You can deal effectively with a micromanaging boss by doing which of the following?

   (a) discussing your technical skills and experience in detail

   (b) requesting that your boss interact with you in the same manner that she or he interacts with other team members

   (c) discussing the specific roles he or she would like team members to assume

   (d) none of the above

8.5 Handling and Avoiding Project-Management Pitfalls

Sometimes a project manager joins a project in progress and finds that things are languishing. Or sometimes, a project just loses its focus. To get back on track, project managers should think of the remaining work as a new project: Develop a revised project plan, announce the plan to the organization, and track performance closely.

8.5.1 Determining How and Why Projects Get Off Track

The first step toward fixing a problem is understanding it. Project managers with floundering projects need to take the time to describe exactly *how* the project is off-track. Possibilities include that the project is

▲ Behind schedule.

▲ Overspending resource budgets.

▲ Not producing the desired outcomes.

Next, project managers need to identify reasons *why* the project is off-track. Possibilities include the following:

▲ Key people left the team or new ones joined it.

▲ Key drivers lost interest or new ones entered the picture.

▲ The business environment changed.

▲ New technology emerged.

▲ Organizational priorities shifted.

▲ Scope creep occurred.

8.5.2 Reaffirming Project Details

Often, after investigating the reasons why projects are off-track, project managers discover the original project plan holds all the information for success. Rather than dismantling projects and building something entirely new, many projects can be put on track by simply reaffirming aspects of the original project plan, including the following:

▲ **The key drivers.** Project managers can identify (or re-identify) the people who stand to benefit from the project (see Section 4.2). Project managers should consider people who originally wanted the project to be performed, as well as others who might have emerged since the project began. Reaffirming the benefits of the project can encourage renewed, active support from key project stakeholders.

▲ **Project objectives.** Project managers can reconfirm a project's objectives with the project's drivers. They can modify or add to the original objectives if people's needs have changed. Of course, all objectives (original and brand new) need to be specific, measurable, and achievable (see Section 2.2.2).

▲ **The activities still to be done.** Project managers should work with team members to reconfirm, modify, or eliminate the activities originally identified or add new ones, as needed. For all activities, clarify required resources, estimated durations, and identified interdependencies (see Section 6.2).

▲ **Roles and responsibilities.** Project managers can work with team members to clarify people's roles and responsibilities for the remaining project activities. They should identify and resolve conflicts that arose during the work performed to date—and eliminate any ambiguities that existed in the original plan. The project manager can also encourage all team members to reaffirm their commitments to project success.

▲ **Personnel assignments.** Project managers should clarify who will be performing the remaining work, how much effort they'll have to invest, and when. Project managers might need to have additional team members assigned to the project.

8.5.3 Introducing New Project Plan Elements

Sometimes reaffirming the original project plan is not enough to jumpstart a failing project. In these instances, project managers need to introduce new project plan elements in an effort to revitalize and refocus the project. Some activities include the following:

▲ **Developing a viable schedule.** If a project is behind schedule, project managers must revise the original schedule to allow for all the work remaining to be completed by the required end date (see Chapter 6 for more on scheduling). Defining meaningful intermediate milestones is a key technique that project managers can use to track ongoing performance.

▲ **Developing a risk management plan.** At this stage of many projects, project managers find that they have additional project activities to perform, new members on the team, and a tight schedule to meet. While a project manager might be able to develop a plan that has a chance of meeting targets, the plan most likely will also have risks. Project managers need to identify, analyze, and plan to minimize the negative impact of those risks (see Chapter 14). The best strategy for addressing risk focuses on minimizing the chances that the risks will

FOR EXAMPLE

The American Society for Quality

What is quality and how can it be encouraged from individuals and teams? These are critical questions for the American Society for Quality (www.asq.org), a nonprofit organization with more than 100,000 members dedicated to improving business processes and results by focusing on quality. Although becoming a member of the Society has many benefits, the Web site offers numerous free online tools to all visitors, including checklists, activities, forms, and charts that any project manager can use to define and promote quality for a specific project. Review the organization's free and downloadable "Quality Tools" at www.asq.org/learn-about-quality/qualitytools.html.

occur, developing contingency plans in case they do occur, and continually updating the project's risk management plan throughout the remainder of the project.

▲ **Holding a midcourse kickoff session.** Project managers can galvanize their teams and reawaken organizational interest in a newly replanned project by holding a midcourse kickoff session. In addition to announcing anticipated results and time frames, the project manager's aim is to convince people that the project now has a viable plan, a unified commitment, and a high likelihood of success.

SELF-CHECK

1. Determining how a project is off-track is critical; determining why a project is off-track is not. True or false?

2. To get a project back on track, what should the project manager do first?

3. When assessing off-track projects, project managers should reaffirm key project details including which of the following?

   (a) vendors and contractors

   (b) client approval procedures and network diagrams

   (c) slack time and expenditures

   (d) project objectives and personnel assignments

SUMMARY

Credibility, sensitivity, and ethics are essential personal characteristics for today's project managers. The leadership and management responsibilities of project management require project managers to recognize and develop various forms of personal power. By working with sources of authority and establishing monitoring processes, project managers can hold project members accountable for project work. Micromanaging the work of others is often a sign that the manager is not fully comfortable or confident in their role; establish clear role expectations and check-in processes to minimize the negative effect of micromanagement. When projects are over-budget or behind schedule, the project manager should assess and reaffirm the still-strong aspects of the project plan and then move on to creating a new schedule, developing a risk management plan, and other mid-project revisions.

KEY TERMS

Achieved power	The project manager earns the respect and allegiance of those whom he or she wants to influence.
Ascribed power	Someone gives the project manager the authority to reward and punish those whom he or she wants to influence.
Micromanagement	A person's excessive, inappropriate, and unnecessary involvement in the details of a task that he or she asks another person to perform.
Position power	Project team members take a project manager's requests more seriously because they feel that it's appropriate for the project manager to direct team members.
Power	The ability to influence the actions of others.
Punishment power	People do what a project manager asks because they don't want what the project manager can give them.
Reward power	People do what a project manager asks because they want the benefits that the project manager can give them.

ASSESS YOUR UNDERSTANDING

Go to www.wiley.com/college/portny to assess your knowledge of the basics of effective project management.
Measure your learning by comparing pre-test and post-test results.

Summary Questions

1. An agreed-upon schedule and system of project status check-ins can increase team member accountability and satisfy a micromanager's concerns. True or false?

2. A project manager with high technical credibility is likely to also have significant:

   (a) position power.

   (b) expertise power.

   (c) personality power.

   (d) all of the above

3. While reaffirming the roles, responsibilities, and personnel assignments of an off-track project, the project manager might consider the following:

   (a) getting a commitment in writing from specific team members

   (b) informing others within and outside the project of commitments

   (c) creating detailed statements of expectation for each team member

   (d) all of the above

4. While unnecessary, the power to punish and reward is very useful in getting a project back on track. True or false?

Applying This Chapter

1. Shannon has just been selected to project manage the rapid prototyping of a new microprocessor. What are specific leadership and management activities she can engage in from the very start of her project?

2. You've worked as a senior-level programmer for six years, participating as a team member on several high-profile computer networking projects. Last month you interviewed for a new project manager position within your company's wireless solutions group. You were selected as project manager and assigned a team of six programmers with varying levels of experience: Some are fresh out of college; others have nearly 25 years in the IT industry. Your team's biggest project is a new wireless routing device that is two months behind schedule. How specifically can you motivate your team based on the six influences outlined in Section 8.2?

3. For her latest project, Tessa has decided to have a brief assignment meeting with each team member and his or her functional manager to review what's expected of the team member in relation to the project. Three team members have balked at Tessa's request for assignment meetings, claiming that Tessa doesn't trust them to do their jobs anymore. What are some things Tessa can say and do with her team members to clarify and support her decision to hold assignment meetings?

4. Your new boss at a mid-size PR firm has 12 years of writing and editing experience. She's managed a few projects but has never managed people. Your new boss seems overly interested in your work as team copywriter and you fear she might be micromanaging you. What might be some reasons for your boss's micromanagement? What are some specific things you can do to minimize your boss's micromanagement?

5. This afternoon Jill was asked to take over a project that has been without a project manager for six weeks. The project has been going for nearly four months and was thoroughly planned and organized by the project's original project manager. Unfortunately, the project has not met any of its objectives or milestones and most of the team members have stopped actively participating in the project. Jill needs to assess the health of the project and present her evaluation of the project plan in two days' time. What key areas of the project plan should she focus her energies on prior to presenting her evaluation?

Your Strongest Characteristics

Consider the characteristics of a successful project manager as outlined in Section 8.1. Although all are essential characteristics for you to develop prior to and while working as a project manager, which two or three do you consider your strongest characteristics? In an interview situation, you will likely only have a few minutes to highlight two or three of these characteristics. Which will you highlight? What specific examples/situations can you cite? Take a look at your resume—are examples of these characteristics included in your resume? (And if you don't have a resume yet, begin drafting one by writing down specific work, school, and personal experiences that exemplify the characteristics in Section 8.1.)

Your Power Profile

Think about your current job, even if it's part-time or non-career employment. (If you aren't currently working, consider the last job you held.) In what ways are you powerful in this job? Write down a list of the powers you have, much like you would a job description. For your power profile, list specific ways you can give out punishments or rewards. Does your position by its very nature have some power? What about your personality increases your power? What expertise do you have that others tend to respect? After you draft your power profile, read through it and consider which areas you're the strongest in—and which need more work. Using the tips in Section 8.2.3, write down three ways you can further develop your base in your current position.

Follow-up and Follow-through

Project managers spend a great deal of time working on project budgets, schedules, and priorities, but they frequenly overlook project follow-up and follow-through. Evaluate a project plan you're currently working on and determine whether your plan includes details on follow-up activities that the project manager and team members are responsible for throughout the actual work of the project. If the plan doesn't include these details, write a new section entitled "Work Follow-Up" and provide specific recommendations for what the project manager and team members can do to ensure that work is being completed on schedule, on budget, and to an appropriate quality level. If appropriate, share your follow-up recommendations with others on the project team and consider consistently adding this section to all project plans.

Getting on Track

Create a three-column grid that summarizes your experiences with problematic projects. In the first column, brainstorm a list of 5 to 10 projects that you've been part of or have led that got off track in some way. You can include work, school, home, and personal projects. In the second column, write down the ways in which the projects were off-track (schedule delays, over-budget, quality was lacking, product expectations changed, and so forth). In the third column, list what specific things you or the project manager did to get the project back on track. If the project never got back on track, list some things you might have considered to get the project on track. Finally, use a highlighter or some other method to indicate those strategies for getting projects on track that actually worked in your opinion.

CASE STUDY: Southern Kentucky University Bookstore

Southern Kentucky University Bookstore

The Southern Kentucky University (SKU) bookstore is beginning a major project of automating its inventory system. The bookstore is organized into four business units: Textbooks, General Merchandise—insignia merchandise (sweatshirts, coffee mugs, etc.), General Books, and Convenience (candy, soft drinks, and so on). Lisa O'Brien, the bookstore manager, has decided to name each business unit supervisor as the project manager of his or her area's automation project. Each department has its own information systems person assigned so Lisa feels that each area can work independently to meet her deadlines for completion. The project is scheduled for completion right before school starts in the fall, with staggered "Go Live" dates for each of the business units. Each unit will do its own data entry and then work with the others on testing and implementation.

Missy Motz is the supervisor of the Textbook division of the bookstore. Missy is concerned that her department will not have enough resources to complete the automation project. The Textbook department is always swamped with book orders from professors right before school starts. Missy thinks she has enough staff to handle the data entry, but is concerned about supplying personnel at the times and quantities required as the implementation is phased in over each of the business units.

Missy knows a little bit about resource allocation techniques. She remembers that one of the most effective allocation techniques is to work first on the activity with minimum slack, so she instructed her staff to approach any tasks they are assigned as members of the project team on that basis.

Questions

1. What is the best way to schedule resources for the Textbook division?
2. What complications are added by making this project four separate projects?
3. How could Missy effectively lead her division and the other divisions—even though the other divisions do not report to her? Who does she need to involve in her project audience?

270

9
INVOLVING THE RIGHT PEOPLE IN PROJECTS
Building Strong Project Stakeholders and Teams

Starting Point

Go to www.wiley.com/college/portny to assess your knowledge of project team members.
Determine where you need to concentrate your effort.

What You'll Learn in This Chapter

▲ Internal and external project audiences and stakeholders
▲ Three types of audience members: drivers, supporters, observers
▲ When and how to engage the three types of audience members
▲ Project authority

After Studying This Chapter, You'll Be Able To

▲ Evaluate and prepare audience and stakeholder lists
▲ Create an audience or stakeholder list template
▲ Categorize project drivers, supporters, and observers
▲ Plan appropriate project activities for drivers, supporters, and observers
▲ Assess project authority

INTRODUCTION

People are critical to any project. Project managers need to identify, understand, and engage each project's diverse audience and stakeholders in order to lead everyone toward a successful project completion. Lists and templates are two tools project managers can use to organize and inspire the people associated with their projects. Various segments of a project audience can and should be engaged and involved in projects in different ways. Understanding who has authority in a project can mean the difference between project success and failure.

9.1 Knowing and Engaging a Project's Audience

In many ways, a project is like an iceberg: Nine-tenths of it lurks below the surface. A project manager receives an assignment and might think he or she knows what it entails and who has to be involved. Then, one by one, new people emerge as the project unfolds—people who affect what the project manager needs to accomplish and how he or she needs to approach the project.

Project managers run three risks when they don't involve key people or groups in projects in a timely manner:

1. They might miss important information that can affect the project's performance and ultimate success.
2. They might insult someone. When people involved in projects feel slighted or insulted, they sometimes take steps to make things more difficult for the project—and ultimately the project manager.
3. They may be sandbagged by a group with a non-project agenda.

From the very beginning, project managers should start to identify people who might play a role in the project. This chapter discusses how to identify these candidates; how to decide whether, when, and how to involve them; and how to determine who has the authority to make critical decisions.

9.1.1 Engaging a Project's Audience

A **project audience** is any person or group that supports, is affected by, or is interested in a project. Project audiences can be inside or outside the organization, and should be identified in a written project audience list.

Knowing a project's audiences helps project managers to do the following:

▲ Plan if, when, and how to involve them.
▲ Determine whether the scope of the project is bigger or smaller than originally anticipated.

Other terms are used to refer to project audiences, but each term addresses only some of the people to include in a complete project audience list.

▲ A **stakeholder list** identifies people and groups who support or are affected by a project. The stakeholder list most often doesn't include people outside of the organization or those who are merely interested in the project (although it can and should).

▲ A **distribution list** identifies people who receive copies of written project communications. Unfortunately, distribution lists are often out of date. Sometimes people are on the list because no one thought to remove them; other times, people are on the list because no one wants to run the risk of insulting them by removing them. In either case, their presence doesn't ensure that they actually support, are affected by, or are interested in a project.

▲ **Team members** are people whose work is directed by the project manager. All team members are part of the project audience, but the audience list includes more than just the team members.

9.1.2 Using Categories to Create an Audience List

Project managers and senior managers should start to develop an audience list as soon as they begin to think about a project and then continue to add and subtract names until the project is finished. Although some projects do not have stakeholders, most do.

To increase the chances of identifying all appropriate people, develop an audience list in categories. For example, Chris is less likely to overlook people

---

FOR EXAMPLE

Dealing with Large Project Audiences

Darlene's boss assigned her a project that had to be finished in two months. Darlene immediately set out to develop an audience list for the project. After realizing that her initial audience list included more than 100 names, she was about to conclude that the audience list was useless. However, as her manager pointed out, developing the audience list had fulfilled its purpose perfectly. Apparently, Darlene felt that each of the people on her list would in some way affect the success of her project. Identifying them at the start of her project gave her three options: (1) plan how and when to involve each person during the project; (2) assess the potential consequences of not involving one or more of her audiences; and (3) if she felt she couldn't ignore any of the audiences, she could discuss with her boss extending the project deadline or reducing its scope.

if he considers exactly who from the accounts payable group in the finance department should be included than if he tries to determine all the people from the entire organization at the same time.

Start an audience list by developing a hierarchical grouping of categories that covers the major areas from which audiences can be identified, such as the following:

▲ **Internal audiences.** Identify specific people and groups inside the organization who have interest in a project. Be sure to consider the following groups:

   ▲ **Upper management:** executive-level management responsible for the general oversight of all organization operations.

   ▲ **Requester:** the person who came up with the idea for a project and all the people through whom the request passed before it was given to the project manager. The requester often serves as the project champion.

   ▲ **Project manager:** the person with overall responsibility for successfully completing the project.

   ▲ **Team members:** people whose work is directed by the project manager.

   ▲ **Groups normally involved:** groups typically involved in most projects in the organization, such as human resources, finance, contracts, and the legal department.

   ▲ **Groups needed just for this project:** groups or people with special knowledge related to this project.

▲ **External audiences.** Identify people and groups outside the organization who have interest in the project. Be sure to consider the following groups:

   ▲ **Clients or customers:** people or groups that buy an organization's products and services.

   ▲ **Collaborators:** groups or other organizations with which team members might pursue joint ventures related to the project.

   ▲ **Vendors, suppliers, and contractors:** organizations that provide human, physical, or financial resources to help perform the project's work.

   ▲ **Regulators:** government agencies that establish regulations and guidelines that govern some aspect of project work.

   ▲ **Professional societies:** groups of professionals that could influence or be interested in a project.

   ▲ **The public:** the local, national, and international community of people who could be affected by or interested in a project.

Table 9-1 lists many of the groups to include in an audience list for the project manager coordinating an example project, an organization's annual blood drive.

Table 9-1: A Portion of an Audience List

Category	Subcategory	Audiences
Internal	Upper management	Executive oversight committee Vice president of sales and marketing Vice president of operations Vice president of administration
	Team members	Customer service representative Community relations representative Administrative assistant
	Groups normally included	Finance Facilities Legal
	Groups or people with special knowledge or interest	Project manager and team from last year's blood drive Public relations
External	Clients, customers	Donors from prior years Potential donors
	Regulatory agencies	Local Board of Health
	Vendors, contractors	Nurses who will be in attendance Food services provider Landlord of facility where the drive will be held
	Professional societies	American Medical Association American Association of Blood Banks
	Public	Local community Local newspapers Local television and radio stations

9.1.3 Ensuring That Audience Lists Are Complete and Useful

To ensure an audience list is useful and complete, consider the following guidelines:

▲ **Eventually identify each audience by position description and name.**
A project manager could, for example, initially identify people from sales

and marketing as part of a project's audience. Eventually, however, the project manager must specify the particular people to be considered from the sales and marketing group, such as the brand manager for XYZ product, Sharon Wilson.

▲ **Speak with a wide range of people.** Check with people in different organizational units, from different disciplines, and with different tenures in the organization. Ask every person for recommendations of other people to speak with. The more people a project manager speaks with, the less likely he or she will overlook someone important.

▲ **Allow sufficient time to develop an audience list.** Start to develop an audience list immediately. The longer a project manager thinks about a project, the more potential audiences he or she will identify. Continue to check with people throughout the project to find out more about additional audiences they might identify.

▲ **Include audiences who might play a role at any time during the project.** A project manager's only job at this stage is to identify names so they aren't forgotten. At a later point, the project manager can decide if, when, and how to involve them (see Section 9.2).

▲ **Include team members' functional managers.** Even though functional managers (that is, the people to whom team members directly report) don't directly perform project tasks, they can help to ensure that the project manager and team members devote all the time they originally promised to the project.

▲ **Separately include a person's name on the audience list for every different role he or she will play.** For example, Jan's boss will also be providing expert technical advice to her project team. Jan should include her boss's name twice—once as her direct supervisor and once as the technical expert. If her boss is subsequently promoted or leaves the company, listing him twice reminds Jan that a new person is now fulfilling the role of her direct supervisor and must be brought up to speed accordingly.

▲ **Continue to add and remove names from the audience list throughout the project.** Audience lists evolve as project managers learn more about their projects and as the projects themselves change. Encourage people involved in a project to continually identify new candidates as they think of them.

▲ **When in doubt, write down a person's name.** The goal is to avoid overlooking someone who might play an important part in the project. Identifying a potential audience member doesn't mean he or she has to be involved; it means that the project managers must consider them. Eliminating a name is easier after a project manager determines that the person isn't part of the audience than it is to add a name (that was initially overlooked) later in the project.

FOR EXAMPLE

Audience List Impact

A bank with U.S. and European locations spent considerable time and money revising its information systems. The people in charge of the project worked closely with special liaisons in Europe who represented the interests of the local bank personnel—the people who would enter and retrieve data from the system. When the system was turned on, a fatal problem was immediately identified: More than 90 percent of the local bank personnel in Europe were non-English speaking, but all the system documentation had been written in English. The system designers had worked with the liaisons to ensure that the interests and needs of the system users were identified and addressed. However, the liaisons had apparently misinterpreted their roles: They thought they were supposed to identify issues from their own experience rather than to identify and share issues raised by the local bank personnel. It turned out that English was the primary language of all the liaisons, so the issue of language was never identified. Putting both the liaisons and the local bank personnel on the audience list would have reminded the project staff to consider the concerns of the local bank personnel.

9.1.4 Developing an Audience List Template

An **audience list template** is a predesigned audience list that contains audiences typically included for similar projects. Using templates can save time and improve accuracy. An audience list template reflects the cumulative experience gained from doing numerous projects of a particular type. As project managers perform more projects, they can add audiences to the template that were overlooked in earlier projects and remove ones that prove not to be needed.

When using templates, keep the following in mind:

▲ **Develop templates for frequently performed tasks, as well as for entire projects.** Templates for kicking off the annual blood drive or submitting a newly developed drug to the Food and Drug Administration are valuable. But so are templates for individual tasks that are part of these projects, such as awarding a competitive contract and having a report printed. Templates for tasks can be incorporated into a larger audience list for an entire project for which these tasks will be performed.

▲ **Focus on position description rather than name of prior audience.** Identify an audience as "accounts payable manager" instead of "Bill Miller." People come and go, but functions endure. For each specific project, a project manager can fill in the appropriate names.

▲ **Develop and modify audience list templates from previous projects that actually worked, not from plans that looked good.** Often, detailed audience lists are developed at the start of projects, but they aren't revised during the project to add overlooked audiences. If a project manager only updates an audience list template with information from the audience list that was prepared at the start of a project, the template doesn't reflect learning acquired during the actual performance of the project.

▲ **Use templates as starting points, not ending points.** Make clear to those involved that the audience list template is the start of the audience list for the project, not the final list. Every project differs in some ways from similar ones in the past. If the template isn't critically examined, a project manager might miss people who weren't involved in previous projects but who need to be considered for this one.

▲ **Continually update templates to reflect the experience gained from performing different projects.** The postproject evaluation (see Section 14.1) is an excellent time to review and critique an original audience list.

FOR EXAMPLE

Drivers, Supporters, and Observers in an Information Technology Project

An information technology group was assigned a project to modify the layout and content of a monthly sales report that's prepared for all sales representatives. The project was requested by the vice president of sales and approved by the chief information officer (CIO), the boss of the head of the information technology group. The drivers for the project include the vice president of sales because he has specific reasons for asking that the report be revised and individual sales representatives because they are looking to get certain specific capabilities from the redesigned report. (The CIO is a potential driver because she might be looking to achieve certain capabilities through the performance of the project.) The supporters for the project include the systems analyst who will design the revised report, the training specialist who will train users, and the vice president of finance who authorizes the funds for printing the changes in the systems operating manual. The observers include the head of the customer service department, who is curious how the project might affect his chances of developing a monthly caller log in the next year.

SELF-CHECK

1. While project team members are part of a project audience:

   (a) project audience members are not always part of the project team.

   (b) project clients and customers are never project stakeholders.

   (c) project audience members are always upper management.

   (d) All the above are correct.

2. While a stakeholder list identifies people within an organization who support or are affected by a project, an audience list includes which of the following?

   (a) people likely to purchase the product or services created by the project

   (b) people who are affected by the project

   (c) people inside and outside the organization who support the project

   (d) all the above

3. Collaborators, contractors, and regulators are specific examples of what type of audience category?

4. Which internal audience category includes the person or people who came up with the original project idea?

5. When developing a project audience list, project managers should do all except which of the following?

   (a) Start the audience list as soon as possible and revise it frequently.

   (b) Include each person's name only once to avoid duplication.

   (c) Use an audience template, if available.

   (d) List each audience member by position and name.

9.2 Identifying Drivers, Supporters, and Observers

After identifying everyone in a project's audience, project managers need to determine which of the following groups the audience members fall into, to decide whether, how, and when to involve them.

▲ **Drivers:** people who have some say in defining the results that the project is to achieve. These are the people for whom the project is being carried out.

▲ **Supporters:** the people who help carry out the project. Supporters include those who authorize the resources for the project as well as those who actually work on it.

▲ **Observers:** people who are interested in the activities and results of the project. Observers have no say in what the project is to accomplish and they're not actively involved in supporting it. However, the project might affect them at some point in the future.

Project managers need to beware of supporters who try to act like drivers. For example, a programmer responsible for formatting and organizing content on a new employee-orientation intranet site might try to include information that he or she thinks might be helpful. However, the drivers (human resources, hiring managers) need to determine whether they want specific content to appear on the site. The programmer determines only the best manner to organize and present the information.

The same person can be both a driver and a supporter. The vice president of operations is a driver for a project to develop a series of safety teams. The vice president of operations is also a supporter if she has to transfer funds from the department budget to pay for developing and training the new teams.

9.2.1 Deciding When and How to Involve Drivers, Supporters, and Observers

As Section 4.1 details, most projects pass through a series of five life stages (conceive, define, start, perform, and close) as they progress from initial idea through completion. Drivers, supporters, and observers have different involvements during each phase of a project.

Involving Drivers

Drivers should be involved in projects from the start to the finish.

▲ **Conceive phase:** heavy involvement. Identify and speak with as many drivers as possible because their desires and the project manager's assessment of feasibility influence whether a project should be pursued. If project managers uncover additional drivers later in planning or while performing project tasks, they should explore with these new drivers the issues that led to the creation of the project and identify and assess any special expectations.

▲ **Define phase:** moderate to heavy involvement. Consult with drivers during this phase to ensure that the project plan addresses their needs and expectations. Have them formally approve the plan before starting the actual project work.

▲ **Start phase:** moderate involvement. Announce and introduce the drivers to the project team. Having the drivers talk about their needs and interests reinforces the importance of the project and helps team members form a more accurate picture of what needs to be accomplished. Having the drivers meet team members increases the drivers' confidence that the project will be successfully completed.

▲ **Perform phase:** moderate involvement. Keep drivers apprised of project accomplishments and progress to sustain their ongoing interest and enthusiasm. Involving drivers during this phase also ensures that the results being achieved are meeting their needs.

▲ **Close phase:** heavy involvement. Have drivers assess the project's results and determine whether their needs and expectations were met. Identify any recommendations they might have for improving performance on similar projects in the future.

Involving Supporters

Just as with drivers, supporters and project champions should be involved with projects from start to finish.

▲ **Conceive phase:** moderate involvement. Wherever possible, have key supporters assess the feasibility of meeting the expectations of the drivers. If key supporters are identified later in the project, have them confirm the feasibility of meeting the expectations that have been set.

▲ **Define phase:** heavy involvement. Supporters are the major contributors to the project plan. Because they perform or facilitate all the work, have them determine technical approaches, schedules, and resources required. Also have them formally commit to all aspects of the plan.

▲ **Start phase:** heavy involvement. Familiarize all supporters with the planned project work. Clarify how the supporters will work together to achieve the project results. Have the supporters decide how they'll communicate, resolve conflicts, and make decisions throughout the project.

▲ **Perform phase:** heavy involvement. By definition, supporters perform the work of the project during this phase. Keep them informed of project progress, encourage them to identify any performance problems encountered or anticipated, and work with them to develop and implement solutions to these problems.

▲ **Close phase:** heavy involvement. Have the supporters conclude their different tasks. Inform them of project accomplishments and recognize their roles in the project's achievements. Elicit their suggestions for how future projects can be performed even more effectively.

Involving Observers

Project managers should choose those observers with whom they want to actively share information about the project. Observers should be involved minimally throughout projects.

▲ **Conceive phase:** minimal involvement. Inform observers that the project exists and tell them what it'll produce.

▲ **Define phase:** minimal involvement. Inform observers about the planned outcomes and time frames.

▲ **Start phase:** minimal involvement. Tell them that the project has started and confirm the dates for planned intermediate and final milestones.

▲ **Perform phase:** minimal involvement. Inform observers of key achievements during the project.

▲ **Close phase:** minimal involvement. When the project is completed, inform observers about the project's products and results.

9.2.2 Using Different Methods to Involve Drivers, Supporters, and Observers

Keeping drivers, supporters, and observers informed as a project progresses is critical to the project's success. The following strategies can encourage the involvement of drivers, supporters, and observers, so they can make the greatest contribution to projects.

Choosing the right method can stimulate a group's continued interest and encourage them to actively support a project. The following communication tools and techniques can help keep project audiences involved throughout a project (Section 12.1 covers communication in detail):

▲ **One-on-one meetings:** formal and informal discussions with one or two other people about project issues. One-on-one meetings are particularly useful for interactively exploring and clarifying special issues of interest to a small number of people.

▲ **Group meetings:** planned sessions for some or all project team members or audiences. Smaller meetings are useful for brainstorming project issues, reinforcing team-member roles, and developing mutual trust and respect among team members. Larger meetings are useful for presenting information of general interest.

▲ **Informal written correspondence:** notes, memos, letters, and e-mail. Informal written correspondence helps the project manager and team members document informal discussions and share important project information.

▲ **Written approvals:** formal, written agreement about a project product, schedule, or resource commitment or a technical approach to project work.

SELF-CHECK

1. In general, when should supporters and drivers of projects be involved?

   (a) only during the define phase

   (b) from start to finish

   (c) during the perform and close phases

   (d) none of the above

2. During the start phase of a project, supporters are highly involved and busy making decisions about group process, while drivers are:

   (a) moderately involved and busy determining schedules and budgets.

   (b) highly involved and busy updating other audience segments.

   (c) moderately involved and busy empowering team members.

   (d) minimally involved and busy confirming project milestones.

9.3 Involving People with Authority in Projects

Authority is the right to make project decisions that others must follow. Having *opinions* about how an aspect of the project should be addressed is different from having the *authority* to decide how it will be addressed. Mistaking a person's level of authority can lead to wasted time and money, as well as to frustration.

When determining a project's audiences, project managers should confirm that the people they've identified have sufficient authority to make the decisions necessary to perform their assigned tasks. If they don't, find out who does and how to bring those people into the process.

For each project, use the following process to define each person's authority:

1. Clarify each person's tasks and decisions.

   (a) Define with each person in the project audience what his or her tasks will be and what his or her role in the task will be. Will she just be working on it? Will he be asked to approve schedules, resource expenditures, or work approaches?

2. Ask each person what authority he or she has regarding each decision and task.

   (a) Ask the person about his or her authority for individual tasks, rather than for all issues in a particular area. It's easier for a person to know

FOR EXAMPLE

Who's in Charge Here?

A committee responsible for planning the renovation of the offices of a mid-size communication firm reached a final decision on the new wall color paint. After intense discussions, all present agreed that the walls would be painted a light gray. One week later, the committee member from the facilities department informed the rest of the committee that his boss decided the color the group had chosen was too expensive and that they would have to choose another color. The meeting a week earlier had been a complete waste of everyone's time. Each person at that meeting had assumed that the others in attendance had the necessary authority to support whatever decision the group made. Had they realized beforehand that the facilities department representative didn't have this authority, the group could have invited the facilities manager who did have the authority to attend the meeting. Or they could have asked the representative from the facilities department to find out what criteria affect the choice of paint products for the company.

with confidence that he or she can approve supply purchases for up to $5000 than that he or she can approve all equipment purchases, no matter what type and how large.

(b) Clarify decisions that the person can make his- or herself. For decisions needing someone else's approval, find out whose approval they need. Be sure to ask—not assume.

3. Ask people how they know what authority they have.

(a) Does a written policy, procedure, or guideline confirm the authority? Did the person's boss tell him or her in conversation? Is the person just assuming?

4. Check the history.

(a) Have you or others worked with this person in the past? Has he or she been overruled on decisions he or she was supposed to be authorized to make?

5. Has anything changed recently?

(a) Is the person new to the organization? To his or her current group? To his or her current position? Has the person recently started working for a new boss?

Reconfirm the information in these steps when the audience's decision-making assignments change. For example, Nina initially expected that individual purchases on her project would total at or under $2500. Bill, the team representative from the finance group, assured her that he has the authority to approve such purchases for the project without checking with his boss. After researching options, Nina finds that she needs to purchase a $5000 piece of equipment. Nina needs to verify with Bill that he can personally authorize this larger expenditure. If he can't, she needs to find out whose approval is also required.

SELF-CHECK

1. The more authority you have in a project, the more responsibility you have to make things happen. True or false?

2. Which of the following is one appropriate way to determine audience members' authority within the context of the project?

   (a) asking them what authority they think they have

   (b) analyzing the project plan for details on the topic

   (c) asking upper management to outline who has authority for the project

   (d) working as a group to determine who has authority

SUMMARY

Project managers need to know all the diverse members of a project audience and how to engage and involve them. Creating an audience list (either from a template or from scratch) helps project managers organize all the individuals who need to be involved in communications and decision making. Depending on a project member's general role—supporter, driver, or observer—and his or her level of authority, the project manager can determine the best way to involve the person.

KEY TERMS

Audience list template	A predesigned audience list that contains audiences typically included for similar projects.
Authority	The right to make project decisions others must follow.
Collaborators	Groups or other organizations in a project audience with which team members might pursue joint ventures related to the project.
Distribution list	Document that identifies people who receive copies of written project communications.

Drivers   People who have some say in defining the results that the project is to achieve; the people for whom the project is being carried out.

Observers   People who are interested in the activities and results of the project but have no say in what the project is to accomplish and are not actively involved in supporting it.

Project audience Any person or group inside or outside the organization that supports, is affected by, or is interested in a project.

Regulators   Government agencies that establish regulations and guidelines that govern some aspect of project work.

Requester   The person who came up with the idea for a project and all the people through whom the request passed before it was given to the project manager.

Stakeholder list Document that identifies people and groups who support or are affected by a project. The stakeholder list most often does not include people outside of the organization or those who are merely interested in the project.

Supporters   People who help carry out the project, including those who authorize the resources for the project as well as those who actually work on it.

Team members   People whose work is directed by the project manager.

ASSESS YOUR UNDERSTANDING

Go to www.wiley.com/college/portny to assess your knowledge of project team members.

Measure your learning by comparing pre-test and post-test results.

Summary Questions

1. A stakeholder list is likely to include which of the following?
   (a) observers
   (b) supporters
   (c) drivers
   (d) all of the above
2. Drivers often have significant authority associated with projects, while supporters have less, but still relevant, authority. True or false?
3. An internal driver for a project might be an upper manager, while an external driver might be which of the following?
   (a) a vendor
   (b) a client
   (c) a regulator
   (d) an adjudicator

Applying This Chapter

1. Liam manages 10 to 15 projects annually that have many of the same goals and audience members. To make his project communications more consistent and efficient, he's developed a list of 25 people who typically are part of his projects' audiences. What can he do to create an effective project template?
2. Two sales representatives for the same company developed audience lists for new projects. The first representative put her audience list template on a set of overheads, using graphic-design software, while the second handwrote her audience list on several sheets of chart paper. Both representatives shared the templates with their teams and asked for feedback. Rep #1 received a few new names, while rep #2 received dozens of recommendations and ended up reorganizing the way she communicated with her project audience. Why was rep #2 more successful in generating a quality audience list?
3. Identify a driver, supporter, and observer for the project of organizing and managing a fundraising bake sale at your child's elementary school.

4. Consider the four methods of involving your audience listed in Section 9.2.2. How appropriate is each method for the specific audience segment of a project's drivers, supporters, and observers?

5. You and your project team need to purchase a major piece of equipment to successfully complete your project. Everyone on your team agrees the equipment is necessary. You've talked with your boss about the purchase and she's on board as well. Yet several weeks go by and you're no closer to ordering the piece of equipment because no one seems able (or willing) to approve the purchase. What are some things you can do as project manager to figure out who has the authority to make the purchase happen for this project?

Your Audience List

In many ways, your ongoing career education is a major project that you are managing. Create an audience list of all the people who are part of the audience for this project. Consider internal and external audiences as you compile your list. After you brainstorm your list, go back and organize the names categorically and by title.

Your Three-Part Plan

Select a real or hypothetical work project that you've managed or would like to manage someday. Think about your project's audience and identify at least two drivers, two supporters, and two observers for your project. Draft a basic audience involvement plan with one specific thing you can expect from each audience segment during the conceive, define, start, perform, and close phases of the project. Refer to Section 9.2.1 for examples of appropriate involvement levels for each audience segment.

Know Your Authority

Brainstorm a short list of what authority you believe you have for a work-related or school-related project. Although you might initially think you have no authority, consider anything you can make a decision on to be your realm of authority. For example, your authority might be as seemingly minor as having the authority to write your research paper on any word-processing program you choose—or as seemingly major as being able to authorize purchase of equipment up to $10,000. Read through the list and ask yourself the critical questions outlined in Section 9.3 to help determine if your understanding of your authority makes sense. Write your statement of authority for the project and keep it handy whenever questions arise.

CASE STUDY: Quantum Bank, Inc.

Quantum Bank, Inc.

Quantum Bank, Inc. is a regional bank with branches throughout the Southeast. In early 1999 the bank launched a Web site that provides its customers with the ability to check account balances, obtain information about the bank's various services, obtain contact information and e-mail questions, and link to a variety of other useful sources of information.

Given the site's tremendous success, competition from both traditional and nontraditional organizations, and the desire to expand its presence beyond its current geographical area, Quantum decided to expand its online offerings significantly. More specifically, Quantum would like to expand its Web site to include an online bill payment service, allow customers to apply for credit cards and loans online, open accounts online, and manage their investment portfolios online.

Vice President of Information Systems Stacey Thomas has been charged with overseeing the project. One of her first tasks was to select the project manager. Because of the strategic importance of the project, she had a strong preference for staffing the project internally as opposed to employing the services of one of the many consulting firms available that specialize in these types of projects. After developing a list of 10 or so possible candidates to serve as project manager, she was finally able to pare the list down to the two finalists described in the following sections.

Bill Fence

Bill joined Quantum in 1995 after graduating from a well-respected small private school with a degree in computer science. His first assignment, as a member of the bank's help desk, provided him with exposure to a variety of areas in the bank. He quickly gained a reputation for being able to solve difficult technical problems. In addition, users of the bank's various computer systems were often heard commenting on how service-oriented Bill was and on his ability to describe concepts in nontechnical terms.

Because of both his technical knowledge related to hardware and his ability to program, Bill was selected to develop the bank's Web site in 1998. Bill worked alone on this project and had frequent meetings with one of the bank's Directors of Information Systems, who supervised the project. Initially, the director did most of the design work and Bill did the computer programming. Bill often proposed alternate ways for incorporating key features into the Web site, and the director would choose among the options Bill identified. Toward the end of the development project, Bill began to take a more active role in proposing features to include in the site.

The development project was largely completed on time and on budget, considering the changes in the scope of the project that were made as the project progressed. Several suggestions that would have extended the site's functionality were tabled to be considered after the site was officially launched.

In his current position as Webmaster, Bill is in charge of maintaining the bank's Web site. Although Bill's staff now includes a programmer and a hardware specialist, his approach is very much hands-on, staying involved with all technical aspects of the site. Bill has developed an excellent rapport with his two direct reports, and they have emulated much of Bill's style, including working long hours and even competing to see who can accumulate the largest number of soft drink cans, empty candy wrappers, and computer printouts on one desk.

Andy Dover

Andy Dover also joined the bank in 1995 after completing his MBA at a large public university. Andy entered graduate school immediately after graduating with a Civil Engineering undergraduate degree at the same university.

Andy spent his first year at the bank rotating between various departments in the bank's management training program. After completing this training, Andy requested permanent assignment to the operations group. His initial assignment was to oversee the check encoding operation. After implementing several process improvements, Andy was eventually promoted to senior operations analyst and worked on several large process improvement projects.

290

Performance evaluations of Andy suggested that one of his greatest strengths is his ability to step back from a problem and understand how the various issues are interrelated. His evaluations further recognized him as "a highly motivated self-starter with very good organizational skills." His organizational skills also helped him effectively present information, and he was often requested to make short presentations related to a particular project's status to senior management.

By almost all accounts, Andy was considered highly competent, completing assigned tasks in a timely fashion with little or no direct supervision. At the same time, Andy always made it a point to communicate regularly with other project team members to keep them abreast of his progress. He was often passionate about his ideas and was typically able to get buy-in from other team members for his ideas.

Andy is almost always seen carrying his planner. As an avid stock investor, he makes it a point to stay abreast of trends in technology. He has a basic understanding of how the Internet works and knows all the important buzzwords. While he has fooled around and created a couple of Web pages, he knows very little about more sophisticated programming languages such as Java, and knows even less about computer hardware beyond its basic purpose.

Questions

1. Who would you recommend Stacey Thomas select to serve as project manager? Why?
2. How would you recommend this project be organized? Functional project? Pure project? Matrix? Why?
3. Do you agree with Ms. Thomas's decision that the project should be staffed internally? What are the major advantages of staffing the project with Quantum employees? Are there any advantages to using the services of an outside consulting firm?

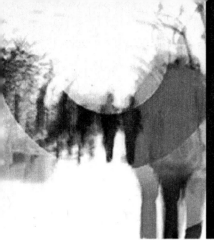

10

MANAGING PROJECT TEAMS
Organizing and Guiding Others to Project Success

Starting Point

Go to www.wiley.com/college/portny to assess your knowledge of the basics of project team management.
Determine where you need to concentrate your effort.

What You'll Learn in This Chapter

- ▲ The effects of authority, responsibility, and accountability on teams
- ▲ The purpose and process of delegating
- ▲ Methods that encourage project accountability
- ▲ Three organizational clusters: teams, groups, and committees
- ▲ Team-management and development techniques
- ▲ Motivational strategies

After Studying This Chapter, You'll Be Able To

- ▲ Build strong project teams through delegation and shared responsibility
- ▲ Create project teams with high levels of responsibility and accountability
- ▲ Compose team and individual project goals and processes
- ▲ Develop and enhance team members' contributions to projects
- ▲ Evaluate the effectiveness of the team and develop tools and techniques to further strengthen teams

INTRODUCTION

Of the many people in a project's audience, the members of the project team are extremely important to the success of the project. Project managers can develop their authority, responsibility, and accountability through a variety of methods, including delegation and sharing responsibility. Early on, project teams need to establish team and individual goals for the project as well as team roles and operating procedures. Project managers can motivate teams through clarifying project benefits, demonstrating project feasibility, and rewarding individual and group progress.

10.1 Defining Team Roles and Responsibilities

Project teams typically include people from different parts of an organization, with different skill sets and operating styles. (And virtual projects can link team members from anywhere around the globe.) A project usually has a tight time schedule, and team members most likely are working on several other projects at the same time. The project manager might not have worked extensively with these people before.

Success in this environment requires that the project manager and team members reach agreements about how they'll work together to maximize everyone's contribution and minimize wasted time and mistakes. Project managers need to develop an approach that gives them and others confidence that everyone will live up to their commitments. Project managers also need to understand the planned roles and be comfortable with them.

10.1.1 Agreeing to Three Team Concepts

The following three concepts define and clarify how team members should relate to each other and to their assigned tasks:

1. **Authority:** the ability to make binding decisions about a project's products, schedule, resources, and activities. Examples include a project manager's ability to sign purchase orders not exceeding $3000 or the ability of a team member to change a scheduled date by no more than two weeks.
2. **Responsibility:** the commitment to achieve specific results. An example is a technical writer's promise to have a draft report ready by March 1.
3. **Accountability:** bringing consequences to bear based on people's performances. Having a boss reflect in an employee's annual performance appraisal that he or she solved a difficult manufacturing problem is an example of accountability. Many people think of accountability as a negative concept—if someone fouls up, he or she pays the price. This

fear often causes people to shun positions in which they would be held accountable for performance. Paying a price for fouling up is only half of the concept. The other half is that when someone does a good job, he or she is rewarded. This positive reinforcement is a far more effective way to encourage high-quality results.

The three preceding terms all address similar issues. However, each one is a distinct element that's required to define and reinforce team relationships. Consider authority and responsibility, as follows:

▲ Similarity: both authority and responsibility are upfront agreements. Before a project starts, the project manager and project team agree on who can make which decisions and who will ensure that particular results are achieved.
▲ Difference: authority focuses on process, while responsibility focuses on outcomes. Authority defines the decisions that can be made but does not mention the results that must be achieved. Responsibility addresses the results to be accomplished, with no mention of the decisions people can make to reach the desired outcomes.

Also, consider responsibility and accountability, as follows:

▲ Similarity: both responsibility and accountability focus on results.
▲ Difference: responsibility is a before-the-fact agreement, while accountability is an after-the-fact process.

People who make promises, fail to keep their promises, and experience no resulting consequences create some of the worst frustrations in a project environment. It's essential that the entire project team keep in mind the following guidelines for accountability:

▲ **If you're responsible, you should be held accountable.** In other words, if you make a promise, you should always face consequences based on how well you honor your promise.
▲ **If you're not responsible, you shouldn't be held accountable.** If something goes wrong but you weren't responsible for ensuring that it was handled correctly, you shouldn't face negative consequences. (Of course, you shouldn't receive positive accolades if things go well in this case, either.)

Holding people accountable when they aren't responsible is **scapegoating.** This process of assigning blame to the closest person when things go wrong only encourages people to avoid dealing with the scapegoating individual in the future.

10.1.2 Assigning Project Roles through Delegation

Although many definitions exist, **delegation** is giving something away. People delegate for three reasons:

1. To free themselves up to do other tasks.
2. To have the most qualified person make decisions.
3. To develop another person's ability to handle additional assignments prudently and successfully.

Follow these two guidelines when assigning project roles:

1. Someone can delegate authority, but he or she can't delegate responsibility.
2. Someone can *share* responsibility.

Project managers can choose to transfer to another person the right to make decisions that they are empowered to make, but they can't rid themselves of the responsibility for the results of those decisions.

For example, Gordon has the authority to sign purchase orders under $5000. Gordon has never been told he can't give this authority to someone else, and no policy specifically prevents him from doing so. Gordon could delegate some or all of this authority to Matt if he wanted to. That is, Gordon could give Matt the authority to sign purchase orders for the project not to exceed $5000. However, if Matt mistakenly bought ten reams of specialty paper for $3000 instead of the five that he really needed, Gordon would be responsible for the poor decision.

Project managers can always take back authority that they delegated to someone else, but they can't blame the person for exercising that authority while he or she has it.

It's critical that project managers actively reinforce and support delegation of authority. For example, Linda has been the leader of a project team for the past two months, and Mary has been her assistant. Mary has been helping to deal with people's technical issues including the following situations:

▲ When someone runs into a technical problem, he or she discusses it with Mary.
▲ Mary analyzes the problem and decides how to address it.
▲ Mary discusses the problem with Linda and explains her proposed solution.
▲ If Linda agrees with Mary's proposed solution, Linda asks her to implement it.
▲ If Linda doesn't agree with Mary's suggestion, Linda works with her to develop a more acceptable approach.

Yesterday, Linda told Mary that she wanted to change the way she deals with technical issues. Linda explained that, from now on, Mary doesn't have to pass her proposed solutions by Linda before implementing them. After discussing this with Mary, Linda told the other team members about the new procedure.

This morning, Joe came to Mary to discuss a problem he was having with a contractor. After listening to the problem, Mary gave Joe very specific instructions for how to deal with it. As soon as Joe left Mary's office, however, he called Linda on the phone. He recounted the problem he had discussed with Mary and her proposed solution, and he asked Linda if she agreed with the approach Mary had recommended.

Linda now has a dilemma. On the one hand, Linda wants to support Mary's newly delegated authority to develop and implement solutions to technical problems on her own. On the other hand, Linda also wants to ensure that things go smoothly and successfully on the project. What should Linda do?

The only appropriate response Linda can make to Joe that supports the delegation of authority to Mary is this: "Do whatever Mary told you to do."

What if Linda responded to Joe, "Yes, Mary's solution sounds good to me"? That won't do it. By declaring that Linda likes Mary's solution, she undercuts Mary's authority to make the decision on her own. Perhaps Linda just wants to tell Joe that she had full confidence in Mary's ability to develop an appropriate solution, and the one Mary proposed was an example of her good judgment. However, in reality, Linda's response suggests to Joe that she is still a part of the approval process because Linda just gave her approval to Mary's decision rather than to her authority to make whatever decision she felt was appropriate.

Additionally, the following situations require further consideration:

▲ **Linda doesn't agree with Mary's recommendation.** If Linda fears that following Mary's recommendation will have catastrophic consequences, Linda must suggest to Joe that he wait until she can discuss the issue with Mary. In this instance, protecting the project and organization is more important than supporting Linda's delegation of authority.

▲ In all other instances, though, Linda should tell Joe to follow Mary's suggestion because she has the authority to make that decision. Here are several reasons to do so even if Linda doesn't agree with Mary's choice:

  ▲ Mary might know more about the situation than Linda learned from her conversation with Joe.

  ▲ Maybe Mary's right and Linda's wrong.

  ▲ Suppose Linda's approach is better than Mary's. How will Mary learn to make better choices in the future if Linda doesn't discuss with Mary why she doesn't agree with Mary's decision?

▲ If Mary believes that Linda will jump in to save her every time she makes a bad decision, Mary will be less concerned about making the correct decision the first time.

▲ Linda can always ask Mary later to explain privately the rationale for her decision, and Linda can offer thoughts and opinions, if she feels it's necessary.

▲ **Joe's call indicates a more general problem with the team's procedures and working relationships.**

    ▲ Perhaps Linda wasn't clear when she explained the new working procedures to the team member. In this case, Linda should explain and reinforce the new procedures to Joe.

    ▲ Perhaps Joe didn't like Mary's answer and is trying to go behind her back to get his way. Again, Linda must reinforce that the decision is Mary's to make.

    ▲ Perhaps Mary wasn't clear enough in her explanation to Joe why she recommended what she did. Linda should suggest to Mary that Mary explain the reasons behind her solutions more clearly and that Mary probe to make sure people understand and are comfortable with the information she shares.

    ▲ Perhaps some interpersonal conflict exists between Joe and Mary. Linda should talk with both Joe and Mary to determine whether such a conflict exists and, if it does, how it came about. Linda should then work with Joe and Mary to help them address and resolve the conflict.

10.1.3 Delegating with Confidence

Delegation always involves some risk—the delegator has to live with the consequences of someone else's decisions. Project managers can take the following steps to increase their comfort level and improve the delegate's chances for successful performance:

▲ **Clarify what is to be delegated.** Describe in unambiguous terms the work the other person is to perform; also explain what the person is not supposed to do.

▲ **Choose the right person.** Determine the skills and knowledge a person must have to perform the task successfully, and don't delegate the task to a person who lacks these skills and knowledge.

▲ **Make the delegation correctly.** Explain the work to be done, how much effort is expected of the person, and the date by which the work is to be completed.

▲ **Monitor performance.** Set up frequent, well-defined checkpoints to monitor performance; monitor according to that schedule.

10.1.4 Sharing Responsibility

The decision to delegate authority is a **unilateral decision;** it doesn't require the agreement of both parties. A project manager can choose to give someone the authority to make a decision.

After the project manager gives authority to another person, he or she is free to pass it on to someone else (if the project manager hasn't specifically told him or her not to). Responsibility, however, is a two-way agreement: Cheryl's boss asks her to respond to a customer inquiry, and Cheryl agrees to do so. Because Cheryl and her boss agreed that Cheryl would handle the inquiry, Cheryl can't decide to give the assignment to someone else and not worry about whether he or she accomplishes it. Cheryl committed to her boss that the inquiry would be addressed; the only way Cheryl can free herself from this responsibility is to ask if her boss would agree to change their original understanding.

10.1.5 Holding People Accountable When They Don't Report to You

What happens when people who don't report to a project manager agree to help him or her? Can the project manager hold people accountable for their performances if the project manager has no direct authority over them?

Suppose Leslie was recently assigned to a new inventory control system project—an effort to design, develop, test, and implement an upgraded inventory control system for her organization. When Leslie learns that her friend Eric

---

FOR EXAMPLE

Can Responsibility be Delegated?

Alice asks Neil to prepare a report highlighting the organization's latest sales figures. Neil figures that he can prepare the text of the report in Microsoft Word and any necessary graphics in Microsoft PowerPoint. Neil knows where to get the raw sales data and how to use Word, but he doesn't know how to use PowerPoint. However, Bill, a member of Neil's staff, does know how to use PowerPoint. Neil accepts Alice's assignment and Bill agrees to help Neil with the project. A week later, Alice asks how Neil's doing on the report. Neil tells her that he's completed the text, but Bill hasn't finished the graphics. Neil suggests that she check with Bill to find out how he's doing and when he'll be finished. After a moment's silence, Alice reminds Neil that he agreed to prepare the report, and, therefore, ensuring that all parts of the work are completed is his responsibility, not hers. In other words, because he accepted responsibility for completing the report, he can't choose to give away part of that responsibility to someone else.

had been working on the project until a month ago, she calls Eric and asks him to fill her in on the project's history. After a few minutes, Leslie realizes that he knows more about the project than anyone else with whom she's spoken to date. Leslie explains to Eric that Chapter 1 of the manual will recount the history and development of the new system. She asks him if he would be willing to write a draft of Chapter 1 by a week from Friday. Eric agrees, and they both hang up the phone. A week from Friday comes and goes, and Leslie never receives the draft from Eric. He never calls to explain why he didn't submit the draft, and Leslie never checks with him to see what's happening.

This situation might sound familiar to many project managers. To avoid this scenario, project managers need to hold people accountable if they accept the responsibility to complete an assignment. Further, a project manager can't hold people accountable if they don't accept responsibility.

Therefore, two questions stand out in the Leslie/Eric situation:

1. After their phone call, was Eric responsible for writing a draft of Chapter 1 for Leslie? Very simply, the answer is yes because he made the commitment. Leslie's responsibility to ensure that the user's manual is prepared hasn't changed, but Eric accepted the responsibility to prepare the Chapter 1 draft. It makes no difference that Eric is no longer assigned to work on the project or that he doesn't report to the same boss. He's responsible because he said that he would be.

2. Did Leslie hold Eric accountable for his failure to perform in accordance with his promise? The answer is no. No consequences resulted from his failure to deliver a draft of Chapter 1 as promised. In fact, Leslie's behavior sends the message that either the assignment wasn't that important or that Eric's behavior was okay. Both are horrible messages.

Unfortunately, these types of behaviors, multiplied many times every day, define an organizational environment where promises mean little and breaking them becomes an accepted element of business as usual.

Project managers might not try to hold people accountable when they have no authority over them because they don't think it's appropriate (after all, the project managers aren't their bosses) or because the project managers don't know how. However, holding people accountable is appropriate and necessary if they've accepted the responsibility to perform. Accountability helps people know that they're on the right track and enables project managers to formally acknowledge when they complete the promised assignments. Project managers don't need authority to hold people accountable; the people just must accept the responsibility.

Project managers can use the following approaches to hold people account-able when the project managers have no direct authority over them:

▲ **Find out who does have direct authority over the person and bring that supervisor into the process.** Consider soliciting the approval of the person's boss. Doing so correctly and at the right time can improve the chances for success.

▲ **Put it in writing.** Put agreements in writing to clarify the terms, to serve as a reminder, and to formalize the agreement. If people ask, explain to them that it has nothing to do with lack of trust. If you didn't trust them, you wouldn't work with them at all.

▲ **Be specific.** The clearer a request, the easier it is for the person to estimate the effort needed to respond to the request and to produce the right result the first time. Some project managers are uncomfortable being too specific because they feel that giving the person orders is inappropriate (after all, project managers rarely have direct authority over others). But being specific makes it easier for the person, not harder.

▲ **Follow up.** Negotiate a schedule to monitor the person's performance and to address any issues or questions that arise. Be sure to negotiate a follow-up schedule at the outset. If a project manager calls unannounced at random times, it appears that he or she is checking up and distrusts the other person.

▲ **Make the person accountable to the team.** A project manager's most valuable professional asset is his or her reputation. When a person promises to do something, let others on the project team know about the promise. When the person lives up to that promise, acknowledge it in front of his or her colleagues. If the person fails to live up to the promise, let him or her know that this information will be shared with others as well.

▲ **Get a commitment.** When a person indicates that he or she will help, be sure to get a firm, specific commitment that the desired result will be achieved by this time for this cost. Beware of declarations like "I'll give it my best effort" or "You can count on me."

▲ **Create a sense of urgency and importance.** Try not to minimize any pressure the person feels by saying, in essence, that it's okay if he or she doesn't perform to expectations because he or she has so many other things going on. Unfortunately, this approach suggests to the person that his or her work is really not that important and actually increases the chances that they won't deliver. Instead, let the person know how his or her work influences other activities and people on the project. Let the person know why it's important that he or she does perform to expectations and what the consequences to the project and the organization will be if he or she doesn't.

A Linear Responsibility Chart (Section 4.5) is a good tool to define, organize, and illustrate various team roles and responsibilities

SELF-CHECK

1. What three critical concepts do all project managers and project teams need to consider early on to ensure clarity for the project?

2. Responsibility and accountability both relate to the results of a project. Accountability focuses on results after the project is completed, while responsibility focuses on which of the following?

   (a) results while the project is happening

   (b) objectives and outcomes

   (c) agreed-to results before the project happens

   (d) liability and expectation

3. Which of the following statements about delegation is untrue?

   (a) People can delegate to develop the other person's skills.

   (b) When you delegate authority, you also delegate responsibility.

   (c) Effective delegation involves ongoing monitoring of the situation by the person delegating authority.

   (d) Delegation can allow the most qualified person to make decisions.

4. An effective way for a project manager to encourage accountability from a team member is to do which of the following?

   (a) Let the entire project team know about the team member's accountability.

   (b) Write down a formal description of the accountability.

   (c) Inform the team member's functional manager of the accountability.

   (d) all the above

10.2 Establishing New Project Teams

Merely assigning people to perform selected tasks on a project does not create a project team. A **project team** is a collection of people who are committed to common goals and who depend on one another to do their jobs. Project teams are based on the premise that every member can and must make a valuable and unique contribution to the project.

A project team is different from other associations of people who work together, as follows:

▲ A **work group** is comprised of people who are assigned to a common task and work individually to accomplish their particular assignments.

▲ A **committee** is comprised of people who come together to review and critique issues, propose recommendations for action, and, on occasion, implement those recommendations.

By contrast, teams entail commitment to common goals, mutually dependent work, and vital and unique contributions from all members.

As soon as project managers identify their project team members, they should take steps to define and establish their teams' identities and operating practices. At the earliest possible time, start to discuss and develop the following, making sure they're well-defined and accepted:

▲ **Goals:** what the team as a whole, as well as each member individually, hopes to accomplish.

▲ **Roles:** each member's individual assignments.

▲ **Processes:** the techniques that team members will use to help them perform their project tasks.

▲ **Relationships:** the feelings and attitudes of team members toward each other.

The following sections cover each of these four aspects of teams.

10.2.1 Developing Team and Individual Project Goals

Team members commit to a project when they believe that their participation can help them achieve worthwhile professional and personal goals. Project managers help team members develop and buy into a shared sense of the project goals by doing the following:

▲ Discussing the reasons for the project, who is supporting the project, and the impact of the planned results. The Statement of Work (see Section 2.5) can be a useful tool for this activity.

▲ Clarifying how the project results could benefit the organization's client populations.

▲ Emphasizing how the results of the project might support the organization's growth and viability.

▲ Exploring how the project results could impact each team member's job.

Project managers can encourage people to think about how their participation in the project might help them to achieve personal goals, such as acquiring new skills and knowledge, meeting new people, increasing their visibility in the organization, and enhancing their opportunities for job advancement. Of course, projects aren't performed solely to help team members achieve personal benefits, but if team members can realize personal benefits and at the same time perform valued services for the organization, their motivation and commitment to project success will be greater. See Section 10.3 for more on creating and sustaining team motivation.

10.2.2 Defining Team Member Roles

Nothing can cause disillusionment and frustration faster than bringing motivated people together and giving them no guidance about how to work with each other. Two or more people often start doing the same activities without coordinating with each other, while other activities are overlooked entirely. Eventually, people either define tasks that they can perform by themselves without having to coordinate with anyone else, or they'll gradually withdraw from the project and work on more rewarding assignments.

To prevent this frustration, work with team members to define the roles that each member will play. Specify which activities they'll work on and define the nature of the roles they'll play. Possible roles include the following:

▲ **Primary responsibility:** has the overall obligation to complete an activity.

▲ **Secondary or supporting responsibility:** has the obligation to complete a part of an activity.

▲ **Approval:** must approve the results of an activity before work can proceed.

▲ **Available for consultation:** can be called on to provide expert guidance and support if needed.

▲ **Must receive output:** is to receive either a physical product produced in an activity or a report of the results of an activity.

Project managers can use a Linear Responsibility Chart (see Section 4.5) as a starting point in discussions of project roles with team members. However, encourage people to raise any questions or concerns about roles portrayed so they're comfortable that the roles are feasible and appropriate.

10.2.3 Defining a Team's Operating Processes

Project managers work with their project teams to develop the procedures that their team members use to support one another's day-to-day work. At a minimum, develop procedures for the following:

▲ **Communication:** sharing project-related information in writing and through face-to-face interactions. Such procedures can include when and how to use e-mail to share project information, which types of information should be in writing, when and how to document informal discussions, how to set up regularly scheduled reports and meetings to record and review progress, and how to address special issues that arise.

▲ **Conflict resolution: conflict resolution** is resolving differences of opinion between team members regarding project work. Project managers need to develop both standard approaches, steps the group normally takes to encourage people to develop a mutually agreeable solution, as well as **escalation procedures,** steps that the group takes when the people involved can't readily resolve their differences. Creating a team environment based on trust can help make conflict resolution possible.

▲ **Decision making:** deciding among alternative approaches and actions. Develop guidelines for choosing the most appropriate decision-making approaches for typical situations, including consensus, majority rule, unanimous agreement, and decision by technical expert; develop escalation procedures as well.

10.2.4 Supporting the Development of Team Member Relationships

In high-performance project teams, members trust each other and have cordial, coordinated working relationships. Developing trust and effective work practices takes time and concerted effort. As project manager, begin to help team members get to know and be comfortable with one other as soon as the project starts. Encourage them to do the following:

▲ Work through conflicts together.
▲ Brainstorm challenging technical and administrative issues.
▲ Spend informal personal time together, such as having lunch or participating in non-work-related activities after hours.

10.2.5 Helping Teams Become Smooth-Functioning Units

Project managers work with teams to help them successfully develop through each of the project life cycle stages (see Section 4.1). Keep the following in mind as you guide a team through its developmental phases:

▲ **If everything goes smoothly on a project, whether or not you have completed the conceive, define, and start stages will make no**

> ## FOR EXAMPLE
>
> ### W.L. Gore & Associates
>
> Founded by William and Vieve Gore in 1958, Gore (www.gore.com) creates products from fluorocarbon polymers, including wire, cable, electronics, and state-of-the-art fabrics such as Gore-Tex. Throughout its history, the company has avoided traditional hierarchy, opting instead for team-based organization. The company has no chains of command or predetermined channels of communication. Instead, associates (not employees) are arranged into general work areas based on skills and experiences. Within multidisciplinary teams focused on a topic, product, or use, associates communicate freely and directly with each other, and are accountable to fellow team members. With the guidance of sponsors (not bosses) and a growing understanding of opportunities and various team objectives throughout the organization, associates commit to projects that match their skills. Extreme collaboration seems to work for Gore: The company has more than 6000 associates worldwide, annual revenues above $1.5 billion, and has been repeatedly named among the best companies to work for in the United States by *Forbes*.

difference. Only if you hit problems will your team become dysfunctional if it hasn't progressed through every stage. Suppose, for example, that the team misses a major project deadline. If team members have not developed mutual trust for one another, they are likely to spend their time searching for someone to blame instead of working together to fix the situation.

▲ **On occasion, teams might have to revisit an earlier developmental stage for the good of the project.** For example, a new person might join the team, or a major aspect of the project plan might change.

▲ **Teams do not automatically pass through the developmental stages; a project manager has to guide them.** Left to their own, teams often fail to move beyond the define stage. People don't like to confront thorny interpersonal issues, so they tend to ignore them.

▲ **Teams need to periodically assess how everyone feels about performance and identify any potential areas for improving.** Managing a team is a project itself. As such, project managers want to periodically assess how the team is doing and consider whether to take any corrective actions to bring the team back on course.

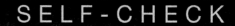

SELF-CHECK

1. As soon as possible, a new project team should take time to discuss and develop which four elements of the team's identity?

2. Within your team, anyone can call on Charlotte, a computer programmer with more than 10 years' experience, to answer technical questions. Which of the following is the best description of Charlotte's role on the team?

    (a) approval

    (b) primary responsibility

    (c) supporting responsibility

    (d) available for consultation

3. Early on, a project manager and project team should take time to define all but which of the following processes?

    (a) documentation

    (b) conflict resolution

    (c) communication

    (d) decision making

10.3 Motivating and Sustaining Project Teams

Efficient processes and smooth working relationships create the opportunity for successful projects. Having team members who are personally committed to a project's success gives everyone the greatest chance of achieving the project's goals. The project manager's major task is to encourage all the people associated with the project to be motivated and committed to its success.

Motivation is a personal choice—the only person you can motivate directly is yourself. Project managers can create the opportunity for others to become motivated, but they can't make the decision for them.

Four factors encourage a person to become and remain motivated to achieve a goal:

1. Desirability: the value of achieving the goal.
2. Feasibility: the likelihood that the goal can be achieved.
3. Progress: how things are proceeding as you try to reach your goal.
4. Reward: the payoff you realize when you reach the goal.

Helping others understand how a project meets their professional and personal needs in each of these areas strengthens their commitment to help the project succeed.

10.3.1 Clarifying Project Benefits

While some people commit to completing an assignment because someone tells them to do so, project managers can achieve much more serious levels of commitment from team members when team members personally recognize and appreciate a project's benefits.

When discussing a project's benefits with a team, consider the things that are important to the organization, its employees, and its clients, including the following:

▲ Improved products and services.
▲ Increased sales.
▲ Improved productivity.
▲ More efficient operations.
▲ Better work environment.

Also consider potential benefits to each of the team members personally, such as the following:

▲ Learning new skills and becoming more knowledgeable.
▲ Working in an enjoyable environment.
▲ Expanding business contacts.
▲ Enhancing career potential.
▲ Successfully meeting a challenge.

Project managers can help people understand and appreciate the benefits that a project can achieve for the organization by doing the following:

▲ Identifying the situation that led to the project.
▲ Identifying the project's key drivers and project champion (see Section 9.2) and clarifying what they hope that you achieve.
▲ Accepting and appreciating the worth of those benefits.
▲ Encouraging others to discuss the expected benefits and recognize their value.
▲ Encouraging others to think about additional benefits that might have been overlooked.

Project managers can encourage people to identify personal benefits that they could realize from participating in the project by doing the following:

▲ Discussing their personal interests and career goals and relating those interests and goals to aspects of the project.

▲ Discussing past projects they have enjoyed and the reasons they have enjoyed them.

▲ Discussing some of the benefits that you and others hope to realize by working on this project.

10.3.2 Demonstrating Feasibility

A project is **feasible** if people think they have a chance to accomplish it. No matter how desirable a project might be, no one gets excited about working on it if he or she thinks that accomplishing it is impossible. Success doesn't have to be guaranteed, but people must believe that the project and project team have a chance of success. Of course, feasibility is a subjective assessment. What seems impossible to one person might appear to be feasible to another.

A project manager's assessment of feasibility can become a self-fulfilling prophecy. If the project manager thinks that an assignment is feasible, the team typically works hard to complete it, and if the team encounters problems it will try to work things out. However, if the project manager believes that the project has no chance of succeeding, the team usually gives up at the first sign of difficulty. Any problems will just confirm what everyone already knew—that the project was doomed from the start.

Project managers help people believe that a project is feasible by working with them to define what will be produced, when, and how. Specifically, project managers can do the following:

▲ Involve the team in the planning process.

▲ Encourage the team to identify potential concerns so the team can analyze them and develop plans to address them.

▲ Explain why the established targets and plans are feasible.

▲ Develop responsive risk management plans.

10.3.3 Reporting and Rewarding Progress

Appreciating a project's value and feasibility helps project managers create initial motivation for their teams. However, if the project lasts for more than a couple of weeks, the initial motivation will die out if the project manager doesn't reinforce it continually.

Team members need to know how they're doing over time for two reasons:

1. Achieving each intermediate milestone provides personal satisfaction.
2. The recognition of successful performance confirms that the team is on the right track, which reinforces the belief that the team can and will succeed.

Have you ever seen a 12-month project in which all the major milestones occur in months 11 and 12? When do you think people get serious about working on this kind of project? Months 10, 11, and 12, if they're still around by then. Project managers keep people on track and excited about a project by doing the following:

▲ Developing meaningful and frequent intermediate milestones in the planning process.
▲ Minimizing slack time in the project schedule.
▲ Continually assessing how people are doing.
▲ Frequently sharing information with people about their performance and accomplishments.
▲ Continually reinforcing the benefits that everyone will realize when they successfully complete the project.

Team members also need to know that what they do makes a difference. Rewards—a public acknowledgment of good work or a quick note or e-mail—can work wonders with a team, confirming that they accomplished the correct results and met their audiences' needs, and that people appreciated the effort they invested.

FOR EXAMPLE

Customized Motivation at Metzger Associates

John Metzger, CEO and founder of the communications consulting firm Metzger Associates (www.metzger.com), motives his 30-employee firm with a "Live Long and Prosper" plan. To better match their personal and professional goals, the company allots each employee a yearly allowance to spend on four different categories: $600 for physical fitness, $500 for outdoor living, $600 for relaxation, and $1000 for education. Metzger empowers his employees to use the funds in any appropriate way they can come up with. The company's turnover rate has decreased to 2 percent.

SELF-CHECK

1. Which of the following are three of the four factors that motivate team members to achieve a goal?

   (a) reward, punishment, and productivity

   (b) feasibility, progress, and reward

   (c) desirability, efficiency, and progress

   (d) power, punishment, and incentives

2. What are four personal benefits that can motivate team members?

SUMMARY

The specific roles and responsibilities related to project teams often come down to three concepts: authority, responsibility, and accountability. Through delegation and techniques to encourage greater accountability, project managers can foster strong teams and develop individual team members' skills. New project teams have several defining topics to discuss early on, including goals, roles, processes, and working relationships. The long-term success and sustainability of project teams require motivating behaviors from project managers.

KEY TERMS

Accountability	Bringing consequences to bear based on people's performances.
Authority	The ability to make binding decisions about a project's products, schedule, resources, and activities.
Committee	People who come together to review and critique issues, propose recommendations for action, and, on occasion, implement those recommendations.
Conflict resolution	Resolving differences of opinion between team members regarding project work.
Delegation	Giving away something (for a project it's often a task assignment or responsibility).
Escalation procedures	Conflict resolution steps that the group takes when the people involved can't readily resolve their differences.
Feasible	Whether people think they have a chance to accomplish a project.

Goals	What a project team as a whole, as well as each member individually, hopes to accomplish.
Processes	The techniques that team members will use to help them perform their project tasks.
Project team	A collection of people who are committed to common goals and who depend on one other to do their jobs.
Relationships	The feelings and attitudes of team members toward each other.
Responsibility	The commitment to achieve specific results.
Roles	Each project team member's individual assignments.
Scapegoating	Holding people accountable when they aren't responsible.
Unilateral decision	A decision that doesn't require an agreement of both parties.
Work group	People who are assigned to a common task and work individually to accomplish their particular assignments.

ASSESS YOUR UNDERSTANDING

Go to www.wiley.com/college/portny to assess your knowledge of the basics of project team management.

Measure your learning by comparing pre-test and post-test results.

Summary Questions

1. When a project manager delegates authority to a team member, the process can actually be motivating to the team member if the project manager emphasizes that the delegation does which of the following?

   (a) improves productivity

   (b) saves the team and larger organization money

   (c) offers the team member the opportunity to learn new skills

   (d) none of the above

2. Creating a sense of urgency and importance for a project is one way that a project manager can do which of the following?

   (a) encourage responsibility and discipline from team members

   (b) use accountability as a motivating force on his or her project

   (c) create a sense of community and togetherness within the project team

   (d) all of the above

Applying This Chapter

1. Consider the following assertion: "A project manager can delegate authority, but he or she can't delegate responsibility; responsibility can only be shared." What is one specific situation that illustrates this assertion?

2. Two team members on the large multidisciplinary product testing team you project manage are consistently late turning in weekly reports. When you spoke with each of the team members individually, they both said, essentially, that you aren't their manager so getting their reports to you is of secondary importance to them. What are two specific things you can do to encourage these team members to contribute to the project on time?

3. Compare and contrast the composition and activities of a work group, a project team, and a committee. List at least one example of each that you've been part of in the last year or two.

4. Think of a team you've recently led or been part of. List the members of the team and then define each member's role. Who had primary responsibility, supporting responsibility, and approval? Who was available for consultation? Who had to receive outputs from the project?

5. Miguel is project managing a research team that will be testing various microprocessor designs for at least the next 18 months. The groups has a strong goal (to develop a processor that works efficiently more than 150 meters below sea level), but Miguel is concerned about keeping the group motivated for the next year and a half—and potentially even longer. What are some specific things Miguel can do to motivate his team over the next months?

YOU TRY IT

Authority versus Accountability

The three essential concepts of making assignments within a project team are authority, responsbility, and accountability. Section 10.1.1 compares authority and responsibility, as well as responsibility and accountability. Write up a comparision of authority versus accountability, using the some format that appears in Section 10.1.1. In what ways do you consider authority and accountability similar? In what ways are they different?

Delegating

In the next week, try to delegate one activity to someone else. The activity might be some task related to a larger work or school project. Or maybe it's an activity that's part of the everyday project of running your home or personal life. Remember that you can delegate authority but not responsibility. What techniques did you use to effectively delegate the activity?

Get Your Team on the Same Page

Before jumping into the actual work of your next school-related group assignment, take 15 to 20 minutes to discuss as a group the goals, roles, processes, and relationships of the project *before* you begin talking about the specifics of the assignment. What did you learn about yourself and your teammates by taking time to discuss goals, roles, processes, relationships? Did the actual work of the project go more smoothly?

Breaking Down Long-Term Projects

Consider a long-term project or goal that you have that's still several years away. A long-term goal might be completing a certain level of higher education, being promoted to a specific position within an organization, writing a novel, or starting your own business. Because long-term goals are important but often overwhelming, divide your long-term goal into specific intermediate milestones. Try to come up with a specific milestone that you can work toward every two to three months. How will you reward yourself when you reach each intermediate milestone? How will you report to others about your intermediate progress toward each milestone? Write down all your intermediate milestones on a single sheet of paper and display it someplace you'll see it every day.

CASE STUDY: Joe Samuel

Joe Samuel was once again asked to be a project manager on a marketing project at GinTech, a small consulting firm. This was the fourth time in the last 14 months, and he was glad to add this type of work experience to his resumé, but he dreaded the interpersonal relationship issues that always came up on projects. He felt like he was the project's babysitter, always checking on progress, making sure everyone on the team was happy and understood each other's roles, handing out assignments, and so on. Joe then remembered an article he had recently read about "tried and true project management practices." He thought "tried and true" had to be more managerially comfortable than his past experiences. He decided to accept the new project so that he could try out the new ideas.

The project Joe accepted was to make a decision on whether or not to close several of a client's distribution centers in order to improve the responsiveness of the client's supply chain. Joe had experiences working on a supply chain service, so he felt qualified to lead the effort. He defined the scope and deliverables of the project and detailed all of the major tasks of the project as well as most of the detail-level steps in the project plan.

At the first project team meeting, Joe felt very comfortable about the control and direction of the project, much more than any of the previous projects he had managed. He had specifically defined objectives and tasks for each member of the project team. He even determined completion dates for each task. He wrote individual "contracts" for each team member to sign as an indication of their commitment to completion of the designated tasks by the assigned schedule dates.

The meeting went smoothly, with almost no comments or questions from the project team. Everyone picked up a copy of their "contract" and went off to work on the project. Joe felt great and was pleased with the success of his new approach to project management.

Questions

1. How do you think Joe will feel six weeks after the project is underway?
2. Compare his new approach to project management with his previous approach.

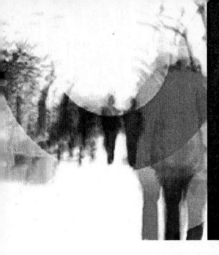

11

TRACKING PROGRESS AND MAINTAINING CONTROL
Monitoring Project Performance and Achieving Desired Results

Starting Point

Go to www.wiley.com/college/portny to assess your knowledge of the basics of project control.
Determine where you need to concentrate your effort.

What You'll Learn in This Chapter

▲ The plan-monitor-control cycle
▲ Systems and tools for monitoring and controlling projects
▲ Data collection, analysis, and reporting
▲ Types of control data and reports
▲ Earned Value Analysis
▲ Scope creep and change control

After Studying This Chapter, You'll Be Able To

▲ Design effective project monitoring and controlling systems
▲ Analyze collected data, including through the use of Earned Value Analysis
▲ Create useful and targeted control reports
▲ Build special control systems for schedule performance, work-effort, and expenditures
▲ Manage a project's scope creep and control its rate of change

INTRODUCTION

Planning, monitoring, and controlling a project's progress is an ongoing project-management responsibility. From the very beginning of a project, a project manager must decide the type of data that needs to be collected, the analyses the data will undergo, and the formats in which pertinent information will be reported. Earned Value Analysis is a popular and useful data analysis tool that determines where a project stands budget- and schedulewise by only tracking expenditures. Project managers can design monitoring and controlling systems specifically targeted for schedule performance, work-effort, and expenditures. Monitoring and managing scope creep and project change are two overarching control responsibilities.

11.1 Understanding the Plan-Monitor-Control Cycle

Project monitoring is the collection, recording, and reporting of project information that is important to the project manager and other relevant stakeholders. Controlling means different things within various organizations, but in general, **project controlling** uses the monitored data and information to bring actual performance into agreement with the project plan. Frequently, the distinction between monitoring and controlling becomes blurred, and the interaction of the two processes sometimes leads project managers to think they are working on a single task. However, the processes are highly distinct and serve significantly different purposes.

The key issue in designing an effective monitoring and control system is to create an information system that gives project managers and others the information they need to make informed, timely decisions that will keep project performance as close as possible to the plan.

11.1.1 Making Time for Planning, Monitoring, and Controlling

Managing a project involves continually planning what to do, checking on progress, comparing progress to plan, taking corrective action to bring progress into agreement with the plan if it is not, and replanning when needed. The fundamental items to plan, monitor, and control are time, cost, and performance so that the project stays on schedule, does not exceed its budget, and meets its specifications.

This **plan-monitor-control cycle** is an ongoing process that happens throughout a project until it is completed. Figure 11-1 shows how information and authority flows for such a cycle in an engineering project. Note that the information generally flows up the organization while the authority typically flows down.

Figure 11-1

	Planning and Scheduling			Reporting and Monitoring		
President and General Manager Director of Engineering Director of Research Director of Manufacturing		Project review and signature approval			Distribution to directors and managers Feeder copy	Review and action as required
Administration		Administration review, type, and prepare final copies	Initiate project records Distribute copies		Post to weekly project status report and project expenditure and control schedule chart	Prepare and forward management reports as required
Responsible Engineer	Rough draft of engineering project authorization and project expenditure and control schedule chart		Copy	Weekly time tickets milestone report	Feeder copy Distribution to responsible engineer	

Source: Dean, 1968.

The plan-monitor-control cycle in an engineering project.

Unfortunately, projects that are particularly complex, challenging, or uncertain are often the first to minimize the importance of planning, monitoring, and controlling effort so the team can focus on "the real work" of the project. Many project managers are tempted to focus on doing something, anything, rather than to spend time on planning, monitoring, and controlling—especially if the stakes are high and the project is a difficult one. It is precisely such projects, however, that most desperately need mature project managers who realize the importance of creating effective planning-monitoring-controlling processes.

11.1.2 Monitoring Projects

For project managers, the key to setting up a monitoring system is to identify the special characteristics of performance, cost, and time that need to be controlled in order to achieve the project goals as stated in the project plan (see Chapter 4).

FOR EXAMPLE

Planning Is Critical

Many organizations have incurred tremendous expense and large losses because the project planning process was inadequate for the tasks undertaken. For instance, a retailer won a bid to supply a regional office of a national firm with a computer, terminals, and software. Due to insufficient planning, the installation was completed far beyond the due date with very inadequate performance. The project failure disqualified the retailer from bidding on an additional 20 installations planned by the national firm. Similarly, a firm in the construction industry ran 63 percent over budget and 48 percent over schedule on a major project because the project manager had managed similar projects several times before and claimed to know what to do "without going into all that detail that no one looks at anyway."

The action plan identifies what is being done and when, and the planned resources for each task and subtask in the project. The project manager must determine the exact boundaries within each task that should be monitored, as well as the specific performance characteristics for each project activity or task.

Project managers must set up systems and processes to gather and store relevant performance data. In addition to technology-based systems for collecting hard data, the monitoring system is likely to include telephone logs, tracking documents, records of significant changes, and documentation processes for both formal and informal communications.

Monitoring can take various forms, including the following:

▲ **An ever-evolving project schedule or chart.** The Gantt chart in Figures 6-15 and 6-16 shows that one way to link planning and control is to monitor project progress. The original Gantt chart provided the baseline. Every time there is a change, the "tracking Gantt chart" can be updated to reflect changes. Project-management software can automatically adjust all information to reflect these changes.

▲ **Earned value charts.** The project manager can create and gauge project progress against a preestablished baseline. See Section 11.3 for more on this technique.

Project managers frequently make several project monitoring errors, including the following:

▲ **Focusing on easy data.** Project managers might be tempted to pay attention to monitoring activities where control data can be easily gathered rather than control data that might be more important but more difficult to collect and interpret. For example, project managers focus on the hard, objective measures (number of units completed per hour, for example) rather than the softer, subjective data revealed in phone calls and water-cooler conversations (new expectations brought up by the client in an e-mail, for instance). Both types of data are typically necessary for proper project control.

▲ **Focusing on inputs.** Because measuring project performance can be difficult, project managers sometimes allow project inputs to serve as measures of output (for example, assuming that if 50 percent of the budget has been spent, then 50 percent of the tasks must be completed).

▲ **Focusing on data that don't change.** In this common error, project managers spend a significant amount of time monitoring data generally related to project performance but that virtually never change from one collection period to the next. With no significant change, there is no significant control activity.

Project managers must remember that monitoring project performance doesn't identify problems—it identifies symptoms. Whenever a symptom is identified, the project manager must investigate the situation to determine the nature of any underlying problems, the reasons for the problems, and how to fix the problems.

11.1.3 Controlling Projects

Project control is the set of activities project managers perform to ensure that projects proceed according to plan and produce the desired results. A project manager performs the following activities throughout the life of a project:

▲ **Reconfirming the plan.** At the beginning of each **performance period** (the interval for which a project is reviewed and assessed), the project manager reaffirms with team members their project responsibilities and commitments for the coming period.

▲ **Assessing performance.** The project manager collects information during the period about what was produced; when activities started and finished; when milestones were reached; and what work-effort, money, and other resources were used. Project managers should compare team performance with the plan and determine the reasons for any differences between planned and actual performance.

▲ **Taking corrective action.** If necessary, the project manager takes steps to bring the project's performance back into conformance with plans or, if doing so isn't possible, to change the existing plans to reflect a new set of expectations.

▲ **Keeping people informed.** The project manager shares information with selected audiences about achievements, problems, and future plans.

Great project plans often fall by the wayside when well-intentioned people start to do what they feel is necessary to achieve the best possible results. They might spend more hours than were allotted because they feel that the additional work will produce better results. They might ask people to work on the project who were not included in the original plan because they feel that these people's expertise will improve the quality of the project results. They might spend more than the amount budgeted to buy an item they believe to be of higher quality. And they might overspend their budgets because they aren't keeping track of how much they're spending.

SELF-CHECK

1. Project controlling uses data to bring actual performance into agreement with project plans, while project monitoring involves which of the following?

   (a) evaluating project objectives, schedules, and budgets

   (b) classifying expenditures and resource allocations

   (c) estimating costs, work-effort, and timelines

   (d) collecting, recording, and reporting project data

2. Useful tools for project monitoring include Gantt charts and tracking documents. True or false?

3. Using an organization's time sheets to track project work-effort even though this tool isn't as detailed as the project demands is poor project monitoring because it focuses on which of the following?

   (a) data that don't change.

   (b) project inputs, rather than outputs

   (c) easily acquired data

   (d) all of the above

4. Although taking corrective action is a form of control, reaffirming the plan can be an effective control as well. True or false?

11.2 Collecting, Analyzing, and Reporting Data

After project managers decide on the type of data they want to monitor, the next question is how to gather the data, interpret it, and turn it into information useful for controlling projects. **Data collection and reporting** is the collective term typically used to refer to these activities.

Data collection raises a number of questions, including the following:

▲ Should special forms be designed and used?
▲ Should data be collected just before or after important milestones?
▲ Should time and cost data always be collected at the same time each month?

These and many other issues are likely to arise, and most questions can only be answered in the context of a specific project. However, the following sections offer some general guidelines to aid project managers in creating their data collection systems.

11.2.1 Data Collecting

The majority of project data to be collected exists in one of the following five formats:

▲ **Frequency counts.** A **frequency count** is a simple tally, or count, of the occurrence of an event—for example, days without an accident. Often a count of events per time period or as a fraction of some standard number is used, such as complaints per month, defects per thousand products, or fraction of luggage lost.

▲ **Raw numbers. Raw numbers** are actual numbers in collected data, usually in comparison to some expected or planned amount, such as dollars spent, hours required, and pounds consumed. The comparison to a project plan might take the form of **variances**, that is, differences between planned and actual. When collecting raw numbers, it is important that the basis, time period, and collection process always be the same.

▲ **Subjective numeric ratings.** These are usually subjective estimates of some quality offered by specialists in the topic, such as numeric rankings of performance. Ratings can be reported in the same ways as raw numbers, but they often cannot be mathematically processed in the same ways raw numbers can.

▲ **Indicators and surrogates.** When it is especially difficult to find a direct measure of a variable, indicators or surrogates are frequently used instead. If this approach is taken, it is important that the indicator or surrogate be as directly related to the variable as possible. For example, body temperature is an indicator of infection and years of experience can be a surrogate for expertise. The number of salespersons, however, would be a poor, and clearly indirect, measure for level of customer service.

▲ **Verbal characterizations.** Other variables that are difficult to measure, such as team spirit or client/supplier cooperation, can take the form of verbal characterizations. These forms of data are acceptable and useful as long as the terminology is limited and is uniformly understood by all parties.

11.2.2 Data Analysis

Following the collection of the data, the project manager (or someone on the project team) needs to analyze or process the data in some manner before reporting it and using it for control purposes. Analysis might take the form of simple aggregation of the data, such as averaging the values, or it might be something complex, such as fitting statistical distribution functions to the data to ascertain a particular trend. Project-management software is frequently required to conduct data analysis.

Quality control/management techniques are often useful at this point. For example, a common graph used in quality management shows the range of sample values taken during a period of time. If the samples' range—the largest value minus the smallest value—appears to be increasing over time, this could indicate that something needs to be adjusted in a project (perhaps a machine is wearing out or needs maintenance). Figure 11-2 illustrates a common charting format that combines a predetermined level of performance (the curving dashed line) with data collected at specific points during the project.

In general, significant differences from plan should be highlighted or flagged in some way so the project manager or other person exercising control cannot overlook the potential problem. Many statistical quality control techniques can

Figure 11-2

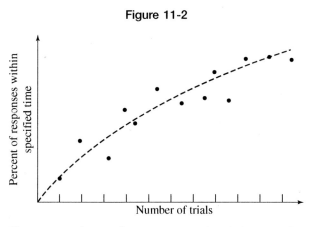

Chart comparing performance to a plan during a series of trials.

help project teams determine how significant variances are, and can often even help determine causes and effects. Unfortunately, these formal approaches are often after-the-fact techniques for correcting or controlling problems; variances occur, are reported, investigated, and then some action is taken. The astute project manager, however, is much more interested in preventing fires rather than putting them out, thus the value of timely data collection and reporting.

Finally, it should be noted that data analysis is sometimes used as a tool to assign blame. Project managers should avoid this endeavor entirely because it does not help in the management of projects. The goal of monitoring and controlling is to achieve project objectives through correcting deviations from plan, not to find scapegoats or assign guilt. The project manager needs all team members performing at the top of their capabilities. Blame encourages team members to avoid taking the risks necessary to achieve a project's goals.

11.2.3 Reporting

After data have been collected and analyzed, it needs to be reported in some form. Project reports provide upper management and project teams an opportunity to see whether a project is on track and to determine whether they should do something differently to ensure the projects meet their goals.

In general, project managers should avoid periodic reports except in those cases in which the flow of data is periodic (such as accounting data). Reports issued routinely—every day, week, month, or quarter—generally do not get read. Instead, let a project's milestones, scope changes, problems, and the project team's need for information dictate the timing of reports.

Choosing Report Types

Project managers primarily have three distinct types of reports to choose from:

1. **Routine reports** are issued on a regular schedule and report on data collected on established aspects of a project. Routine reports often review schedule and budget commitments and ensure upper management and the project team that a project is on track. Routine performance reports include status reports, progress reports, and forecasts, but many other possible formats exist, including time/cost reports, variance reports, and update presentations. Section 12.2 covers the process of preparing progress reports.

2. **Exception reports** are primarily intended for special decisions or unexpected situations in which affected team members and outside managers need to be made aware of a change, and the change itself needs to be documented.

3. **Special analysis reports** are prepared to disseminate the results of a special study in a project concerning a particular opportunity or problem

for the project. They might be distributed to top management, other project managers who can benefit from the knowledge, functional managers, or anyone who might be affected or interested. Typical subjects include studies of new materials, capabilities of new software, and descriptions of the impact of new government regulations.

In addition to reports, on an ongoing basis, project managers should update all tables, network diagrams, Gantt charts, and action plans to reflect current reality. In addition to alerting team members to potential problems, such updates help maintain team morale. (And whenever project documents are updated, project managers should take care to preserve all documents from earlier stages of the project's life. These materials will be invaluable when the project is completed and a project final report is written.)

Customizing Reports

Although everyone concerned with the project should be tied into the reporting system in some fashion, not everyone needs to receive the same information. Reports can and should vary in terms of the frequency of distribution and detail, as well as the particular measures being reported. For example, a client might wish to receive reports on cost or schedule while functional management might wish to see reports on technical performance. Project team members might need information at the task or subtask level on a frequent, perhaps daily, basis.

The explosion of electronic tools for both collecting and disseminating project information can lead project managers to overreporting, which can be just as dangerous as underreporting. Important events, problems, and trends tend to be hidden in a mountain of detail. Thus, it is crucial that the reporting system

---

FOR EXAMPLE

Report Frequency

Project managers should time the frequency of reports to suit the time required for team members to exercise control over a project task. For instance, drug efficacy tests required by the Food and Drug Administration require a long time—often months or years—to conduct. For a pharmaceutical manufacturer, frequent control-related reports would not be appropriate because testers would not be able to work with the information for months. In contrast, performance verification tests on silicone chips for a microprocessor manufacturer can result in hundreds of discrepancies within a matter of hours. Daily or even more frequent reports are often necessary.

be well designed to make use of such modern technological marvels without abusing the recipient with their capabilities.

In addition to their control-related benefits, reports do the following:

▲ Provide an opportunity for mutual understanding between stakeholders in a project regarding the goals, progress, difficulties, successes, and other ongoing project events.

▲ Help communicate the need for coordination among team members working on the tasks and subtasks of the project.

▲ Communicate changes to the goals and functioning of projects in a timely and appropriate fashion, thus minimizing the confusion often encountered during such changes.

▲ Help maintain the visibility of the project and the project team to top management, functional managers, colleagues, and clients.

SELF-CHECK

1. What are five formats of data that a project manager can collect?

2. Raw number data can be compared to estimates to figure out how far off-plan a certain project aspect is. This type of data is known as which of the following?

   (a) biased data

   (b) variance

   (c) outlying

   (d) trending data

3. Regularity should drive the timing of project reporting. True or false?

4. A new steel processing procedure holds the possibility of cutting two months from your standard manufacturing process. To appropriately consider the new procedure in relation to your project, you should consider producing which of the following?

   (a) a routine report

   (b) an exception report

   (c) a special analysis report

   (d) none of the above

11.3 Performing Earned Value Analysis

Earned Value Analysis is a technique that helps project managers determine whether a project is ahead or behind schedule and whether it's over or under budget, while only tracking resource expenditures. It's particularly useful on larger projects to identify those areas where project managers might need to investigate further for potential problems.

Unfortunately, just comparing a project's actual expenditures with those planned normally doesn't indicate whether a project is over or under budget. For example, Ilena is three months into a project and has spent $50,000. According to her plan, she shouldn't have spent $50,000 until the end of the fourth month of the project. It appears that the project is over budget at this point, but actually Ilena can't tell for sure. A variety of situations could have produced this result, including the following:

▲ Ilena's team might have performed all the work planned but paid more for it than expected. This means the project is on schedule and over budget.

▲ Ilena's team might have performed more work than they planned but paid exactly what was expected for the work completed. This mean the project is on budget and ahead of schedule.

Earned Value Analysis is necessary for Ilena to truly assess her project's schedule and resource expenditure performance, based on resource expenditures to date.

11.3.1 Defining the Key Elements of Earned Value Analysis

With Earned Value Analysis, a project manager determines the following critical pieces of information:

▲ **Cost variance:** the portion of the difference between what was planned to be spent by a certain date and what has really been spent that's true cost savings or loss.

▲ **Schedule variance:** the difference between what was planned to be spent by a certain date and what was really spent that's due to the project being ahead of or behind schedule.

▲ **Estimate at completion:** the total amount that will be spent to perform a task, if a project's spending pattern to date continues until the task is finished.

Figure 11-3 depicts the key information used and produced in an Earned Value Analysis. As illustrated, the difference between planned and actual expenditures

Figure 11-3

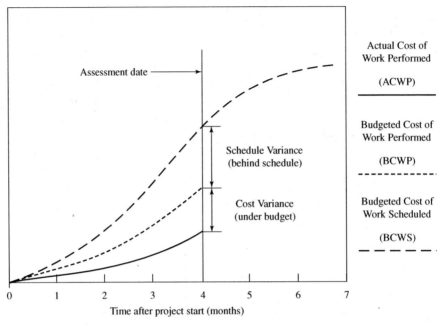

Monitoring using Earned Value Analysis.

on the date of the report is due to the combined effects of a schedule delay and a cost savings.

Cost and schedule variances and the estimate at completion are calculated from the following information:

▲ **Budgeted cost of work scheduled (BCWS):** the planned cost for work due to be completed by a specified date.

▲ **Actual cost of work performed (ACWP):** the amount of funds actually spent for work actually done by the specified date.

▲ **Budgeted cost of work performed (BCWP):** the planned cost for work actually done by the specified date.

The **earned value** of a piece of work is defined to be equal to the amount the project manager planned to spend to perform it.

Cost and schedule variances are defined in mathematical terms, as follows:

$$CV = \text{Cost variance}$$
$$= BCWP - ACWP$$

In other words, the cost variance as of a certain date is the difference between what the project manager planned to spend for the work that was actually completed and what was really spent.

$$SV = \text{Schedule variance}$$
$$= BCWP - BCWS$$

The schedule variance is the difference between planned expenditures for the work actually completed and what the project manager planned to do.

The cost and schedule variances can be expressed as percentages, using the following formulas:

$$CVP = \text{Cost variance percentage}$$
$$= CV \div BCWP \times? 100$$
$$SVP = \text{Schedule variance percentage}$$
$$= SV \div BCWS \times 100$$

Although the preceding method of calculating variance is relatively standard, another way of handling the data is more useful for making comparisons at different points in time or across different projects. This procedure is simply to take the ratios of the measures as a number, rather than a percentage. Thus, the spending or cost variance becomes the Cost Performance Index (CPI), where CPI = BCWP/ACWP, and the schedule variance becomes the Schedule Performance Index (SPI), where SPI = BCWP/BCWS. Values less than 1.0 are undesirable.

Table 11-1 illustrates that a positive variance indicates something desirable (that is, either that the project is under budget or ahead of schedule), while a negative variance indicates something undesirable (either that the project is over budget or behind schedule).

Finally, the estimate at completion is defined as follows:

$$EAC = \text{Estimate at completion}$$
$$= ACWP \div BCWP \times \text{total budget}$$

This is a simplistic estimate because it assumes that the spending patterns through the end of the project will be the same as they've been up until now. Of course,

Table 11-1 Interpretations of Values of Cost and Schedule Variances

Variance	Negative	Zero	Positive
Cost	Over budget	On budget	Under budget
Schedule	Behind schedule	On schedule	Ahead of schedule

circumstances could change the expenditure pattern or the project manager might choose to alter the pattern if he or she has been overspending and wants to get back on track. Project managers and organizations often use more specific and complex estimate, such as the estimated cost to completion (ETC).

11.3.2 Considering an Example

The terms and definitions of Earned Value Analysis become easier to understand when a simple example is considered.

Suppose Portia is planning to conduct a series of telephone interviews. The interview guide is already prepared, and each phone interview is independent of the others. Portia states the following in the project plan:

▲ The project will last 10 months.
▲ The team will conduct 100 interviews each month.
▲ Each interview will cost $300 to conduct.
▲ The total project budget is $300,000.

During the first month, Portia's team does the following:

▲ Conducts 75 interviews.
▲ Spends a total of $15,000.

In reality, this little project is so simple that Earned Value Analysis isn't necessary to gauge progress. Because Portia planned to conduct 100 interviews in the first month and the team only conducted 75, the project is behind schedule. Because Portia planned to spend $300 per interview and the team has only spent $15,000 ($15,000 ÷ 75 interviews = $200 per interview), the project is under budget. However, calculating the earned value information offers a variety of additional insights.

1. Calculate the three information items from which the schedule and cost variances and the estimate at completion are determined:

   BCWS = What Portia planned to spend for what she planned to do during the month
   = $300/interview × 100 interviews = $30,000
   ACWP = What Portia actually spent during the month
   = $15,000
   BCWP = What Portia planned to spend for what the team really did during the month
   = $300/interview × 75 interviews = $22,500

2. Determine the cost and schedule performance (cost variance and schedule variance) during the month, as follows:

$$CV = BCWP - ACWP$$
$$= \$22,500 - \$15,000 = \$7500$$
$$SV = BCWP - BCWS$$
$$= \$22,500 - \$30,000 = -\$7500$$

3. The cost variance and schedule variance percentages are as follows:

$$CVP = CV \div BCWP \times 100$$
$$= \$7500 \div \$22,500 \times 100 = 33\%$$
$$SVP = SV \div BCWS \times 100$$
$$= -\$7,500 \div \$30,000 \times 100 = -25\%$$

The cost variance percentage and schedule variance percentage make sense when considering the actual numbers for the month. Portia had originally planned to spend $300 per interview, but in the first month she actually spent $200 per interview ($15,000 ÷ 75). The difference between the planned per interview cost and the actual is $100, which is 33 percent less than planned (100 ÷ 300 × 100), meaning that the project is 33 percent under budget. Additionally, Portia originally planned to conduct 100 interviews in the first month, but her team only finished 75. The difference between the planned and actual performance is 25 interviews, which is 25 percent less than planned (25 ÷ 100 × 100), meaning that the project is 25 percent behind schedule.

If Portia's work continues in the same fashion for the remainder of the project, the total project expenditures at completion will be the following:

$$EAC = ACWP \div BCWP \times \text{total budget}$$
$$= \$15,000 \div \$22,500 \times \$300,000 = \$200,000$$

In other words, if Portia's team continues to perform interviews for $200 each rather than the planned $300 each, they will spend 2/3 of the total planned budget to complete all the interviews.

While it makes no sense to do a formal Earned Value Analysis to monitor a project that's this simple, if a project has 50 to 100 activities (or more), an Earned Value Analysis can help the project manager consider jointly the performance on individual activities to identify general trends that might suggest that the entire project will come in over budget or behind schedule. The earlier a project manager identifies such trends, the more easily he or she can take steps to counteract them.

11.3.3 Determining the Reasons for Observed Variances

Cost and schedule variances suggest project performance isn't going exactly as planned. After a project manager determines that a variance exists, he or she needs to figure out the reason(s) for the variance so that the necessary corrective actions can be taken.

Possible reasons for cost variances include the following:

▲ More or less work is required to complete a task than originally planned.
▲ The people performing the work are more or less productive than planned.
▲ The actual costs of labor and materials are more or less than planned.
▲ Actual organization indirect rates are higher or lower than originally planned.

Possible reasons for schedule variances are as follows:

▲ Work scheduled is performed earlier or later than planned.
▲ More or less work is required than originally planned.
▲ People performing the work are more or less productive than planned.

11.3.4 Calculating Budgeted Cost of Work Performed

The key to an accurate Earned Value Analysis lies in the accuracy of the BCWP.

To determine BCWP, first estimate how much of a task is completed to date and how much of the task's total planned budget has been spent for the amount of work achieved. Usually, project managers can assume that there's a direct relationship between the portion of a task completed and the amount of funds spent. In other words, if you've completed 60 percent of the task, a project manager can figure that 60 percent of the total task budget should be spent.

For tasks with separate components, like printing brochures or conducting telephone surveys, determining how much of a task has been completed is straightforward. However, if a project task entails an integrated work or thought process with no easily segmentable parts, such as designing the brochure, the best a project manager can do is to make an educated guess.

Figure 11-4 illustrates three alternate approaches that are typically used to estimate budgeted cost of work performed:

1. **Percent-complete method.** BCWP is the product of the fraction of the activity completed and the total activity budget.
2. **Milestone method.** BCWP is zero until the activity is completed and 100 percent of the total activity budget after it's completed.
3. **50/50 method.** BCWP is zero before the activity is started, 50 percent of the total activity budget after it's started but before it's finished, and 100 percent of the total activity budget after the activity is finished.

The milestone method and 50/50 method allow project managers to approximate BCWP without requiring them to estimate the portion of a task that is completed.

Figure 11-4

Activity				Budget Cost of Work Performed		
Work Breakdown Structure code	Budget Cost at completion			% Complete	50/50	Milestone
1.2.1	$10,000		Today	$10,000	$10,000	$10,000
1.2.2	$20,000		75% done	$15,000	$10,000	$0
1.2.3	$30,000		20% done	$6,000	$15,000	$0
				$31,000	$35,000	$10,000

Months after project start

Three ways to define budgeted cost of work performed.

Figure 11-4 also compares the accuracy of the three different methods for a simple example. Task 1.2 is comprised of three subtasks: 1.2.1, 1.2.2, and 1.2.3. For this illustration, it's assumed that project manager knows accurately the following amount of work that has been done on each subtask:

▲ Subtask 1.2.1 is complete.
▲ Subtask 1.2.2 is 75 percent complete.
▲ Subtask 1.2.3 is 20 percent complete.

The BCWP of Task 1.2 is calculated by adding up the BCWP for each of the three subtasks that comprise Task 1.2. The actual BCWP, as determined with the percent-complete method, should be $31,000. (Again, this method can only be used if the project manager knows accurately the percent of the task that's completed.)

▲ The milestone method is the most conservative and the least accurate. You'd expect that you would spend some money while you're working on the task. However, this method doesn't allow you to declare BCWP greater than $0 until the activity is completed. Therefore, it'll always appear the project is over budget while the activity is being performed.
▲ The 50/50 method is a closer approximation to reality than the milestone method, because you're allowed to declare a BCWP greater than $0 while

performing the task. However, it's possible that this approximation can inadvertently mask an overspending situation.

Project managers should observe the following guidelines to improve the accuracy of estimates of BCWP when using either the 50/50 method or the milestone method:

▲ Define activities to be of relatively short duration: usually two weeks or less.

▲ Define at least seven subelements that can be added together to give the BCWP of a higher-level activity.

SELF-CHECK

1. Earned Value Analysis enables project managers to determine what three specific aspects of a project?

2. Which of the following schedule variance formulas is correct?

   (a) SV = BCWP − ACWP

   (b) SV = BCWS − BCWP

   (c) SV = CV ÷ BCWP × 100

   (d) SV = BCWP − BCWS

3. In Earned Value Analysis, ACWP stands for the actual cost of work performed. True or false?

4. To find out an estimate at completion (EAC) for a project, you need to know which of the following?

   (a) the ACWP, BCWS, and cost variance

   (b) the ACWP, BCWP, and total budget

   (c) the BCWS, BCWP, and total budget

   (d) none of the above

5. In calculating BCWP, the milestone method generally produces a closer approximation to reality. True or false?

11.4 Designing Monitoring and Control Systems

A **project-management information system (PMIS)** is a set of procedures, equipment, and other resources for collecting, analyzing, storing, and reporting on information that describes project performance. To support ongoing management and control of the project, project managers want to collect and maintain information about activity status, labor hours spent, and funds expended.

Figure 11-5

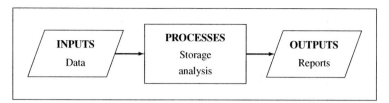

Three elements of a project-management information system.

As Section 11.1 explains, project managers can sometimes use existing systems to track, analyze, and report on control information. Other times they have to design, develop, and maintain their own systems. In either case, the system must include the following three components illustrated in Figure 11-5:

1. **Inputs:** raw data collected to describe selected aspects of project performance.
2. **Processes:** storage and analysis of the data collected to compare actual performance with planned performance.
3. **Outputs:** reports presenting the results of the analyses performed.

In addition to defining the data items to collect, project managers specify how the data will be collected, by whom it will be collected, when it will be collected, and how it will be entered into the system. All these factors can affect the timeliness and accuracy of the data and any project performance assessments.

Although project managers monitor and control any number of project aspects, three specific areas that most project managers must deal with are schedule performance, work-effort expended, and expenditures. Sections 11.4.1, 11.4.2, and 11.4.3 cover control system concerns related to these three areas.

11.4.1 Monitoring Schedule Performance

Project managers can assess project schedule status by comparing the actual dates on which activities start and end (or on which events are reached) to the planned dates. Figures 11-6, 11-7, and 11-8 present various formats that support ready comparisons of this data.

Figure 11-6 depicts a key-events report. The information in this report is based on the project plan and includes key event identifiers and descriptions, the person responsible for ensuring that the event is reached, and the date on which the event is supposed to be reached. The collected data describe performance during the period covered by the report, including the date on which the event is actually reached and any relevant comments about the event.

Figure 11-7 illustrates an activities report. Like a key-events report, the majority of the information in this report comes from the project plan. Particular data

Figure 11-6

Key Event	Person Responsible	Date Due	Date Due	Comments
KE 2.1.1 Questionnaire design approved	F. Smith	Feb 28	Feb 28	
KE 2.2.2 Questionnaire pilot test completed	F. Smith	Apr 30	Apr 25	
KE 2.2.1 Instructions printed	R. Harris	May 15		

A key-events report.

from a project plan include activity identifiers and descriptions, the person responsible for ensuring that the activity is performed, and the dates on which the activity is supposed to start and end. The collected data describe performance during the period covered by the report, including the dates on which the activity actually starts and ends and any relevant comments about the activity.

Figure 11-8 shows a combined activities and key-events report, which presents information for both activities and events. This report uses the same format as the activities report; however, a project manager can enter the planned and actual event achievement dates in the "End Date" columns.

Figure 11-7

Activity	Person Responsible	Start Date Planned	Actual	End Date Planned	Actual	Comments
2.1.1 Design Questionnaire	F. Smith	Feb 14	Feb 15	Feb 28	Feb 28	
2.2.2 Pilot test Questionnaire	F. Smith	Apr 20	Apr 21	Apr 30	Apr 25	Critical path
2.2.1 Print instructions	R. Harris	May 6	May 6	May 15		

An activities report.

Figure 11-8

Activity	Person Responsible	Start Date		End Date		Comments
		Planned	Actual	Planned	Actual	
2.1.1 Design questionnaire	F. Smith	Feb 14	Feb 15	Feb 28	Feb 28	
2.2.2 Questionnaire design approved	F. Smith			Feb 28	Feb 28	
2.2.1 Pilot test questionnaire	F. Smith	Apr 20	Apr 20	Apr 30		Critical path

A combined activities and key-events report.

Project managers must remember that the purpose of control is to encourage people to perform according to the plan, not just to collect data on how people are doing. The more involved and aware the people performing the work are of how they're progressing in relation to the schedule, the greater the likelihood that they'll hit the schedule. If they don't know or care what the target date is, they're unlikely to hit it.

FOR EXAMPLE

Collecting Schedule Performance Data

Project-management author and consultant Stanley E. Portny uses the following strategies to consistently collect schedule performance data. At the beginning of a performance period, he prints separate reports for each team member that include their activities and events for the period. He then asks team members to record in the appropriate columns on their reports when they start or end an activity during the performance period or when they reach an event, together with any comments they want to share. He finally asks team members to send him a copy of the report by the close of the first business day following the end of the performance period. Portny believes that recording achievements at the time they occur increases the likelihood that the data will be accurate and that having an agreed-upon schedule for submitting information minimizes the chances that he as project manager has to surprise people with unexpected requests for progress data.

FOR EXAMPLE

Manual Schedule Tracking Systems

Many project managers have to develop their own systems to track schedule performance. Even in today's technology-rich workplace, some project managers opt for manual (rather than computer-software-based) systems. Manual systems include day planners, personal calendars, and handwritten project logs. Manual systems are inexpensive and can be appropriate for small projects with limited resources. But manual systems require physical space to store data, and the more data collected, the more space required. Furthermore, analyzing and reporting generated data almost always take longer when done manually.

Project managers can do the following to improve the accuracy of schedule performance data collection:

▲ **Tell people how the requested data will be used.** People are always more motivated to perform a task if they understand the reasons for it.

▲ **Provide schedule performance reports to the people who supply the data.** People are even more motivated to perform a task if they get direct benefits from it.

▲ **Publicly acknowledge those people who supply timely and accurate data.** Positive reinforcement of desired behavior confirms to people that they're meeting expectations and emphasizes to others what constitutes desirable behavior.

▲ **Clearly define activities and events.** Doing so helps the project manager understand where a project stands, when a milestone is achieved or missed, and when an activity is or isn't performed.

▲ **Don't collect more data than can be used—and use all the data that's collected.** Collect only the data needed to assess schedule performance.

11.4.2 Monitoring Work-Effort Expended

A project manager can assess a project's work-effort expenditures by comparing the actual expenditures with those planned. (However, project managers must always keep in mind that effort does not necessarily equal completeness.)

Figure 11-9 shows an example labor report that describes the work-effort expended by each team member working on each lowest-level project activity (as defined by a project plan and Work Breakdown Structure).

Figure 11-9

WBS Code	Description	Employee		Work Effort Expended (Person-hours)					
				Budget	Week 1	Week 2	Week 3	Week 4	. . .
3.1.2	Design questionnaire	H. Jones	Planned	130	20	40	20	30	. . .
			Actual	0	10	30	5	25	. . .
			Remaining	130	120	90	85	25	. . .
			Difference	0	+10	+20	+35	+40	. . .
		F. Smith	Planned	70	0	20	20	15	. . .
			Actual	0	0	25	10	15	. . .
			Remaining	70	70	45	35	20	. . .
			Difference	0	0	−5	+5	+5	. . .

A labor report.

The project manager obtains or calculates the following information from data submitted during the period covered by the report:

▲ The actual number of hours spent by each team member on each activity.

▲ The total number of hours remaining to be spent by each team member on each activity.

▲ The running difference between the total number of hours budgeted to be spent and those actually spent by each team member on each activity.

Actual expenditures do not always agree with those planned. Typically, variances of 10 percent above or below the expected numbers in any month are normal. For example, in Figure 11-9, the labor charges presented for team members indicate that Smith appears to be working in accordance with the plan. He charged more hours in Week 2 than planned, less in Week 3, and the same as planned in Week 4. However, Jones is spending less time on the project than planned, and the total shortfall of hours is building steadily. It's not clear whether this shortfall indicates a problem, but the systematic undercharging does point to a situation that should be investigated further.

Having project team members fill out time sheets is the most effective way to collect work-effort expenditure data.

A time sheet should include the following data:

▲ The number of hours spent working on each activity during the day.

▲ In most instances, recording the time spent on an activity to the nearest half hour is sufficient. Some people might have to record time in intervals smaller than half an hour. Lawyers, for example, often allocate their time on different jobs in six-minute segments. Their clients would have it no other way, given that a lawyer might charge $300 per hour.

▲ A team member's signature verifying that the recorded information is correct.

▲ A project manager's or team leader's approval signature verifying that the time charges made are valid and appropriate.

Project managers can take the following steps to increase the accuracy of the work-effort expenditure data collected:

▲ **Make sure team members understand the purpose of the time-recording system.** A project manager needs work-effort information to compare actual performance with planned performance and to help determine when aspects of the plan need to be changed. However, team members often fear that the project manager is looking to criticize them for not spending time exactly in accordance with a plan or for not spending enough hours on project work (as opposed to other administrative duties). If team members believe that these are a project manager's motives, they'll allocate work hours among activities to show what they think the project manager wants to see rather than what's really happening.

▲ **Encourage people to record the actual hours they work during the period rather than requiring their total hours recorded for a week to equal 40.** If people must record a total of 40 hours per week and they work overtime, they'll omit hours or reduce them proportionately to ensure that their weekly total equals 40. Project managers want them to record accurate data.

▲ **Include categories for time spent on nonproject work activities, such as "unallocated," "administrative overhead," and so on.** If project managers want people to honestly record the activities on which they work, they must provide them with appropriate categories.

▲ **Collect time sheets weekly if possible, and no less often than once every two weeks.** No matter how often people are asked to fill out time sheets, many wait until the sheet is due to complete it.

▲ **Don't ask people to submit their time sheets for a performance period before the period is over.** On occasion, people are asked to submit time sheets by the end of the day Thursday for the week ending on Friday. This practice immediately reduces the accuracy of the data because it's impossible to know with certainty what team members will be doing tomorrow. More important, though, it suggests to people that, if it's okay to estimate their time for Friday, perhaps they don't have to be too concerned with the accuracy of the rest of the week's data, either.

11.4.3 Monitoring Expenditures

Project managers monitor a project's financial expenditures to verify that they're in accordance with the project plan and, if not, to determine how to address any deviations. Earned Value Analysis (see Section 11.3) is frequently used to determining whether a project is over or under budget, as well as if it is ahead of or behind schedule.

Responsive project monitoring requires a project manager to have a picture of the amount of project funds available at each stage of the project. To do this, project managers must typically monitor purchase requisitions, purchase orders, commitments (that is, purchase orders or contracts agreed to by the project manager and the contractor or vendor), accounts payable, and expenditures. Each of these topics is often organization-specific.

Figure 11-10 shows a sample cost report that presents project expenditures individually for lowest-level activities and summed to provide totals for higher-level activities for the current period and for the entire project to date. The actual numbers for the period are derived from data submitted during the period covered by the report. Because no definition is given, "actual" in this illustration could mean the value of purchase requisitions, purchase orders, commitments, accounts payable, and/or expenditures.

Project managers can take the following steps to increase the accuracy of a project's expenditure data:

▲ Check to see that purchase orders are removed from totals after a bill has been received (or a check has been written) to avoid counting the expenditure twice.

Figure 11-10

| WBS Code | Activity | Performance Period | | To Date | | Total |
		Budget	Actual	Budget	Actual	Budget
	Total	$8,500	$8,200	$15,500	$15,100	$200,000
1.0	Finalize requirements	5,000	4,400	12,300	11,400	45,000
1.1	Conduct focus groups	3,000	2,900	7,500	7,100	10,000
1.2	Review documents	1,500	1,200	4,000	3,800	5,000
1.3	Prepare report	500	300	800	500	4,000

A cost report.

▲ Be sure to include the correct Work Breakdown Structure charge code on each purchase requisition. Verify that the purchase order includes the correct Work Breakdown Structure charge code.

▲ Periodically remove from lists old purchase requisitions and purchase orders that have been voided or canceled.

Most organizations have financial systems that maintain records of all expenditures. Often, the system also maintains records of accounts payable. Unfortunately, many financial systems categorize expenses by cost center but don't have the capacity to classify them by project or activity within a project. Even if the organization's financial system can classify expenditures by activity within a project, project managers often choose to develop their own system for tracking purchase requisitions and purchase orders. A spreadsheet program or database software can typically support this tracking.

11.4.4 Developing Comprehensive Monitoring and Control Procedures

Savvy project managers develop a set of procedures (typically early on in their projects) to collect information on schedule performance, work-effort expended, expenditures, and perhaps other project aspects. Project managers then use this gathered information to analyze the work and results.

The following outlines a basic control system that project managers can use throughout a project's life:

1. At the start of a project performance period, the project manager reconfirms with people the activities they're expected to perform during the period, the start and end dates they agreed to for these activities, the dates on which they agreed to achieve key events, and the work-effort they'll have to spend to complete their activities.

   (a) If any people disagree with the project manager or plan about any of this information, the project manager should work with them to come up with an acceptable modification to the existing plan.

2. During each project performance period, the project manager has people record the following performance data:

   (a) The dates on which activities start and end and on which events are reached.

   (b) The work hours they spend on individual project activities.

   (c) Purchase requisitions they submit and purchase orders they send out.

3. At agreed-upon intervals during or at the end of the period, the project manager has people submit the following data either to all relevant

organizational systems or to systems specially maintained for the project:

(a) Their activity achievement data.

(b) Their work hour records.

(c) Their purchase requisition and purchase order information.

4. At the end of the period, the project manager does the following:

(a) Confirms that all acceptance tests, peer reviews, and other assessments of work produced during the period have been successfully passed.

(b) Enters schedule and resource information into the appropriate information systems.

(c) Produces reports from project-specific systems or obtains reports from organizational systems that compare planned and actual schedule and resource performance for the period.

(d) Identifies differences between planned and actual performance and determines the reasons for those variances.

(e) Formulates corrective actions to get back on track or, as needed, to change selected aspects of the existing plan.

(f) Obtains all required approvals to make needed changes to existing plans.

(g) Takes any corrective actions developed.

(h) Reports on achievements, problems, corrective actions, and the results of the corrective actions taken.

5. At the beginning of the next performance period, the cycle starts again.

11.4.5 Identifying Possible Causes of Delays and Variances

If an activity is running behind schedule, it might be due to one or more of the following reasons:

▲ People are spending less time on the activity than was budgeted.

▲ The activity is taking more work-effort than estimated.

▲ People are expanding the scope of the activity.

▲ Work that wasn't identified is required to perform the activity.

▲ The people working on the activity have less experience with similar activities than anticipated.

▲ People are not accurately recording their schedule performance.

The following situations might result in people charging more or less time to activities than planned:

▲ The person performing the work is more or less productive than assumed when the plan was developed.

▲ The project manager allowed insufficient time for becoming familiar with the activity before starting to work on it.

▲ The person is more or less efficient than the project manager estimated.

▲ The activity is requiring more or less work than anticipated.

▲ People are recording their time incorrectly.

Spending more or less money to support project activities than planned can occur because of the following:

▲ The bills for goods or services were received late.

▲ Someone prepaid for certain items to receive special discounts.

▲ Certain goods or services that were included in the plan weren't ultimately needed.

▲ Goods or services that weren't included in the plan were ultimately needed.

▲ Expenditures were allocated to the wrong accounts.

11.4.6 Identifying Possible Corrective Actions

If actual performance deviates from project plan, project managers can consider taking corrective action. However, the later in a project corrective actions are taken, the more difficult and less likely the possibility of successful recovery. Possible corrective actions include the following:

▲ **If the variance results from a one-time difficulty, try to take steps to get back on the plan.** For example, Karla planned to spend 40 hours to buy a piece of equipment. She figured she'd have to visit four stores before finding the equipment, but she found exactly what she wanted for a good price at the first store. She shouldn't change the project plan because most likely she'll wind up requiring slightly more time on some future activities and it'll tend to even out.

▲ **If the variance suggests a situation that will lead to similar variances in the future, consider modifying the plan accordingly.** Suppose Karla's team finished a task with half the allotted work-effort because her team was more experienced than anticipated. If the specific team and its experience enable everyone to be more efficient on future assignments, Karla should revise the plan to reduce the amount of effort she plans to spend on all assignments that use her team.

A **baseline** is the current version of a project plan that guides project performance and against which the project manager compares actual project performance.

Rebaselining is officially adopting a new project plan to guide activities and serve as the comparative basis for future performance assessments.

If a project manager feels that revising the plan and adopting a new baseline is necessary, he or she should do the following:

▲ Consult with key project audiences to explain why the changes are needed and to solicit their approval and support.

▲ Make sure that all key project audiences know about the new baseline.

▲ Keep a copy of the original plan and all subsequent modifications to support the final performance assessment when the project is over.

Rebaselining is a last resort when project work is not going according to plan. Project managers should exhaust all possible strategies and approaches to get back on track before attempting to change the plan itself.

SELF-CHECK

1. A combination activities/key-events report can help project managers collect data for what type of control?

2. Unallocated work hours diminish the usability of work-effort data. True or false?

3. Expenditures worth monitoring include purchase orders, accounts payable, and commitments. True or false?

4. In a comprehensive project monitoring system, team members should submit which of the following on an agreed-upon schedule?

   (a) quality control reports, time sheets, and material requests

   (b) time logs, exception reports, and schedule variances

   (c) activity achievement data, work hour records, and purchases

   (d) none of the above

5. Rachael takes three hours longer to complete a task than her project manager's original estimate. Rachael's performance affects which of the following?

   (a) the project's schedule performance

   (b) the project's work-effort

   (c) both a and b

   (d) neither a nor b

11.5 Responding to Scope Creep and Change Control

Input from more than 500 project managers regarding the most important single problem facing project managers indicates that coping with change is at the top of their list.

New technologies and materials become available or new requirements and needs become apparent during a project; any of these can lead to changed projects. The later these changes are made in the project, the more difficult and costly they become. Another common source of change is the natural tendency of the client, as well as project team members, to try to improve the project's output as the project progresses, a phenomenon known as **scope creep**. The most common result of scope creep is an upset client who was not (or claims not to have been) told how long the change delays the project and how much it raises the project's cost.

A major source of trouble with changes is typically that the project manager, in an attempt to avoid bureaucracy, adopts an informal process of handling requests for change. Such a process leads to misunderstanding on the part of the party requesting the change, and before the project manager can undo the damage, the organization is committed to extending the scope of the project but without the additional resources and time to do it.

Project managers must expect change and be prepared to deal with it. Fighting change is not appropriate. The best approach is to set up a well-controlled, formal process whereby changes can be introduced and accomplished with as little distress as possible. This process is known as the **change control system**. Figure 11-11 shows a graphic depiction of a change control system.

The purpose of a change control system is to do the following:

▲ Review all requested changes (either content or procedural changes).

▲ Identify all impacts the change might have on other project tasks.

Figure 11-11

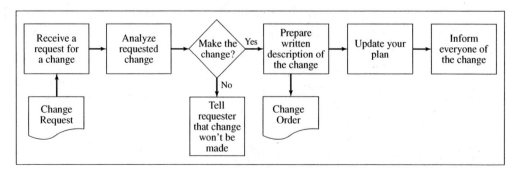

A change control system.

▲ Translate these impacts into alterations of project performance, schedule, and cost.

▲ Evaluate the benefits and disadvantages of the requested changes.

▲ Identify and evaluate alternative changes that might accomplish the same ends with greater benefits and/or fewer disadvantages.

▲ Install a process so that individuals with appropriate authority can accept or reject the proposed changes.

▲ Communicate accepted changes to all concerned parties.

▲ Ensure that the changes are implemented properly.

▲ Prepare reports that summarize all changes to date and their impacts.

Avoiding scope creep is not possible. However, monitoring it, controlling it, and thereby reducing some of the pain is possible—if the project manager follows a few guidelines:

▲ Include a change control system in every project plan.

▲ Insist that every project change is introduced by a change order that includes a description of the agreed-upon change together with any resulting changes in the plan, processes, budget, schedule, or deliverables.

▲ Require changes be approved in writing by the client as well as by a representative of senior management.

▲ Amend and update all project plans and schedules to reflect the change after the change order has been approved.

FOR EXAMPLE

Change Control Boards

Large, long-term projects frequently include a change control board, which is a committee of interested parties that makes decisions whether a proposed change should be implemented. The authority of change control boards varies from project to project and organization to organization, but board decisions are typically accepted as final and binding. Although change control boards are most common on software-development projects, the U.S. government in 2004 established a change control board as part of Vista, a new veterans' electronic health record system (www.worldvista.org). The control board is staffed by members of four interested organizations—Veterans' Affairs, Centers for Medicare & Medicaid, the Health Resources and Services Administration, and the Indian Health Service.

SELF-CHECK

1. Who is responsible for scope creep?
2. Project managers can monitor and control change by doing which of the following?
   (a) requiring clients to approve all changes in writing
   (b) updating plans and schedules to reflect change
   (c) developing a change order to document all change requests
   (d) all of the above

SUMMARY

Project managers are continually planning, monitoring, and controlling various project aspects. Project data for productive monitoring and control must be defined, appropriately collected, systematically analyzed, and tactfully reported. Although numerous analysis tools and techniques exist, Earned Value Analysis is especially effective and popular because project managers can gauge schedule and budget based on a review of expenditures. Project managers should monitor schedule performance, work-effort, and expenditures and make control decisions accordingly. Scope creep is inevitable with projects, but a change control system can lessen its stressful aspects.

KEY TERMS

Actual Cost of Work Performed (ACWP)	The amount of funds actually spent for work actually done by the specified date.
Baseline	The current version of a project plan that guides project performance and against which the project manager compares actual project performance.
Budgeted Cost of Work Performed (BCWP)	The planned cost for work actually done by the specified date.
Budgeted Cost of Work Scheduled (BCWS)	The planned cost for work due to be completed by a specified date.
Change control system	A formal process whereby changes can be introduced and accomplished with as little distress as possible.

Cost variance	The portion of the difference between what was planned to be spent by a certain date and what has really been spent that's true cost savings or loss.
Data collection and reporting	Gathering project information and turning it into information useful for controlling projects.
Earned value	The earned value of a piece of work is defined to be equal to the amount the project managers plan to spend to perform it.
Earned Value Analysis	A technique that helps determine whether a project is ahead or behind schedule and whether it's over or under budget, while only tracking resource expenditures.
Estimate at completion	The total amount that will be spent to perform a task, if a project's spending pattern to date continues until the task is finished.
Exception reports	Report intended for special decisions or unexpected situations in which affected team members and outside managers need to be made aware of a change.
Frequency count	A simple count of the occurrence of an event.
Inputs	Raw data collected to describe selected aspects of project performance.
Outputs	Reports presenting the results of the analyses performed.
Performance period	The interval for which a project is reviewed and assessed.
Plan-monitor-control cycle	An ongoing project-management process of continually planning what to do, checking on progress, comparing progress to plan, and taking corrective actions.
Project controlling	Using monitored data and information to bring actual performance into agreement with the project plan.
Project-management information system (PMIS)	A set of procedures, equipment, and other resources for collecting, analyzing, storing, and reporting on information that describes project performance.
Project monitoring	Collecting, recording, and reporting project information that is important to the project manager and other relevant stakeholders.
Raw numbers	Actual numbers in collected data.

Rebaselining	Officially adopting a new project plan to guide activities and serve as the comparative basis for future performance assessments.
Routine reports	Reports issued on a regular schedule that report on data collected on established aspects of a project.
Schedule variance	The difference between what was planned to be spent by a certain date and what was really spent that's due to the project being ahead of or behind schedule.
Scope creep	The natural tendency of the client, as well as project team members, to try to improve the project's output as the project progresses.
Special analysis reports	Report that disseminates the results of a special study in a project concerning a particular opportunity or problem.
Variance	The difference between planned and actual figures.

ASSESS YOUR UNDERSTANDING

Go to www.wiley.com/college/portny to assess your knowledge of the basics of project control.
Measure your learning by comparing pre-test and post-test results.

Summary Questions

1. The project monitoring system is the direct connection between:
   (a) project planning and project evaluation.
   (b) project organizing and project evaluation.
   (c) project control and project organizing.
   (d) project planning and project control.
2. Earned Value Analysis requires project managers to create which of the following?
   (a) detailed invoices and accounts payable records during the planning phase
   (b) detailed budgets and schedules during the planning phase
   (c) detailed action plans and objectives during the defining phase
   (d) detailed budgets and schedules during the evaluation phase
3. Monitoring and control systems must follow an organization's budget- and time-tracking systems in order for the monitoring and controlling to carry adequate authority. True or false?
4. The accuracy of schedule performance, work-effort, and expenditure data can all be improved when which of the following occurs?
   (a) Each project team member logs his or her individual work contribution.
   (b) Upper management regularly reviews reported data.
   (c) The project manager tells team members how the data will be used.
   (d) all of the above
5. All but which of the following are control activities?
   (a) reconfirming the plan
   (b) taking corrective action
   (c) creating data tracking forms
   (d) rebaselining

Applying This Chapter

1. After several years of successfully managing projects at an automotive parts manufacturer, Sean decided to skip formally planning and monitoring his latest project because he believes he has adequate experience to respond to any problem that might arise. He also contends that no one in the organization ever looks at plans anyway. As Sean's manager, what might you tell him to convince him of the importance of ongoing planning and monitoring?

2. You're managing the design and installation of a new machine on a computer hardware assembly line. How might each of the following types of control data be used for project control: frequency counts, raw numbers, subjective numeric ratings, and indicator and surrogate measures?

3. Harry's organization has effective systems in place to track work-effort and expenditures, but he wants to begin measuring other project aspects. How might Harry collect data for and monitor team morale during the course of his project?

4. Consider the data report from several weeks of collecting the number of programming bugs identified weekly during a software development project. The curve indicates the project plan estimates for bugs. What specifically would you say in a report to upper management about this data? Would you say anything different in a report to team members?

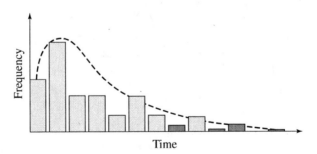

Number of bugs reported versus plan.

5. Janice is planning the frequency of the period reports she'll issue for her project. She's considering timing project reports with the schedule of her organization's regular accounting reports, sending out reports on the same day of the month, or sending out reports whenever a project milestone is reached. What are the pros and cons of Janice's three report-timing options?

6. The Acme Company has awarded a contract for the production of two specialized corporate brochures to Copies 'R' Us. The contract calls for Copies 'R' Us to produce 500 copies of Brochure A and 1,000 copies of Brochure B. It further states that Copies 'R' Us will produce Brochure A at the rate

of 100 per month and Brochure B at the rate of 250 per month. Production of Brochure A is to start on January 1 and production of Brochure B on February 1. The project plan is depicted in the following table:

Activity	Start	End	Elapsed Time	Total Cost
Brochure A	Jan 1	May 31	5 months	$100,000
Brochure B	Feb 1	May 31	4 months	$100,000
Total				$200,000

The following table summarizes what has happened as of March 31:

Activity	Start	Elapsed Time	Number Produced	Total Cost
Brochure A	Jan 1	3 months	150	$45,000
Brochure B	Feb 1	2 months	600	$30,000
Total				$75,000

What is the project schedule and cost performance to date? What's likely to happen if expenditure patterns stay the same for the remainder of the project (estimate at completion)?

7. You've been asked to include a section on your project's monthly status report about schedule performance. You've identified the type and frequency of data you need to collect from your team of six technicians and have even created an online form for team members to fill out each Friday. Still, you can't get your team members to consistently submit weekly progress reports to you. What are some strategies you can consider to improve the efficacy of your schedule performance data collection?

8. Marcia is heading a project to produce four new 30-second television ads for a small liberal arts college. After two months of work, Marcia and her team of PR and marketing representatives at the college are off track in terms of work-effort planned. The group has put in 60 percent of the effort estimated in the project plan up to this point. This level of work-effort is beginning to affect project schedule performance. What more does she need to know about the situation to determine whether she should try to get the project back on plan or modify the plan?

9. Your organization recently introduced a new change control system. How might the existence of this new system affect the behavior of you as project manager, a client, or a project team member whenever a change in the project is considered?

YOU TRY IT

Cycling Through

Read through a detailed Work Breakdown Structure for a job. If you don't have a Work Breakdown Structure of your own, brainstorm a detailed list of tasks required to complete a project you know well (planning a party, planning and going on vacation, selecting and attending a college). Evaluate the list of tasks and identify activities that have planning, monitoring, and/or controlling aspects. (Some tasks might have multiple aspects; you might want to consider breaking down these tasks into multiple subtasks.) After you identityfing tasks, look for clusters of tasks that illustrate the plan-monitor-control cycle found in project management. In what ways does planning feed into monitoring and then feed into controlling in your project?

Targeting a Report

Find a set of data that spans over several months or years. Data of this type that you probably have lying around your home or office include several old bank statements, your employee evaluations from the last few years, or several report cards. Read through the data and analyze it to the best of your ability. Do the data match your objectives and goals? Draft two versions of one-paragraph reports about the data, focusing the content, organization, and tone of your report to two different audiences. For example, write a brief explanation of your last three report cards for your parents, for a scholarship decision committee, and/or for a good friend. How is your content, tone, and organization different for each audience?

Monitoring the Big Three

Consider a large but everyday project you encounter—maintaining a home or car, raising and caring for a child

or pet, and so on. Even though these activities aren't traditional projects, they can benefit from ongoing monitoring and controlling based on the strategies outlined in Section 11.4. For your everyday project, brainstorm a list of activities that contribute to each of the three major categories of monitoring and control: schedule performance, work-effort, and expenditures. Create a list of specific pieces of data that you need to assess schedule performance, work-effort, and expenditures. What are some specific ways that you (and perhaps others in your family life) can participate in the ongoing collection of important data related to schedule performance, work-effort, and expenditures? Write down all your thoughts to create a comprehensive monitoring and control procedure for your everyday project. (See Section 11.4.4 for specifics.)

Change Control

Many plans neglect to include change control systems or its details. Review a project plan that doesn't include change control details. (If you don't have a plan of your own, review the wastewater management plan for Southern Boone County, Missouri, a detailed plan that does not include change control details, at www.missouri.edu/~wwpsbc/workplan.html.) First write a definition of what constitutes a significant change for your project. Next, draft a description of the process that everyone must go through to make project changes. Finally, detail how everyone involved with the project will be informed of change requests and changes that are actually enacted. If possible, share your change control plans with someone who can help you get these details officially incorporated into the plan—or into future plans of a similar nature.

CASE STUDY: Cable Tech

Cable Tech

Cable Tech is a contract cable wiring company. It provides support to local cable companies in seven states in the Midwest. Cable Tech has one operation in each state, and each varies in size from 60 to 250 employees. A disturbing trend has been developing for the last couple of years that Cable Tech management wishes to stop. Incidences of tardiness and absenteeism are on the increase. Both are extremely disruptive in a contract wiring operation. Cable Tech is non-union in all seven locations, and since management wants to keep it this way, it wants a careful, low-key approach to the problem. Assistant Personnel Manager Jean Alister has been appointed project manager to recommend a solution. All seven operations managers have been assigned to work with her on this problem.

Jean has had no problem interfacing with the operations managers. They quickly agreed that three steps must be taken to solve the problem:

1. Institute a uniform daily attendance report that is summarized weekly and forwarded to the main office. (Current practice varies from location to location, but comments on attendance are normally included in monthly operations reports.)

2. Institute a uniform disciplinary policy, enforced in a uniform manner.

3. Initiate an intensive employee education program to emphasize the importance of good attendance.

In addition, the team decided that the three-point program should be tested before a final recommendation is presented. They thought it would be best to test the program at one location for two months. Jean wants to control and evaluate the test by having a daily attendance report transmitted to her directly at headquarters, from which she will make the final decision on whether or not to present the program in its current format.

Questions

1. Does this monitoring and control method seem adequate?

2. What are the potential problems?

12

COMMUNICATING AND DOCUMENTING PROJECT PROGRESS

Reporting on and Meeting about Project Status

Starting Point

Go to www.wiley.com/college/portny to assess your knowledge of the basics of project communication.

Determine where you need to concentrate your effort.

What You'll Learn in This Chapter

▲ Forms of communication
▲ Informal versus formal communication
▲ Meeting preparation, conduct, and follow-up
▲ Content for project progress reports
▲ Types and expectations of various project meetings

After Studying This Chapter, You'll Be Able To

▲ Produce more effective written communication
▲ Plan and lead project meetings
▲ Create detailed meeting agendas
▲ Write appropriate progress reports for various audiences
▲ Customize meetings for various audiences and purposes

INTRODUCTION

In today's workplace, communication takes numerous forms. For the project manager, both written and verbal communications—as well as informal and formal communications—are useful, meaningful ways to share and collect important project information. The project progress report is an important, formal written piece of communication for which project managers are typically responsible. Strategic planning and strong writing can help increase the likelihood that these documents are actually read. Planning and strategic thinking can similarly improve the quality and effectiveness of communication produced in project meetings.

12.1 Forms of Communication

The key to successful project management is effective **communication**—sharing the right messages with the right people in a timely manner. Through communication people exchange and share information with one another, and influence one another's attitudes, behaviors, and understandings.

The ability to communicate well, both orally and in writing, is a critical skill for project managers. Planning project communications up-front enables project managers to choose the appropriate type of communication for sharing different messages.

12.1.1 Choosing the Best Communication Approach

Project communications can be both formal and informal.

▲ **Formal communications** are preplanned and conducted in a standard format in accordance with an established schedule.
▲ **Informal communications** occur as people think of information they want to share.

Informal communications occur continuously in the normal course of business. However, project managers must take care not to rely on these informal interchanges to share thoughts about all aspects of projects because they often tend to involve only a small number of the people who might benefit from the topics being addressed. To minimize the chances for misunderstandings and hurt feelings, project managers should do the following:

▲ Confirm in writing the important information that was shared in informal discussions.
▲ Avoid having an informal discussion with only some of the people who are involved in the topic being addressed.

12.1.2 Sharing Information in Writing

Written reports enable project managers to present factual data more efficiently, choose their words carefully in order to minimize misunderstandings, provide historical records of the information shared, and share the same message with a wide audience. However, written reports don't do the following:

▲ Allow the intended audience to ask questions to clarify the content, meaning, and implication of the message being sent.

▲ Enable project managers to verify that their audiences received and interpreted their message in the way intended.

▲ Enable project managers to pick up nonverbal signals that suggest an audience's reactions to the message.

▲ Support interactive discussion and brainstorming about a message.

Most important, project managers might never know whether the intended audience even read the reports. Project managers can take the following steps to improve the chances that people read and understand their written reports:

▲ Prepare regularly scheduled reports in a standard format. Doing so makes it easier for audiences to know where to look for specific types of information.

▲ Stay focused. Preparing several short reports to address different topics is better than combining several topics into one long report.

▲ Minimize the use of technical jargon and acronyms.

FOR EXAMPLE

Communications Resources at the Center for Creative Leadership

Nearly a third of project managers report some difficulties in dealing with communication and interpersonal relations. The Center for Creative Leadership (www.ccl.org), a not-for-profit training center in Greensboro, North Carolina, helps project managers and other leaders address communication issues via role-playing exercises, self-evaluative tools, classes, online resources, and group exercises. Although participants in CCL programs come from a variety of disciplines, developing good communication skills is part of every CCL program. As CCL's Michael Wakefield notes, "Leaders who are trusted—even in times of great difficulty—are skilled communicators."

▲ Use written reports to share facts, and identify a person for people to contact to clarify or discuss further any information included in those reports.

▲ Clearly describe any actions that people should take based on the information in the report.

▲ Use novel approaches to emphasize key information, such as printing key sections in a different color or on colored paper, or mentioning particularly relevant or important sections in a cover memo.

▲ After a report is sent, project managers should discuss with the people who received it one or two key points that were addressed in the report. Doing so will tell a project manager quickly whether the intended audience read the report.

▲ Keep reports as brief as possible. Say what needs to be said and then stop. If a report must run several pages, consider including a short summary at the beginning of the report.

12.1.3 Sharing Information through Meetings

Most people view meetings as being anything from the last vestige of interpersonal contact in an increasingly computer and technology-focused society to the biggest time-waster in business today.

Following are some of the most common frustrations about meetings that people express:

▲ Not being given sufficient advance notice.

▲ Not having the right people attend.

▲ Not starting on time.

▲ Not having an agenda.

▲ Not sticking to the agenda if one exists.

▲ Having no actions result from the meeting.

▲ Rehashing issues that were supposedly resolved at a previous meeting.

▲ Having people represent that they have the authority to make a decision and then having their decision reversed after the meeting.

▲ Reading written material aloud that people could've read themselves beforehand.

▲ Having a large portion of the meeting deal with issues in which most of the participants are not interested or involved.

▲ Knowing that the next meeting will be no better than the last one.

Meetings can be valuable, though, if they are planned and managed effectively. When handled correctly, meetings can help project managers learn about other team members' backgrounds, experience, and styles; stimulate brainstorming, problem analysis, and decision making; and provide a forum for people to explore the reasons for and interpretations of a message.

Project managers can improve their meetings by taking the steps discussed in the following sections.

Premeeting Preparation

▲ Clarify the purpose of the meeting and include meeting agenda.

▲ Circulate the written agenda and any background material in advance so that people can prepare for the meeting.

▲ Decide who needs to attend and why. If the purpose of the meeting is to share information, figure out beforehand who has it. If decisions are to be made during the meeting, decide who has the necessary authority— and make sure that those people attend.

▲ Give plenty of advance notice of the meeting.

▲ Tell others the purpose of the meeting.

▲ Prepare a written agenda that includes topics and times. Doing so helps people to see why attending is in their interests. The agenda also serves as the guideline for conducting the meeting.

▲ Keep meetings to one hour or less. If necessary, schedule multiple meetings to discuss complex issues or topics. However, if the purpose of the meeting is to solve a problem, plan to work until the problem is solved.

Meeting Conduct

▲ Start on time, even if people are absent. After people see that the project manager will wait for latecomers before starting, everyone will come late.

▲ Assign a timekeeper—someone who will remind the group when allotted times for topics have been exceeded.

▲ Take written minutes of who attended, what items were discussed, and what decisions and assignments were made.

▲ Keep a list of action items to be explored further after the meeting, and assign responsibility for all entries on that list.

▲ If the right information isn't available or the right people aren't in atten- dance to resolve an issue, stop the discussion and put it on an action item list to deal with later.

▲ End on time.

Follow-up

▲ Promptly distribute meeting minutes to all attendees.

▲ Monitor the status of all action items to be performed.

▲ Don't just think about these suggestions; act on them!

Section 12.3 discusses various types of meetings project managers should plan to incorporate during the life of projects.

SELF-CHECK

1. Informal communications can be an effective way to share information, but project managers need to supplement informal communication with what?

2. Although written project reports are useful communication tools, project managers must take care that team members do which of the following?

    (a) agree with the reports

    (b) read the reports

    (c) do not share the reports

    (d) all of the above

3. Scheduling multiple meetings to deal with topics that take longer than an hour to discuss is an example of which of the following?

    (a) good premeeting preparation behavior

    (b) good meeting conduct behavior

    (c) good meeting follow-up behavior

    (d) none of the above

12.2 Preparing Progress Reports

The most common regularly scheduled, written project communication is the project progress report. A **project progress report** reviews what has happened during a performance period, describes problems and the corrective actions needed, and previews what is planned for the next period.

A project progress report is a convenient way to keep key audiences involved in a project and informed of anything they have to do to support the project's ongoing performance. In addition, preparing the report gives the project manager an opportunity to step back and review all aspects of the project so that he or she can recognize accomplishments and identify situations that might require early intervention.

Project managers can determine the audience for regularly scheduled project progress reports by answering the following questions:

▲ Who needs to know about the project?
▲ Who wants to know about the project?
▲ Who else does the project manager want to know about the project?

At a minimum, project managers should consider providing project progress reports to supervisors, upper management, the client or customer, project team members, others who are helping on the project, and others who are interested in or will be affected by the project's results.

Project progress reports include some or all of the following content:

▲ **Performance highlights.** Always begin a report with a summary of highlights. Try to keep it to no more than one page.
▲ **Performance details.** Describe in detail the outcomes produced, activities performed, milestones reached, labor hours worked, and funds expended.
▲ **Problems and issues.** Highlight special issues or problems encountered during the period and propose any needed corrective actions.
▲ **Approved changes to the plan.** Report all approved changes made to the existing project plan.
▲ **Risk management status.** Update project risk assessments by reporting on changes in project assumptions or the likelihood that they will come to pass, as well as their impact on existing project plans.
▲ **Plans for the next period.** Summarize major work and accomplishments planned for the next performance period.

Project managers can improve the quality of project progress reports by following these tips and techniques:

▲ **Tailor reports to the audience's interests and needs.** Provide only the information that the audience wants and/or needs. If necessary, prepare separate reports for different audiences.
▲ **When preparing different progress reports for different audiences, prepare the most detailed one first and extract information from that report to produce the others.** This approach ensures consistency among the reports and reduces the likelihood of performing the same work more than once.

▲ **Make sure that all the product, schedule, and resource information included in a report is for the same time period.** Doing so might not be easy for project managers who depend on different organization systems for raw performance data. For example, if Marcia tracks project schedule performance on a system that she maintains herself, she might be able to produce a status report by the end of the first week after the performance period ends. However, her organization's financial system, which she uses to track project expenditures, might not generate performance reports for the same period until a month after the period ends.

▲ **Always compare actual performance with respect to the performance planned.** Presenting the information in this format highlights issues to be addressed.

▲ **Include no surprises.** If something significant occurs during the period that requires prompt action, tell all the people involved immediately and work to address the problem. Mention the occurrence and

FOR EXAMPLE

Virtual Reports

Using the Internet to communicate and report on a project's status is now easily accomplished whether project team members are in the next cubicle or across the world. More and more companies are using secure Web pages on the Internet to collect, store, and disseminate project information. Software programs such as Microsoft Project enable project managers to use an organization's local area network or intranet, as well as the Internet, to help with project communication and monitoring. Some pages are specifically designed to communicate project information to and from clients, while others are designed for the sole use of members of the project team or for use by the organization's senior management team. Web pages can hold any information that the project manager wants to share, such as progress to date on a project, resources assigned to a task, status of a particular task, and expenses to date. Project managers can electronically check the status of a task or any resource on the team and have updated information automatically entered into a project plan. Electronic work groups can be set up to monitor task completion, resource usage, and to provide reports to a group of individuals who have an interest in the project's status. For example, milestone reports can be sent to a senior management work group, and up-to-date personnel usage reports can be sent to the human resources department.

any associated corrective actions in the progress report to provide a record.

▲ **Use regularly scheduled team meetings to discuss issues and problems raised in the project progress report.**

SELF-CHECK

1. The three general audiences for a project progress report include people who need to know about the project, people who want to know about the project, and which of the following?

   (a) people who are involved in similar projects

   (b) people auditing the project

   (c) people who are funding the project

   (d) people the project manager wants to know about the project

2. To efficiently prepare multiple project progress reports, you should begin by drafting the report to upper management and then move on to creating other versions for other audience sections. True or false?

12.3 Holding Key Project Meetings

Active, ongoing support from all major project audiences gives a project its greatest chance for achieving success. A savvy project manager continually reinforces a project's vision and how everyone is progressing toward it, which helps the project's audience understand when and how they can most effectively support the project.

Project managers use some or all of the following types of meetings during a project:

▲ **Regularly scheduled team meetings:** opportunities for team members to share progress and issues and to sustain productive and trusting interpersonal relationships.

▲ **Ad hoc team meetings:** special sessions for team members to address problems and issues as they arise.

▲ **Upper-management reviews:** periodic summary of project status, major accomplishments, and issues with which upper management's help is required. This type of meeting enables the project manager to keep the project fresh in upper management's minds and note ways to keep the project in line with major organization initiatives.

The following sections cover each meeting type in detail.

12.3.1 Regularly Scheduled Team Meetings

Project teams should have the opportunity to meet periodically to reaffirm the project's focus and keep abreast of activities within and outside the project that affect their work and the project's ultimate success. Recognizing that most people work on several projects at the same time, these meetings can reinforce the team's identity and working relationships.

Project managers should consult with team members to develop a meeting schedule that is convenient for as many people as possible. If some people can't attend in person, try to have them participate in a conference call.

In addition to the general suggestions for ensuring productive meetings (see Section 12.2), observe the following guidelines when planning and conducting team meetings:

- ▲ Even though the meetings are regularly scheduled, always prepare a specific agenda, distribute it beforehand, and solicit comments and suggestions.
- ▲ Distribute progress reports for the most recent performance period before the meeting.
- ▲ Distribute beforehand any other background information related to topics that will be discussed at the meeting.
- ▲ Limit discussions that require more in-depth consideration; deal with them in other forums.
- ▲ Start on time and end on time.
- ▲ Prepare and distribute brief minutes of the meeting.

FOR EXAMPLE

www.manager-tools.com

As an outgrowth from weekly podcasts on effective management and leadership skills, manager-tools.com focuses less on management theory and more on what project managers are actually doing in their jobs today. Along with each podcast (all of which are available for free download), the site provides an accompanying tool, such as a project delegation worksheet, meeting agenda templates, and organizing outlines for effective e-mail communication, to illustrate the topics presented during the show.

12.3.2 Ad Hoc Team Meetings

Ad hoc team meetings address specific issues that arise during a project. An ad hoc meeting could involve some or all of a team's members, depending on the issues to be addressed. Because issues often arise unexpectedly, it's important that project managers do the following:

▲ Clarify the issue and what they hope to achieve at the meeting.

▲ Identify and invite all people who might be interested in, affected by, or working on the issue.

▲ Clearly explain the meeting's purpose to all invitees.

▲ Carefully document all action items developed at the meeting and assign responsibility for their completion.

12.3.3 Upper-Management Progress Reviews

Project managers should take every opportunity to help upper management remember why a project is important to them. They might have approved a project months ago, but chances are it's now only one of many things going on in a busy organization.

An upper-management progress review is typically presided over by a senior manager and run by the project manager. Team members and representatives from all functional areas attend. This meeting provides an opportunity to highlight the progress and status of a project, acknowledge any support that functional managers have provided, remind upper management of future project plans, determine whether major priorities that initially led to the creation of the project have changed and whether the project should change accordingly, and discuss specific ways in which upper management can support the project to ensure its continued successful performance.

Make upper-management progress review effective by observing the following tips:

▲ Identify the audience's interests and explain how the project is meeting those interests.

▲ Keep presentations short; choose a few key messages and emphasize them.

▲ Highlight key information, but be prepared to go into more detail on issues if asked to do so.

▲ Allow time for questions.

▲ Present updated information on project risks and how they're being addressed.

▲ Distribute brief handouts at the meeting that summarize the key points of any presentations.

▲ After the meeting, distribute notes that highlight issues raised and actions agreed upon at the session.

SELF-CHECK

1. Your boss is currently faced with a round of budget cuts and has requested an update of your project. Which of the following should you should begin preparing for?

    (a) a project audit

    (b) an upper-management review

    (c) an annual report

    (d) an ad hoc meeting

2. Given their more familiar tone and approach, regularly scheduled team meetings can use a standard agenda. True or false?

3. Because project problems can arise quickly, an ad hoc meeting can be conducted in which of the following ways?

    (a) with some of the project team

    (b) with all of the project team

    (c) with someone outside the team and someone on the team

    (d) all of the above

SUMMARY

Project managers are responsible for a variety of communication activities during the life of a project. Communication can be formal or informal, written or verbal. Whatever form communications take, however, project managers should plan and prepare so their messages are received and correctly interpreted by project audiences. The project progress report is an opportunity for project managers to highlight performance, assess problems, and point projects toward the next period. Project meetings—including regularly scheduled team meetings, ad hoc meetings, and upper-management reviews—are all tools for project managers to share information and gather support and solutions from others.

KEY TERMS

Ad hoc team meeting	Special session for team members to address problems and issues as they arise.
Communication	Sharing the right messages with the right people in a timely manner.

Formal communications	Preplanned communication, conducted in a standard format in accordance with an established schedule.
Informal communications	Communication that occurs as people think of information they want to share.
Project progress report	Regularly scheduled written communication that reviews what has happened during a performance period, describes problems and the corrective actions needed, and previews what is planned for the next period.
Regularly scheduled team meetings	Opportunities for team members to share progress and issues and to sustain productive and trusting interpersonal relationships.
Upper-management review	Periodic summary of project status, major accomplishments, and issues with which upper management's help is required.

ASSESS YOUR UNDERSTANDING

Go to www.wiley.com/college/portny to assess your knowledge of the basics of project communication.

Measure your learning by comparing pre-test and post-test results.

Summary Questions

1. Effectively drafted project progress reports can serve as part of the agenda for regularly scheduled team meetings. True or false?

2. Celia's project is 10 weeks behind schedule and a major piece of equipment needed for the next phase will be delayed another two months before arriving at Celia's warehouse. Which of the following is an appropriate place for Celia to notify the team about these events?

   (a) the next project progress report

   (b) the next team meeting

   (c) an ad hoc meeting

   (d) any of the above

3. Because an ad hoc meeting can involve some or all of a project team, it can be considered informal project communication. True or false?

Applying This Chapter

1. You find that your project team asks some of its best questions and provides useful observations while you're doing your weekly walk-through of the various cubicle clusters that house your project team members. Rather than simply telling team members to bring their questions and comments to your project's weekly status meeting, what are some proactive things you can do make these informal communications more effective and efficient?

2. Nancy's new team members have been members of various other projects at the data-processing company that they all work for. Nancy has suggested that her team meet every time their new project reaches a major milestone (as defined in the project plan), but several members of her team have complained the meetings are a waste of time. The team members feel that a well-written report from Nancy is all that's necessary to keep the team updated and the project moving along smoothly. What specifically might Nancy tell her team about the importance of team meetings and potential downsides of written reports?

3. In the last week, Hannah's project crossed a major milestone: The Web site she and her team are developing was put online as a fully functional beta version of the site. The Web site, however, is having major difficulties in processing credit card data from testers. In which sections of the project progress report can Hannah most effectively highlight the project's recent activities?

4. Next week, you will be facilitating an upper-management review for the new product development team you lead. Your boss already knows that your project is on-schedule and on-budget, so what can you do to make the meeting valuable and useful for all parties?

Shaping Your Communications

Consistent, well-organized communication increases the likelihood that your message will be received and understood by others. Consider the various pieces of written and verbal communications you must produce on a weekly or monthly basis for your job. Brainstorm a list of communications by type (e-mails, printed reports, PowerPoint presentations, status updates, verbal check-ins, and so on) as well as by topic (sales figures, productivity, work hours, and so on). For each of these specific types of communication, develop templates that organize your message into logical, recurring sections. Use headlines and an outline format to further establish organization. Leave main body sections unwritten; you'll supply specific details in these sections when data become available. Save your templates electronically in one central place on your computer or server for easy access. For inspirational examples of literally hundreds of communication templates, search online for "communication templates." Many templates are available for purchase, but most organizations offer a few examples for free evaluation.

Meetings Made Easy

Evaulate the project manager responsbilities for meetings outlined in Section 12.1.3. Which of the listed responsibilities are appropriate for the meetings you're typically asked to lead? Create a customized checklist based on the responsibilities in Section 12.1.3, adding responsibilities for premeeting preparation, meeting conduct, and follow-up to suit your organization and management style. Save your checklist as a word-processing file or simply make photocopies of your list. Whenever you're assigned another meeting to lead, print out and use the checklist to ensure your next meeting runs smoothly before, during, and after the actual gathering.

Test and Improve Your Writing Skills

While managers today typically write fewer memos than 10 years ago, nearly all project managers must write some type of report on a regular basis—as well as dozens of e-mails each day to team members, functional managers, clients, vendors, and other audiences. Each of these messages needs to effectively and efficiently communicate your meaning. Good grammar is essential to writing a report or a quick e-mail. Assess your grammar skills with more than 100 free, interactive quizzes available at http://grammar.ccc.commnet.edu/grammar/quiz_list.htm. The main site (grammar.ccc.commnet.edu/grammar) is also a good resource if you have a question while writing a message.

St. Dismas Assisted Living Facility

Four months before the Assisted Living Facility project at St. Dismas Assisted Living Facility was to be completed (see the Case Study at the end of Chapter 4 for information about the planning phase of this project), the project team was excited. They could see the construction of the facility and felt they were moving toward the end of this project.

Every week since construction began, the construction project manager, Kyle Nanno, held a project team meeting. At the meetings, Kyle invited representatives of the construction company, the facilities manager from St. Dismas, the Director of Security, and other key people. The meetings are scheduled every Friday at 1:00 p.m. and last no longer than one hour. No matter who is or is not there, Kyle starts the meetings exactly at 1:00 p.m. Kyle developed the following standing agenda:

1. Review schedule and budget as of today's date.
2. Review schedule and budget for next two weeks.
3. Discuss issues impacting schedule or budget.
4. Discuss next steps and action items to be completed.

The construction project update presented at the April 11 meeting is included in this case study.

After each meeting, the construction project manager e-mails the minutes of the meeting and the action item list generated to each member of the Construction Project team. He also sends the information to Fred Splient, the president of St. Dismas, as well as to each member of the Assisted Living Facility Project Steering Team.

Following the update is the most recent copy of the action items generated at the 4/11/01 construction project meeting.

Upon reading the minutes and action items from the week's meeting, Fred got quite angry. Fred read the minutes every week and would immediately phone Kyle to ask why certain decisions still had not been made.

This week he wanted to know why the location of the security panel had not been picked out yet, and what the hair salon issue was about. Kyle decided that these matters would be better discussed face to face.

In Fred's office, Kyle explained that the Director of Security, Frank Geagy, had not attended the construction project update meeting in weeks. Kyle said that Frank informed him that in light of cost cutting going on in the hospital, he is short-staffed and cannot hire a new security guard. Frank states that he personally has to cover shifts during the time when the update meetings take place. Kyle told Fred that he was not comfortable making the security panel decision without the head of security's input, and that Frank has not returned his phone calls or answered his e-mails. Fred Splient proceeded to tell Kyle in a very loud and angry voice, "That guy is not short-staffed and is not busy covering anyone's shift. Who does he think he is?" Fred instructed Kyle to tell Frank to answer the contractor's questions immediately or the decisions would be made for him. Kyle said he would do so and then changed the subject.

Kyle then told Fred that they were still waiting for city officials to approve the parking lot construction permit. St. Dismas's legal officer estimated that it would take 8–10 weeks to hear back on approval. Kyle allocated that amount of time in the schedule. Kyle received notice from Fred to proceed with the parking lot project on January 11. On February 9, he submitted the application for a permit, complete with appropriate plans and descriptions of the proposed lot, and allocated 10 weeks to wait for the county to notify him. He expected approval on or before April 19 and scheduled construction to begin April 20. Privately, he doubted he would hear from the county by his target date.

The lot would take three weeks to build, two weeks to install the lighting and add landscaping, and one week to pave and stripe. The lot had to be completed by the end of June so that parking spaces would be available when Marketing wanted to begin showing the facility to potential residents. This was a tight schedule, but the marketing people insisted that residents had to begin preparing for this kind of move

Assisted Living Facility
Construction Project Update
As of 4/11/01

ID	Task Name	Baseline Start	Actual Start	Baseline Finish	Actual Finish	Baseline Duration	Actual Duration	Remaining Variance	Dur. Variance	Finish Variance
1	Construction & furnishings	03/01/00	03/01/00	07/30/01	NA	369 days	278.76 days	104.24 days	14 days	14 days
2	Facility construction	03/01/00	03/01/00	06/04/01	NA	329 days	285.12 days	57.88 days	14 days	14 days
3	Phase 1- Foundation & Excavation	03/01/00	03/01/00	07/11/00	08/01/00	95 days	110 days	0 days	15 days	15 days
4	Phase 2- Structure	04/19/00	05/24/00	09/22/00	10/09/00	113 days	99 days	0 days	14 days	11 days
5	Phase 3- Enclosure	07/12/00	08/01/00	01/15/01	01/15/01	134 days	120 days	0 days	14 days	0 days
6	Phase 4- Interiors	07/12/00	08/01/00	06/04/01	NA	234 days	139 days	95 days	0 days	14 days
7	First 45 (light-assisted) units ready to prepare for occupancy	05/01/01	NA	05/01/01	NA	0 days	0 days	0 days	0 days	14 days
8	First 45 units ready for residents	05/01/01	NA	06/25/01	NA	8 wks	0 wks	8 wks	0 wks	14 days
9	Remaining 57 units (light & heavy) ready to prepare for occupancy	06/04/01	NA	06/04/01	NA	0 days	0 days	0 days	0 days	14 days
10	Construction complete	06/04/01	NA	06/04/01	NA	0 days	0 days	0 days	0 days	14 days
11	Building ready for residents	06/05/01	NA	07/30/01	NA	8 wks	0 wks	8 wks	0 wks	14 days

Project Manager: K. Nanno

373

CASE

St. Dismas—Assisted Living Facility
Construction coordination meeting 4/11/01
ACTION ITEM LIST

Item	Date Initiated	Date Required	Date Resolved	Required From	Comments
Provide notice to proceed on parking lots	01/10	ASAP	02/11/2001	St. Dismas	Proposal to St. Dismas 1/18/00
Provide P.S. # for designer to purchase accessories	11/9	12/1/2000	02/8/2001	St. Dismas	
What are the security requirements? There are fire doors, and they do not have locks. We have rough-in for card readers, but no electric hardware.	11/9	12/1/2000		St. Dismas Security	Cost proposal to St. Dismas 1/13/00
Lighting review—will exterior lighting in addition to the building mounted lights be required?	12/14	03/15/2001	03/15/2001	St. Dismas lighting consultant & electrician	
Location of security panel	09/28	ASAP		St. Dismas security	
Room number style and placement	01/18	01/27/2001	02/11/2001	St. Dismas designer	Part of signage discussion
Parking lot permit	02/9	ASAP		Contractor	Permit application 2/9/2001, waiting for City to approve
Fire alarm connection to hospital panel	02/11	ASAP		St. Dismas electrician	Conduit required
Hair salon decision	02/11	ASAP		St. Dismas	
Updated fire alarm drawings	02/7	07/1/01		Contractor & electrician	

374

at least a month before they took residence. Potential residents needed to see the facility, get familiar with apartment layouts, and they needed a place to park. Also, Marketing insisted on having some occupancy by the opening date.

Kyle told Fred that Legal was calling the county weekly to follow up. Fred wanted to know why the parking lot construction was not outlined on the action plan for facility construction. Fred asked Kyle to add it to the Gantt chart and to do a what-if analysis on the assumption that the county did not respond until May 1. Fred also wanted to know the latest date that they could be notified and still meet a June 15 deadline for completion of the lot.

As Kyle was leaving Fred's office, Fred asked him about the hair salon. Kyle explained that the COO and VP of Marketing had come up with an idea to build and operate a hair salon in the facility for the residents. They thought this might be a great selling point that could generate revenue. They came to Kyle just two months ago and asked him to include a hair salon on the first floor of the facility. Kyle explained that he did not have enough information to be able to determine the impact this would have on the construction schedule or the cost of this addition. Fred listened and then wondered if the members of his team had done any analysis to determine if this was a good idea or not. Fred told Kyle he would get back to him on that one. He then made a phone call to the COO and VP of Marketing.

Questions

1. What do you think the construction project manager should have done when the Director of Security stopped attending the project meetings?

2. Do you think it is an effective communications tool to send the construction project meeting minutes to the Assisted Living Facility steering team and the president? Support your answer.

3. How much time has to be made up for the original, baseline schedule to be met?

4. Develop an action plan and draw a Gantt chart for the Parking Lot phase of the project as originally planned by Kyle. Answer Fred's questions.

5. What information does Fred need to make a decision about building a hair salon?

13

MANAGING RISK
Identifying Uncertainty and Preparing Responses

Starting Point

Go to www.wiley.com/college/portny to assess your knowledge of the basics of risk management.
Determine where you need to concentrate your effort.

What You'll Learn in This Chapter

▲ Risk management process
▲ Risk identification, assessment, and analysis
▲ Risk management plans
▲ Risk control
▲ Risk management groups

After Studying This Chapter, You'll Be Able To

▲ Evaluate a risk's likelihood and impact
▲ Produce effective risk communications
▲ Formulate risk management plans

INTRODUCTION

All projects have risks, which project managers need to be aware of and actively manage. Using a detailed project plan, project managers can identify risks by recognizing specific risk factors throughout the life of a project. After identification, risk must be assessed and analyzed based on the likelihood of the risk happening and the magnitude of the consequences if a risk were to happen. Project managers can respond to risk in various ways, including creating risk management plans and working with risk control groups.

13.1 Understanding Risk and Risk Management

The first step toward a successful project is to develop a plan that allows the project team to do the work required to produce the desired results in the available time for the available resources. If a project will last a relatively short time, and if the project planners were thorough and realistic in their planning, things should have a high likelihood of working out as planned.

However, the larger and more complex the project and the longer it lasts, the more likely that some aspects of a project will not work out as envisioned.

Project managers give themselves the greatest chance for success if they confront head-on the possibility that some things might change. They need to prepare at the outset for how to minimize any associated negative consequences and maximize any positive consequences. Project managers should consider potential project risks when deciding whether to undertake projects, when developing project plans, and continually while performing project work.

13.1.1 Defining Risk and Risk Management

Risk is the possibility that a project might not achieve its product, schedule, or resource targets because something unexpected occurs or something planned does not. By contrast, **uncertainty** is a lack of sureness that something will come to pass. Because it's impossible to predict the future with certainty, all projects have some degree of risk and uncertainty. However, project risk is greater in the following conditions:

▲ The longer the project lasts.
▲ The longer the time span between when a project plan is prepared and when the project begins.
▲ The less experience the project manager, team members, or the organization has had with similar projects in the past.
▲ The newer the technology or work approaches that will be used.

Risk management is the process of identifying possible risks, assessing their potential impact on a project, and developing and implementing plans for minimizing their negative effects. Risk management doesn't eliminate risks, but it gives project teams their best chance of successfully accomplishing their projects, despite the uncertainties of a changing environment.

The following risk management strategies don't work:

▲ **The ostrich approach:** ignoring risks or pretending they don't exist.

▲ **The prayer approach:** looking to a higher being to solve all a project's problems or to make them disappear.

▲ **Denial:** recognizing that certain situations might cause problems for a project, but refusing to accept that these situations could occur.

Project managers consider the potential impact of risks on the chances for project success when they do the following:

▲ Decide whether to undertake the project in the first place.

▲ Develop project objectives, strategies, responsibility assignments, schedules, and resource budgets.

▲ Monitor ongoing performance and respond to problems that might arise.

▲ Consider making changes to a project after it's underway.

Likewise, project managers manage risks and minimize the negative impacts of risk on projects when they do the following:

▲ **Identify risks.** Determine which aspects of a plan or envisioned project environment might change.

▲ **Assess potential impacts of risks on a project.** Assess what will happen if things don't work out as envisioned.

▲ **Develop plans for mitigating the impacts of the risks.** Decide how to protect the project from the possible negative consequences of risks.

▲ **Monitor the status of a project's risks throughout performance.** Determine whether existing risks continue to be risks, whether the likelihood they'll occur changes, and whether other risks arise.

▲ **Keep others informed.** Explain to all key audiences the status and potential impact of all project risks from the exploration of the initial concept through the completion of all project work.

13.1.2 Choosing the Risks to be Managed

All identified risks affect a project in some way if they occur (after all, that's the definition of a risk). However, project managers may determine that trying to anticipate and avert problems that can be caused if a particular risk comes to pass takes more time and effort than just dealing with the problems, should they arise.

The first step in developing a risk management strategy is to choose those risks that need to be addressed proactively. When making this choice, project managers should do the following:

▲ **Consider together the likelihood of a risk and its potential impact on the project.** If the impact of a risk would be great and the chances it will occur are high, the project manager will probably want to develop plans to manage it. If the impact is low and the likelihood is low, the project manager might decide not to worry about it.

   ▲ When either the impact would be high but the likelihood is low or vice versa, project managers must consider the situation more carefully. A more formal approach for considering the combined effect of likelihood of occurrence and potential impact is to define the expected value of the risk, as follows:

Expected value of the risk = Quantitative measure of the impact, if it occurs
× Probability it will occur

▲ **In certain instances, a potential consequence is so totally unacceptable that, even if it has a low likelihood of occurrence, the project manager is not willing to take the chance.** At a minimum in such a situation, develop a plan to manage the risk. In fact, the project manager might actually want to reconsider whether to undertake the project at all.

13.1.3 Developing a Risk Management Process

Recognizing those risks that pose a potential threat to a project's successful completion is the first step a project manager can take toward controlling the risks. However, project managers must also develop specific plans for reducing the potential impacts of risk on their projects.

After project managers decide they want to manage specific risks, they can choose one of the following approaches for dealing with the risks:

▲ **Minimize the chances the risk will occur.** Take actions to reduce the chances that an undesirable situation will come to pass. For example, if Natalie has a new employee assigned to a task, she might feel there's a risk the person could take longer to do the task than she's planned. She can consider taking the following steps to reduce the chances that the person will require more time:

   ▲ Explain the task and the desired results very clearly to the person before he or she begins to work on it.

▲ Develop frequent milestones and monitor the person's performance often so that Natalie can identify and deal with any problems as soon as they occur.

▲ Have the person attend training to refresh the skills and knowledge he or she will need to perform the assignment.

▲ **Develop contingencies.** Develop one or more alternative action plans to follow in the event an undesirable situation does come to pass. For example, Ryan is counting on having his organization's publication department reproduce 100 copies of the manual he's using in an upcoming training program. If he's concerned that the department might be working on other higher priority projects at the time he'll need the manuals, he can consider locating an external vendor that can reproduce the manuals if the need arises.

▲ **Buy insurance.** Pay a price to reduce the potential impact of an undesirable situation if it comes to pass. As an example, Paul needs a piece of equipment on a specified date. He might decide to order the same part from two different vendors to increase the likelihood that at least one of the parts arrives on time.

13.1.4 Communicating about Risks

People often share information about project risks ineffectually or not at all. As a result, projects suffer problems and setbacks that could have been avoided had proper actions been taken beforehand.

Many project managers are reluctant to deal with risk because the concept is hard to grasp. If they're only doing their projects once, what difference does it make that a particular situation would occur 40 times out of 100? Some project managers feel that focusing on possible risks suggests that they're looking

FOR EXAMPLE

Risk Management Plans at EPA

The U.S. Environmental Protection Agency, or EPA (www.epa.gov), was established in 1970 to research, monitor, and enforce environmental policies throughout the United States. Major EPA projects have included banning the use of DDT and cleaning up toxic waste. The organization publishes and updates its numerous risk management plans online for its ongoing projects. Although most project managers do not need to plan for the type and number of risks that EPA staffers are responsible for, the thoroughness and organization of EPA plans are worth considering. To evaluate an EPA risk management plan in detail, visit www.epa.gov/ebtpages/enviriskmanagement.html.

for why a project will fail rather than how to make it succeed. Developing a **risk bank,** a file or database in which multiple project managers note risks and solutions, can make the most of a broad range of project experiences.

Project managers must communicate about project risks early and often. In particular, they need to share information with both drivers and supporters (see Section 4.2) at the following points during projects:

▲ **Concept:** to support the decision whether to undertake the project.

▲ **Definition:** to guide the development of all aspects of a project plan.

▲ **Start:** to allow team members to discuss and understand potential risks and to encourage them to recognize and address potential problems as soon as they occur.

▲ **Perform:** to update the likelihood identified risks will occur, to reinforce what people should do to minimize the negative impacts of project risks, and to guide the assessment of whether or not to make requested changes to the project.

Project managers can improve their communications by doing the following:

▲ Explaining in detail the nature of a risk, how it would impact the project, and the basis on which the project manager estimated its likelihood of occurrence.

▲ Telling people the most recent assessment of the current chances that risks will come to pass, what is being done to minimize the chances of problems for the project, and what they can do to reduce the chances of negative consequences for the project.

▲ Encouraging people to think and talk about risks, always with an eye toward figuring out ways to minimize their negative impacts on the project.

▲ Documenting in writing all the information about the risk.

SELF-CHECK

1. All projects have risks. However, risks are generally lower on projects that have shorter durations. True or false?

2. Although Michael knows his team is $10,000 over budget, he continues authorizing spending for additional materials and services, including some expenses that are not in the project budget. Michael's risk response can be characterized as which of the following?

(a) the risk-adverse approach

(b) the prayer approach

(c) denial

(d) none of the above

3. The expected value of a risk can be defined as which of the following?

   (a) the cost of countering the risk × the probability that it will occur

   (b) a quantitative measure of a risk's impact × the cost of not responding

   (c) the likelihood that a risk will happen × the likelihood it will not happen

   (d) a quantitative measure of a risk's impact × the probability that it will occur

13.2 Identifying Risks

Project managers discover potential project risks by identifying conditions or situations that might lead to risks and by determining the specific risks associated with these conditions or situations.

13.2.1 Recognizing Risk Factors

A **risk factor** is a situation that might give rise to one or more project risks. A risk factor itself doesn't cause a project team to miss a product, schedule, or resource target. However, it increases the likelihood that the project team *might* miss one.

For example, the fact that neither Steve nor his organization has undertaken projects similar to the one he's planning is a possible risk factor. Because Steve has no direct prior experience, he might overlook activities he'll need to perform or he might underestimate the time and resources required to perform them. However, just because Steve has no prior direct experience doesn't guarantee he'll have these problems. However, it might increase the chances that he will.

Project managers identify possible risk factors by reviewing written materials and interviewing people who know about or were involved in the development of the project. Specifically consider the following:

▲ How the different phases of the project have been handled.
▲ The information developed in each of the phases.

Risk factors arise from a project's evolution. As Section 4.1 discusses, all projects progress through the five phases (conceive, define, start, perform, and close). Table 13-1 illustrates possible risk factors that could arise, depending upon how the project manager handles a project's progression, in these phases.

Table 13-1: Possible Risk Factors during a Project's Evolution

Life Cycle Phase	*Possible Risk Factors*
All	Insufficient time was devoted to one or more phases.
	Key information wasn't written down.
	You moved to a subsequent phase without completing one or more of the earlier ones.
Conceive	Not all background information and plans were recorded in writing.
	No formal cost-benefit analysis was performed.
	No formal feasibility study was performed.
	You don't know who first came up with the idea for the project.
Define	People preparing the plan hadn't done similar projects in the past.
	The project plan wasn't written down.
	Parts of the plan were omitted.
	Some or all aspects of the project plan weren't approved by all key audiences.
Start	The people assigned to perform the project aren't the ones who prepared the plan.
	Members who didn't participate in the development of the project plan don't review the plan and raise any questions they might have.
	No effort was made to help the team establish its identity and focus.
	Project team procedures for resolving conflicts, reaching decisions, or ongoing communication weren't developed.
Perform	The needs of your primary clients change.
	Incomplete or incorrect information is collected regarding schedule performance and resource expenditures.
	Project progress reporting is inconsistent.

Table 13-1: *(continued)*

Life Cycle Phase	Possible Risk Factors
	One or more of your key project supporters is reassigned.
	Project team members are replaced during performance.
	Market place characteristics or demands change.
	Changes are made informally, with no consistent analysis of their impact on the overall project.
Close	One or more of your project's drivers don't formally approve the project's results.
	People are assigned to new projects before all the work on this project is completed.

Table 13-2 suggests potential risk factors that might arise in conjunction with the different information addressed in a project plan.

Table 13-2: Possible Risk Factors

Planning Information	Possible Risk Factors
Project audiences	You haven't dealt with this client before.
	You've had problems when you've dealt with this client before.
	Upper management or other key drivers are only mildly interested in your project.
	Your project has no champion.
	You haven't specifically identified project audiences at all.
Project background	The project is the result of a spontaneous decision, rather than a well-thought-out assessment.
	No one has proven conclusively that success-fully completing the project will eliminate the problem it was designed to address.

	The project requires other planned activities to be completed before work can be performed.
Project scope	The project is unusually large.
	The project will require a variety of skills and knowledge.
	The project will involve different organizational units.
Project strategy	There is no declared strategy at present.
	You plan to use a new, untested technology or approach.
Project objectives	One or more objectives are missing.
	Performance measures are unclear or missing.
	Performance measures are difficult to quantify.
	Performance targets or specifications are missing.
Constraints	No constraints are identified.
	Constraints are vague.
	In general, all constraints might lead to potential project risks.
Assumptions	Assumptions are vague.
	In general, every assumption leads to a potential risk.
Work packages	Work packages aren't sufficiently detailed.
	Some or all people who will be doing the work didn't participate in developing the work package descriptions.
Roles and responsibilities	Not all supporters were involved in developing the roles and responsibilities.
	You're overly dependent on one or more people.
	No primary responsibility is assigned for one or more activities.
	Two or more people have primary responsibility for the same activity.
	No one person has overall responsibility for the entire project.

Table 13-2: *(continued)*

Planning Information	Possible Risk Factors
Schedule (activity-time estimates)	Time estimates were developed by backing into an established end date.
	The organization has no historical database of how long it took to perform similar activities in the past.
	Part of the project work entails procedures or technologies that haven't been used before.
	Some activities will be performed by people who haven't worked together before.
Schedule (activity interdependencies)	Interdependencies aren't specifically considered when developing the schedule.
	Partially related activities are scheduled to be done simultaneously, in the hopes of saving time.
	No formal analytical approach is used to assess the impact of interdependencies on the schedule.
Personnel	No estimates have been made of the actual work-effort required to perform individual activities.
	No formal consideration has been given to availability and efficiency.
	No plans have been prepared for when people working less than full time on the project will invest their effort.
	New or inexperienced personnel will be performing project activities.
Other resources	No plans have been prepared to identify the type, amount, and timing of nonpersonnel resources needed.
Funds	No project budget has been prepared.

13.2.2 Defining Risks

After risks have been identified, project managers need to separately describe how each risk factor might cause project team members to miss their product, schedule, or resource targets.

For example, Helen plans to use a new technology in her project. The fact that she'll use a new technology is a risk factor. Possible product, schedule, and resource risks arising from this risk factor are as follows:

▲ **Product risk:** the technology might not produce the desired results.

▲ **Schedule risk:** tasks using the new technology might take longer than anticipated.

▲ **Resource risk:** the existing facilities and equipment might not be adequate to support the use of the new technology.

When identifying potential risks, project managers should do the following:

▲ Review past records of problems encountered in similar situations.

▲ Brainstorm with experts and people with related experience.

▲ Be specific. The more specific the description of a risk, the better able a project manager and project team are to assess its potential impact. As an example,
  ▲ Weak: "Activities could be delayed."
  ▲ Strong: "Delivery could take three weeks instead of two."

FOR EXAMPLE

Objectives-based Risk Identification

Well-planned projects always include clear, specific objectives. In objectives-based risk identification, anything that might positively or negatively impact these objectives is considered a risk. COSO (www.coso.org) is a voluntary private sector group (with representatives from the American Accounting Association, the American Institute of Certified Public Accountants, and other accounting organizations) that is dedicated to improving financial reporting processes. Among its numerous recommendations to companies is its Enterprise Risk Management–Integrated Framework, or ERM, which recommends organizations generate their risk management plans based on project objectives. For more details on ERM and whether it's an appropriate tool for your projects, visit www.coso.org/publications.htm.

Try to eliminate as many potential risk factors as soon as possible in projects. As an example, a key audience for Maria's project hasn't approved the project's objectives. Rather than just noting that there's a risk that the project might not correctly address the audience's needs, Maria can (and should) do anything necessary to get the audience to approve the objectives.

SELF-CHECK

1. No feasibility study was conducted for Jerome's current project. This introduces a risk factor to which of the project's phases?

   (a) conceive phase

   (b) start phase

   (c) close phase

   (d) define phase

2. A risk factor associated with project objectives is that two or more people on the team have primary responsibility for the same activity. True or false?

3. A single risk can affect a project in terms of which of the following?

   (a) team members, upper management, and project champions

   (b) audiences, objectives, and timelines

   (c) planning, monitoring, and controlling

   (d) product, schedule, and resources

13.3 Assessing and Analyzing Risks

Project managers determine the potential impact a risk poses for their projects by determining the likelihood that a risk will occur and the magnitude of the consequences if it does occur.

13.3.1 Assessing the Likelihood of a Risk Occurring

Any of the following schemes can help project managers describe the chances that a risk will come to pass:

▲ **Probability of occurrence.** Expresses the likelihood a risk will occur as a probability. **Probability** is a number between 0 and 1 indicating the likelihood that a given situation will come to pass. A probability of 0 means that the situation will never occur and a probability of 1 means that it

---

FOR EXAMPLE

Using Experience to Determine Likelihood

Gordon estimates the likelihood that a risk will occur on his current software-development project by comparing the number of times the risk actually did come to pass on similar projects he's managed before. Gordon and his team have designed 20 computer-generated reports during the past year for clients with whom they hadn't worked before. Eight times, when his team submitted a design for final approval, the client wanted at least one change made. If he's planning to design a computer-generated report for a client with whom he hasn't worked before, Gordon concludes—and plans appropriately schedule- and budgetwise—that there's about a 40 percent chance (8 ÷ 20 × 100 = 40%) that the team will have to make changes to the final report design when it is submitted to the client for approval.

---

will always occur. (Project managers could also express likelihood as a percentage instead of a fraction. In this case, a likelihood of 100 percent means the situation will always occur.)

▲ **Category ranking.** Classifies risks into categories that represent the likelihood they will occur. Project managers often use "High," "Medium," and "Low" or "Always," "Often," "Sometimes," "Rarely," and "Never."

▲ **Ordinal ranking.** Orders the risks so the first is the most likely to occur, the second is the next most likely, and so on.

▲ **Relative likelihood of occurrence.** If two possible risks exist, the project manager can, for example, declare that the first is twice as likely to occur as the second.

When using objective information to determine the likelihood of different risks occurring on a project, project managers should do the following:

▲ Consider previous experience with projects similar to the current one, as well as previous indicators of problems.

▲ Ensure as many as possible of the associated conditions are the same as for the current project.

▲ Make sure any conclusions are based on a sufficient number of prior situations.

▲ Keep in mind that the greater the number of similar situations considered, the greater the confidence in any conclusions.

In the absence of objective data, project managers should solicit the opinions of experts and people who have worked on similar projects in the past.

To increase the accuracy of likelihood estimates based upon the opinions of others, do the following:

▲ Define as clearly as possible what the category names mean. A project manager might suggest, for example, that "low" means the likelihood the risk will occur is between 0 and 33 percent, "medium" means it's between 33 and 66 percent, and "high" means it's between 66 and 100 percent.

▲ Consider the opinions of as many people as possible.

▲ Be sure that the projects from which the consulted people draw their opinions and the conditions surrounding those projects are truly similar to the project at hand.

▲ Don't allow people to discuss their estimates with each other before they share them. Initially, the project manager is looking for individual opinions, not a group consensus.

▲ After they submit their initial estimates, consider having the people discuss with each other their reasons for their estimates and whether they would like to revise them.

Precision is different from accuracy. **Precision** refers to the detail with which a number or measurement is expressed. **Accuracy** refers to how correct the number or measure actually is. Jill might estimate the likelihood of a particular risk occurring on a project to be 67.23 percent. However, even though she expressed the risk to two decimal places, her guess has little chance of being accurate if she's had no prior experience with similar projects in the past. Unfortunately, people often assume that numbers expressed with greater precision are also more accurate. Project managers can avoid misinterpretations when sharing assessments of likelihood with others by using round numbers, categories, or relative rankings.

The more factors that suggest a particular risk could occur, the higher the likelihood that it will occur. Ordering from a vendor with whom Marissa hasn't worked before could raise the possibility that delivery times will be longer than initially promised. However, the likelihood of delays in delivery time is greater if, in addition, this is a special-order item, Marissa asks for delivery during a busy period for the vendor, and/or the vendor has to order several parts to make the item she's requested.

13.3.2 Assessing the Magnitude of the Consequences

In addition to assessing the likelihood of a risk, project managers also need to determine the specific effect that each risk would have on a project's product, schedule, and resource performance. Consider the following when evaluating these effects:

FOR EXAMPLE

Using Numerical Scales

You can estimate the likelihood that a particular risk will come to pass on a project by soliciting the opinions of 10 people who have worked on similar projects in the past. You can ask them to estimate the likelihood of a risk as being "high," "medium," or "low." Suppose six choose "high," two choose "medium," and two choose "low." You could then develop your estimate of the likelihood as follows by assigning values of 3, 2, and 1, to "high," "medium," and "low," respectively. Determine the weighted average of your responses as follows: $(6 \times 3 + 2 \times 2 + 2 \times 1) \div 10 = (18 + 4 + 2) \div 10 = 2.4$. This result suggests the likelihood of occurrence is between medium and high.

▲ **Consider the impact of a risk on the total project, rather than on just a portion of it.** Project-management software can effectively simulate the impact of a risk. For example, taking one week longer to complete an activity than originally planned might cause intermediate milestones to be missed and cause the personnel who were waiting for the results of this activity to start their work to sit idly. However, the impact to the project would be even greater if the delayed activity is on the project's critical path (see Section 6.2), which would mean that the one-week delay would cause the final completion date for the entire project to be delayed by one week.

▲ **Consider the impact of related risks when assessing their impact on the overall project.** The likelihood that a project schedule will slip is greater if three activities on the same critical path have a significant risk of slippage instead of just one.

Project managers should take care to describe risks and their associated consequences as specifically as possible. As an example, Wilmer feels there's a risk that a key piece of equipment he ordered for his project might arrive later than expected. He can express that risk as follows:

▲ Weak: "Delivery could be delayed."
▲ Strong: "Delivery could be delayed by two weeks."

Just stating that delivery could be delayed doesn't give Wilmer (or anyone on the project team) enough information to determine the impact of that delay on the overall project. It also makes it harder to estimate the risk of that delay actually occurring. Is he talking about a delay of one day? One month? Stating that delivery might be delayed by two weeks allows Wilmer to determine more precisely the impact on the overall project schedule and resources. It also makes it easier for Wilmer to decide how much he's willing to spend to avoid that delay.

Risk estimation and assessment can be supported with a variety of more formal techniques, including the following:

▲ **Decision trees:** diagrams illustrating different situations that could occur as a project unfolds, the likelihood of each situation occurring, and the consequences to the project if it does.

▲ **Risk assessment questionnaires:** formal data-collection instruments for eliciting expert opinions about the likelihood that different situations might come to pass on a project and the associated impacts.

▲ **Automated impact assessments:** computerized spreadsheets that consider in combination both the risk that different situations will occur and the consequences if they do.

SELF-CHECK

1. You ask your team to review a list of project risks and grade their concern for each item on the list. You're assessing risk by which of the following means?

    (a) category ranking

    (b) ordinal ranking

    (c) probability of occurrence

    (d) relative likelihood of occurrence

2. Data from past projects can help a project manager calculate probabilities of similar risks for current projects. True or false?

3. Data from past projects are the preferred way a project manager can calculate probabilities of similar risks for current projects. True or false?

4. In calculating probabilities, precision is the level of detail with which a number is expressed, while accuracy refers to which of the following?

    (a) how calibrated the measure is

    (b) how correct the number is

    (c) how the number varies from plan

    (d) all of the above

5. What are three formal, advanced tools project managers can use to assess risks?

13.4 Selecting the Appropriate Response Mechanism

Risk response typically involves the project manager making decisions about which risks to prepare for and which to ignore and simply accept as potential threats.

13.4.1 Creating Risk Management Plans

The main preparation for risk is the development and maintenance of a **risk management plan**, which lays out specific strategies to minimize the potential negative consequences that uncertain occurrences will have on a project. (Also, risk management plans help foster positive outcomes.) Project managers develop risk management plans in the define phase of projects, refine them in the start phase, and continually update and maintain them during the perform phase (see Section 4.1 for more on these phases).

The risk management plan includes the following:

▲ Risk factors (see Section 13.2.1).

▲ Associated risks.

▲ An assessment of the likelihood of occurrence and the associated consequences for each risk.

▲ Plans to manage selected risks.

▲ Plans to keep people informed about the status of the selected risks throughout the project.

Table 13-3 illustrates a portion of a risk management plan.

Table 13-3: A Portion of a Risk Management Plan

Plan Element	Description
Risk factor	You haven't worked with this client before.
Risks	Product: chance for miscommunication, leading to incorrect or incomplete understanding of client's needs.
	Schedule: incomplete understanding of client's business operation, leading to an underestimate of how long it'll take to survey the current operations.
	Resources: inaccurate understanding of client's technical knowledge, leading to assigning tasks to the client that he or she

Table 13-3: *(continued)*

Plan Element	Description
	won't be able to perform; the need to have additional staff assigned to the project to perform these tasks.
Analysis	Chances of misunderstanding the client's needs = high.
	Chances of underestimating the time to survey operations = low.
	Chances of misunderstanding the client's technical knowledge = low.
Strategy	Only deal with the risk of misunderstanding the client's needs. Reduce the chances of this happening by
	• Using approaches such as reviewing past correspondence or reviewing written problem reports to identify the client's needs.
	• Having at least two team members present in every meeting with the client's staff.
	• Speaking with different staff in the client's organization.
	• Putting all communications in writing.
	• Sharing progress assessments with the client every two weeks throughout the project.

Risk management plans often includes specific contingency plans and logic charts detailing exactly what to do depending on particular events. Sometimes, it is helpful to conduct actual tests of the risk management plan by conducting simulations, including the following:

▲ **Tabletop exercises,** which simulate the decision-making process and any actions to be taken in response to specific risks. Tabletop exercises are primarily "soft simulations" where the project team simply states various actions, rather than executing actions.

▲ **Dress rehearsals,** which involve more realism and require participants to partially (or fully) take the actions. Fire drills are dress rehearsals. Practice in taking these actions can be helpful in the event the risk actually comes to pass. More detailed simulations might include full dress rehearsals where even more fully realistic actions are taken.

13.4.2 Risk Monitoring and Control

Like risk management planning, risk monitoring and control are tasks for the larger organization, as well as for the project team.

Many organizations have **risk management groups** or teams, which maintain records on how all projects within the organization deal with risks. These individuals are often involved along with a project team in performing the tasks of recording and maintaining records of what risks were identified, how they were analyzed and responded to, and what resulted from the responses. Without the participation of a risk management group, the risk-related records have a high probability of being lost forever when the project is completed. If records are lost or not easily available, the chance that other projects can learn from the experiences of others is very low.

A risk management group is not merely a passive record holder. Fundamentally, the group is devoted to the improvement of the organization's risk management activities. It should be involved in the search for new risks, for developing new and better techniques of measuring and handling risk, and estimating the impacts of risks on projects. Thus, the group should become an advisor to project risk management teams. It should provide an ongoing evaluation of current risk identification, measurement, analysis, and response techniques.

FOR EXAMPLE

Scenario Planning

Scenario planning combines known facts about the future with possibilities, trends, and risks to aid groups in making strategic plans. Scenario planning can take numerous forms: The Pentagon is famous for using "war games" to map out future military strategies; top product designers at Apple frequently attend off-site brainstorming sessions to respond to new technologies and consumer insights. Numerous online resources and communities, including ScenarioThinking.org (www.scenariothinking.org), offer project managers from around the world opportunities to report on and publish their scenario planning activities for a wide range of industries.

SELF-CHECK

1. What type of risk planning activity requires participants to respond to risk situations and discuss their possible actions?

2. Risk monitoring and control is the responsibility of which of the following?

    (a) a risk management group

    (b) project team members

    (c) project managers

    (d) all of the above

3. Effective risk management groups include representatives from each project where risk is being monitored and controlled. True or false?

SUMMARY

Project managers pay attention to project risks and appropriately communicate these risks throughout their project leadership. An effective risk management process involves first identifying and defining risk factors that could affect the various stages of the project's development as well as specific aspects of the project. Through probability, ranking, and other methods, project managers assess and analyze the likelihood and impact of risk. Assessed risks can then be responded to effectively, as part of a comprehensive risk management plan.

KEY TERMS

Accuracy	How correct a number or measurement is.
Automated impact assessments	Computerized spreadsheets that consider in combination both the risk that different situations will occur and the consequences if they do.
Decision trees	Diagrams illustrating different situations that could occur as a project unfolds, the likelihood of each situation occurring, and the consequences to the project if it does.
Dress rehearsal	Realistic risk-preparing activity that requires participants to take action.

Precision	The detail with which a number or measurement is expressed.
Probability	A number between 0 and 1 indicating the likelihood that a given situation will come to pass. (A probability of 0 means the situation will never occur; a probability of 1 means that it will always occur.)
Risk	The possibility that a project will not achieve its product, schedule, or resource targets because something unexpected does or doesn't occur.
Risk assessment questionnaires	Formal data-collection instruments for eliciting expert opinions about the likelihood that different situations will come to pass on a project and the associated impacts.
Risk bank	A file or database in which multiple project managers note risks and solutions.
Risk factor	A situation that might give rise to one or more project risks. A risk factor itself doesn't cause a project team to miss a product, schedule, or resource target. However, it increases the likelihood that the project team might miss one.
Risk management	The process of identifying possible risks, assessing potential impact on a project, and developing and implementing plans for minimizing negative effects.
Risk management groups	Teams that maintain records on how all projects within the organization deal with risks.
Risk management plan	Document that lays out specific strategies to minimize the potential negative consequences that uncertain occurrences will have on a project.
Tabletop exercise	An activity that simulates the decision-making process and any actions to be taken in response to specific risks.
Uncertainty	A lack of sureness that something will come to pass.

ASSESS YOUR UNDERSTANDING

Go to www.wiley.com/college/portny to assess your knowledge of the basics of risk management.
Measure your learning by comparing pre-test and post-test results.

Summary Questions

1. Effective risk management activities focus on the early stage of a project—particularly activities that can be accomplished during the conceive and define phases. True or false?

2. A risk and a risk factor differ in which of the following ways?

   (a) A risk is the possibility that a project will not achieve a goal, while a risk factor is a situation that might give rise to one or more project risks.

   (b) A risk is manageable over time with planning, while a risk factor is hypothetical and does not require managing.

   (c) A risk can affect multiple aspects of a project, while a risk factor typically only affects one aspect of the project.

   (d) none of the above

3. Formal tools like decision trees help project managers identify project risks. True or false?

Applying This Chapter

1. You and your team are designing and installing a new machine for an automotive assembly line. You identify the top risk for the project as a high likelihood that a critical material you're planning to use will no longer be available if the EPA enacts new regulations. How can you respond to this risk based on the three main categories of risk response in Section 13.2.2?

2. In her project's risk management plans, Lisa lists several risks including "the project is too large," "tasks are under-budgeted," and "not enough workers." What can Lisa do to improve the effectiveness of the risks she's identified? How might she reword her risk identification statements for greater specificity?

3. Risk identification reveals that a top risk for your project is that the cost of outsourced labor on several tasks will increase and the project will end up going over budget. You, however, think a much more likely possibility is that the project will lose multiple team members; this

would require you to find new team members, which affects the schedule and the budget. How can you assess these risks using probability, category rankings, and ordinal rankings? Which form or forms of assessment do you think will be most useful?

4. You interview 25 people associated with your project and discuss project risks. You ask your interviewees to rate risk on a scale of 1 to 5, with 1 meaning "no risk" to 5 meaning "extremely high risk." Of your interviewees, 4 rate the risk as 1, 5 rate the risk as 2, 11 rate the risk as 3, 4 rate the risk as 4, and 1 rates the risk as 5. What is the weighted average ranking of the risk?

YOU TRY IT

Risk ID by Phase and Function

Many work projects with detailed project plans lack risk management details. The first step to creating a risk management plan is identifying the associated risks. Start with a project plan you're familiar with and develop a list of risks associated with each phase of the project's life cycle (see Table 13-1). Then consider the plan based on the list of elements in Table 13-2. Evaluate your list of risks one last time, identifying each risk in terms of its effects on the project's product, schedule, and/or resources.

Assessing your Everyday Risks

Consider an everday activity you regularly engage in (perhaps commuting to work or school, preparing dinner, and so on). Although your selected activity is probably not considered risky, it does have some risks associated with it. Brainstorm a list of as many risks as you can think of (even outlandish ones) associated with each task of your everyday project. Evaluate your list of risks based on the two-part guideline in Section 13.3—the likelihood of the risk happening and the magnitude of the risk's consequences. Risks with high magnitude and high likelihood probably require a response strategy; risks with low magnitude and low likelihood can probably

be passed over. If either magnitude or likelihood is high, assess the risk further to determine whether you need to establish a risk response.

Hands-on Risk Practice

Tabletop exercises and dress rehearsals are two risk-preparing activities that are used most often with high-risk, life-threatening projects and positions, such as within the military, emergency health care, and fire and police forces. However, hands-on practice can be useful in responding to any non-life-threatening risk. Consider the top risks you've identified for a work project (or that a project's risk management plan has identified). Develop a 30-minute tabletop exercise that you and your team members can work through together to prepare for your project's most likely risks. How can you effectively simulate a risk happening? How will you encourage your team to collaborate and work together? What responses and actions do you ultimately hope your team members will reach while working through the exercise? Write down the details and steps of your exercise and then create any support material you'd need for the exercise. Consider using your exercise at an upcoming team meeting as a group training and development activity.

CASE STUDY: NutriStar

NutriStar

NutriStar produces a line of vitamins and nutritional supplements. It recently introduced its Nutri-Sports Energy Bar, which is based on new scientific findings about the proper balance of macronutrients. The energy bar has become extremely popular among elite athletes and other people who follow the diet. One distinguishing feature of the Nutri-Sports Energy Bar is that each bar contains 50 milligrams of eicosapentaenoic acid (EPA), a substance strongly linked to reducing the risk of cancer but found in only a few foods, such as salmon. NutriStar was able to include EPA in its sports bars because it had previously developed and patented a process to refine EPA for its line of fish-oil capsules.

Because of the success of the Nutri-Sports Energy Bar in the United States, NutriStar is considering offering it in Latin America. With its domestic facility currently operating at capacity, the president of NutriStar has decided to investigate the option of adding approximately 10,000 square feet of production space to its facility in Latin America at a cost of $5 million.

The project to expand the Latin American facility involves four major phases: (1) concept development, (2) definition of the plan, (3) design and construction, and (4) startup and turnover. During the concept development phase, a program manager is chosen to oversee all four phases of the project and the manager is given a budget to develop a plan. The outcome of the concept development phase is a rough plan, feasibility estimates for the project, and a rough schedule. Also, a justification for the project and a budget for the next phase are developed.

In the plan definition phase, the program manager selects a project manager to oversee the activities associated with this phase. Plan definition consists of four major activities that are completed more or less concurrently: (1) defining the project scope, (2) developing a broad schedule of activities, (3) developing detailed cost estimates, and (4) developing a plan for staffing. The outputs of this phase are combined into a detailed plan and proposal for management specifying how much the project will cost, how long it will take, and what the deliverables are.

If the project gets management's approval and management provides the appropriations, the project progresses to the third phase, design and construction. This phase consists of four major activities: (1) detailed engineering, (2) mobilization of the construction employees, (3) procurement of production equipment, and (4) construction of the facility. Typically, the detailed engineering and the mobilization of the construction employees are done concurrently. Once these activities are completed, construction of the facility and procurement of the production equipment are done concurrently. The outcome of this phase is the physical construction of the facility.

The final phase, startup and turnover, consists of four major activities: pre-startup inspection of the facility, recruiting and training the workforce, solving startup problems, and determining optimal operating parameters (called centerlining). Once the pre-startup inspection is completed, the workforce is recruited and trained at the same time that startup problems are solved. Centerlining is initiated upon the completion of these activities. The desired outcome of this phase is a facility operating at design requirements.

The following table provides optimistic, most likely, and pessimistic time estimates for the major activities.

Activity	Optimistic Time (months)	Most Likely Time (months)	Pessimistic Time (months)
Concept Development	3	12	24
Plan Definition			
Define project scope	1	2	12
Develop broad schedule	0.25	0.5	1
Detailed cost estimates	0.2	0.3	0.5
Develop staffing plan	0.2	0.3	0.6
Design and Construction			
Detailed engineering	2	3	6
Facility construction	8	12	24
Mobilization of employees	0.5	2	4
Procurement of equipment	1	3	12
Startup and Turnover			
Pre-startup inspection	0.25	0.5	1
Recruiting and training	0.25	0.5	1
Solving startup problems	0	1	2
Centerlining	0	1	4

Questions

1. Draw a network diagram for this project. Identify all the paths through the network diagram. Which aspects of the project carry the greatest risks? Support your answer.
2. How would you characterize the various risks associated with the project?
3. What risks would you include in a risk management plan for this project?

14

EVALUATING AND ENDING PROJECTS
Assessing Projects and Moving On

Starting Point

Go to www.wiley.com/college/portny to assess your knowledge of the basics of project evaluations.
Determine where you need to concentrate your effort.

What You'll Learn in This Chapter

▲ Criteria for project evaluations
▲ Postproject evaluations
▲ Project audit preparation and conduct
▲ Reasons for and type of project termination

After Studying This Chapter, You'll Be Able To

▲ Plan for project evaluations throughout the life of a project
▲ Create project evaluation criteria
▲ Prepare the project manager's portion of a project audit
▲ Determine when to end projects
▲ Conduct effective, appropriate project terminations

INTRODUCTION

By their very nature, projects must end at some point. To ensure a smooth ending, project managers can and should prepare for termination throughout each phase of the project. Based on the evaluation criteria, project managers write the postproject evaluation, which can offer insights for the project team, upper management, and other project managers. A project audit is a more formal final review of a project by a group outside the project team. Projects can end in a variety of ways, and savvy project managers will work to smooth the transition of resources to other projects by carefully writing a final project report.

14.1 Evaluating Projects

One of the ongoing frustrations of the project environment is that people make the same mistakes over and over again. While a project manager might have the opportunity to learn firsthand what works and what doesn't while managing a project, the lessons often appear to be forgotten as soon as they're learned.

Of course, project managers don't do this on purpose. Chances are, successful project managers are in demand and are off to their next assignments before they can completely finish current projects. In today's fast-paced workplace, project managers rarely have the luxury of reflecting on their experiences so that they can enhance and improve their approaches in the future.

14.1.1 Preparing for a Postproject Evaluation

Project managers should plan to conduct and hold postproject evaluations after any project is performed. A **postproject evaluation**, or project postmortem, is an assessment of project results, activities, and processes in order to do the following:

▲ Recognize project achievements and acknowledge people's contributions.
▲ Identify techniques and approaches that worked and devise steps to ensure they're used again in the future.
▲ Identify techniques and approaches that didn't work and devise steps to ensure that things are handled differently in the future.

Because the primary purpose of a project evaluation is to give feedback to senior management for decision and control purposes, project evaluations need to have credibility in the eyes of both senior management and the project team. From a control standpoint, evaluations are meant to improve the process of carrying out projects; from a decision-making standpoint, they are intended to improve the selection process.

FOR EXAMPLE

Project-Management Manuals

Postproject evaluations can help organizations improve the project-management skills of their employees on future projects. An organization-specific project-management guide or manual is an effective tool for detailing standardized project-management practices. Such manuals commonly cover best practices for planning, monitoring, and controlling projects and can include advice on both selecting and terminating projects. For instance, at auto parts and building controls manufacturer Johnson Controls (www.johnsoncontrols.com), internal benchmarking determined that the organization's most successful project managers used four sets of detailed project-management procedures. These procedures were compiled into a manual that is regularly updated with new project experiences.

Projects evolve through stages (see Section 4.1). During the project, forward-thinking project managers take steps in each stage to lay the groundwork for the postproject evaluation:

▲ **Conceive phase:**
 ▲ Identify key project drivers: the people for whom the project is being performed (see Section 4.2).
 ▲ Determine the benefits that people thought they would realize when they decided to authorize the project.
 ▲ If the project is designed to change an existing situation, take "before" measures of key characteristics to compare to "after" outcomes.
 ▲ If a formal cost-benefit analysis was performed (see Section 2.1), find out which benefits people considered they would achieve through this project.

▲ **Define phase:**
 ▲ Identify any additional project drivers.
 ▲ Develop clear and detailed descriptions of all project objectives, including performance measures and performance targets to be achieved.
 ▲ Include the activity "Conduct a postproject evaluation" in Work Breakdown Structure (see Section 4.4) and allow time and resources to perform it.

▲ **Start phase:**
 ▲ Tell team members that there will be a postproject evaluation at the end of the project.

▲ Encourage team members to record issues, problems, and successes throughout their project involvement.

▲ **Perform phase:**

   ▲ Maintain files of cost, labor-hour charges, and schedule performance reports throughout the project.

   ▲ Maintain project logs, which identify and describe situations and problems encountered, unexpected occurrences that affected project performance, and techniques or approaches that were unusually successful.

▲ **Close phase:**

   ▲ If the project is designed to change an existing situation, take "after" measures of key outcome characteristics.

   ▲ Obtain final cost, labor-hour, and schedule performance reports for the project.

   ▲ Hold a postproject evaluation session.

   ▲ Distribute minutes from the postproject evaluation session.

14.1.2 Determining Evaluation Criteria

Many different measures can be applied in a project evaluation. Senior management might have particular areas it wants evaluated for future planning and decisions, and these should be indicated in the instructions to whoever is evaluating the project. Beyond that, project managers should also consider the following:

▲ **The original criteria for selecting and funding the project.** For example, was the project initiated for greater profitability, acquiring new competencies for the organization, or getting a foothold in a new market segment, to name a few possibilities?

▲ **Any special reasons for selection.** Was the project someone's sacred cow? Was the project a competitive necessity?

▲ **The project's efficiency in meeting the budget and schedule.** This includes meeting the formal technical and operational specifications of the project.

▲ **The project's level of customer impact/satisfaction.** Efficiency does not necessarily translate into performance or effectiveness, so the project manager needs to consider whether the project met less tangible aspects of fulfilling the customer's needs. A key question is asking whether the customer actually uses the project results.

▲ **The project's direct, business success.** For external projects, project managers can consider factors such as the level of commercial success and market share; for internal projects, project managers should consider the achievement of the project's goals such as improved yields or reduced throughput time.

▲ **The project's future potential.** This can include establishing a presence in a new market, developing a new technology, and so forth.

▲ **The project's contribution to the organization's goals.** This includes the unstated objectives of the organization (see Section 2.1.3), as well as the project's contributions to the objectives of project team members.

SELF-CHECK

1. Postproject evaluations assess which of the following?

   (a) project results

   (b) project activities

   (c) project processes

   (d) all of the above

2. Although postproject evaluations provide project managers with an opportunity to identify techniques and approaches that did and didn't work, the primary purpose of evaluations is to provide feedback for upper management. True or false?

3. At the end of her project, Maya plans to administer a questionnaire to the client who is paying for her finished product. Which evaluation criteria are Maya's questionnaire based on?

   (a) the original project criteria

   (b) the efficiency in meeting budget and schedule

   (c) the level of client impact/satisfaction

   (d) the project's future potential

14.2 Project Auditing

A special type of evaluation is the **project audit,** a thorough examination of the management of a project, its methodology and procedures, its records, properties, inventories, budgets, expenditures, progress, and so on. Additionally, the following are characteristics of a project audit:

▲ **A project audit is usually not a financial audit.** Project audits are far broader in scope and can deal with the whole or any part of the project.

▲ **A project audit is flexible.** Project audits can focus on any issues of interest to senior management.

▲ **A project audit is broader than the traditional management audit.** Management audits focus on an organization's management systems and operation; project audits can cover management performance as one of many topics.

Although the format and approach of project audits differ from postproject evaluations (see Section 14.1), both processes have similar overarching goals—to provide project team members and other project audiences with summary data at the end of projects for the purpose of evaluating current projects and planning future ones.

14.2.1 The Project Audit Process

The timing of a project audit depends on the purpose of the audit. Because early problem identification leads to easier solutions, having an audit early in the project's life is often helpful. Such audits are usually focused on technical issues. Later audits tend to focus more on budget and schedule because most of the technical issues are resolved by this time. Thus, these later audits are typically of less value to the project team and of more interest to general management.

While audits can be performed at any level of depth, three levels are common.

1. **General audits** are usually constrained by time and cost and limited to a brief investigation of project essentials.
2. **Detailed audits** are often initiated if a general audit finds something that needs further investigation.
3. **Technical audits** are usually performed by a person or team with special technical skills.

The following are the typical steps in a project audit:

1. Familiarize the audit team with the requirements of the project, including its basis for selection and any special charges by upper management.
2. Audit the project on-site.
3. Write up the audit report in the required format (see Section 14.2.2).
4. Distribute the report.

Project managers can expedite the collection of necessary data by developing forms and procedures ahead of time, such as the example in Figure 14-1.

To be effective, the audit team must have free access to all information relevant to the project. Most of the information will come from the project team's records or from various departments such as accounting, human resources, and purchasing.

Figure 14-1

DATA COLLECTION FORM

Date: _____   *Auditor:* _____ _____

MANAGERIAL DATA:

Project: _____ _____ _____ _____
Project manager: _____ _____
Start date: _____
Due date: _____
•

•

•

FINANCIAL DATA:
Allocated budget, $: _____
Spent to date, $: _____
•

•

•

TECHNICAL DATA:
% User involvement in design: _____
User training, hours:
        -Planned: _____
        -Completed to date: _____
Software complexity:
        -Lines of code: _____
        -# Modules: _____
Organizational complexity:
        -# Departments involved: _____
•

•

•

A sample audit form (for use with a software installation project).

Other valuable information will come from documents that predate the project such as the Request for Proposal (RFP), minutes of the project selection committee, and minutes of senior management committees that initiated the project.

Special attention needs to be given to the behavioral aspects of the audit. While the audit team must have free access to anyone with knowledge of the project, except the customer, the audit team's primary source of information should be the project team. Unfortunately, project team members rarely trust auditors. Even if the auditor is a member of the project team, his or her motives will be distrusted and thus the information needed by the auditor can be difficult to obtain. The project team's worry about the outcome of an audit can produce self-protective activity, which distracts the team from project work activities.

The audit team needs to understand the politics of the project team and the interpersonal relationships of the team members, and it must deal with all confidential knowledge respectfully. As much as possible, the audit team should attempt to remain neutral and not become involved in debates. If information is given to the audit team in confidence, discreet attempts should be made to confirm such information through nonconfidential sources. If it cannot be so confirmed, it should not be used. The audit team must beware of becoming a conduit for unverifiable sources of criticism of the project.

14.2.2 Participating in an Audit Report

If the audit is to be taken seriously, all the information must be credibly presented by the audit team. Data should be carefully checked and all calculations verified. Deciding what to include and what to exclude is also important. The audit report should be written with a constructive tone, or project morale might suffer to the point of endangering the project. (Bear in mind, however, that constructive criticism never feels constructive to the criticized individuals.) An example audit report is shown in Figure 14-2.

Information in the report should be arranged so as to facilitate the comparison between planned and actual results. Significant deviations should be highlighted and explained in a set of footnotes or comments. Doing so tends to keep questions focused on important issues rather than trivia. Negative comments about individuals or groups associated with the project should be avoided. The report should be written in a clear, professional, unemotional style, and its content restricted to information and issues relevant to the project.

At a minimum, the following information should be contained in the report:

▲ **Introduction:** describe the project, including its direct goals and objectives.
▲ **Current status:** compare the work actually completed to the project plan along several measures of performance.
  ▲ If total costs must be reported, including allocated overhead charges, total costs should be presented in addition to the direct charges, not in place of them.

Figure 14-2

AUDIT REPORT

Auditor: <u>Fred Williams</u>

Audit Team: <u>Sarah Smith, Mustafa Tudesco</u>

Date of Audit: <u>March 5-12, 2001</u>

Project Audited: <u>Software Installation Project</u>

Project Manager: <u>Craig Stoutheart</u>

-
-
-

INTRODUCTION

The aim of this project was to install a limited-version ERP system in our corporate office, Greenville production plant, and our southeastern field offices. This included testing of functionality, training of user personnel, and hand-off to the users.

CURRENT STATUS

Direct charges on the project are slightly in excess of the planned budget, as shown in the attached Gantt charts (*not included here*). The planned milestones have been achieved to date but task 451, Interface to Warehouse Inventory System, is experiencing difficulty and is both behind schedule and over budget, as seen in the earned value charts (*not included*). . . .

FUTURE PROJECT STATUS

At this time, it would appear that the project is progressing satisfactorily. Attention is currently being given to task 451 but it appears that a new approach is needed for interfacing the vendor's system with our current system. However, this appears to be a normal and temporary dilemma; progress is expected to catch up to plan within six–seven weeks, and the budget may also. At this time, no recommendations for changes in schedule, scope, or budget appear to be necessary. . . .

CRITICAL MANAGEMENT ISSUES

Interfacing with our existing systems seems to be more difficult than we anticipated. Although the vendor's software is reputed to be one of the easiest to tie in with a firm's existing systems, the difficulties were greater than expected. It is recommended that all upcoming interfacing tasks be examined in greater detail in advance so that these kinds of difficulties do not take us by surprise again. . . .

RISK ANALYSIS AND RISK MANAGEMENT

There does not seem to be any reason at this point to expect either project failure at this stage of the program or serious monetary loss. (The next stage, Implementation, is a separate and higher risk project, however.) As noted above, the major risks in the project do not seem to be equipment compatibility, as we had assumed, but rather software interfacing. If more serious interface issues arise, this could delay the project and/or substantially increase the cost of the project. As noted, it is recommended that

---

A software installation audit report.

Figure 14-2 (*continued*)

future projects with significant software interfaces be examined much more carefully before decisions are made. . . .

FINAL COMMENTS

This report has assumed that the software interface issue will in fact be resolved without significant further delay or cost. If this assumption proves to be incorrect, it could have a major effect on the success of the project, and future projects, not only with this software system but other systems as well. . . .

A software installation audit report.

▲ The completed portions of the project (planned events and milestones) should be clearly noted. The percent completion of unfinished tasks should also be noted if estimates are available.

▲ A comparison of work completed with resources expended should be offered. This information can help pinpoint specific problems and lead to specific projections about the timing and amounts of remaining expenditures required for success.

▲ If there are detailed quality specifications for the project, a full review of quality control procedures and the results of quality tests conducted to date must be reported.

▲ **Future project status:** make conclusions regarding project progress as well as recommendations for changes in technical approach, schedule, or budget.

▲ It is not appropriate at this point to try to rewrite the project proposal. The audit report should consider only work that has already been completed or is well under way.

▲ **Critical management issues:** identify any issues that senior management should monitor. The relationship between these issues and the project objectives should be briefly described.

▲ **Risk analysis and risk management:** address the potential for project failure or monetary loss. The major risks associated with the project and their projected impact on project schedule/cost/performance should be identified. If alternative courses of action exist that might significantly change future risks, they should be noted at this point.

▲ **Final comments:** note any caveats, assumptions, limitations, and information applicable to other projects. Any assumptions or limitations that affect the data, accuracy, or validity of the audit report should be noted here, as well as lessons learned from this audit that might apply to other projects in the organization.

FOR EXAMPLE

Ongoing Project Audits at Chiquita

Since 1899, Chiquita (www.chiquita.com) has grown, harvested, and shipped Central and South American tropical fruit to grocery stores around the world. As part of its ongoing corporate responsibility initiative, Chiquita began self-auditing its operations and publicly reporting its findings in 2000. The reports evaluate specific Chiquita projects (such as the Nogal Nature and Community Project, a successful community development and rainforest restoration project in Costa Rica) as well as comprehensive assessments of the company's environmental, social, and financial performance. All reports are available at www.chiquita.com/corpres/CRReports.asp.

SELF-CHECK

1. An internal committee has identified some inconsistencies in the expenditures for Rebecca's project and has requested additional evaluation in the form of which of the following?

   (a) mediation session

   (b) detailed audit

   (c) technical audit

   (d) tax audit

2. Effective project audits must have compliance from which of the following?

   (a) the project team

   (b) the client

   (c) upper management

   (d) none of the above

3. According to project auditors, two team members are responsible for exceeding a project budget. Which of the following is the most appropriate place to note the team members and their actions?

   (a) the current status section

   (b) the future project status section

   (c) the critical management issues section

   (d) none of the above

14.3 Terminating Projects

Eventually, all projects are terminated. The manner in which a project is closed out has significant impact on the quality of life within an organization, and the way project termination is managed can occasionally have an impact on the success of the project.

In some project-organized industries (construction or software development, for example), project termination is a less serious problem because the teams often remain relatively intact, moving on to the next project. In other industries, however, the termination of a project, particularly a long and difficult one, is akin to the breakup of a family and could be stressful, even to the point of grieving. Therefore, a project manager's skill and management of the termination process can have a major impact on the working environment of the larger organization.

14.3.1 Deciding When to Terminate a Project

The criteria commonly applied for deciding whether to terminate a project fall into two general categories:

1. The degree to which the project has met its goals and objectives.
2. The degree to which the project qualifies against a set of factors generally associated with success or failure.

In terms of the first category, if a project has met its goals, the time has come to shut it down. The most important reason for the early termination of a project is the likelihood it will be a technical or commercial failure.

The factors associated with project failure, however, vary for different industries, different project types, and different definitions of failure. However, project failure can usually be attributed to four fundamental reasons:

1. A project was not required for this task in the first place.
2. Insufficient support from senior management (especially for unanticipated resources).
3. Naming the wrong project manager (often a person with excellent technical skills but weak managerial skills).
4. Poor up-front planning.

14.3.2 Types of Project Termination

There are several fundamentally different ways to close out a project: extinction, addition, integration, and starvation.

Project extinction occurs when the project activity suddenly stops, although there are still property, equipment, materials, and personnel to disburse or reassign. The project might be terminated either because it was successfully completed or because the expectation of failure was high. Successful projects are completed and delivered to the client. Failures occur when the project no longer meets cost/benefit criteria, or when its goals have been achieved by another project, often in another firm.

An example of the former cause of failure is the cancellation of the superconducting super collider (SSC). The SSC project's tremendous costs relative to the lack of clear benefits doomed the project, and it was canceled during President Clinton's term in office. Other examples of projects facing extinction are when a project's process yield are too low or a drug fails its efficacy tests.

Termination-by-addition occurs when an in-house project is successfully completed and institutionalized as a new, formal part of the organization. This could take the form of an added department, division, subsidiary, or other such organizational entity, depending on the magnitude and importance of the project. For example, 3M Corporation often uses this technique to reward successful innovation projects (the invention of Post-It Notes led to an entirely new production division).

Sometimes, project team members become the managers of the new entity, though some team members might request a transfer to new projects within the organization. Although the new entity will often have a protected status for the first year or so of its life, it eventually has to learn to live with the same burden of overhead charges, policies, procedures, and bureaucracy that the rest of the organization enjoys.

With **termination-by-integration**, the output of the project becomes a standard part of the operating systems of the sponsoring firm, or the client. (With termination-by-addition, the project property often is simply transferred to the new organizational entity.) For example, new software becomes the standard, or a new machine becomes a normal part of the production line. Project property, equipment, material, personnel, and even functions are distributed among the existing elements of the parent or client organization.

Whether the personnel return to their functional positions within the organization or become a part of the integrated system, all functions of the project need consideration in the transition from project to integrated operations, including human resources, manufacturing, accounting, engineering, information systems, marketing, purchasing, distribution, legal, and so on.

Termination-by-starvation often occurs when it is impolitic to terminate a project but its budget can be squeezed until it is a project in name only. The termination-by-starvation project might have been suggested by a special client or a senior executive—or perhaps officially terminating the project would be an embarrassing acknowledgment of managerial failure.

14.3.3 The Termination Process

It is best for a broadly based committee of reasonably senior executives to make the termination decision in order to diffuse and withstand the political pressures that often accompany such decisions. In general, projects do not take kindly to being shut down.

To the extent possible, senior management should detail the termination criteria used and explain the rationale for its decision.

The activities required to ensure a smooth and successful project termination should be included in the initial project plan. The termination process will have much better results for all concerned if it is planned and managed with care—even treating it as a project in itself.

Usually, the project manager is asked to close out the project, but this can raise a variety of problems because the project manager is not a disinterested bystander in the project. An appointed specialist might be more appropriate, such as an experienced **termination manager,** or project undertaker, who completes the long and involved process of shutting down a project. The primary duties of the termination manager include the following:

▲ Ensuring completion of the work, including that of subcontractors.

▲ Notifying the client of project completion and ensuring that delivery and installation are accomplished. Acceptance of the project must be acknowledged by the client.

▲ Ensuring that documentation is complete, including the project final report.

▲ Clearing all accounts and documentation for final billings and client invoicing.

▲ Redistributing personnel, materials, equipment, and other project resources to appropriate places, including the return of client-provided resources.

▲ Clearing the project with legal counsel, including filings for patents and recording and archiving all nondisclosure documents.

▲ Determining what records to keep and delivering them to safe and responsible people, such as the organization's archivist, or storing them in the organization's archives.

▲ Overseeing the closing of the project's books.

Many of the preceding tasks will be handled, or at least initiated, by the project manager. Some might be provided for in the project proposal or contract.

One of the more difficult termination duties is reassigning project personnel. In a functional organization, reassignment usually entails a simple transfer back to duty in the individual's parent department; but at those times when a large project is shut down, team members might be laid off. In a pure project organization (see Section 3.1), there might be more projects to which project personnel can be transferred but no "holding area" such as a home functional department. As a result, layoffs are more common. The matrix organization, having both aspects, might be the least problematic in terms of personnel reassignments.

FOR EXAMPLE

Well-handled Termination

The termination process can be handled well or poorly. A well-handled termination project is exemplified by steel industry giant Nucor's (www.nucor.com) use of a termination-by-addition strategy at its Crawfordsville, Indiana, steel plant. Working from a detailed multiphase plan, Nucor transitioned the plant's traditional steel operation to thin slab casting technology, a revolutionary processing technique that Nucor developed and that substantially reduces the cost to produce sheet steel. While termination resulted in the loss of some specific jobs, many new jobs and opportunities were created by the termination-by-addition strategy.

14.3.4 Preparing the Project Final Report

The project final report is not another evaluation, though the audits and evaluations have a role in it. The **project final report** is a history of the project. It is a chronicle, typically written by the project manager, of what went right and what went wrong, who served the project in what capacity, what was done, how it was managed, and the lessons learned. The report should also indicate where source materials can be found—the project proposal, action plan, budget, schedule, earned value charts, audit reports, scope-change documents, all updates of any of the above documents, and so on.

How the report is written, and in what style, is a matter of taste and preference. In any case, project managers should address the following topics:

▲ **Project performance.** Perhaps the most important information is what the project attempted to achieve, what it did achieve, and the reasons for the resulting performance. Because this is not a formal evaluation of the project, these items can be the project manager's personal opinion on the matter. The lessons learned in the project should also be included here.

▲ **Administrative performance.** Administrative practices that worked particularly well, or poorly, should be identified and the reasons given. If some modification to administrative practices would help future projects, this should be noted and explained.

▲ **Organizational structure.** Projects could have different structures, and the way the project is organized could either aid or hinder the project. Modifications that would help future projects should be identified.

▲ **Project teamwork.** A confidential section of the final report should identify team members who worked particularly well, and possibly those who worked poorly with others. The project manager might also recommend that individuals or groups who were particularly effective when operating as a team be kept together on future assignments.

▲ **Project-management techniques.** Project success depends on the skill and techniques for forecasting, planning, budgeting, scheduling, resource allocation, control, risk management, and so on, so procedures that worked well or badly should be noted and commented upon. Recommendations for improvements in future projects should be made and explained.

The fundamental purpose of the final report is to improve future projects. Thus, recommendations for improvements are especially appropriate and valued by the organization. Of course, none of the recommendations for improvement of future projects will be of any help if the recommendations are not circulated among other project managers, as well as the appropriate senior managers. The project manager should follow up on any recommendations made to make sure that they are accepted and installed, or rejected for cause.

Because most of the information and recollections for the final report come from the project manager, the project manager should consider keeping a project diary. This is not an official project document but an informal collection of thoughts, reflections, and commentaries on project happenings. Not only does a diary help the project manager construct the final report, but also it can be a source of wisdom for new, aspiring project managers. Above all, it keeps good ideas from getting lost amid the jumble of project activities and crises.

SELF-CHECK

1. Projects can fail for all except which of the following reasons?

   (a) unrealistic upper management expectations

   (b) poor up-front planning

   (c) the project wasn't required for the task in the first place

   (d) naming the wrong project manager

2. In termination-by-integration, the product or process associated with the project is sold or transferred to the client or customer. True or false?

3. A project can be terminated effectively by which of the following?

   (a) an official termination manager

   (b) the project manager

   (c) both a and b

   (d) neither a nor b

SUMMARY

Because even the best managed of projects must end one day, proactive project managers should always be preparing for the final reports and analyses that accompany a project termination. While project managers are typically responsible for preparing postproject evaluations, an outside group of experts conducts a project audit and writes an audit report (with involvement from the project manager, of course). Project termination is difficult, but it doesn't have to be painful; project managers can ease the transition to other assignments.

KEY TERMS

Detailed audit	Project audit initiated if a general audit finds something that needs further investigation.
General audit	Project audit constrained by time and cost and limited to a brief investigation of project essentials.
Postproject evaluation	An assessment of project results, activities, and processes in order to recognize achievements and identify what did and didn't work; also known as project postmortem.
Project audit	A thorough examination of the management of a project, its methodology and procedures, its records, properties, inventories, budgets, expenditures, and progress.
Project extinction	Project activity suddenly stops and property, equipment, materials, and personnel must be disbursed or reassigned.
Project final report	A history of the project, typically written by the project manager.
Technical audit	Project audit performed by a person or team with special technical skills.
Termination-by-addition	Project termination process in which an in-house project is successfully completed and institutionalized as a new, formal part of the organization.
Termination-by-integration	Project termination in which the output of the project becomes a standard part of the operating systems of the sponsoring firm or the client.
Termination-by-starvation	Project termination in which a project's budget is squeezed until it is a project in name only.
Termination manager	An appointed specialist who completes the process of shutting down a project.

ASSESS YOUR UNDERSTANDING

Go to www.wiley.com/college/portny to assess your knowledge of the basics of project evaluations.
Measure your learning by comparing pre-test and post-test results.

Summary Questions

1. Technical projects are audited; nontechnical projects are evaluated. True or false?

2. It is appropriate for project managers to have responsibilities in both project audits and project evaluations, even though these termination activities sometimes achieve different final results. True or false?

3. The project final report summarizes the information gathered in the post-project evaluation. True or false?

Applying This Chapter

1. Rose was asked just this week to lead a project to develop a new line of electronic greeting cards. Rose's boss has completed some initial planning work, but the project is still in its conceive stage or define stage. Why should Rose think about project termination when her project is just beginning? What are some specific pretermination activities she can plan for and begin immediately to make the actual termination more efficient and effective?

2. Your boss recently notified you that the project you've been leading for nearly 18 months will be audited by a group within your organization. Several of your project team members are concerned about the nature of the audit. What can you tell them about the audit to calm their fears? Additionally, what can you as project manager do to make the audit proceed quickly and effectively?

3. Bruce's Web site development project is nearing an end, and upper management must decide what to do with the resources associated with the project. Bruce's team met all schedule and expenditure goals, but the product they produced (a video-swapping online destination) has underperformed in terms of ad revenue and visitors. Which form of termination would you recommend upper management consider for Bruce's project?

Always Ending

Few project plans include recommendations of activities for preparing to terminate a project. Review a project plan that's organized by project life phases (conceive, define, start, perform, close) and write down specific actions and activities you as project manager can do during each phase to collect information to make project termination easy and effective. Draft an additional section to include at the end of the project plan that details pretermination activities/responsibilties. List not only things that you think the project manager and team members should be responsible for in the final days of a project, but also termination-related activities to conduct throughout the project. Update your working project plan template to include this new section of pretermination activities/responsibilities.

So How Did You Do?

Consider a work, school, or personal project that is finished but that no one officially evaluated. (Perhaps it's a room you redecorated, your reorganization of your department's filing system, or a prefinals study session you organized.) Even though you weren't graded on this project, you can assess your performance and the performance of others. Consider the evaluation criteria listed in Section 14.1.2. Which of these are appropriate for evaluating your project? Write down additional ways you believe you can effectively evaluate your project. Conduct a quick project evaluation, writing a brief statement for each criterion or question. Consider developing a numeric scale to give your evaluation data that can be easily analyzed.

Choose Your Own End

Many projects just cease, and project resources (both human and materials) are assigned to other projects. Brainstorm a list of completed projects you've participated in or led. Which type of project termination (see Section 14.3.2) did each project undergo? Do you think these were the best termination options? Why or why not? Then envision each of the projects in your list going through the other termination options. Did any better options appear?

CASE STUDY: Datatech Inc.

Datatech Inc.

Steve Bawnson joined Datatech's engineering department upon obtaining his B.S. in Electrical Engineering almost six years ago. He soon established himself as an expert in analog signal processing and was promoted to Senior Design Engineer just two years after joining the firm. After serving as a Senior Design Engineer for two years, he was promoted to Project Manager and asked to oversee a product development project involving a relatively minor product line extension.

As Steve was clearing his desk to make room for a cup of coffee, his computer dinged indicating the arrival of yet another e-mail message. Steve usually paid little attention to the arrival of new e-mail messages, but for some reason this message caught his attention. Swiveling in his chair to face the computer on the credenza behind his desk, he read the subject line of the message: Notebook Computer Development Project Audit Report. Steve then noticed that the message was addressed to the Vice President of Product Development and was copied to him. He immediately opened and read the message.

Datatech had recently adopted a policy requiring that all ongoing projects be periodically audited. Last week this policy was implemented, and Steve was informed that his project would be the first one audited by a team consisting of internal and external experts.

Datatech Inc. is a full-line producer of desktop and notebook computers that are distributed through a network of value-added resellers. After completing the desktop product line extension project about nine months ago, Steve was asked to serve as the project manager for a project to develop a new line of notebook computers.

In asking Steve to serve as the project manager for the notebook computer development project, the Vice President of Product Development conveyed to Steve the importance of completing the project within a year. To emphasize this point, the Vice President noted that he personally made the decision to go forward with this project and had not taken the project through the normal project selection and approval process in order

to save time. Steve had successfully completed the desktop project in a similar time frame, and told the Vice President that this target was quite reasonable. Steve added that he was confident that the project would be completed on time and on budget.

Steve wasted no time in planning the project. Based on the success of the desktop project, he decided to modify the work breakdown structure he had developed for the desktop project and apply it to this new project. He recalled the weeks of planning that went into developing the Work Breakdown Structure for the desktop project. The entire project team had been involved, and that was a relatively straightforward product line extension. The current project was more complicated, and there simply was not sufficient time to involve all team members. What was the point of wasting valuable time and resources to reinvent the wheel?

After modifying the Work Breakdown Structure, Steve scheduled a meeting with the Vice President of Product Development to discuss staffing the project. As was typical of other product development projects at Datatech, Steve and the Vice President agreed that the project should be housed within the engineering division. In his capacity as project manager, Steve would serve as liaison to other functional areas such as marketing, purchasing, finance, and production.

As the project progressed, it continued to slip behind schedule. Steve found it necessary to schedule a meeting each week to address how unanticipated activities would be completed. For example, last week the team realized that no one had been assigned to design the hinge system for attaching the screen to the base.

Indeed, Steve found himself increasingly in crisis mode. For example, this morning the manufacturing group sent a heated e-mail to Steve. The manufacturing group noted that they just learned of the notebook computer project and based on the design presented to them, they would not be able to manufacture the printed circuit boards because of the extensive amount of surface mount components required. Steve responded to this message by noting that the engineering group was doing its job and had designed a state-of-the-art notebook computer. He added that it was the manufacturing group's problem to decide how to produce it.

Just as troubling was the crisis that had occurred earlier in the week. The Vice President of Product Development had requested that the notebook computer incorporate a new type of interface that would allow the notebook computer to synchronize information with a personal digital assistant Datatech was about to introduce. Steve explained that incorporating the interface into the notebook computer would require changes to about 40 percent of the computer and would delay the introduction by a minimum of several months. Nevertheless, the Vice President was adamant that the change be made.

As Steve laid down the audit report, he reflected on its conclusion that the project be terminated immediately. In the judgment of the auditing team, the project had slipped so far behind schedule that the costs to complete it were not justified.

Questions

1. To what extent were the problems facing the notebook computer development project avoidable? What could have been done to avoid these problems?

2. Would it make sense to apply a project selection model or process to this project to determine if it should be terminated?

3. In your opinion, are the types of problems that arose in this situation typical of other organizations? If so, what can organizations in general do to avoid these types of problems?

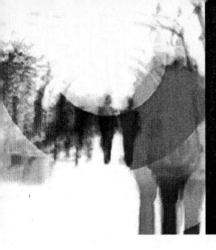

GLOSSARY

Accountability   Bringing consequences to bear based on people's performances.

Accuracy   How correct a number or measurement is.

Achieved power   The project manager earns the respect and allegiance of those whom he or she wants to influence.

Activities report   A table that lists activities and the dates on which you plan to start and end them.

Activity   Work required to move from one event to the next in a project.

Activity-in-the-box   A type of network diagram; also referred to as activity-in-the-node or precedence diagramming.

Activity-on-the-arrow   A type of network diagram; also referred to as the classical or traditional approach.

Actual Cost of Work Performed (ACWP)   The amount of funds actually spent for work actually done by the specified date.

Ad hoc team meeting   Special session for team members to address problems and issues as they arise.

Aggregate project plan   A summary of the various types of projects an organization engages in. Also known as portfolio project plan.

Annual budget   Detailed list of the categories and individual initiatives on which all organization funds will be spent during the year.

Approved project budget   A detailed project budget that essential people agree to support.

Ascribed power   Someone gives the project manager the authority to reward and punish those whom he or she wants to influence.

Assumptions Statements about uncertain information the project manager is taking as fact while conceiving, planning, and performing the project; part of the Statement of Work.

Audience list template A predesigned audience list that contains audiences typically included for similar projects.

Authority **1.** The ability to make binding decisions about a project's products, schedule, resources, and activities.

2. The right to make project decisions others must follow.

Automated impact assessments Computerized spreadsheets that consider in combination both the risk that different situations will occur and the consequences if they do.

Availability When on the calendar a resource will be available.

Backing in The schedule process of starting the end of a project and working back toward the beginning, identifying activities as you go and estimating durations that eventually will add up to the amount of time the project has been given.

Backward pass Finish-to-start analysis by a project manager to determine critical paths and earliest start and finish dates.

Baseline The current version of a project plan that guides project performance and against which the project manager compares actual project performance.

Biased In estimating, when either the chance of over- or underestimates are not about equal or the size of over- or underestimates are not approximately equal.

Bottom-up budgeting Financial estimating process in which a Work Breakdown Structure or action plan identifies elemental tasks, which are then converted to costs and combined to determine an overall direct cost for the project.

Breakthrough projects Projects involving newer technology that may disrupt the status quo in an industry or marketplace.

Bubble-chart format A format for displaying a Work Breakdown Structure that presents activities, tasks, and subtasks as linked circles.

Budget The financial plans for allocating organization resources to project activities.

Budgeted Cost of Work Performed (BCWP) The planned cost for work actually done by the specified date.

Budgeted Cost of Work Scheduled (BCWS)   The planned cost for work due to be completed by a specified date.

Capacity   Productivity per unit time period.

Capital appropriations plan   Itemized list of all expenditures over an established minimum amount planned for facilities and equipment purchases, renovations, and repairs during the year.

Centrally organized structure   Traditional organizing structure for handling projects within an organization; individual units are established to handle all work in particular specialty areas; also known as a *fixed group organization*.

Change control procedure   A statement within a project contract that allows for renegotiation of price and schedule for client-ordered changes in performance.

Change control system   A formal process whereby changes can be introduced and accomplished with as little distress as possible.

Client   The entity for whom the project is being done; **can be** someone or some organization outside or within the company performing the project.

Collaborators   Groups or other organizations in a project audience with which team members might pursue joint ventures related to the project.

Committee   People who come together to review and critique issues, propose recommendations for action, and, on occasion, implement those recommendations.

Communication   Sharing the right messages with the right people in a timely manner.

Concurrent engineering (CE)   Work processes in which two or more steps are carried out at the same time to save time and costs.

Conditional activity   A work activity that's performed only if certain conditions come to pass.

Conflict resolution   Resolving differences of opinion between team members regarding project work.

Constraints   Restrictions that others place on the results, time frames, resources, and ways a project team can approach its tasks; part of the Statement of Work.

Controlling   Project management responsibility that includes reconfirming people's expected performance, monitoring actions and results, addressing problems encountered, and sharing information with interested persons.

Cost variance   The portion of the difference between what was planned to be spent by a certain date and what has really been spent that's true cost savings or loss.

Cost-benefit analysis   Formal identification and assessment of all the benefits that are anticipated from a project plus all of the costs for performing project.

Critical path   A sequence of activities in a project that takes the longest time to complete.

Critical path method (CPM) charts   A network diagram that uses deterministic, certain estimates but includes both time and cost estimates to allow time/cost trade-offs to be used.

Data collection and reporting   Gathering project information and turning it into information useful for controlling projects.

Decision trees   Diagrams illustrating different situations that could occur as a project unfolds, the likelihood of each situation occurring, and the consequences to the project if it does.

Delegation   Giving away something (for a project it's often a task assignment or responsibility).

Dependency diagram   Another term for a network diagram in either activity-on-the-arrow or activity-in-the-box format.

Derivative projects   Projects with objectives or deliverables that are only incrementally different in both product and process from existing offerings.

Detailed audit   Project audit initiated if a general audit finds something that needs further investigation.

Detailed budget estimate   An itemization of the estimated costs for each project activity. Prepared by a project manager based on a Work Breakdown Structure.

Direct costs   Expenditures for resources that are used solely to perform project activities.

Discretionary relationships   Relationships the project manager or project team chooses to establish between activities.

Distribution list   Document that identifies people who receive copies of written project communications.

Dress rehearsal   Realistic risk-preparing activity which requires participants to take action.

Drivers   1. People in a project who have some say in defining the results that a project is to achieve; the people for whom the project work is being performed.

2. People who have some say in defining the results that the project is to achieve; the people for whom the project is being carried out.

Dummy activities   1. Activities on network diagrams that have duration but do not require any resources; also known as pseudoactivities.

2. Activities with 0 span time that are used to represent a required dependency between events.

Duration   How long each individual activity will take in a project.

Earliest finish date   The earliest date that someone can possibly finish an activity.

Earliest start date   The earliest date that someone can possibly start an activity.

Earned value   The earned value of a piece of work is defined to be equal to the amount the project managers plan to spend to perform it.

Earned Value Analysis   A technique that helps determine whether a project is ahead or behind schedule and whether it's over or under budget, while only tracking resource expenditures.

Escalation procedures   Conflict resolution steps that the group takes when the people involved can't readily resolve their differences.

Estimate at completion   The total amount that will be spent to perform a task, if a project's spending pattern to date continues until the task is finished.

Event   A significant occurrence in the life of the project; also called a milestone or a deliverable. Events take no time and consume no resources; they occur instantaneously.

Exception dates   Dates that a resource is unavailable.

Exception reports   Report intended for special decisions or unexpected situations in which affected team members and outside managers need to be made aware of a change.

Fast tracking   Schedule process in which you perform two or more activities at the same time to reduce the overall time to complete a project.

Feasibility study   Formal investigation and documentation of the likelihood of a project being successful.

Feasible   Whether people think they have a chance to accomplish a project.

Formal communications   Preplanned communication, conducted in a standard format in accordance with an established schedule.

Forward pass   Start-to-finish analysis by a project manager at the beginning of the project to see how fast the activities can be completed.

Frequency count   A simple count of the occurrence of an event.

Fudge factor   An amount of time project managers add to an estimate of span time just to be safe.

Functional employees   Individuals within projects who must satisfy the requests of both their functional managers and their project manager; also known as project team members.

Functional managers   Individuals in an organization or company who are responsible for orchestrating their staffs' assignments among different projects, as well as providing the resources to allow their staffs to perform their assignments in accordance with the highest standards of technical excellence.

Functionally organized structure   Organizing structure in which separate units addressing the same specialty are established in the organization's different functional groups.

Gantt chart   A graph illustrating on a time line when each activity will start, be performed, and end.

General and administrative costs   Indirect costs that keep the organization operational.

General audit   Project audit constrained by time and cost and limited to a brief investigation of project essentials.

Goals   What a project team as a whole, as well as each member individually, hopes to accomplish.

Graphical evaluation and review technique (GERT)   A network diagram technique that combines structures such as flowgraphs, probabilistic networks, and decision trees, creating a complex schedule.

Human Resources Matrix   A graphic display that project managers can use to show individual resources that will work on an activity and the work effort that each resource will invest in the activity.

Immediate predecessor   Term given to an activity that, upon completion, can allow someone to start on the following activity.

Indented-outline format   A format for displaying a Work Breakdown Structure that presents activities, tasks, and subtasks as a hierarchically organized list.

Indirect costs   Expenditures that are incurred to support project activities but that aren't tracked individually.

Informal communications   Communication that occurs as people think of information they want to share.

Inputs   Raw data collected to describe selected aspects of project performance.

Integration management   Coordinating the work of groups and the timing of their interactions.

Interest   On a Skills Roster, the "interest" descriptor indicates that the person would like to work on assignments involving this skill or knowledge.

Interface coordination   The process of managing the way groups work together.

Key-events report   A table that lists events and the dates on which you plan to reach them.

Known unknown   Information that you don't have but someone else does.

Latest finish date   The latest date someone can finish an activity and still finish the project in the shortest possible time.

Latest start date   The latest date that someone can start an activity and still finish the project in the shortest possible time.

Learning rate   The percentage at which unit performance improves each time the total production quantity doubles.

Legal requirements   Federal, state, and local laws or regulations that require certain project activities to be done before others.

Limitations   Restrictions that others place on the results, time frames, resources, and ways a project team can approach its tasks; also known as constraints.

Linear Responsibility Chart (LRC)   A matrix that depicts the role that each project team and stakeholder plays in the performance of different project activities.

Logical relationships   Choosing to do certain activities before others because it seems to make the most sense.

Long-range plan   Formal report that identifies an organization's overall direction, specific performance targets, and individual initiatives for the next one to five years.

Lowest-level activity   An activity in a Work Breakdown Structure that's not divided into further detail.

Management reserve   A designated amount of time and money to account for parts of the project that cannot be predicted, such as major disruptions in the project caused by serious weather conditions or an accident.

Managerial choices   Arbitrary decisions to work on certain activities before others.

Managers' annual performance objectives   Specific tasks and desired accomplishments that will be considered when conducting each manager's annual performance appraisal.

Matrix organization   Combination organization of both centrally and functionally organized projects, devised to enable a quick and efficient response to projects that must be performed under today's dynamic business conditions.

Measures   One or more indicators project managers use to assess achievement.

Micromanagement   A person's excessive, inappropriate, and unnecessary involvement in the details of a task that he or she asks another person to perform.

Mixed organization   Central, functional, and matrix project organizations exist side by side in a company; also known as *hybrid organizations*.

Multidisciplinary teams (MTs)   Work groups comprised of individuals from various departments or divisions, with varying backgrounds and expertise; also known as transdisciplinary teams.

Needs   Requirements the project manager determines must be met in order to achieve project success.

Network diagram   A flowchart that illustrates the order in which activities need to be performed in a project.

Noncritical path   A sequence of activities that can be delayed by some amount while still allowing the overall project to finish in the shortest possible time.

Objectives   Results to be achieved through the performance of a project; part of the Statement of Work.

Observers   1. People who are interested in the activities and results of the project but have no say in what the project is to accomplish and are not actively involved in supporting it.

2. People who are interested in a project but will not define what the project should accomplish or directly support efforts.

Organization-chart format   A format for displaying a Work Breakdown Structure that portrays an overview of the project and the hierarchical relationships of different work assignments (and perhaps tasks) at the highest levels.

Organizing   Project management responsibility that includes defining people's roles and responsibilities.

Outcome   A project-specific goal related to creating a specific product, service, or result.

Outputs   Reports presenting the results of the analyses performed.

Overhead costs   Indirect costs associated with resources used to perform project activities, but which are difficult to subdivide and allocate directly.

Parkinson's Law   States that work will expand to fill the amount of time allotted.

Performance period   The interval for which a project is reviewed and assessed.

Performance targets   The value of each measure that defines success in a project objective.

Person effort   See work effort.

Person Loading Chart   A graphic display that shows a detailed allocation of work effort by time period.

Plan-monitor-control cycle   An ongoing project management process of continually planning what to do, checking on progress, comparing progress to plan, and taking corrective actions.

Planning   Project management responsibility that includes specifying results to be achieved, determining schedules, and estimating resources required.

Platform projects   Projects that represent major departures from existing offerings in terms of either the product or service itself or the process used to make and deliver it.

Portfolio project plan   See aggregate project plan.

Position power   Project team members take a project manager's requests more seriously because they feel that it's appropriate for the project manager to direct team members.

Postproject evaluation   An assessment of project results, activities, and processes in order to recognize achievements and identify what did and didn't work; also known as project postmortem.

Power   The ability to influence the actions of others.

Precedence diagram   Another term for a network diagram in the activity-in-the-box format.

Precision   The detail with which a number or measurement is expressed.

Predecessor   An activity that must be completed before someone can work on another activity.

Primary capability   On a Skills Roster, the "primary capability" descriptor indicates that the person can assume a lead role in an assignment requiring this skill or knowledge.

Probability   A number between 0 and 1 indicating the likelihood that a given situation will come to pass. (A probability of 0 means the situation will never occur; a probability of 1 means that it will always occur.)

Procedural requirements   Company policies and procedures that require certain project activities to be done before others.

Process   A series of steps by which a particular job function is routinely performed.

Processes   The techniques that team members will use to help them perform their project tasks.

Program   Work (often multiple projects) performed towards achieving a long-range goal.

Program evaluation and review technique (PERT) chart   A network diagram in the activity-on-the-arrow format that allows project managers to assign optimistic, pessimistic, and most likely estimates for an activity's span time.

Project   A temporary endeavor undertaken to create a unique product or service.

Project audience   1. A person or group who will support, be affected by, or be interested in a project.

2. Any person or group inside or outside the organization that supports, is affected by, or is interested in a project.

Project audit   A thorough examination of the management of a project, its methodology and procedures, its records, properties, inventories, budgets, expenditures, and progress.

Project champion   A person in a high position in the organization who strongly supports a project.

Project controlling   Using monitored data and information to bring actual performance into agreement with the project plan.

Project extinction   Project activity suddenly stops and property, equipment, materials, and personnel must be disbursed or reassigned.

Project final report   A history of the project, typically written by the project manager.

Project management   The process of guiding a project from its beginning through its performance to its closure. Project management requires planning, organizing, and controlling.

Project management information system (PMIS)   A set of procedures, equipment, and other resources for collecting, analyzing, storing, and reporting on information that describes project performance.

Project managers   Individuals responsible for seeing that all aspects of projects are completed satisfactorily.

Project monitoring   Collecting, recording, and reporting project information that is important to the project manager and other relevant stakeholders.

Project plans   Formal plans that describe the roles project managers anticipate people will play and the amount of effort team members will have to invest.

Project progress report   Regularly scheduled written communication that reviews what has happened during a performance period, describes problems and the corrective actions needed, and previews what is planned for the next period.

Project strategy   The general approach project managers plan to take to perform the work necessary to achieve a project's outcomes.

Project team   A collection of people who are committed to common goals and who depend on one other to do their jobs.

Project team members   See functional employees.

Punishment power   People do what a project manager asks because they don't want what the project manager can give them.

Purpose   How and why a project came to be, the scope of the project, and the general approach to be followed; part of the Statement of Work.

R&D projects   Projects that are visionary and use newly developed technologies or existing technologies in a new manner.

Raw numbers   Actual numbers in collected data.

Rebaselining   Officially adopting a new project plan to guide activities and serve as the comparative basis for future performance assessments.

Regularly scheduled team meetings   Opportunities for team members to share progress and issues and to sustain productive and trusting interpersonal relationships.

Regulators   Government agencies that establish regulations and guidelines that govern some aspect of project work.

Relationships   The feelings and attitudes of team members toward each other.

Requester   The person who came up with the idea for a project and all the people through whom the request passed before it was given to the project manager.

Required relationships   Relationships between project activities that must be observed if project work is to be successfully completed.

Resource allocation   The process by which project managers assign specific, limited resources to specific activities (or projects) when there are competing demands for limited resources.

Resource loading   The amounts of specific resources that are scheduled for use on specific activities or projects at specific times.

Resource schedules   Tables that list the availability of all resources—including personnel and non-personnel resources. Resource schedules can list pay rates, typical work hours, and exception dates.

Resource-loading table   A list that shows the amounts of various specific resources that are scheduled for use on specific activities at specific times during the life of the project.

Resources   The amount of people, funds, equipment, facilities, and information needed for a project.

Responsibility   The commitment to achieve specific results.

Reward power   People do what a project manager asks because they want the benefits that the project manager can give them.

Risk   The possibility that a project will not achieve its product, schedule, or resource targets because something unexpected does or doesn't occur.

Risk assessment questionnaires   Formal data-collection instruments for eliciting expert opinions about the likelihood that different situations will come to pass on a project and the associated impacts.

Risk bank   A file or database in which multiple project managers note risks and solutions.

Risk factor   A situation that might give rise to one or more project risks. A risk factor itself doesn't cause a project team to miss a product, schedule, or resource target. However, it increases the likelihood that the project team might miss one.

Risk management   The process of identifying possible risks, assessing potential impact on a project, and developing and implementing plans for minimizing negative effects.

Risk management groups   Teams that maintain records on how all projects within the organization deal with risks.

Risk management plan   Document that lays out specific strategies to minimize the potential negative consequences that uncertain occurrences will have on a project.

Roles   Each project team member's individual assignments.

Rough order-of-magnitude (ROM) estimate   An initial estimate of costs that is based on a general sense of the type of work the project will likely entail; also known as a ballpark estimate.

Routine reports   Reports issues on a regular schedule which report on data collected on established aspects of a project.

Scapegoating   Holding people accountable when they aren't responsible.

Schedule   Plan that lists specific, established dates for work to begin and end.

Schedule slippage   A measure of the amount by which a project, or a set of projects, is delayed by leveling a resource.

Schedule variance   The difference between what was planned to be spent by a certain date and what was really spent that's due to the project being ahead of or behind schedule.

Scope creep   The natural tendency of the client, as well as project team members, to try to improve the project's output as the project progresses.

Secondary capability   On a Skills Roster, the "secondary capability" descriptor indicates that the person has some training or experience in the skill or knowledge area but should work under another person's guidance.

Sequence   The order in which the activities will be performed in a project.

Simple event   One that represents the completion of a single activity.

Skills Roster   A graphic format project managers can use to display the skills and knowledge of people who might work on a project; also known as a Skills Inventory.

Slack time   The maximum amount of time that someone can delay an activity and still finish the project in the shortest possible time.

Span time   The actual calendar time required to complete an activity; also called duration or elapsed time.

Span time estimate   A project manager's best sense of how long it'll actually take to perform an activity.

Special analysis reports   Report that disseminates the results of a special study in a project concerning a particular opportunity or problem.

Stakeholder list   Document that identifies people and groups who support or are affected by a project. The stakeholder list most often does not include people outside of the organization or those who are merely interested in the project.

Statement   A brief narrative description in a project objective that notes what is to be achieved.

Statement of Work (SOW)   Written confirmation of what a project will produce and the terms and conditions under which the project team will perform the work.

Supporters   1. People who help carry out the project, including those who authorize the resources for the project as well as those who actually work on it.

2. People in a project who help to perform project work, including the people who authorize the resources for a project as well as those who work on it.

Tabletop exercise   An activity that simulates the decision-making process and any actions to be taken in response to specific risks.

Team members   People whose work is directed by the project manager.

Technical audit   Project audit performed by a person or team with special technical skills.

Termination manager   An appointed specialist who completes the process of shutting down a project.

Termination-by-addition   Project termination process in which an in-house project is successfully completed and institutionalized as a new, formal part of the organization.

Termination-by-integration   Project termination in which the output of the project becomes a standard part of the operating systems of the sponsoring firm or the client.

Termination-by-starvation   Project termination in which a project's budget is squeezed until it is a project in name only.

Top-down budgeting   Financial estimating process in which top and middle managers estimate the overall project cost by estimating the costs of the major tasks.

Tracking signal   A number project managers can calculate to reveal whether cost estimates have a systematic bias in cost and whether the bias is positive or negative.

Uncertainty   A lack of sureness that something will come to pass.

Unexpected contingency   Budget allowance for surprising, unplanned incidents.

Unilateral decision   A decision that doesn't require an agreement of both parties.

Unknown unknown   Information that you don't have because it doesn't yet exist.

Upper management   The people in charge of the organization's major business units.

Upper-management review   Periodic summary of project status, major accomplishments, and issues with which upper management's help is required.

Variance   The difference between planned and actual figures.

Virtual projects   Geographically dispersed projects that can be managed through e-mail, Web sites, and other high-technology methods.

Work Breakdown Structure (WBS)   An organized, detailed, and hierarchical representation of all work to be performed in a project.

Work effort   The actual time a person spends working on an activity, expressed in person-hours, person-days, or person-weeks; also known as person effort.

Work group   People who are assigned to a common task and work individually to accomplish their particular assignments.

Work-order agreement   A written description of work that a person agrees to perform on a project, the dates the person agrees to start and finish the work, and the number of hours the person agrees to spend on it.

INDEX